(416) 477-5555

p 1 8241 - 9795 - 3071

Arata
THE LEGEND
9

WE ARE MAN, BORN OF HEAVEN AND EARTH,
MOON AND SUN AND EVERYTHING UNDER THEM.

EYES, EARS, NOSE, TONGUE, BODY, MIND...

PURITY WILL PIERCE EVIL AND
OPEN UP THE WORLD OF DARKNESS.

ALL LIFE WILL BE REBORN AND INVIGORATED.

APPEAR NOW.

STORY & ART BY
YUU WATASE

Arata
THE LEGEND

CHARACTERS

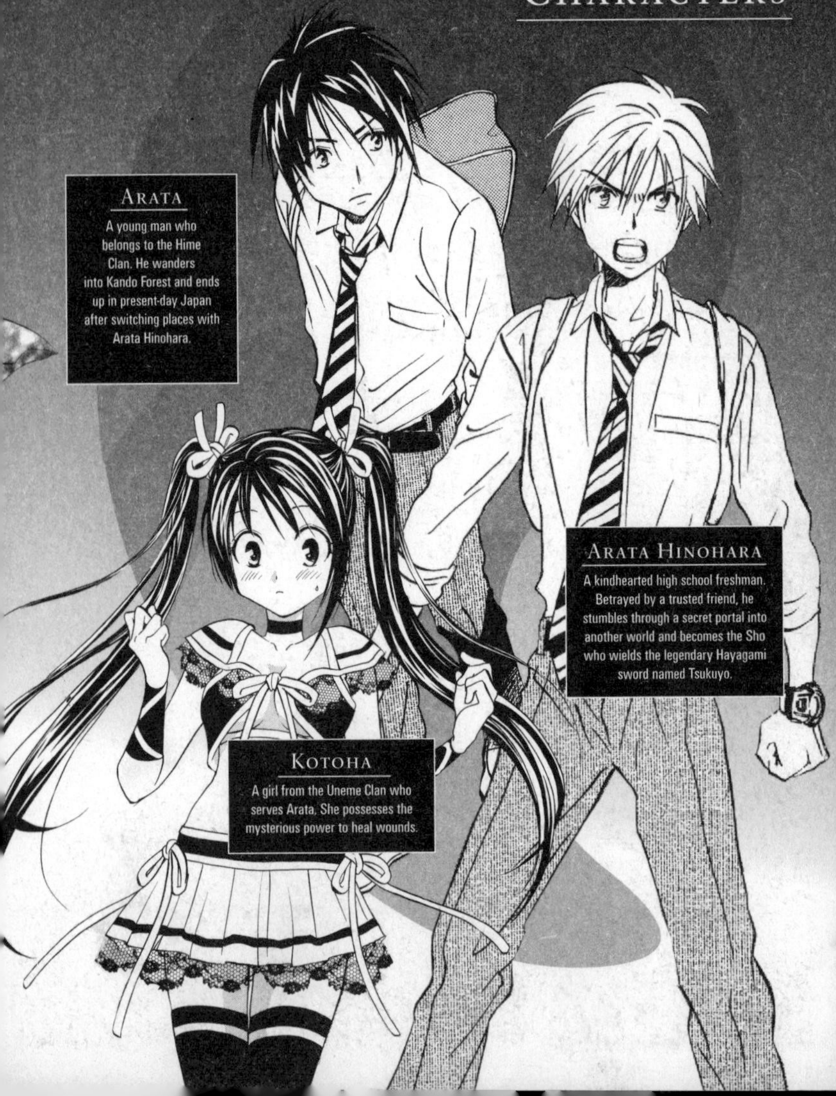
ARATA
A young man who belongs to the Hime Clan. He wanders into Kando Forest and ends up in present-day Japan after switching places with Arata Hinohara.
ARATA HINOHARA
A kindhearted high school freshman. Betrayed by a trusted friend, he stumbles through a secret portal into another world and becomes the Sho who wields the legendary Hayagami sword named Tsukuyo.
KOTOHA
A girl from the Uneme Clan who serves Arata. She possesses the mysterious power to heal wounds.

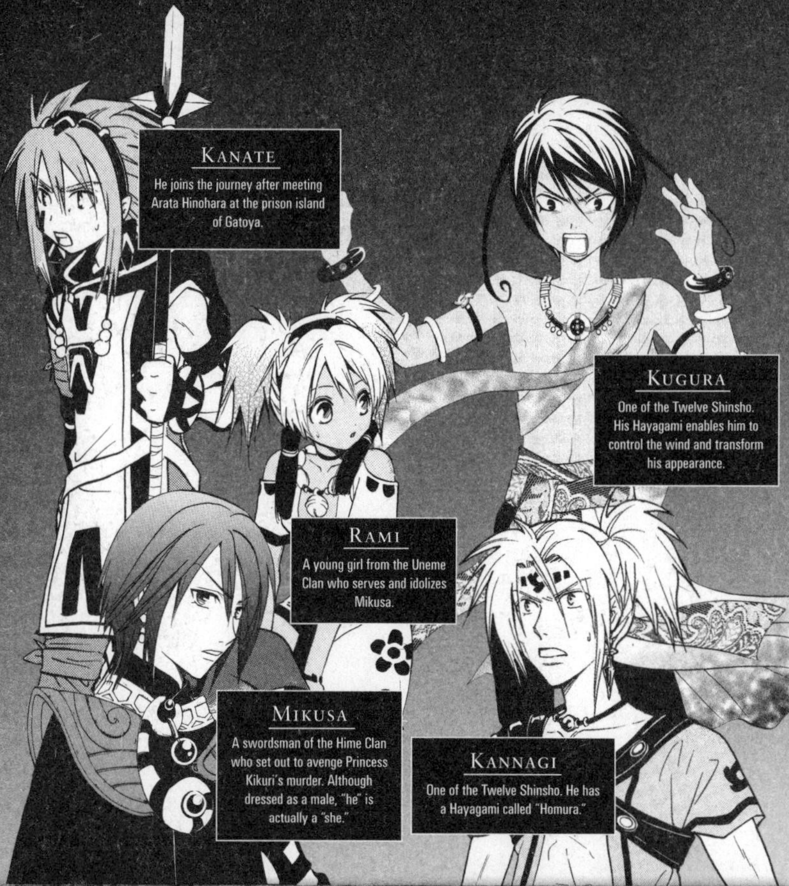
KANATE
He joins the journey after meeting Arata Hinohara at the prison island of Gatoya.
KUGURA
One of the Twelve Shinsho. His Hayagami enables him to control the wind and transform his appearance.
RAMI
A young girl from the Uneme Clan who serves and idolizes Mikusa.
MIKUSA
A swordsman of the Hime Clan who set out to avenge Princess Kikuri's murder. Although dressed as a male, "he" is actually a "she."
KANNAGI
One of the Twelve Shinsho. He has a Hayagami called "Homura."

THE STORY THUS FAR

Betrayed by his best friend, Arata Hinohara—a high school student in present-day Japan—wanders through a portal into another world where he and his companions journey onward to deliver his Hayagami sword "Tsukuyo" to Princess Kikuri.

Hinohara's rival Kadowaki is summoned to Amawakuni and proclaimed the Sho of the Hayagami "Orochi." He fights Hinohara, but their showdown is halted when Hinohara "demonizes"... Later, Hinohara and company enter the territory of Kugura, one of the Twelve Shinsho. There, Kanate meets the ailing Zokusho Futai and agrees to become his successor. Meanwhile, Hinohara infiltrates Kugura's palace in disguise as a girl. Much to his dismay, Kugura falls in love with him at first sight!

Arata 9
THE LEGEND

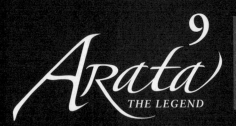

CONTENTS

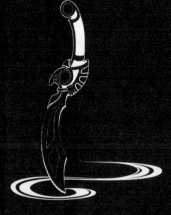

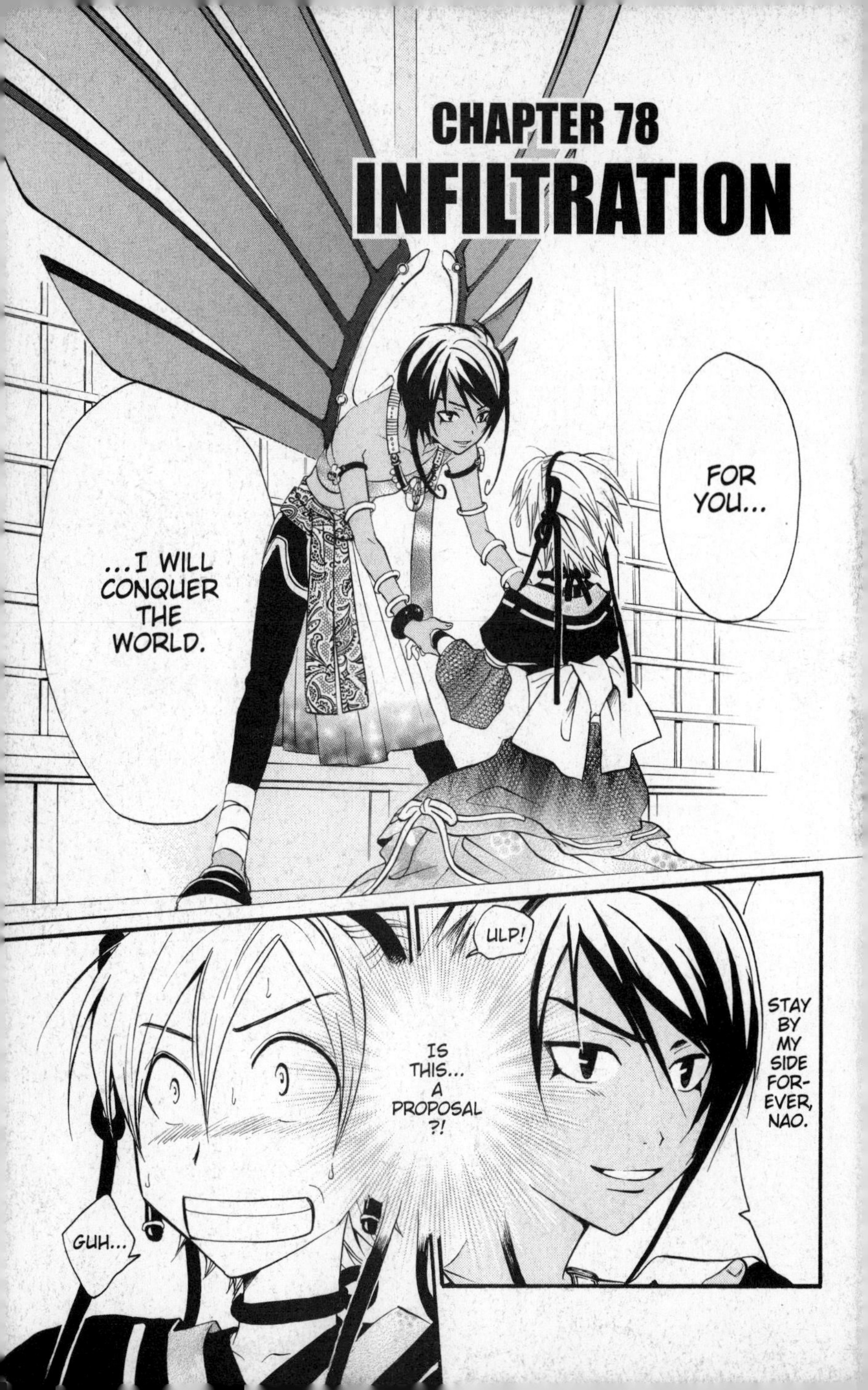
CHAPTER 78
INFILTRATION
FOR YOU...
...I WILL CONQUER THE WORLD.
STAY BY MY SIDE FOREVER, NAO.
ULP!
IS THIS... A PROPOSAL?!
GUH...

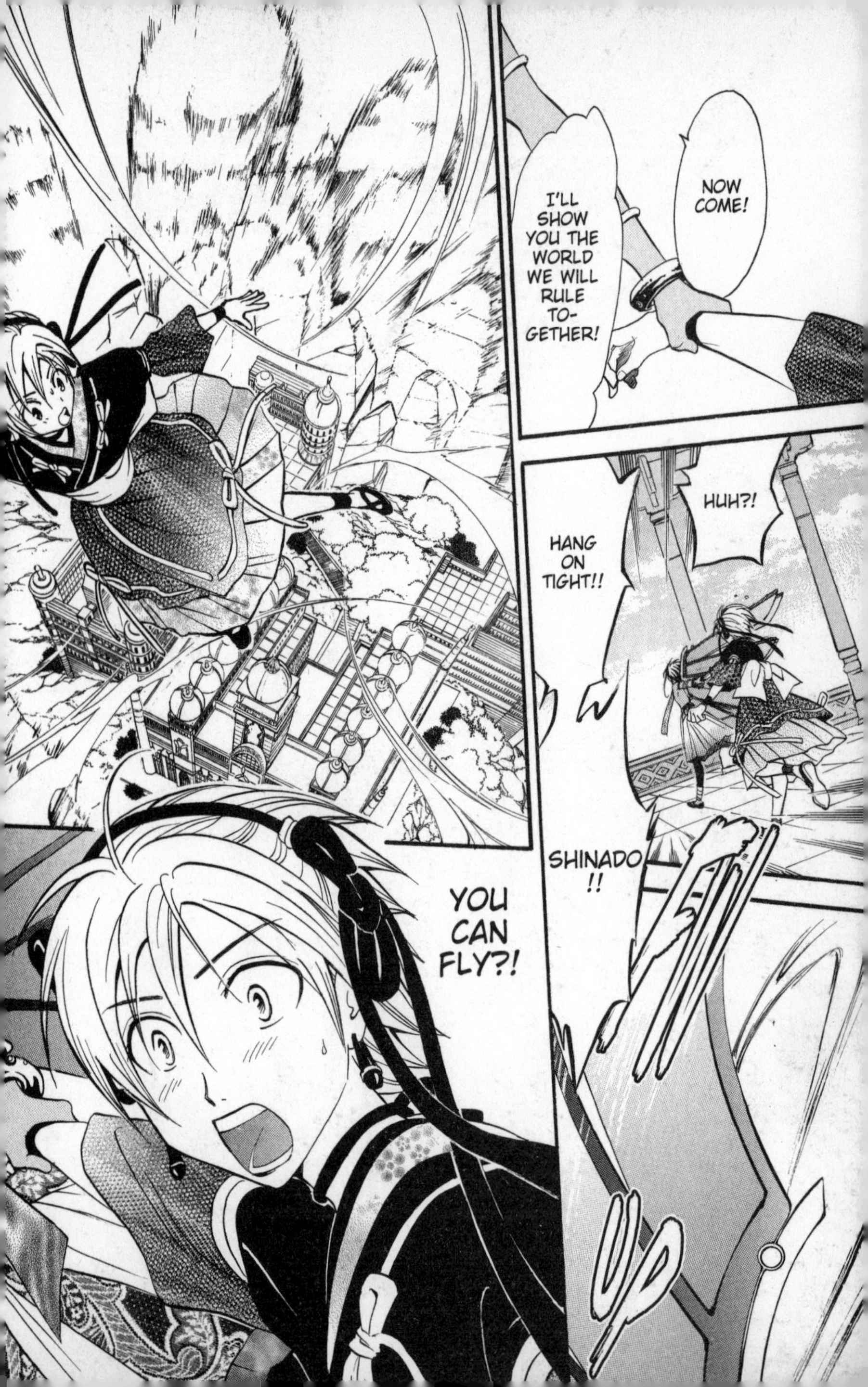
NOW COME!
I'LL SHOW YOU THE WORLD WE WILL RULE TO-GETHER!
HUH?!
HANG ON TIGHT!!
SHINADO!!
YOU CAN FLY?!

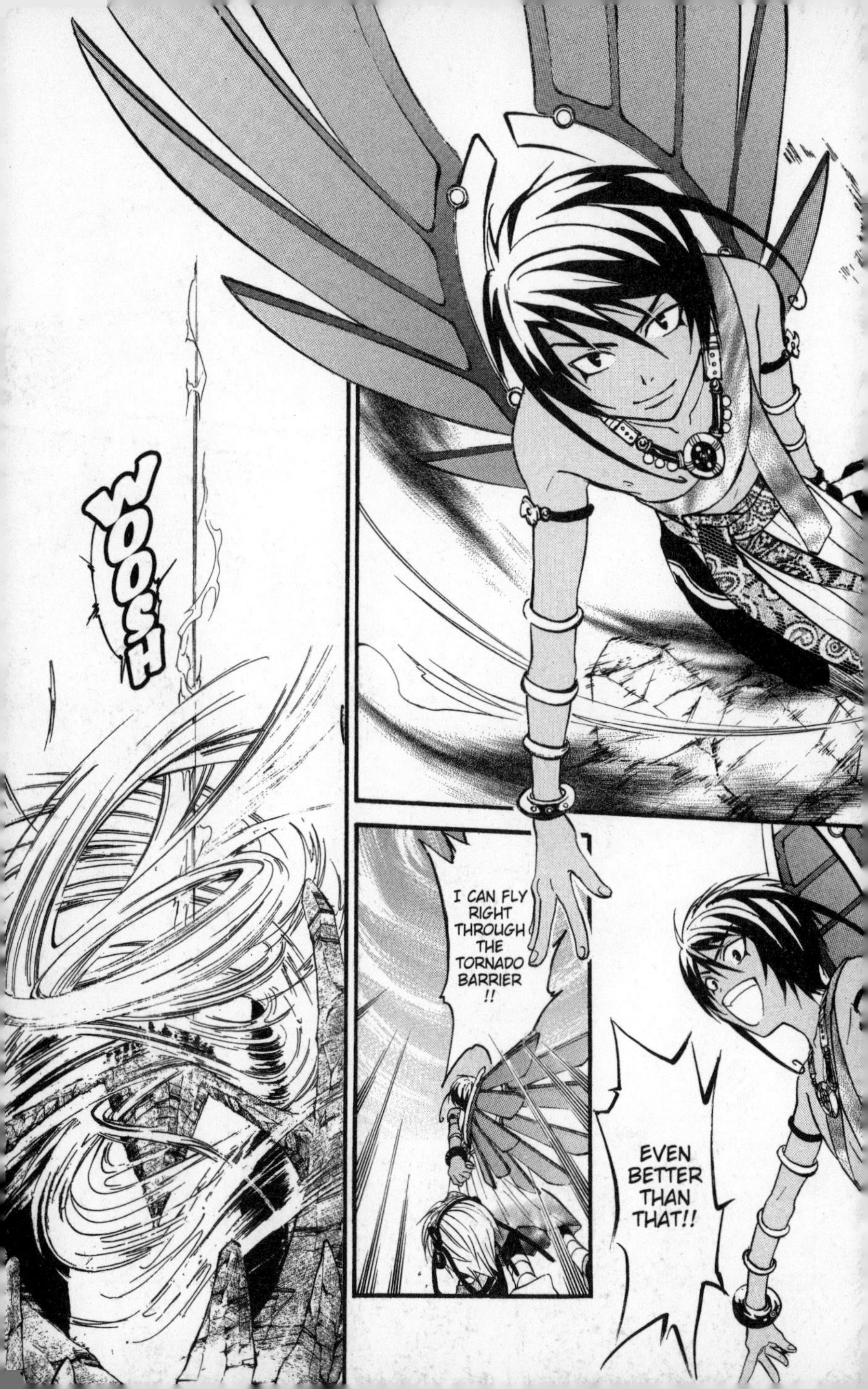
EVEN BETTER THAN THAT!!
I CAN FLY RIGHT THROUGH THE TORNADO BARRIER!!
WOOSH

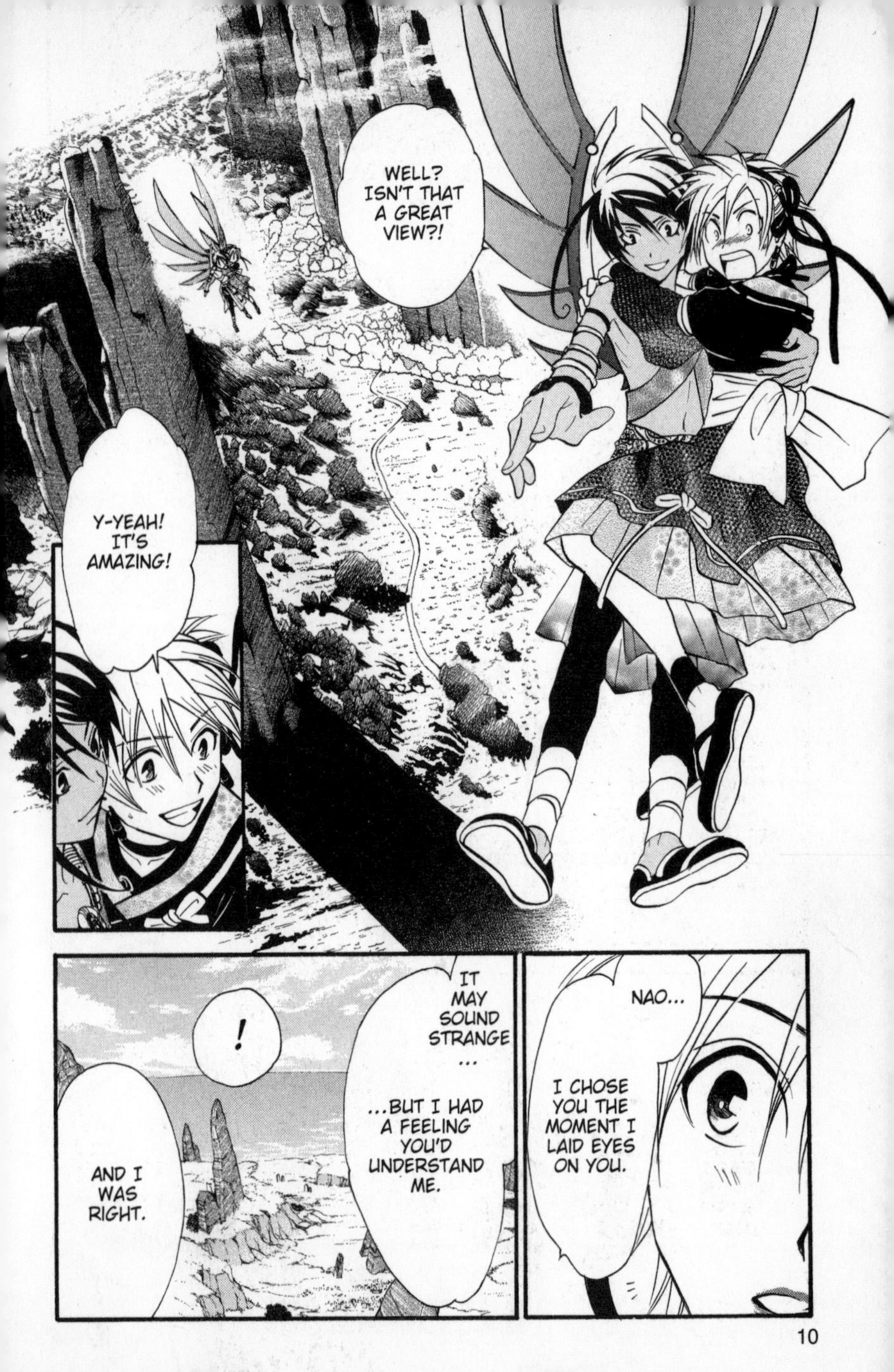
WELL? ISN'T THAT A GREAT VIEW?!
Y-YEAH! IT'S AMAZING!
NAO...
I CHOSE YOU THE MOMENT I LAID EYES ON YOU.
IT MAY SOUND STRANGE...
!
...BUT I HAD A FEELING YOU'D UNDERSTAND ME.
AND I WAS RIGHT.

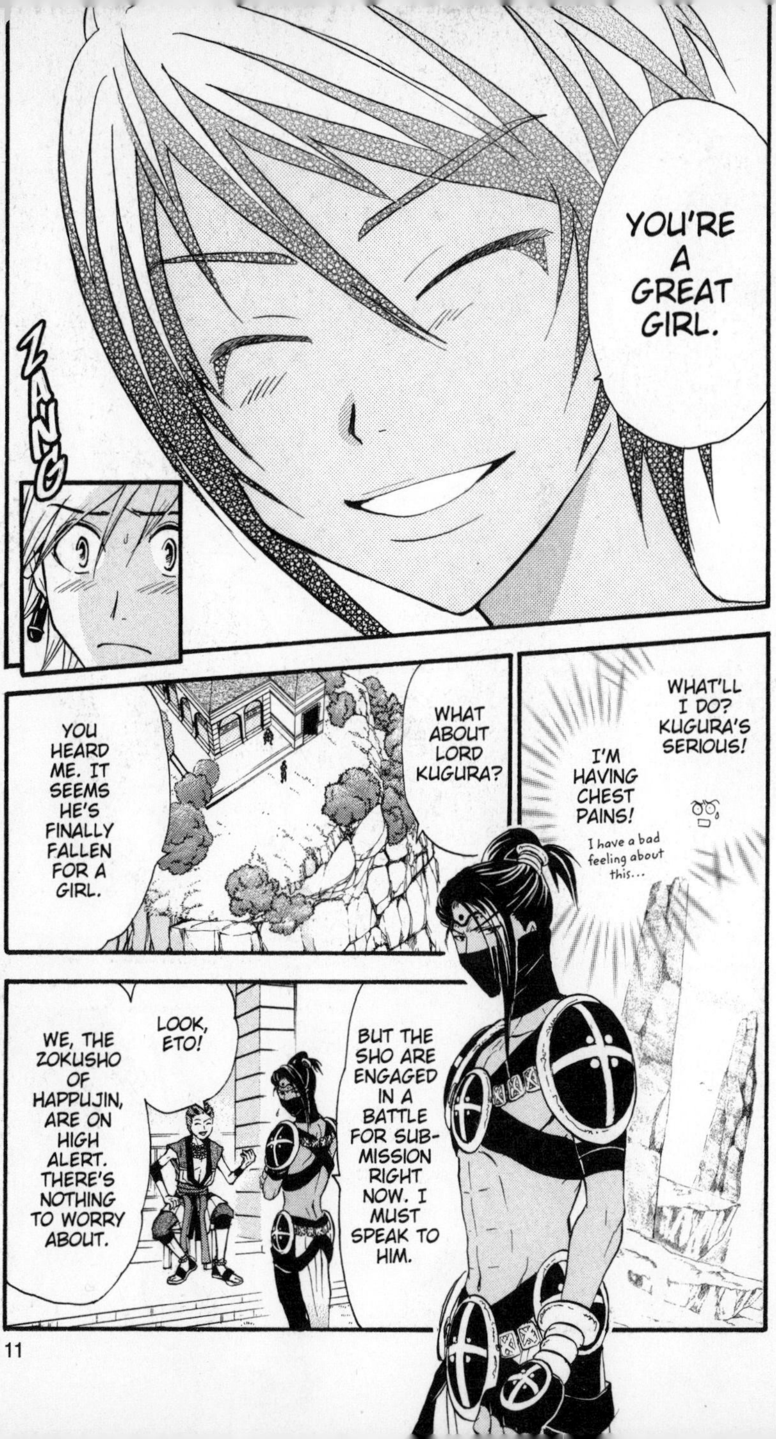
YOU'RE A GREAT GIRL.
ZANG
WHAT'LL I DO? KUGURA'S SERIOUS!
I'M HAVING CHEST PAINS!
I have a bad feeling about this...
WHAT ABOUT LORD KUGURA?
YOU HEARD ME. IT SEEMS HE'S FINALLY FALLEN FOR A GIRL.
BUT THE SHO ARE ENGAGED IN A BATTLE FOR SUB-MISSION RIGHT NOW. I MUST SPEAK TO HIM.
LOOK, ETO!
WE, THE ZOKUSHO OF HAPPUJIN, ARE ON HIGH ALERT. THERE'S NOTHING TO WORRY ABOUT.

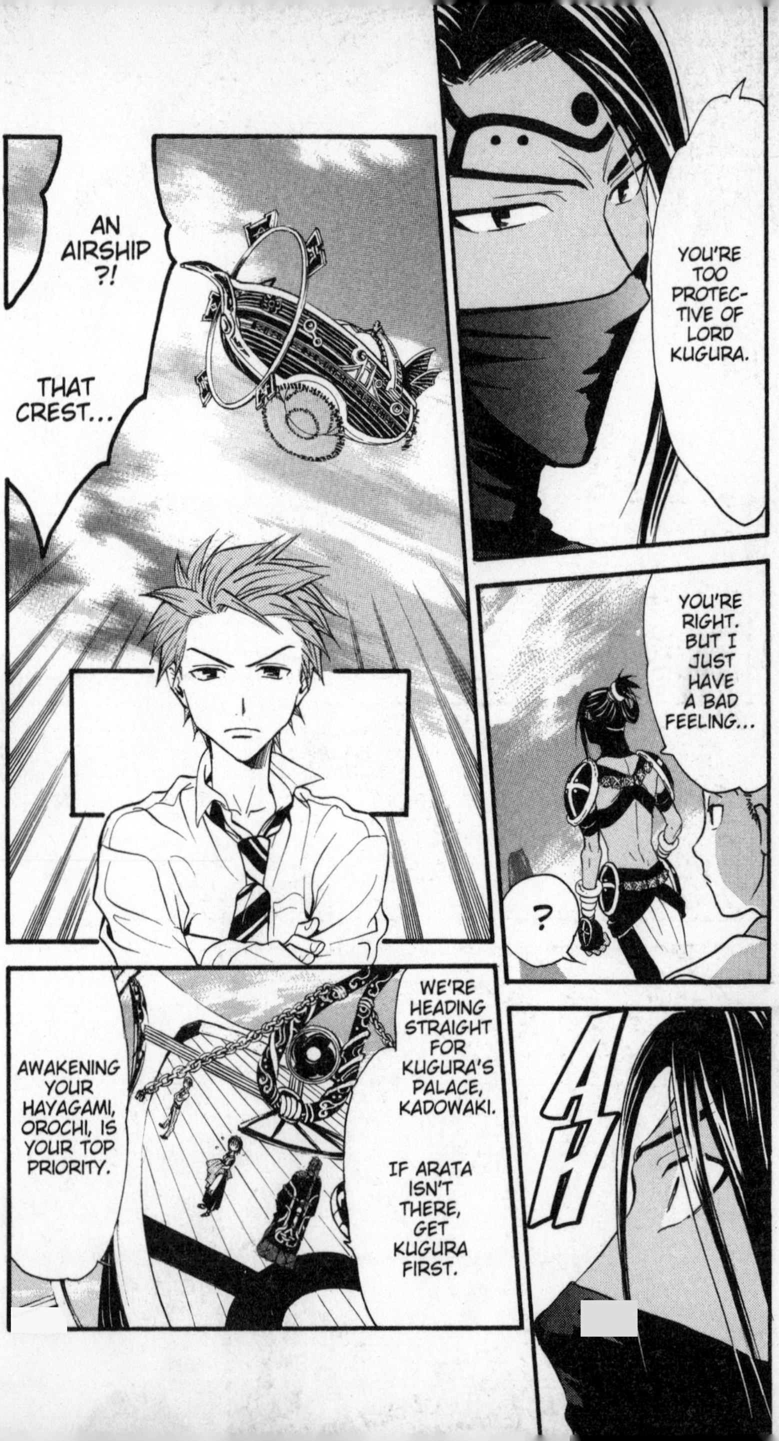
YOU'RE TOO PROTECTIVE OF LORD KUGURA.
YOU'RE RIGHT. BUT I JUST HAVE A BAD FEELING...
?
AN AIRSHIP ?!
THAT CREST...
AH
WE'RE HEADING STRAIGHT FOR KUGURA'S PALACE, KADOWAKI.
IF ARATA ISN'T THERE, GET KUGURA FIRST.
AWAKENING YOUR HAYAGAMI, OROCHI, IS YOUR TOP PRIORITY.

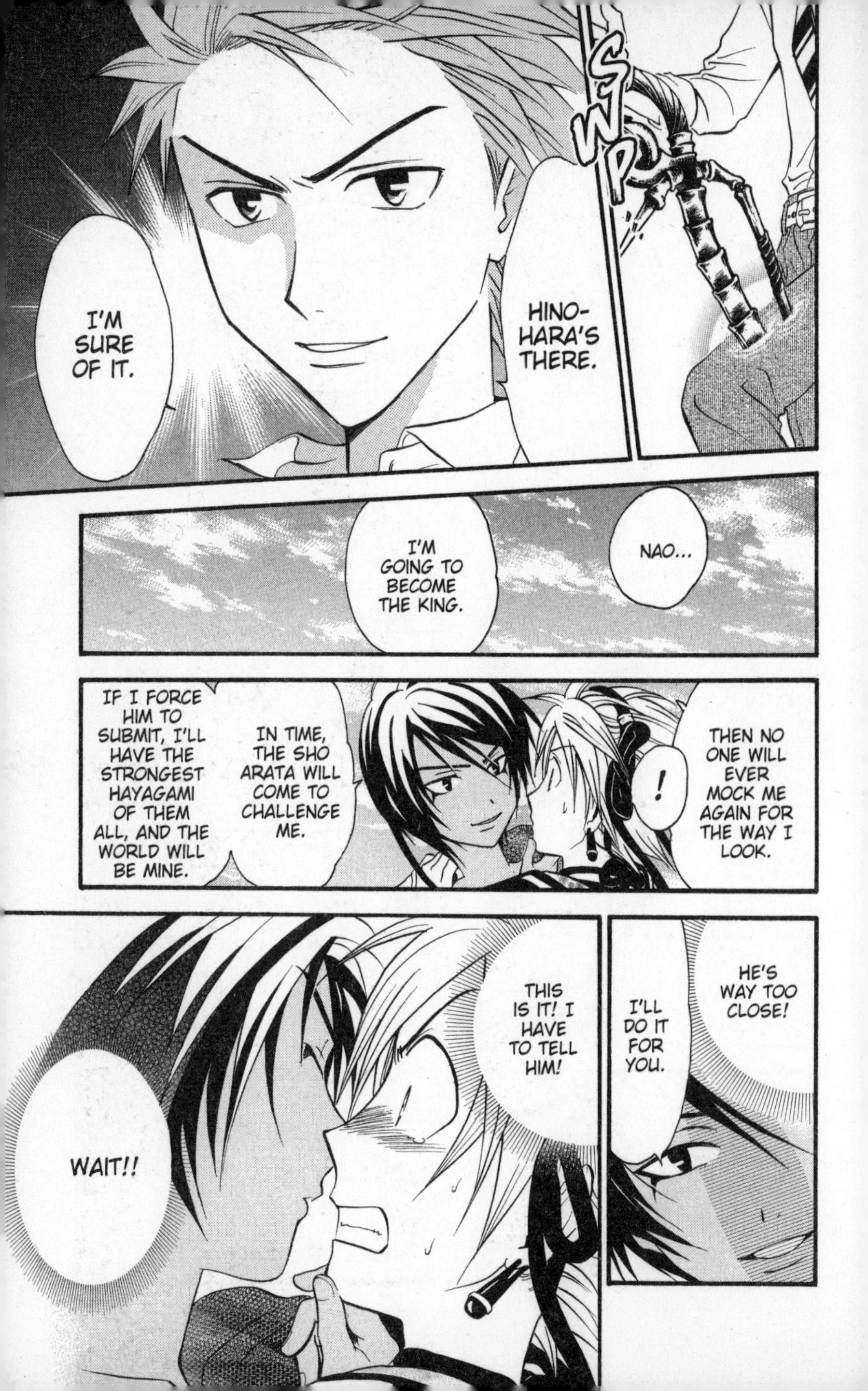

SWP
HINO-HARA'S THERE.
I'M SURE OF IT.
NAO...
I'M GOING TO BECOME THE KING.
THEN NO ONE WILL EVER MOCK ME AGAIN FOR THE WAY I LOOK.
!
IN TIME, THE SHO ARATA WILL COME TO CHALLENGE ME.
IF I FORCE HIM TO SUBMIT, I'LL HAVE THE STRONGEST HAYAGAMI OF THEM ALL, AND THE WORLD WILL BE MINE.
HE'S WAY TOO CLOSE!
I'LL DO IT FOR YOU.
THIS IS IT! I HAVE TO TELL HIM!
WAIT!!

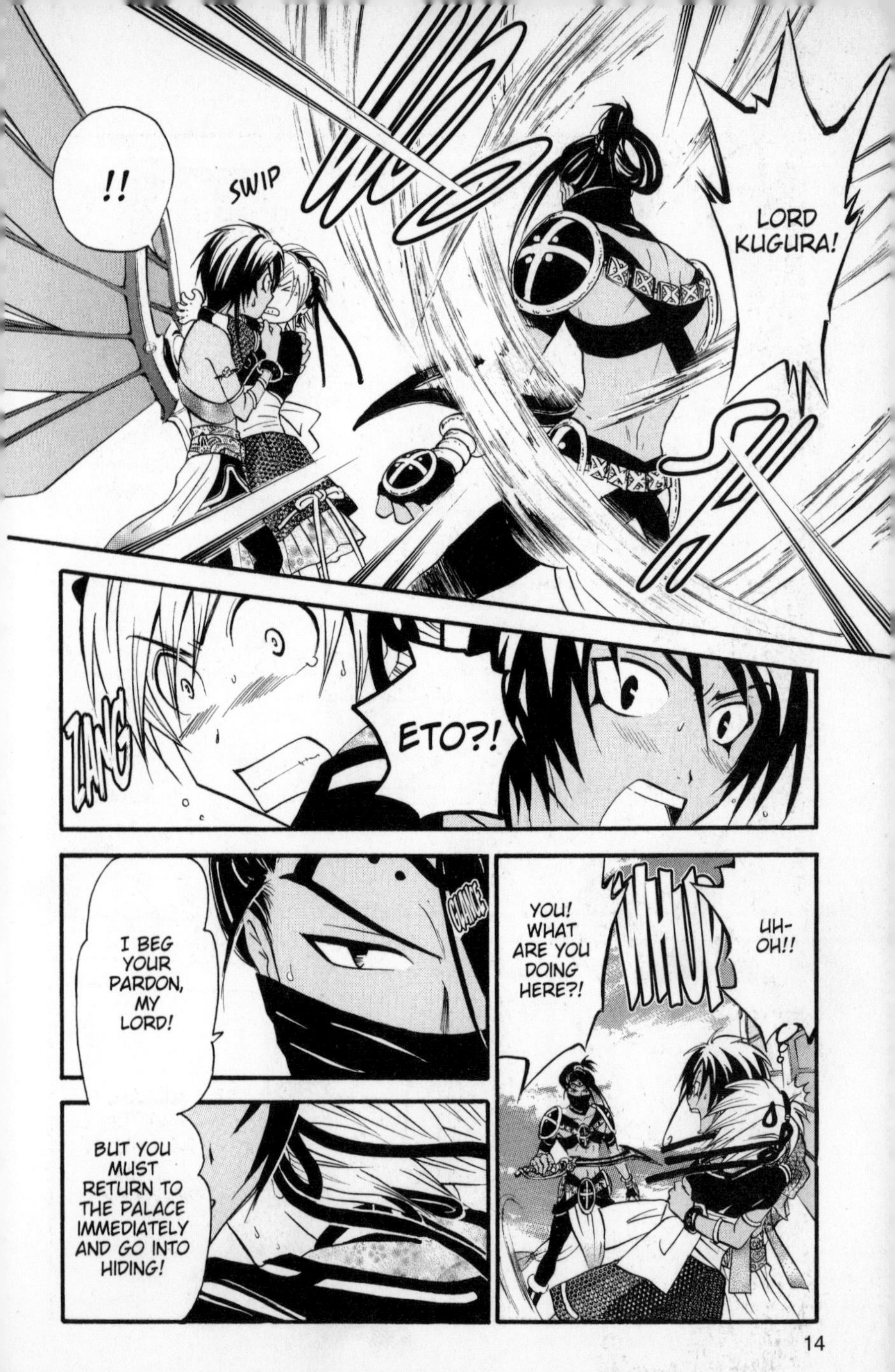
LORD KUGURA!
SWIP
!!
ETO?!
UH-OH!!
WHUP
YOU! WHAT ARE YOU DOING HERE?!
GLANCE
I BEG YOUR PARDON, MY LORD!
BUT YOU MUST RETURN TO THE PALACE IMMEDIATELY AND GO INTO HIDING!

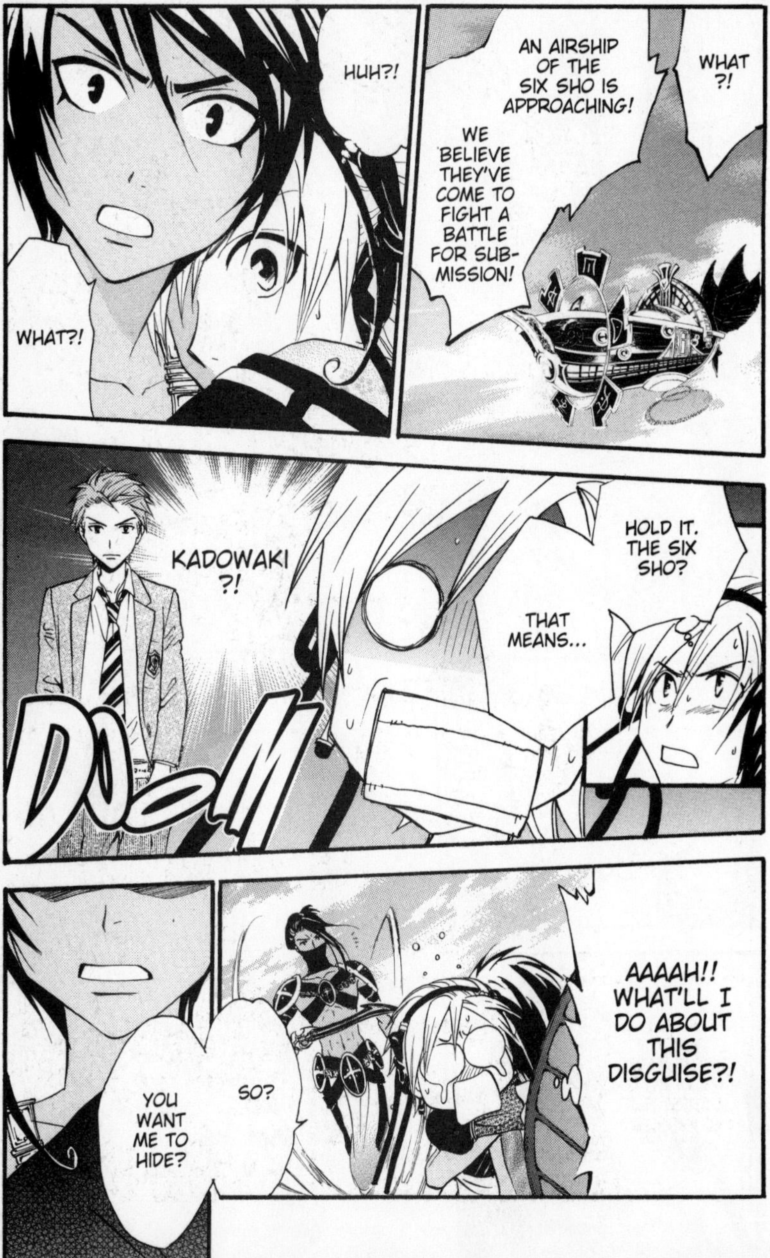
WHAT ?!
AN AIRSHIP OF THE SIX SHO IS APPROACHING!
WE BELIEVE THEY'VE COME TO FIGHT A BATTLE FOR SUB-MISSION!
HUH?!
WHAT?!
HOLD IT. THE SIX SHO?
THAT MEANS...
KADOWAKI ?!
DOOM
AAAAH!! WHAT'LL I DO ABOUT THIS DISGUISE?!
SO?
YOU WANT ME TO HIDE?

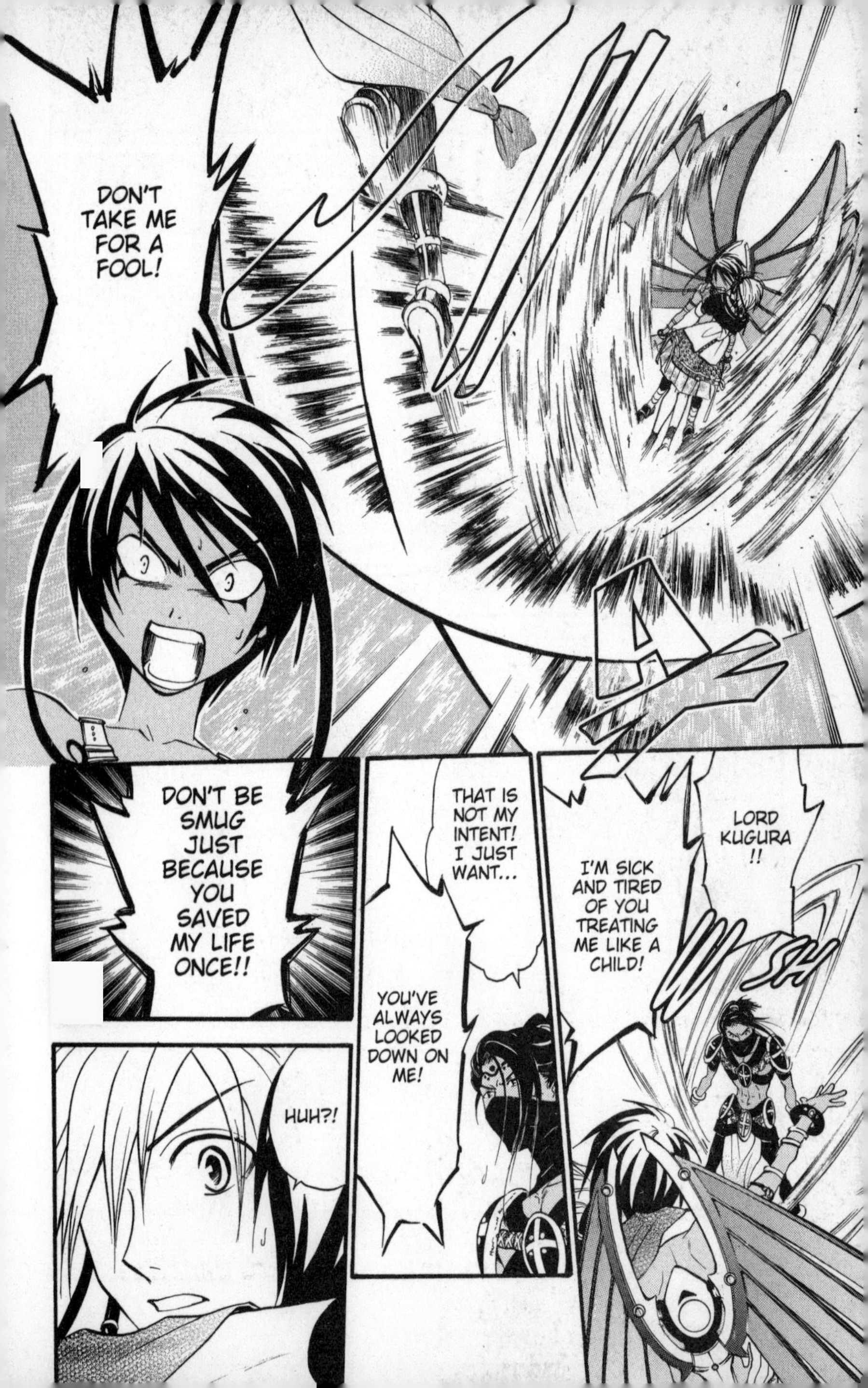
DON'T TAKE ME FOR A FOOL!
LORD KUGURA !!
I'M SICK AND TIRED OF YOU TREATING ME LIKE A CHILD!
THAT IS NOT MY INTENT! I JUST WANT...
YOU'VE ALWAYS LOOKED DOWN ON ME!
DON'T BE SMUG JUST BECAUSE YOU SAVED MY LIFE ONCE!!
HUH?!

LORD
KUGURA
...

WO OO!

THAT'S
...

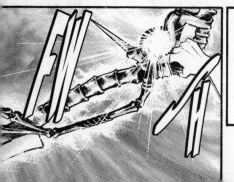

FW

HEH

APPEAR
...

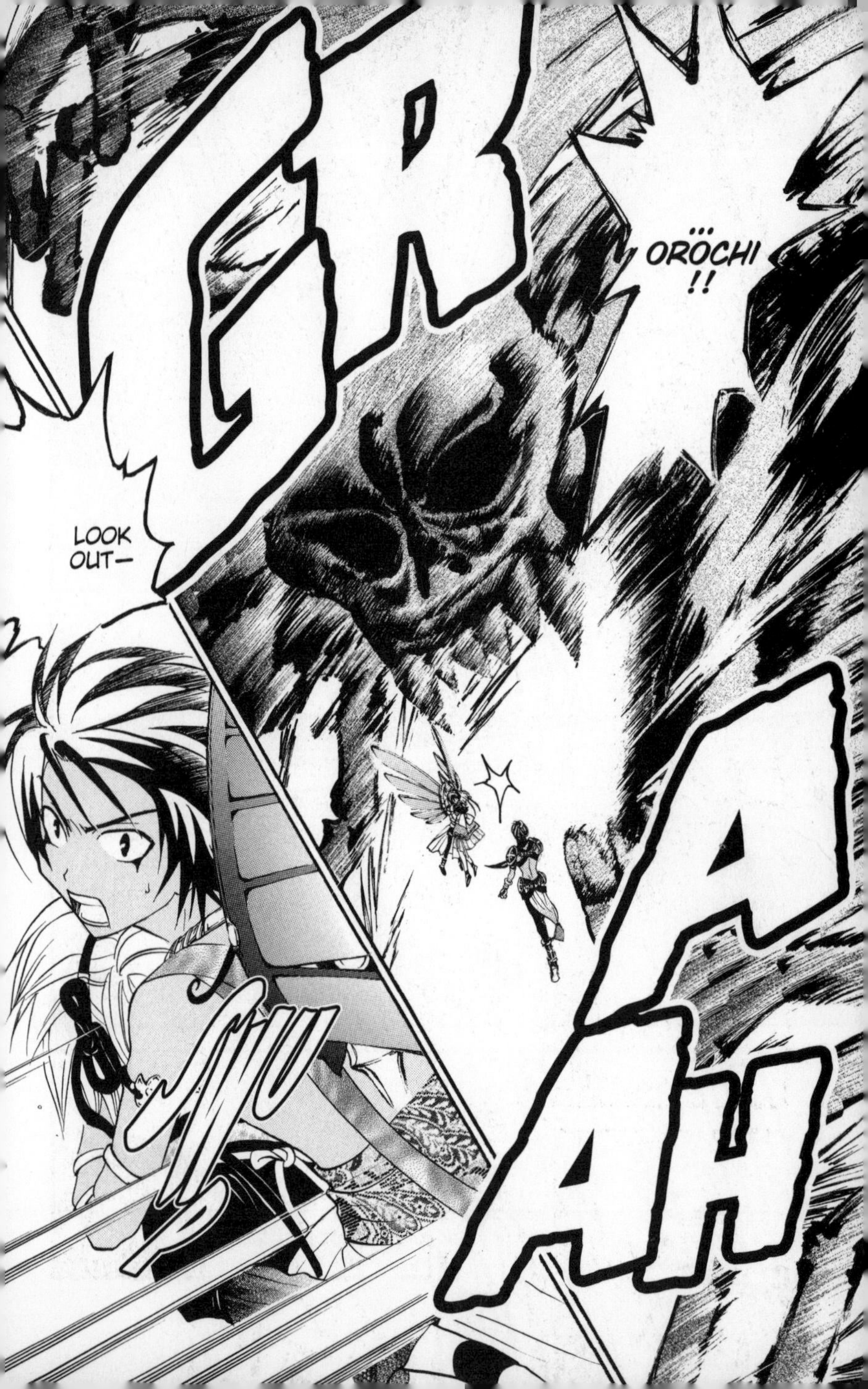
...ORÖCHI !!
LOOK OUT–

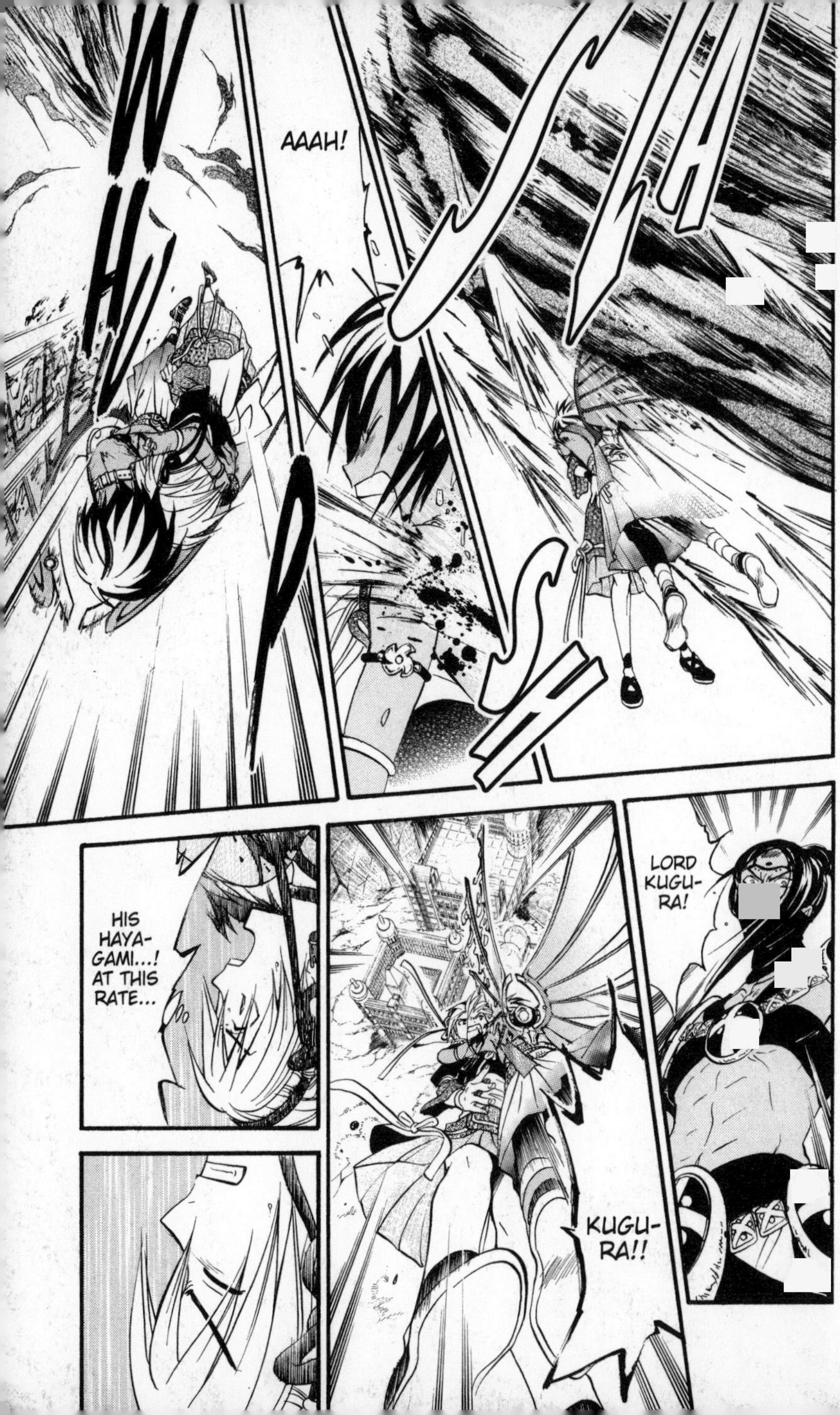
AAAH!
LORD KUGU-RA!
KUGU-RA!!
HIS HAYA-GAMI...! AT THIS RATE...

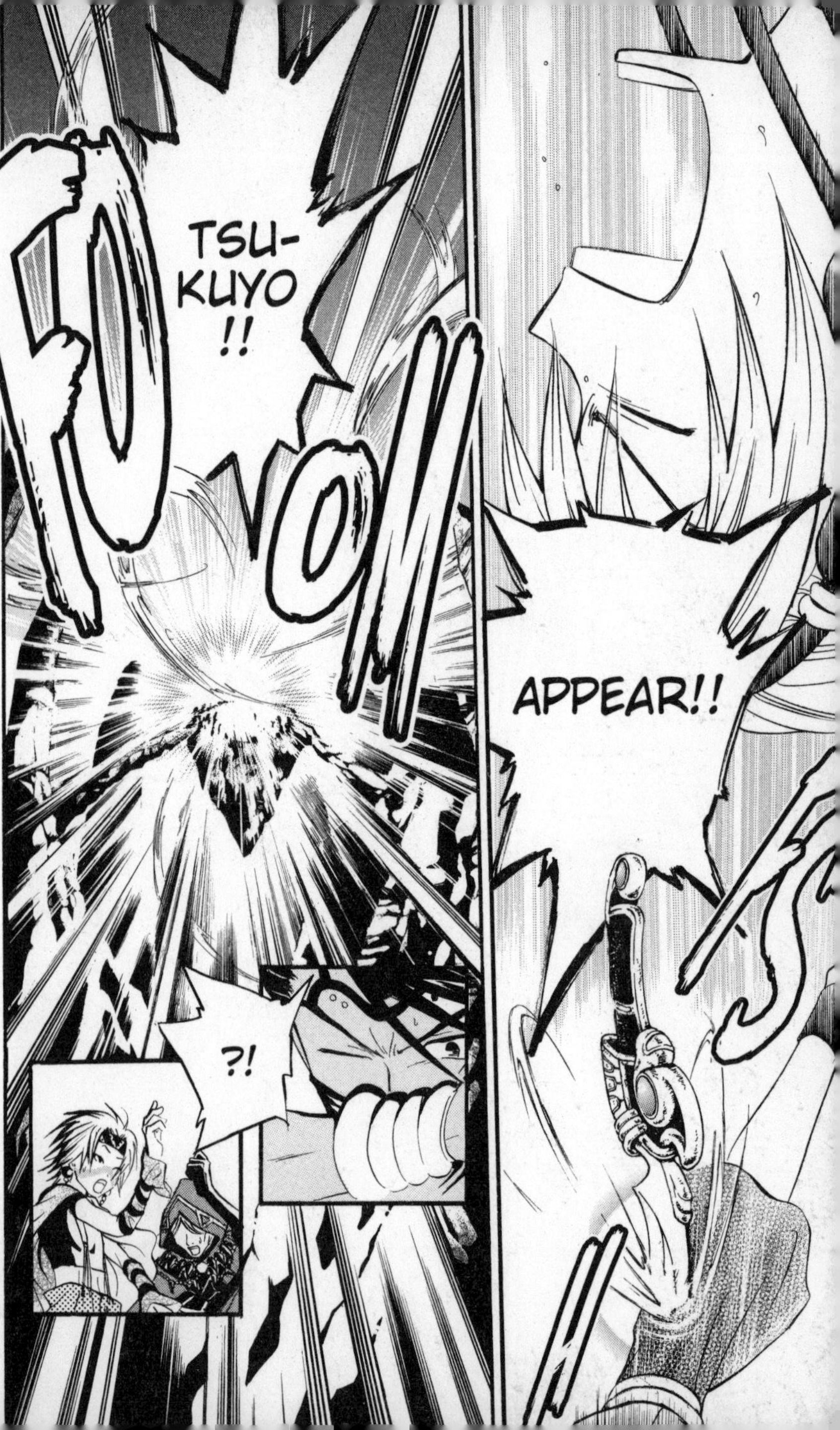
APPEAR!!
TSU-KUYO!!
?!

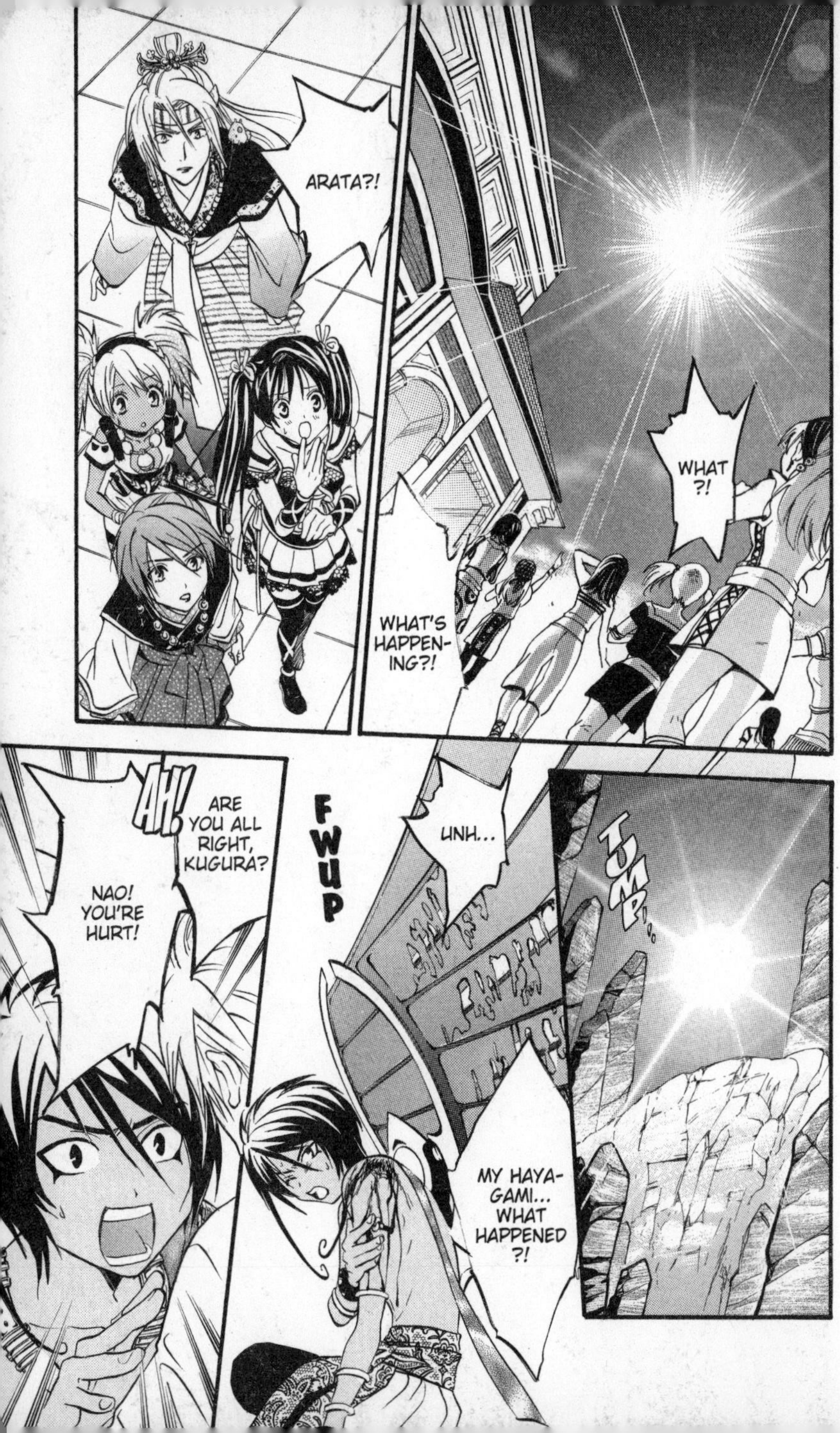
WHAT ?!
WHAT'S HAPPEN-ING?!
ARATA?!
TUMP
UNH...
FWUP
MY HAYA-GAMI... WHAT HAPPENED ?!
AH!
ARE YOU ALL RIGHT, KUGURA?
NAO! YOU'RE HURT!

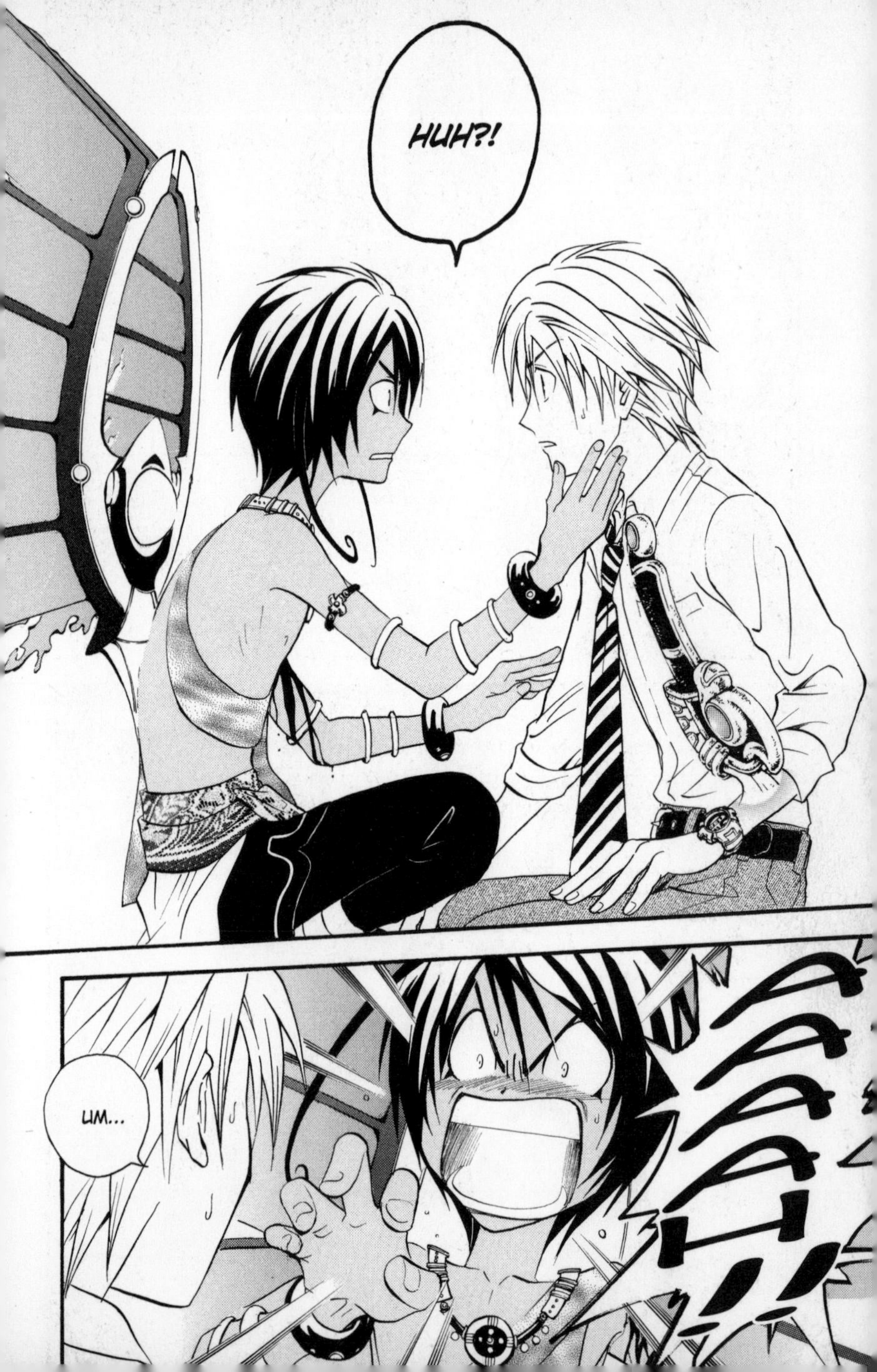
HUH?!
UM...

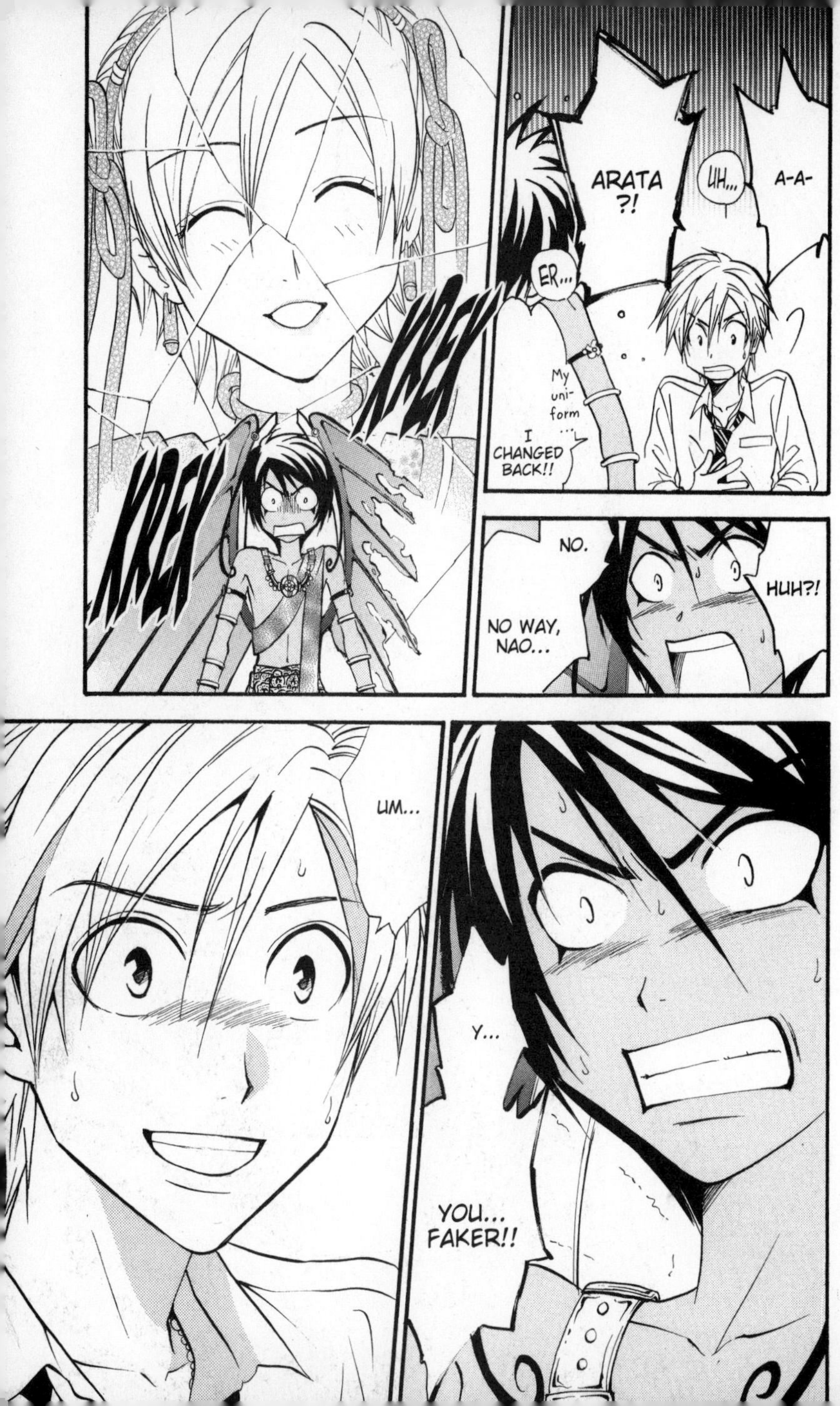
A-A-
UH...
ARATA ?!
ER...
My uni-form...
I CHANGED BACK!!
HUH?!
NO.
NO WAY, NAO...
Y...
YOU... FAKER!!
UM...

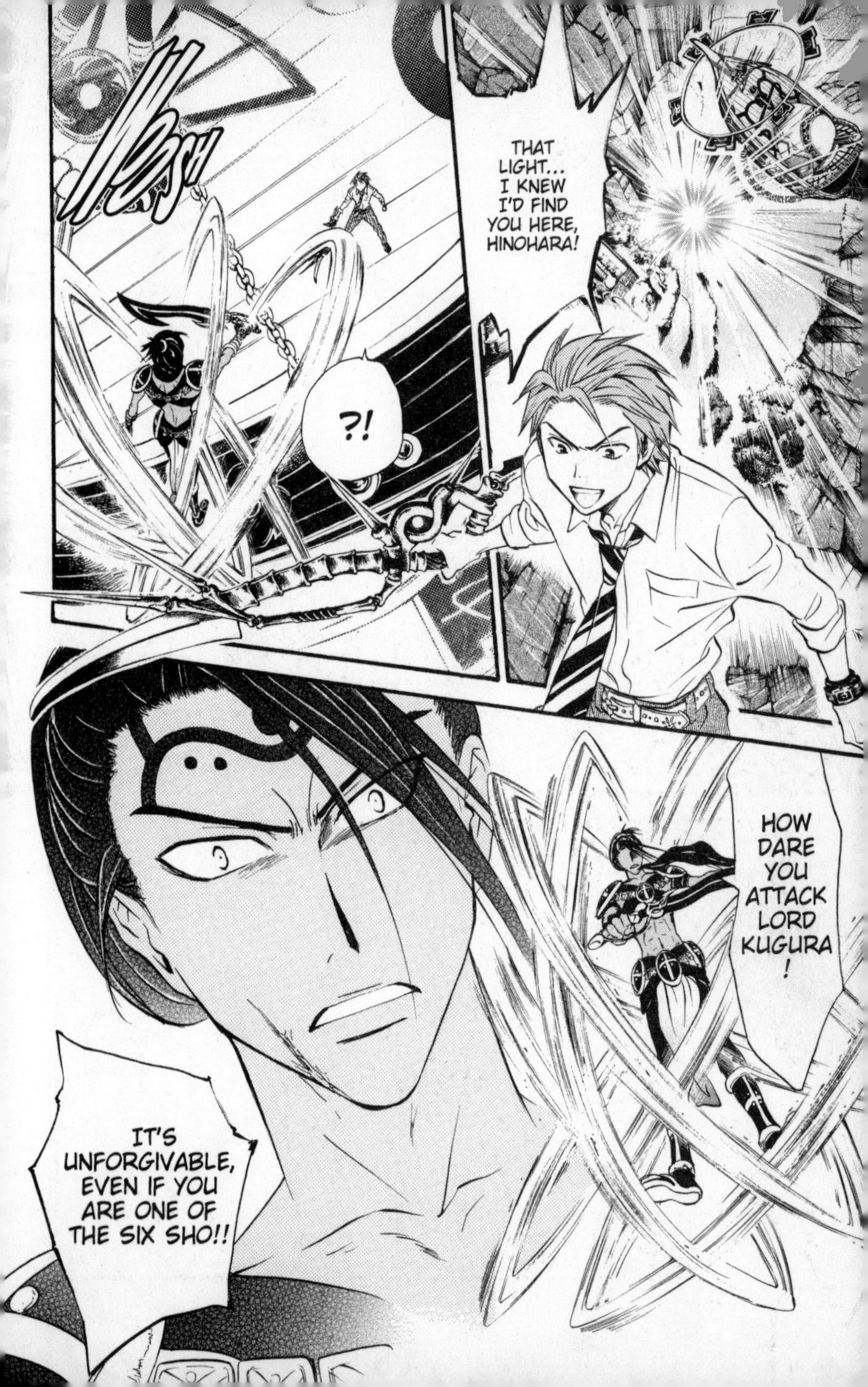
THAT LIGHT... I KNEW I'D FIND YOU HERE, HINOHARA!
VOSH
?!
HOW DARE YOU ATTACK LORD KUGURA!
IT'S UNFORGIVABLE, EVEN IF YOU ARE ONE OF THE SIX SHO!!

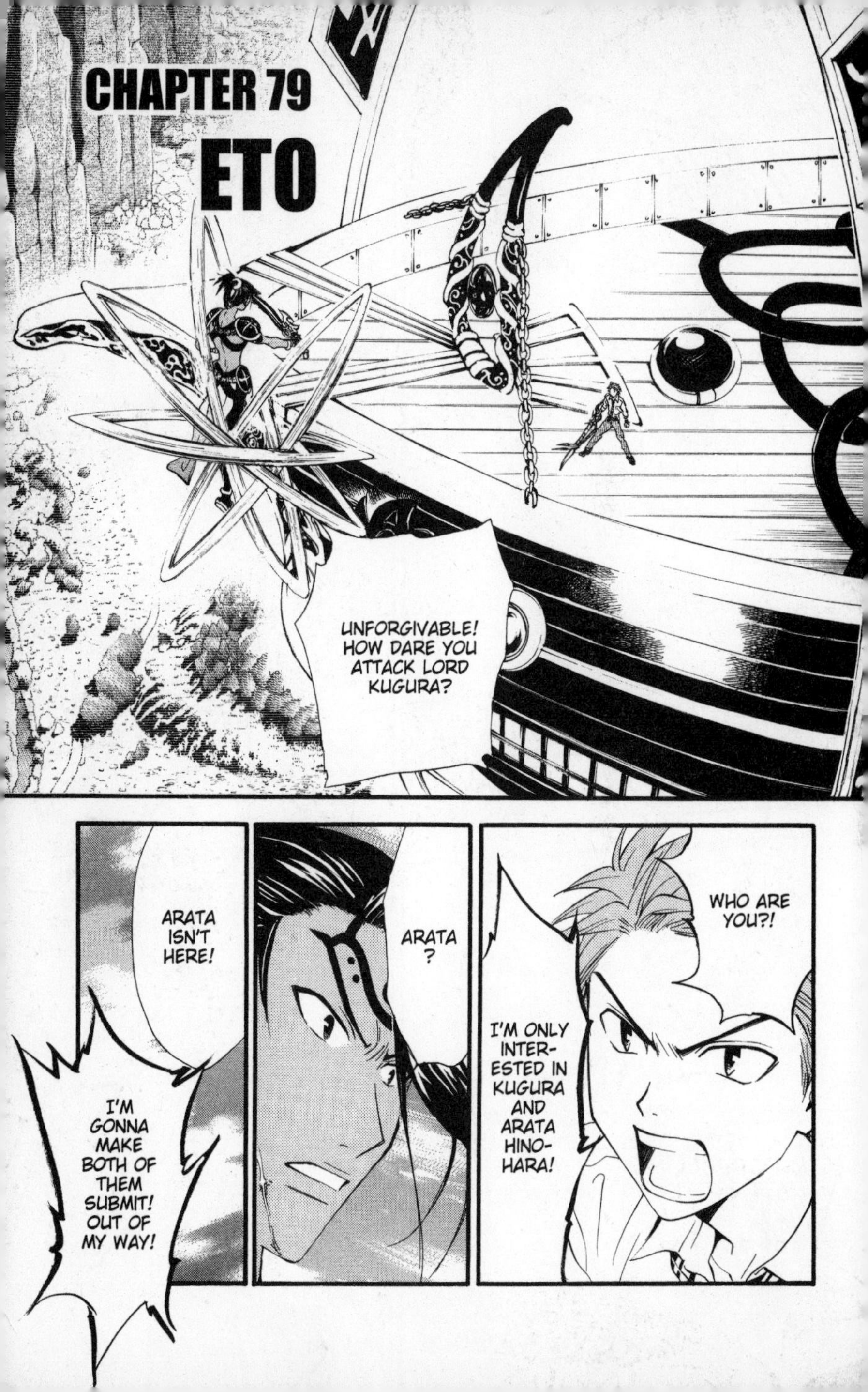
CHAPTER 79
ETO
UNFORGIVABLE! HOW DARE YOU ATTACK LORD KUGURA?
WHO ARE YOU?!
I'M ONLY INTER-ESTED IN KUGURA AND ARATA HINO-HARA!
ARATA?
ARATA ISN'T HERE!
I'M GONNA MAKE BOTH OF THEM SUBMIT! OUT OF MY WAY!

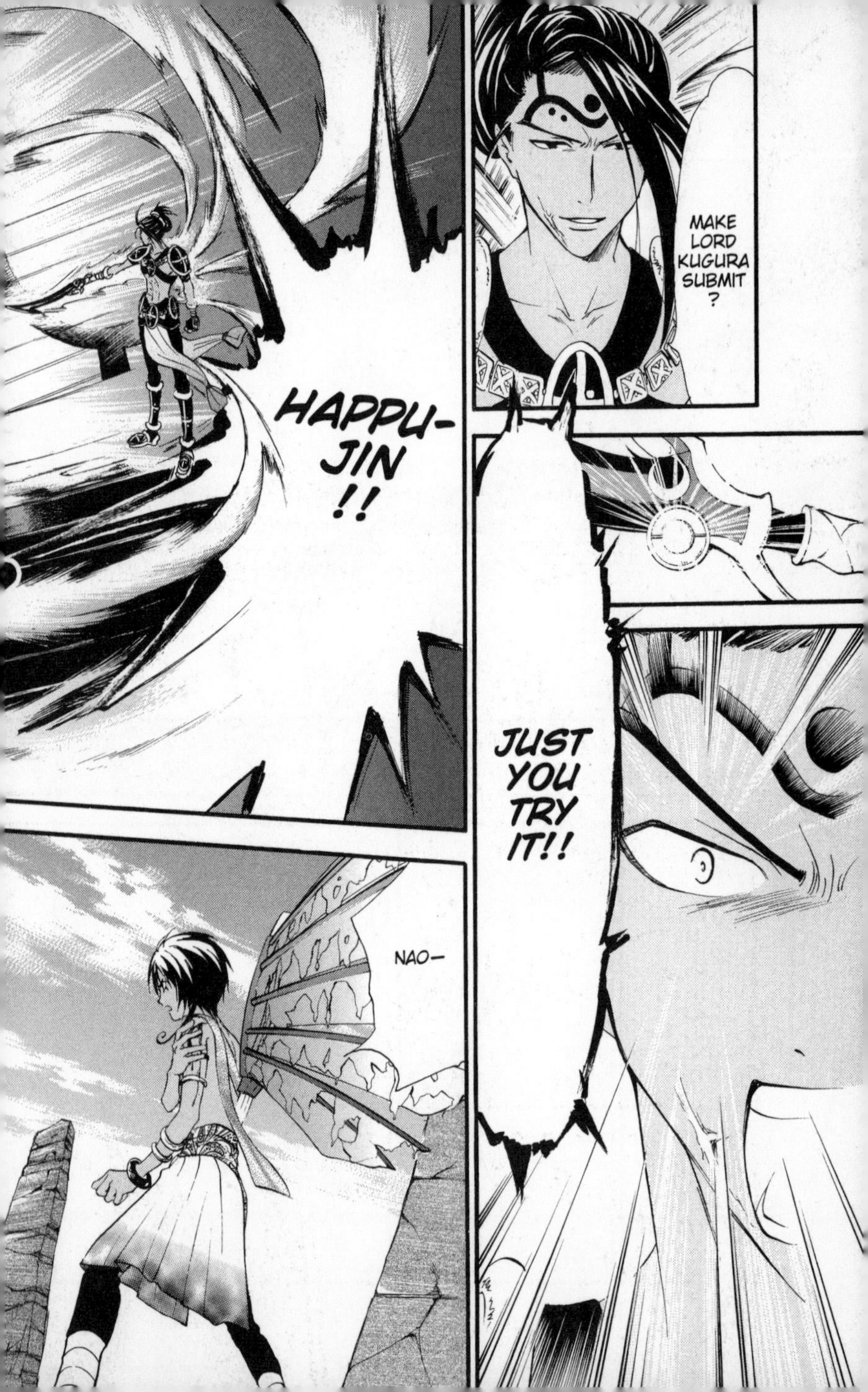
MAKE LORD KUGURA SUBMIT?
HAPPU-JIN!!
JUST YOU TRY IT!!
NAO-

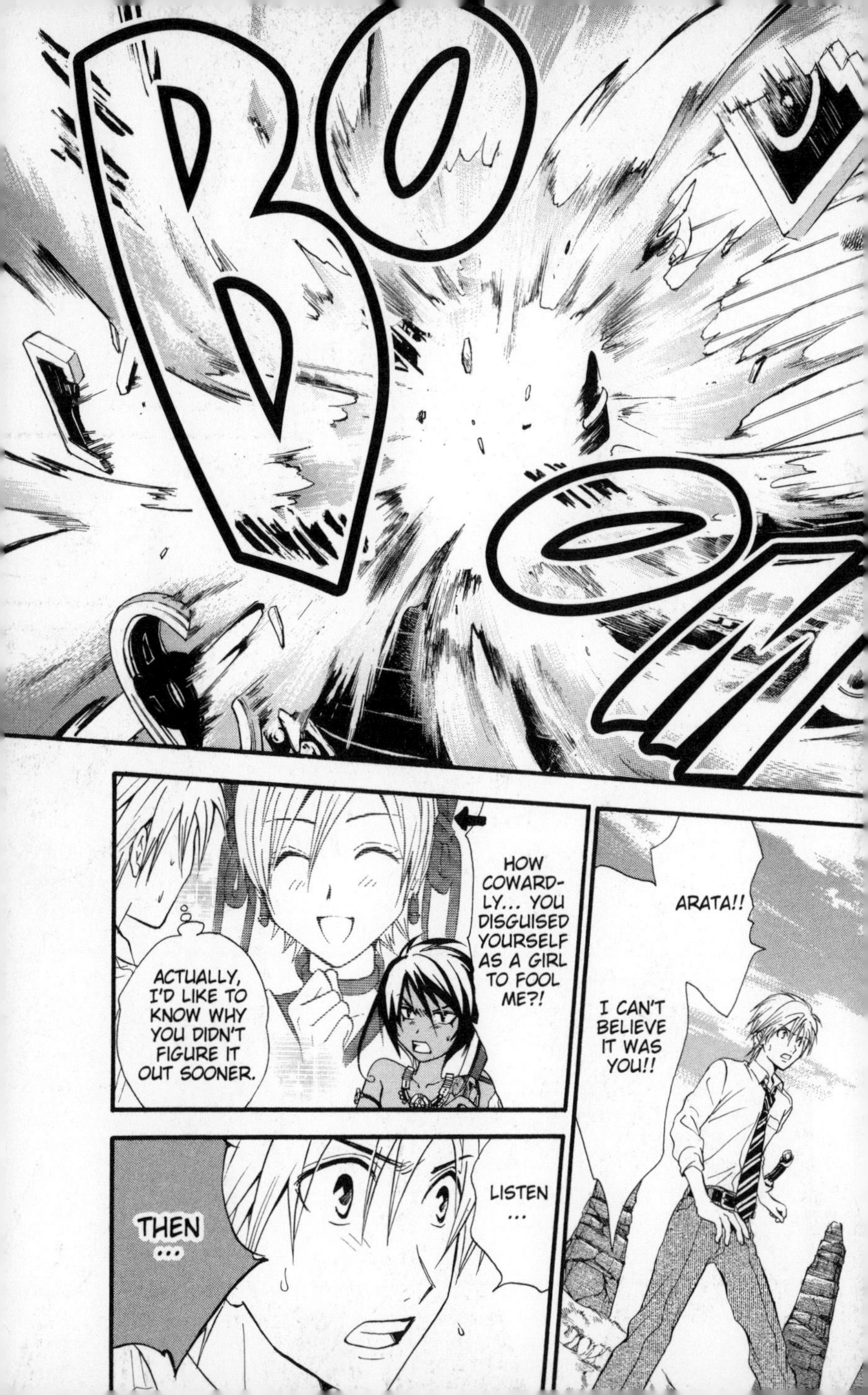

BOOM
ARATA!!
I CAN'T BELIEVE IT WAS YOU!!
HOW COWARDLY... YOU DISGUISED YOURSELF AS A GIRL TO FOOL ME?!
ACTUALLY, I'D LIKE TO KNOW WHY YOU DIDN'T FIGURE IT OUT SOONER.
LISTEN...
THEN...

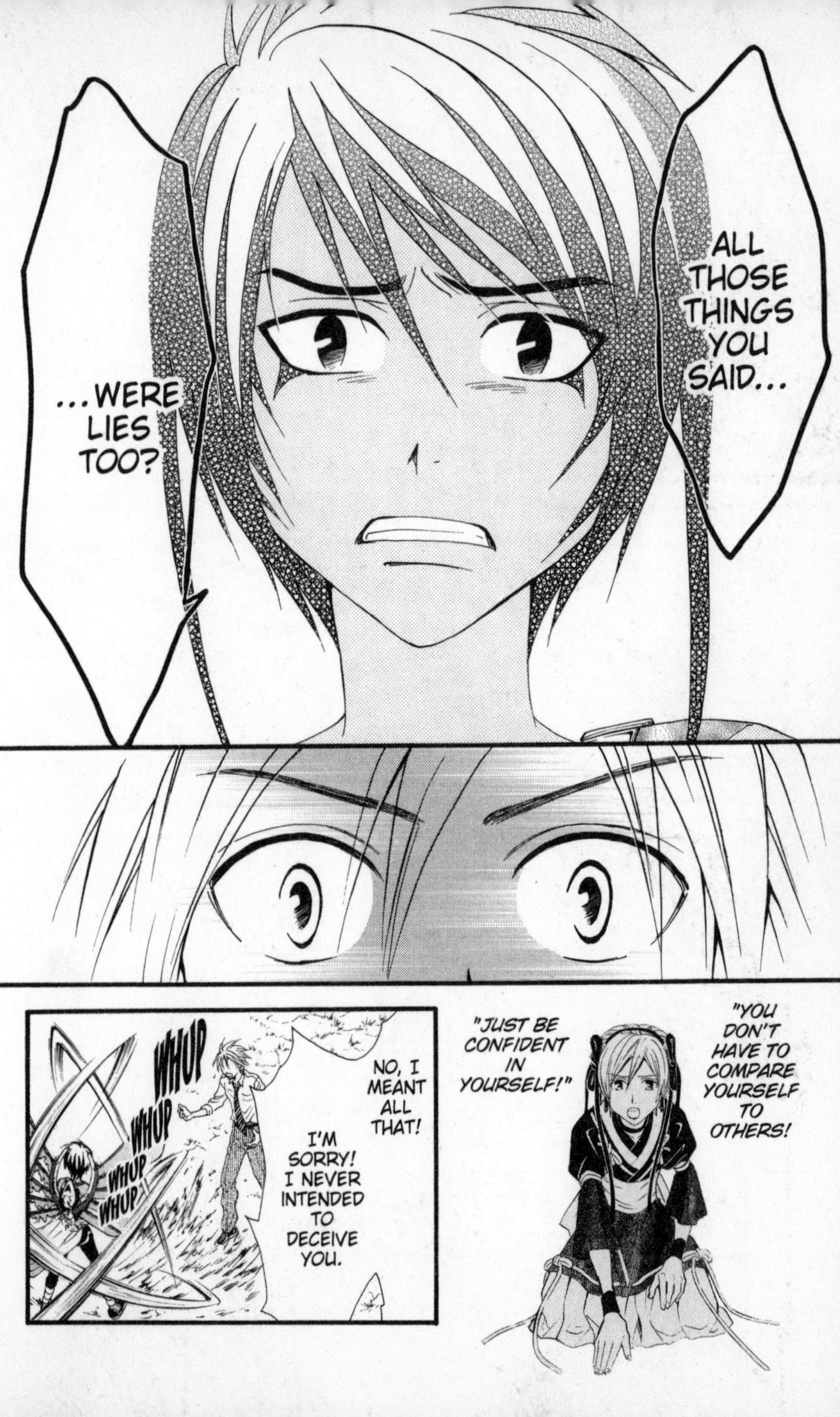
ALL THOSE THINGS YOU SAID...
...WERE LIES TOO?
"YOU DON'T HAVE TO COMPARE YOURSELF TO OTHERS!
"JUST BE CONFIDENT IN YOURSELF!"
NO, I MEANT ALL THAT!
I'M SORRY! I NEVER INTENDED TO DECEIVE YOU.
WHUP
WHUP
WHUP
WHUP

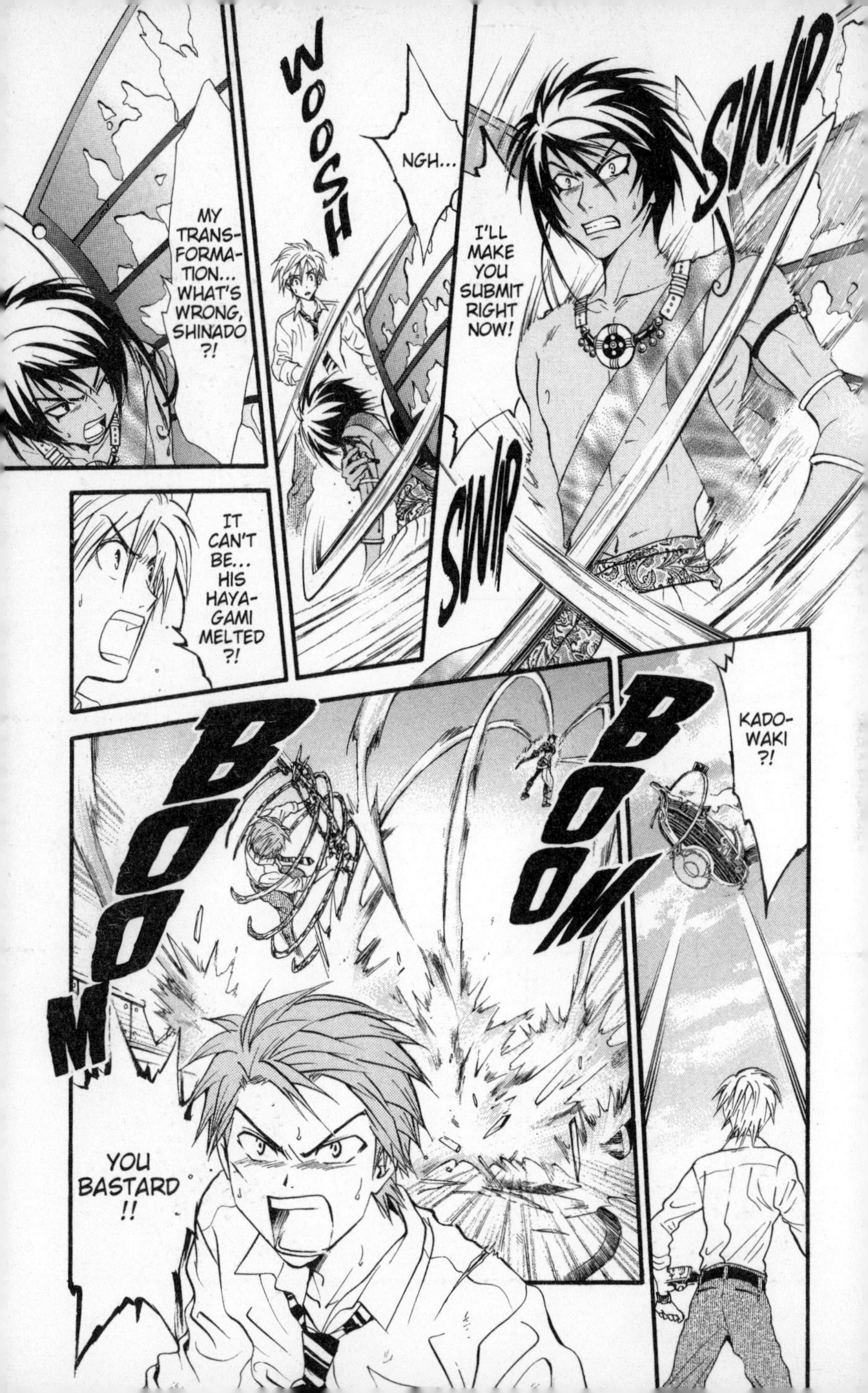
SWIP
I'LL MAKE YOU SUBMIT RIGHT NOW!
SWIP
WOOSH
NGH...
MY TRANSFORMATION... WHAT'S WRONG, SHINADO?!
IT CAN'T BE... HIS HAYAGAMI MELTED?!
BOOM
KADOWAKI?!
BOOM
YOU BASTARD!!

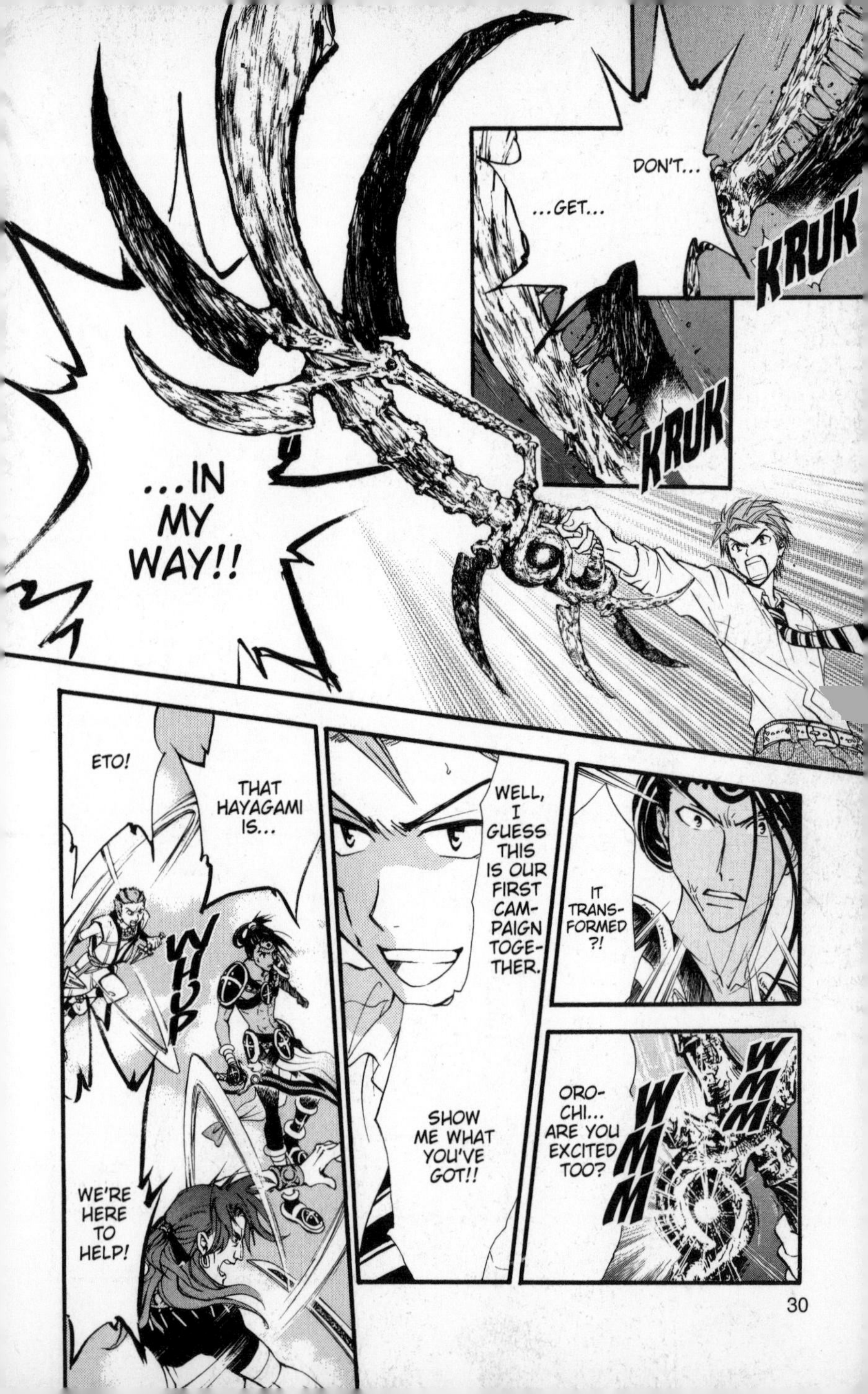
DON'T...
...GET...
KRUK
KRUK
...IN MY WAY!!
IT TRANSFORMED?!
WMM
WMM
ORO-CHI... ARE YOU EXCITED TOO?
WELL, I GUESS THIS IS OUR FIRST CAMPAIGN TOGETHER.
SHOW ME WHAT YOU'VE GOT!!
ETO!
THAT HAYAGAMI IS...
WHUP
WE'RE HERE TO HELP!

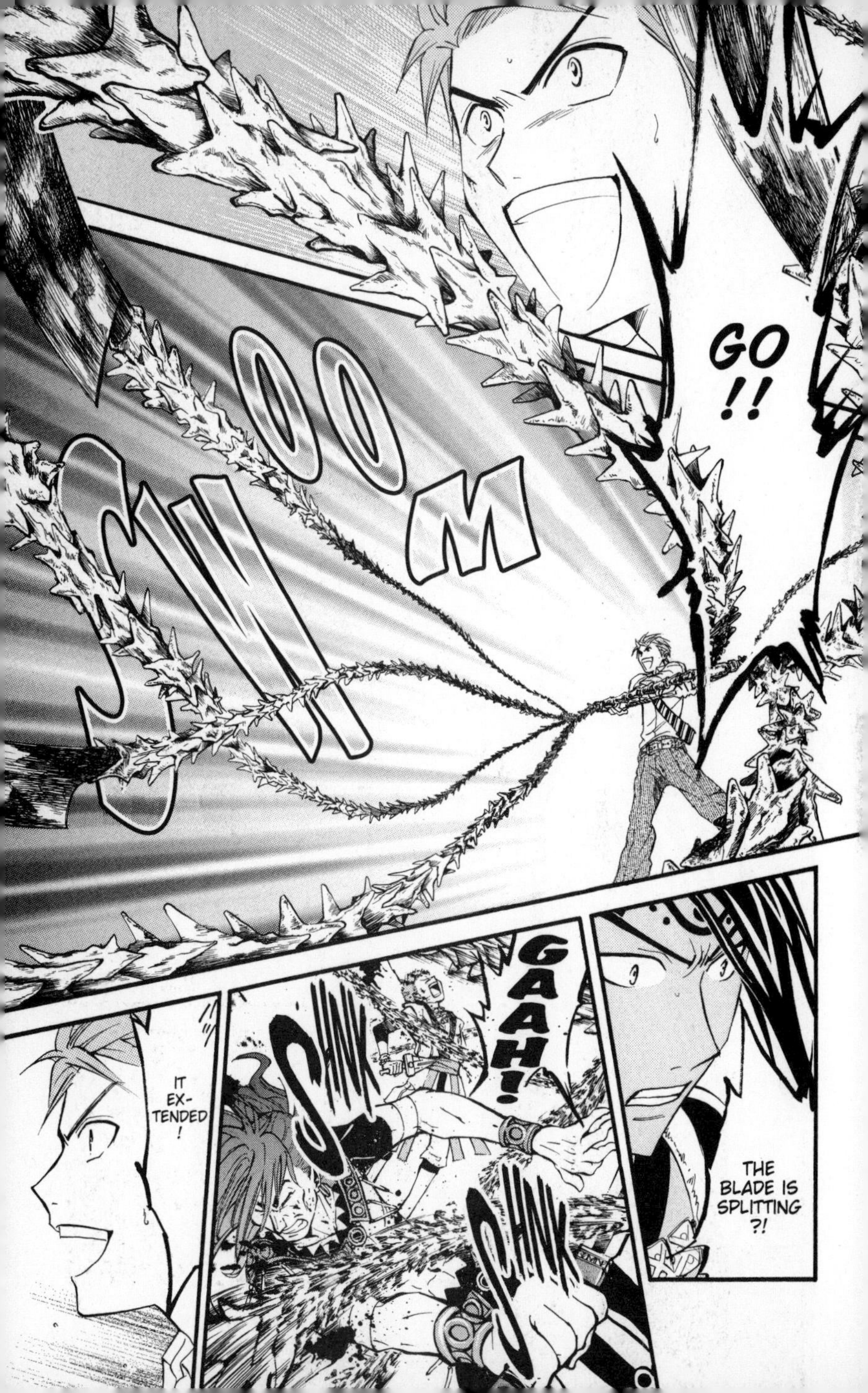
GO!!
SHWOOM
THE BLADE IS SPLITTING?!
GAAH!
SHINK
SHINK
IT EXTENDED!

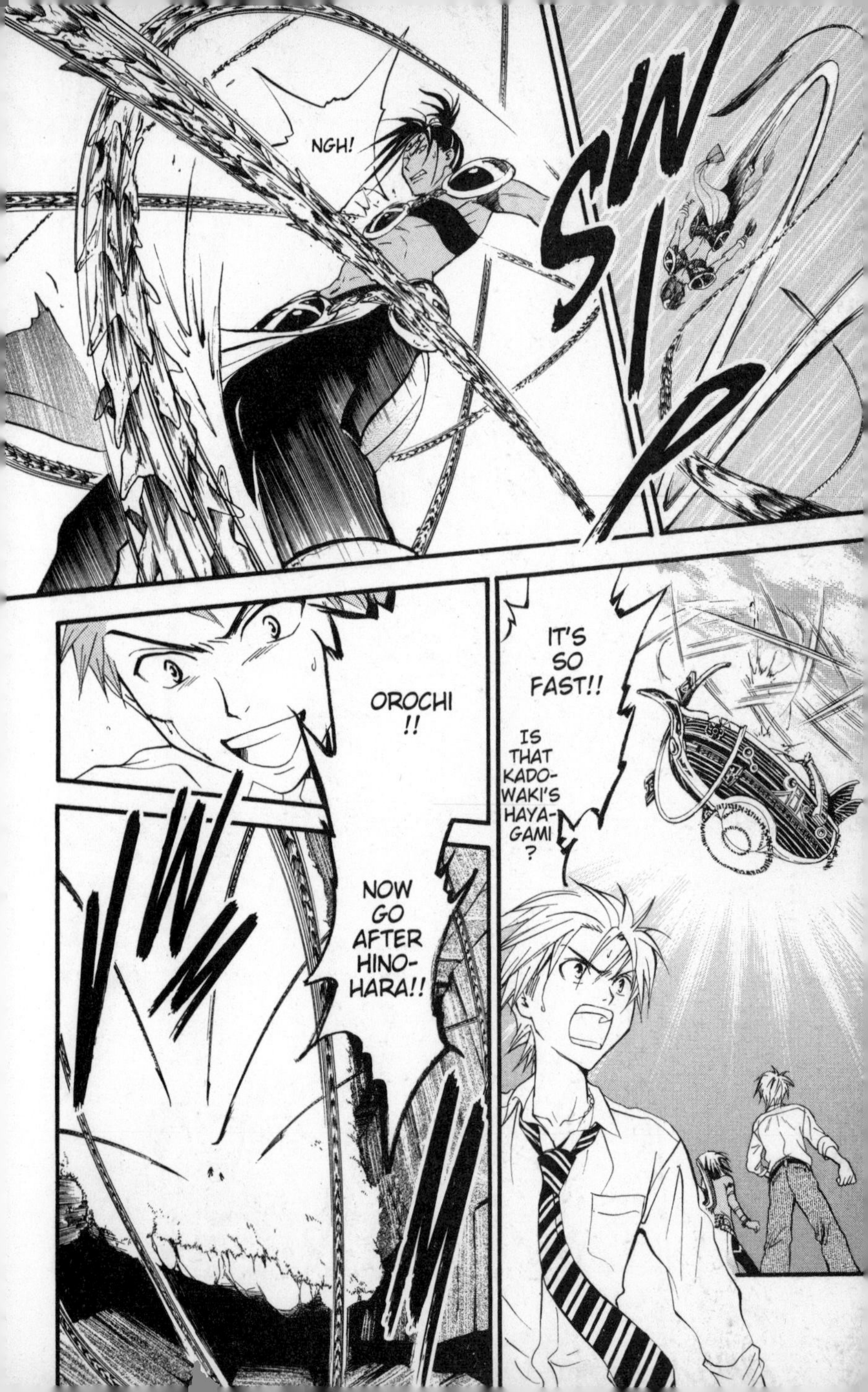
NGH!
IT'S SO FAST!!
IS THAT KADO-WAKI'S HAYA-GAMI?
OROCHI!!
NOW GO AFTER HINO-HARA!!

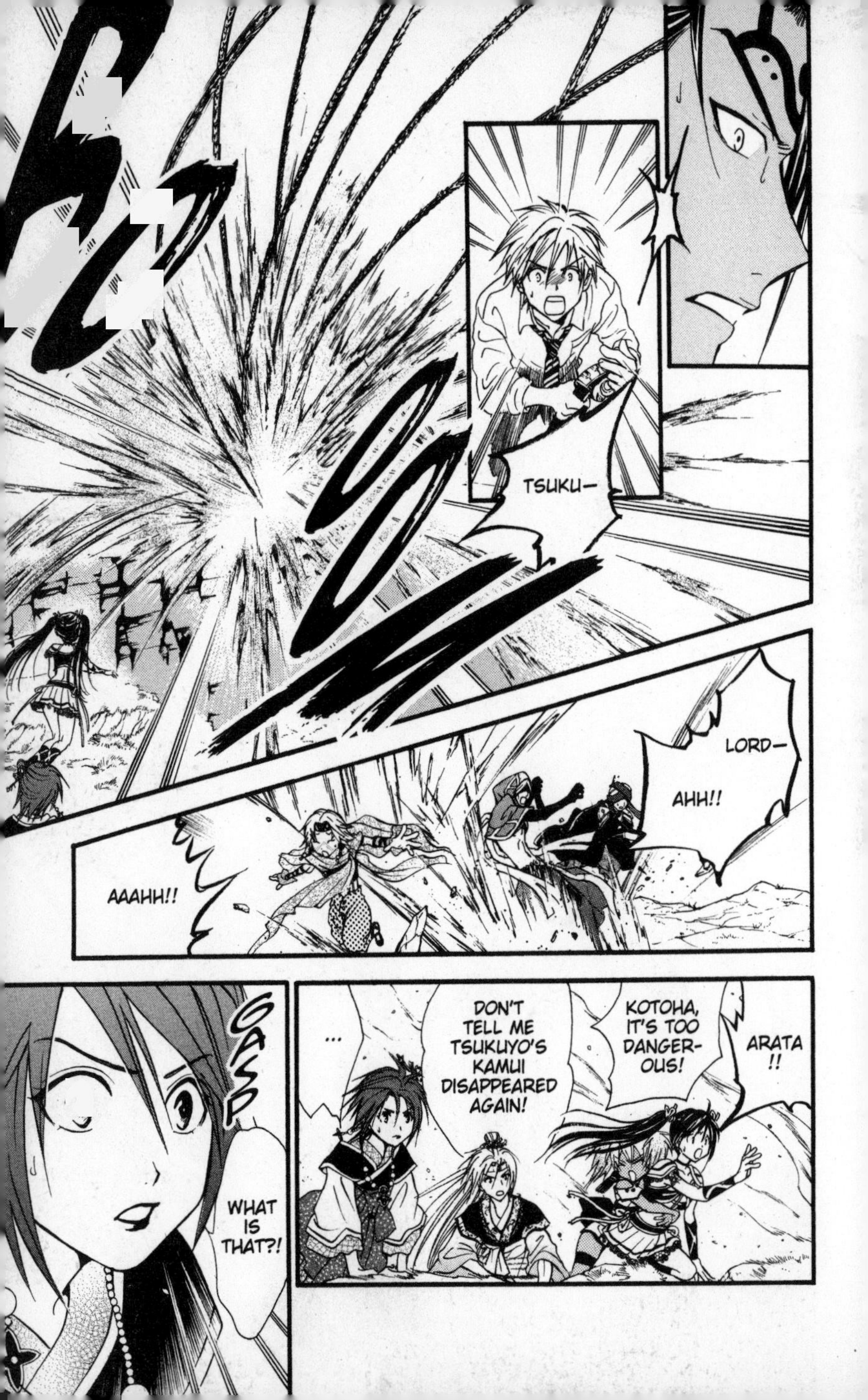
TSUKU—
LORD—
AHH!!
AAAHH!!
ARATA !!
KOTOHA, IT'S TOO DANGER-OUS!
DON'T TELL ME TSUKUYO'S KAMUI DISAPPEARED AGAIN!
...
GASP
WHAT IS THAT?!

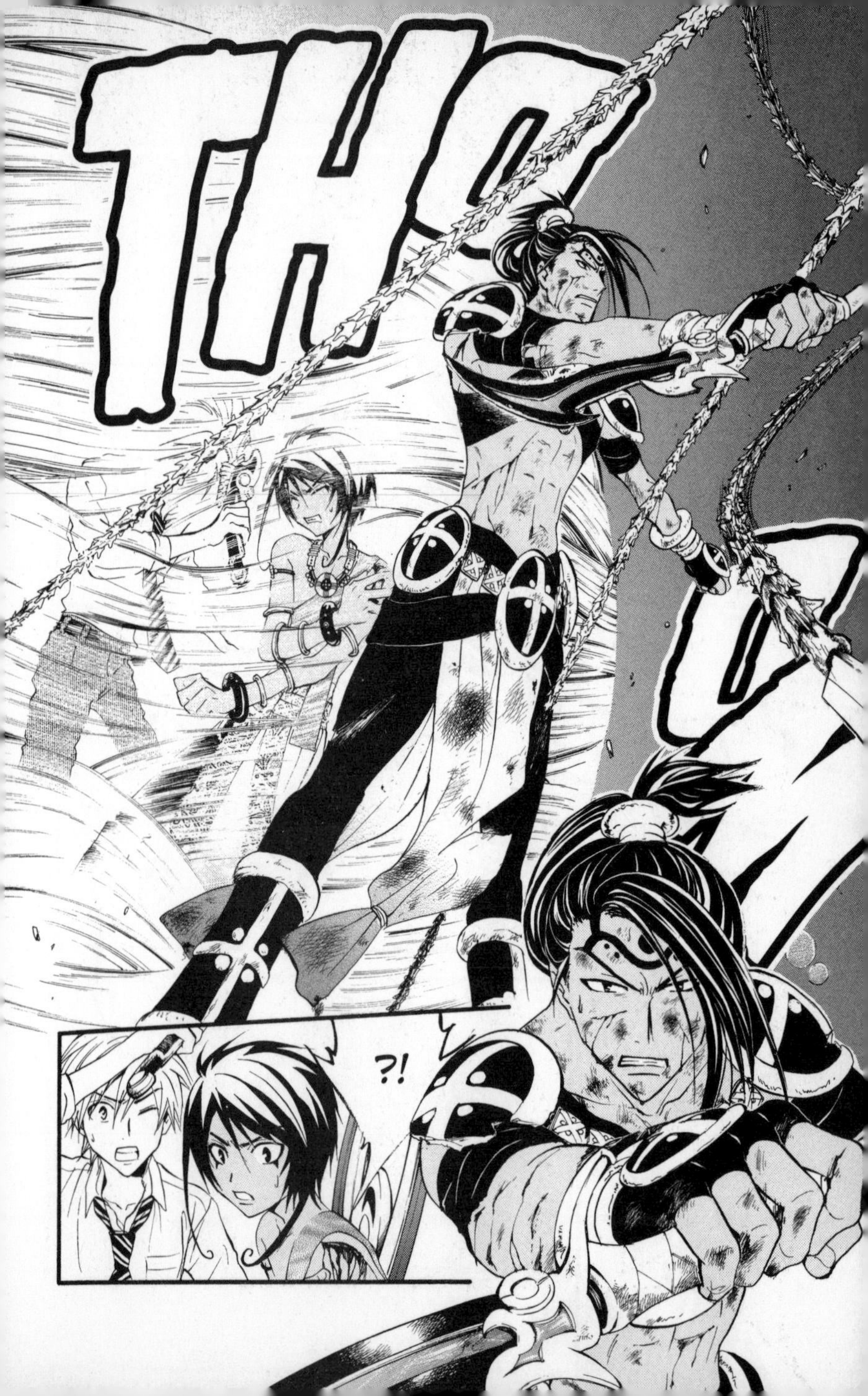

THO
?!

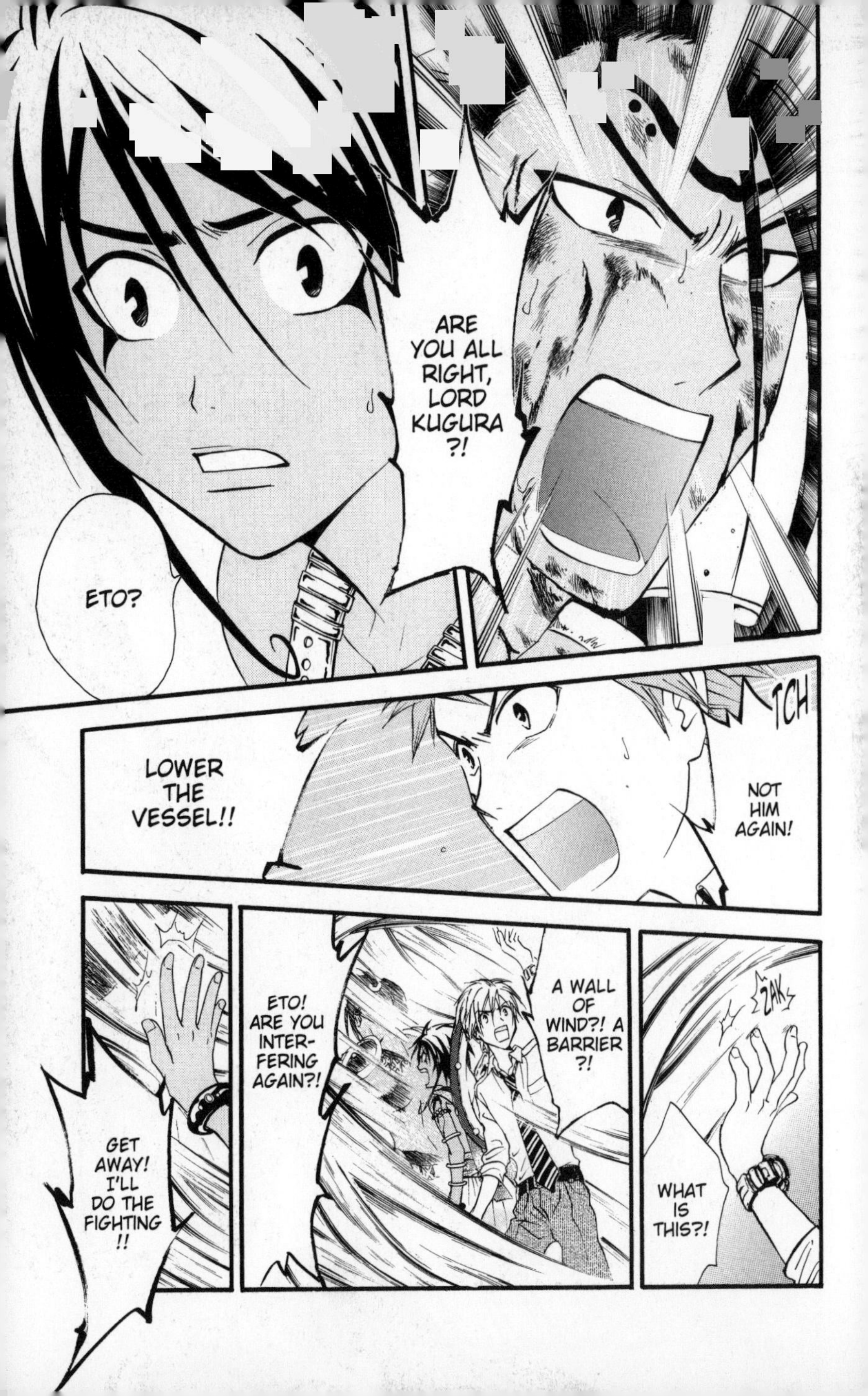
ARE YOU ALL RIGHT, LORD KUGURA?!
ETO?
TCH
NOT HIM AGAIN!
LOWER THE VESSEL!!
ZAK
WHAT IS THIS?!
A WALL OF WIND?! A BARRIER?!
ETO! ARE YOU INTER-FERING AGAIN?!
GET AWAY! I'LL DO THE FIGHTING!!

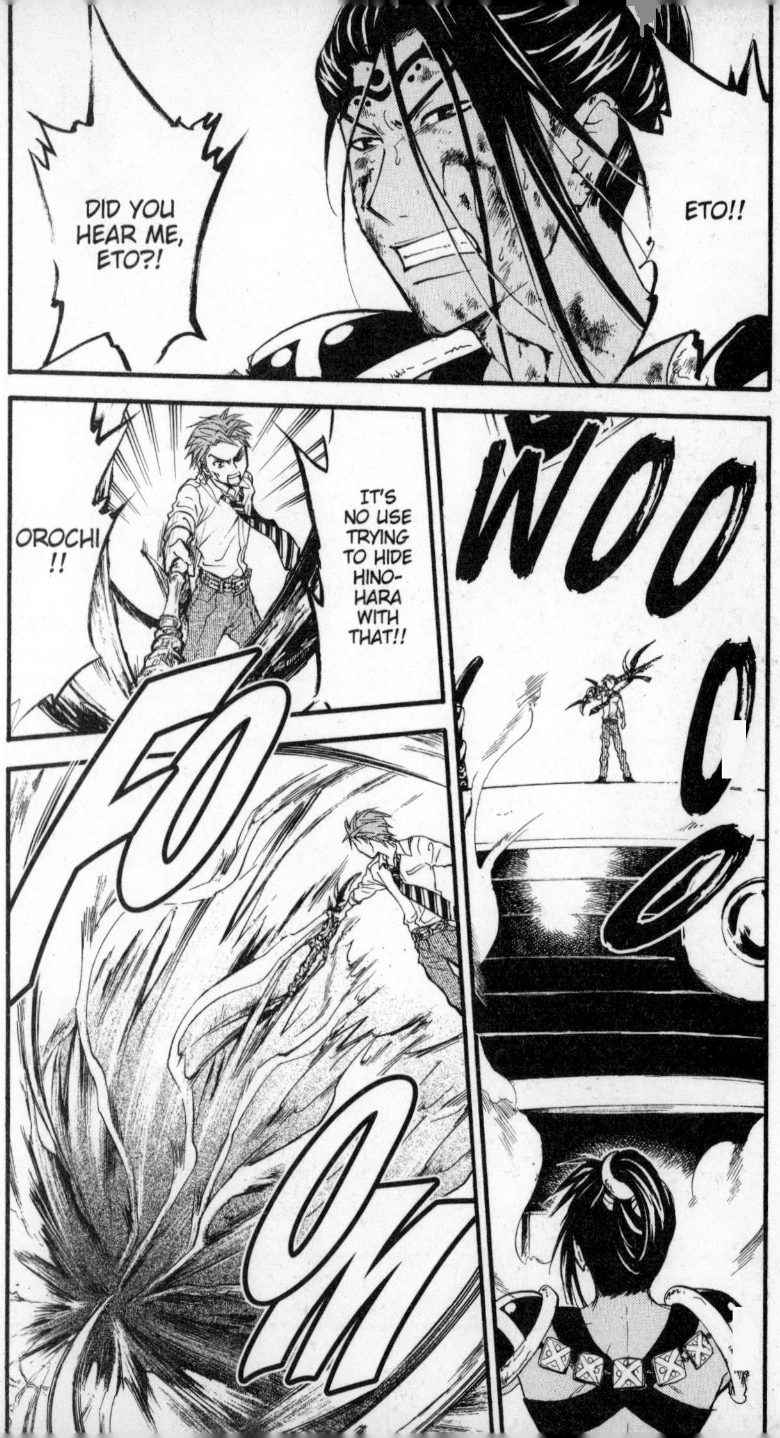
ETO!!
DID YOU HEAR ME, ETO?!
WOOOOOO
IT'S NO USE TRYING TO HIDE HINO-HARA WITH THAT!!
OROCHI!!
FOOM

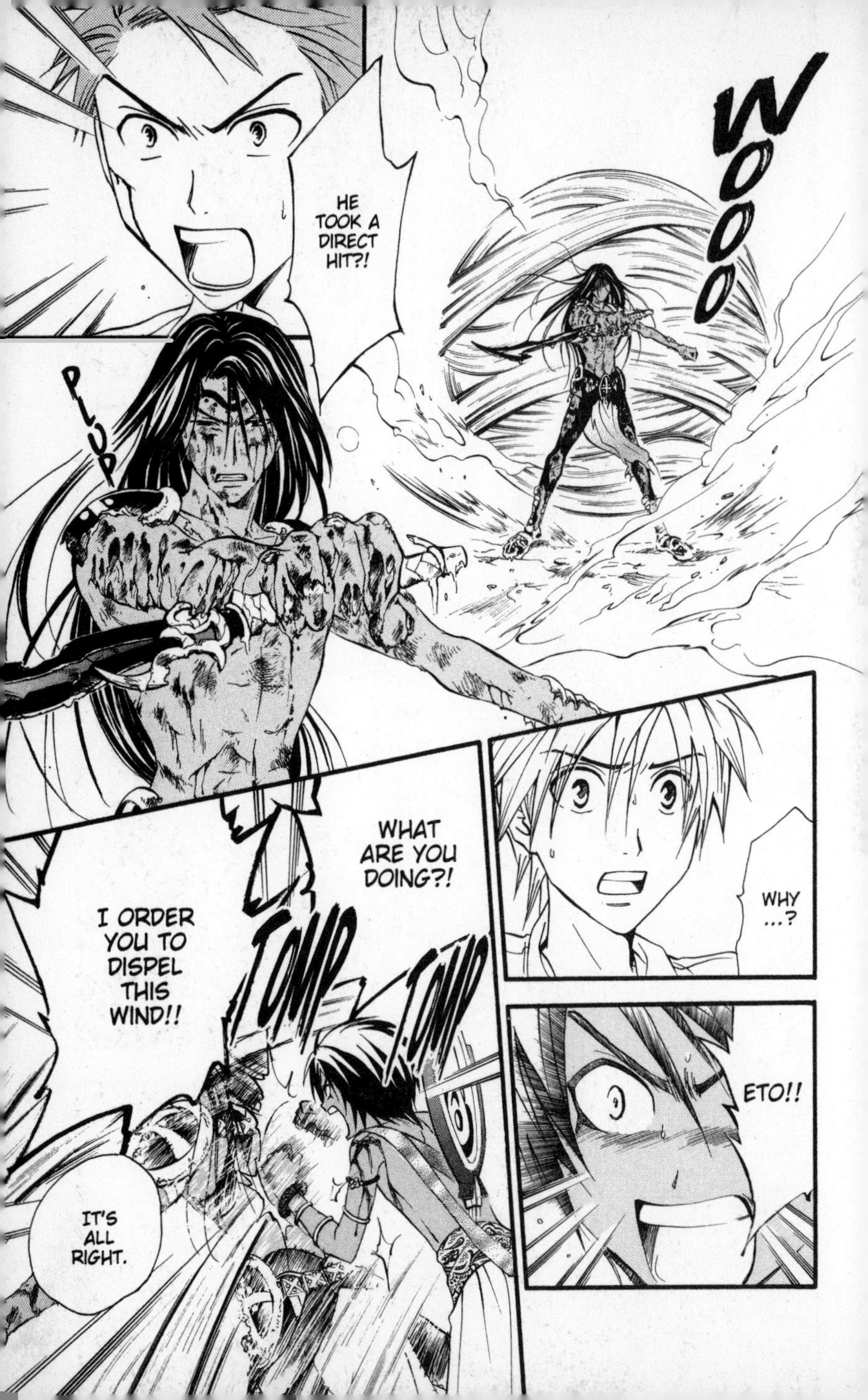
WOOO
HE TOOK A DIRECT HIT?!
PLUP
WHY ...?
ETO!!
WHAT ARE YOU DOING?!
I ORDER YOU TO DISPEL THIS WIND!!
TOMP
TOMP
IT'S ALL RIGHT.

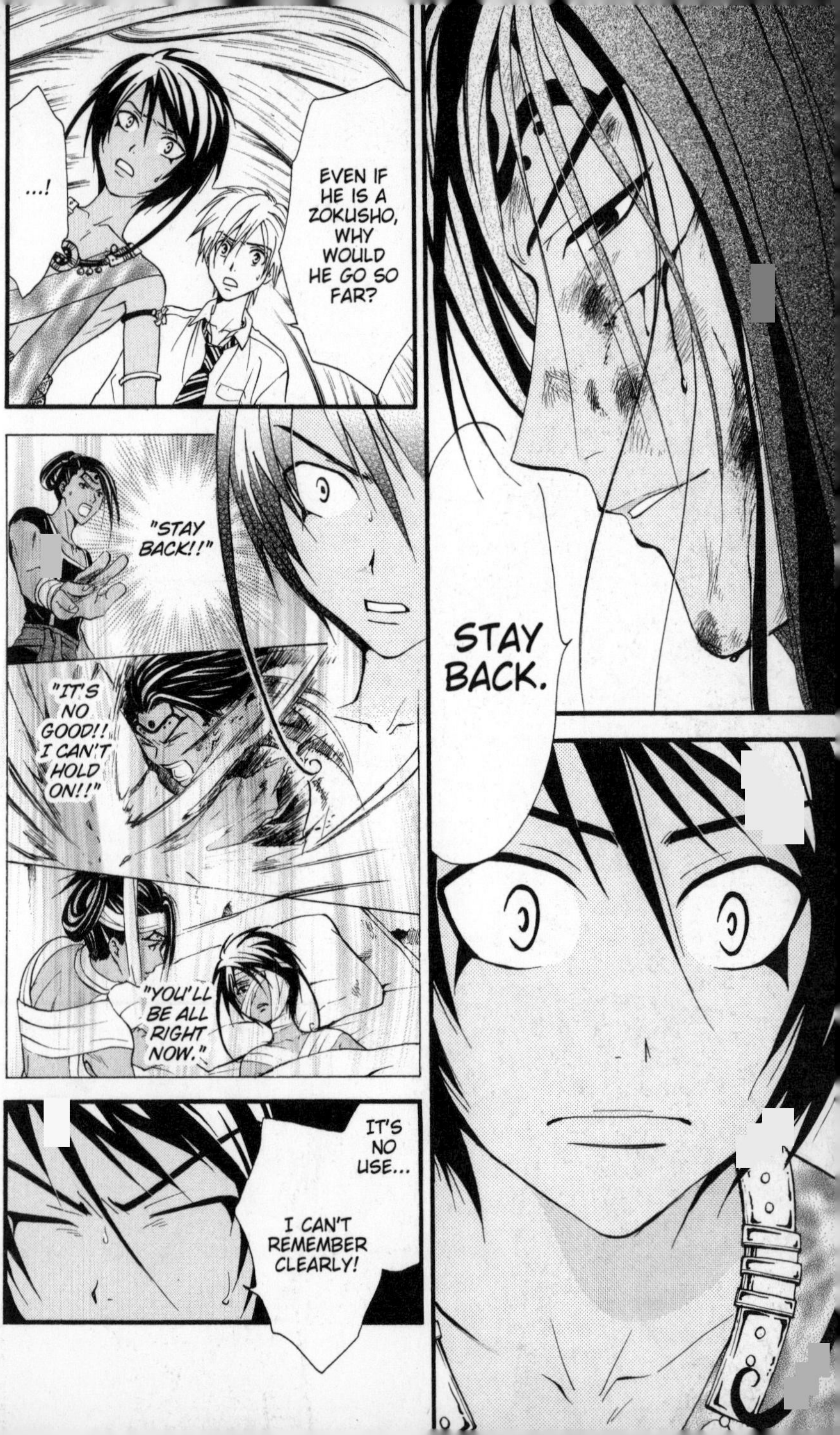
STAY BACK.
EVEN IF HE IS A ZOKUSHO, WHY WOULD HE GO SO FAR?
...!
"STAY BACK!!"
"IT'S NO GOOD!! I CAN'T HOLD ON!!"
"YOU'LL BE ALL RIGHT NOW."
IT'S NO USE...
I CAN'T REMEMBER CLEARLY!

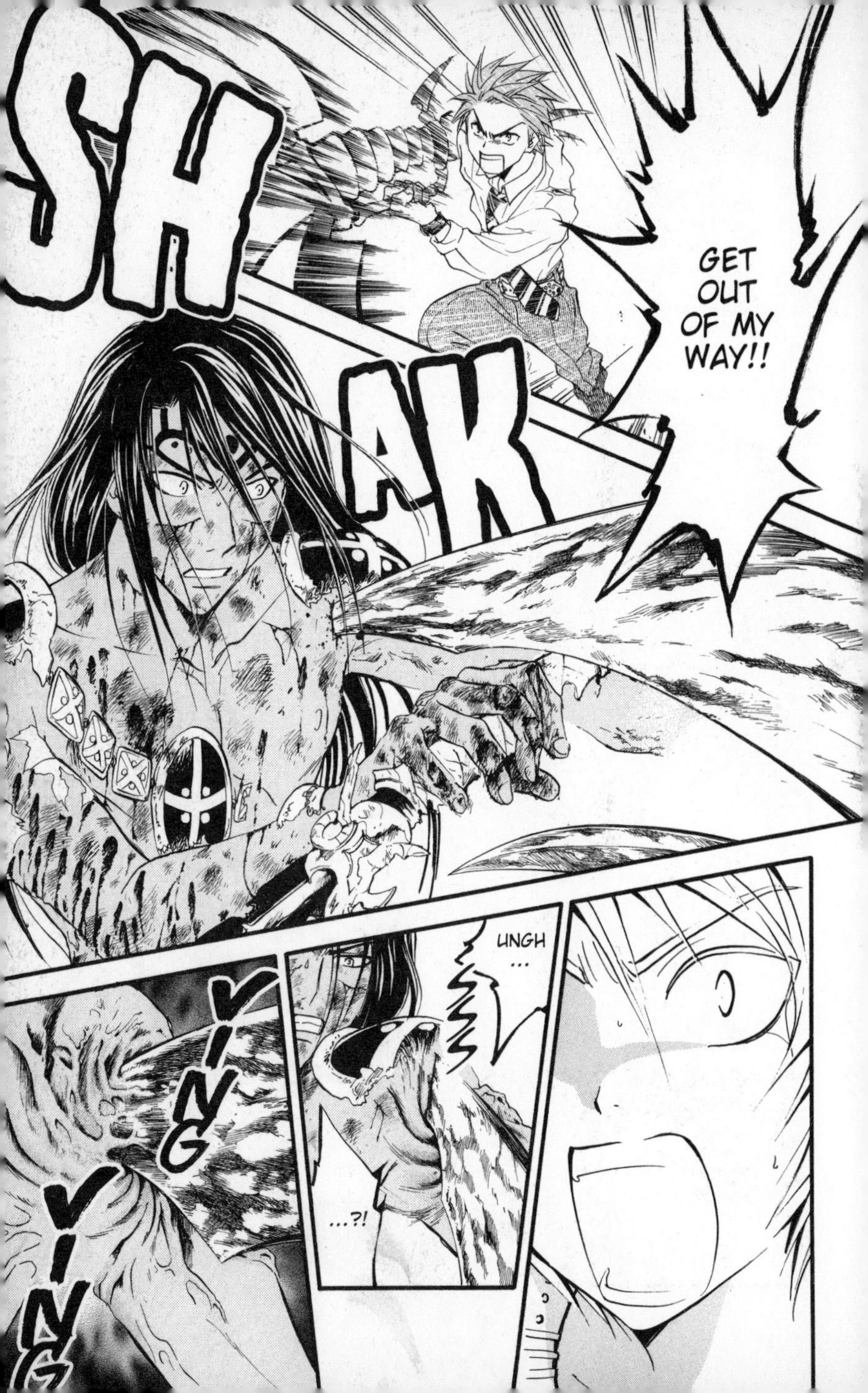
GET OUT OF MY WAY!!
SHAK
UNGH ...
...?!
VING
VING

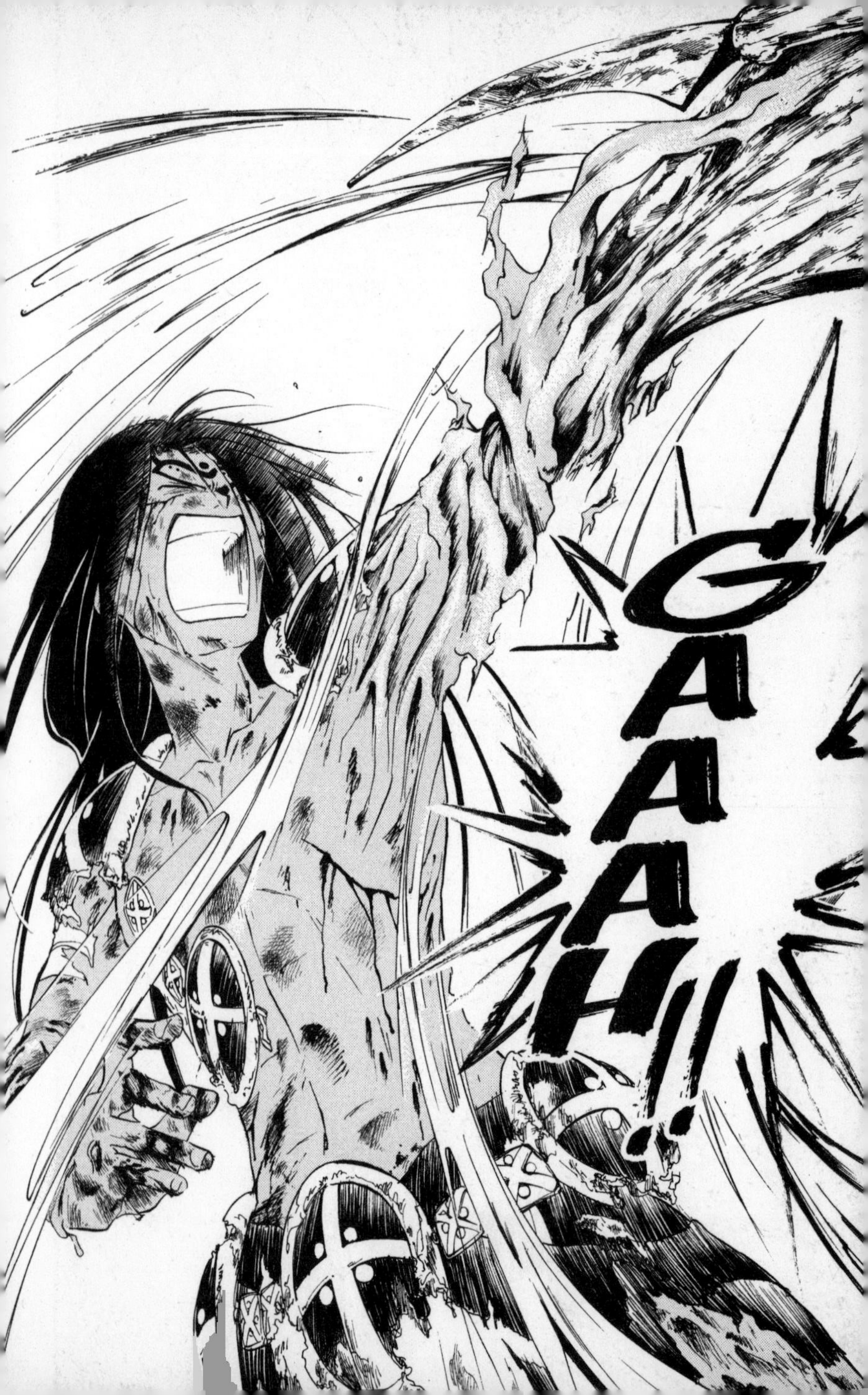
GAAAAH!!

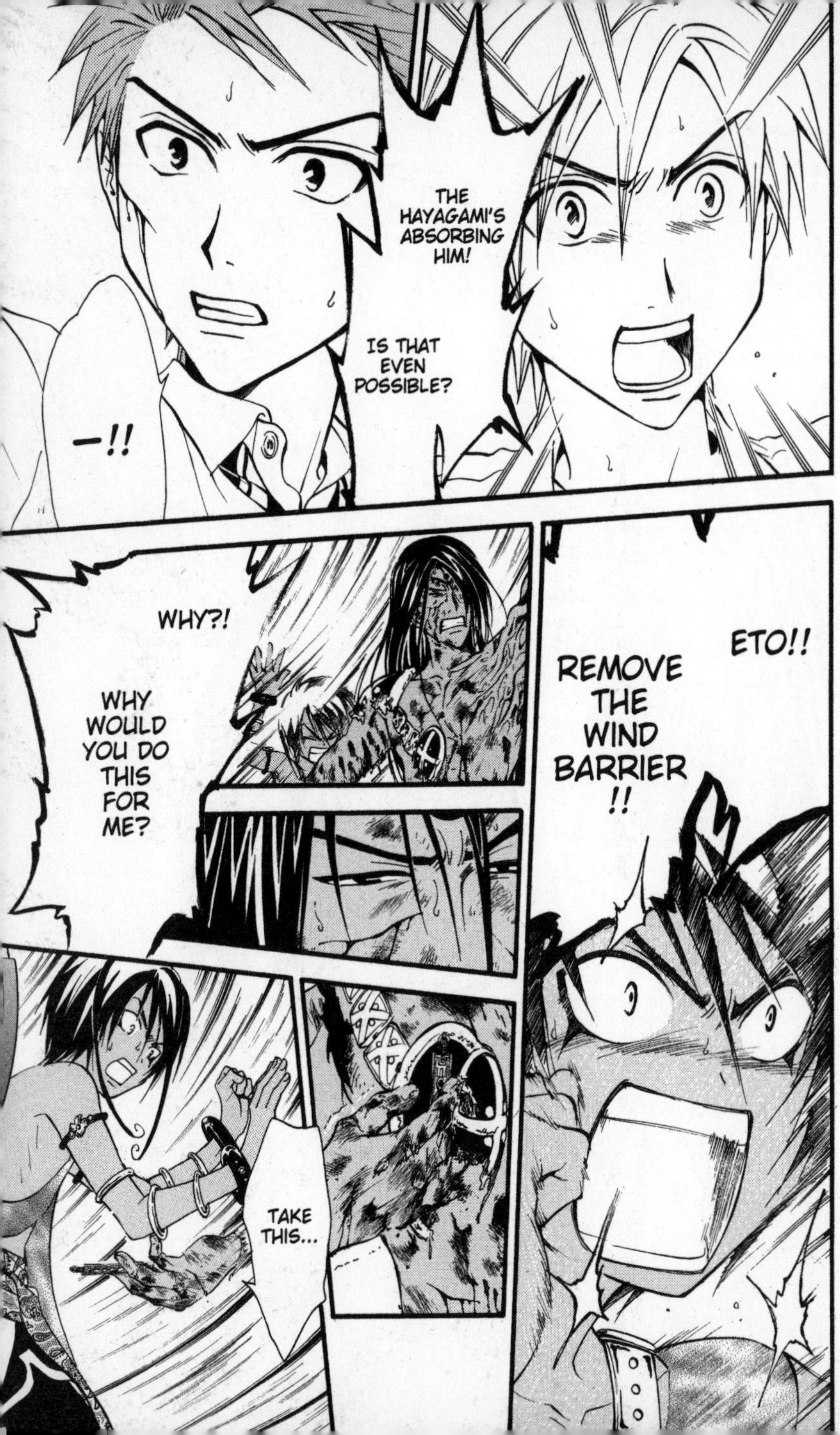
THE HAYAGAMI'S ABSORBING HIM!
IS THAT EVEN POSSIBLE?
—!!
ETO!!
REMOVE THE WIND BARRIER!!
WHY?!
WHY WOULD YOU DO THIS FOR ME?
TAKE THIS...

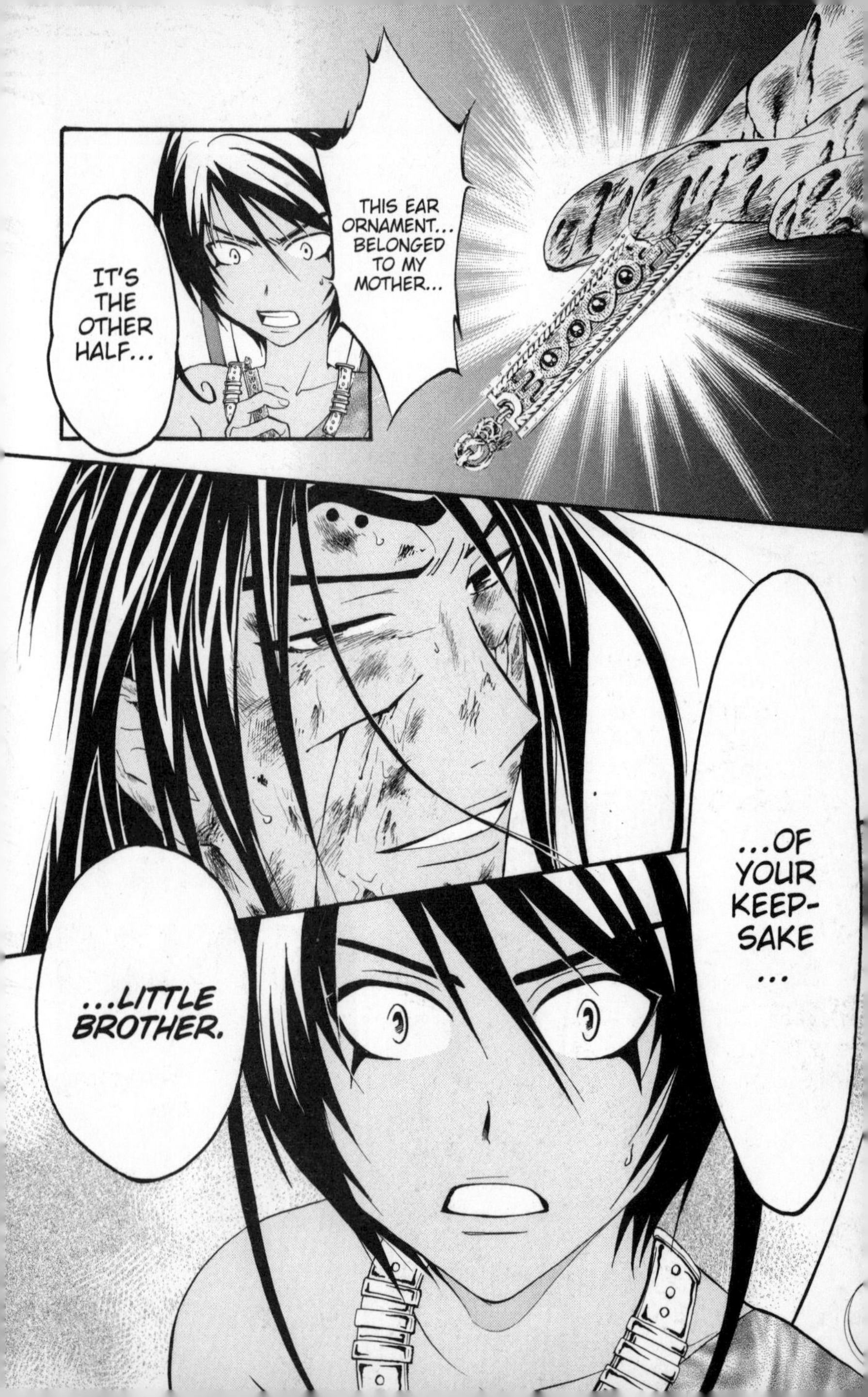
THIS EAR ORNAMENT... BELONGED TO MY MOTHER...
IT'S THE OTHER HALF...
...OF YOUR KEEP-SAKE...
...LITTLE BROTHER.

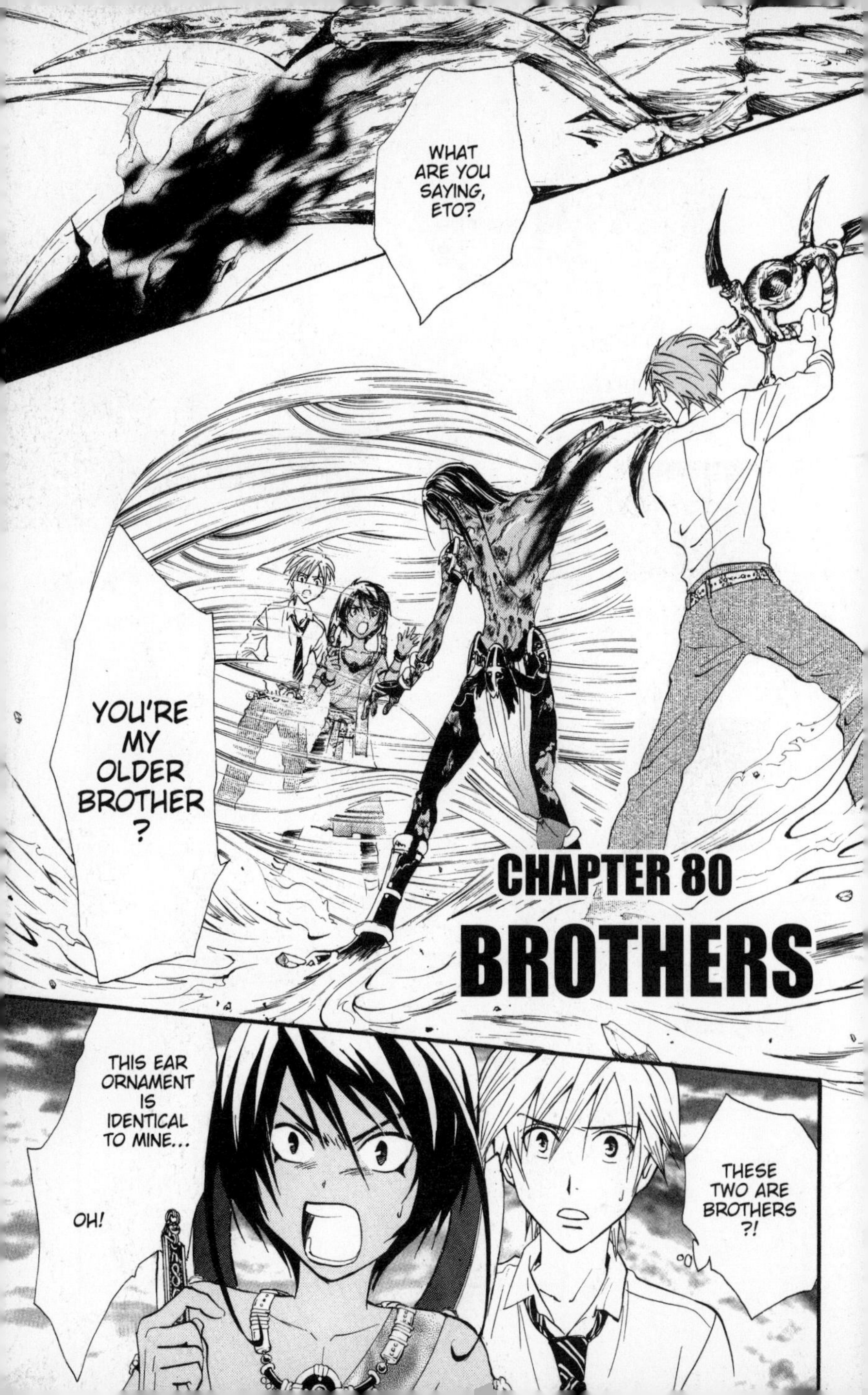
WHAT ARE YOU SAYING, ETO?
YOU'RE MY OLDER BROTHER?
CHAPTER 80
BROTHERS
THESE TWO ARE BROTHERS ?!
THIS EAR ORNAMENT IS IDENTICAL TO MINE...
OH!

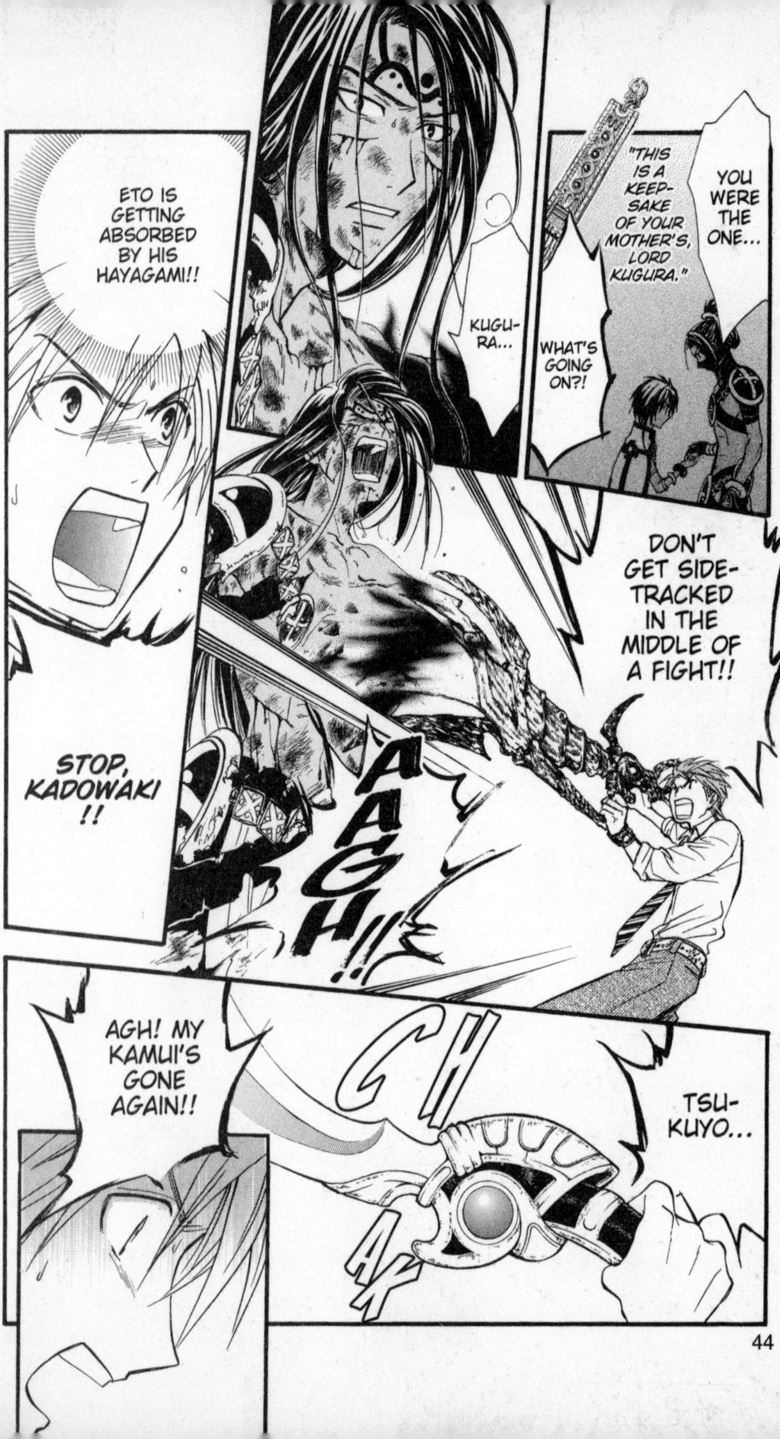
YOU WERE THE ONE...
"THIS IS A KEEPSAKE OF YOUR MOTHER'S, LORD KUGURA."
WHAT'S GOING ON?!
KUGU-RA...
ETO IS GETTING ABSORBED BY HIS HAYAGAMI!!
DON'T GET SIDE-TRACKED IN THE MIDDLE OF A FIGHT!!
AAAGH!!
STOP, KADOWAKI!!
TSU-KUYO...
CHAK
AGH! MY KAMUI'S GONE AGAIN!!

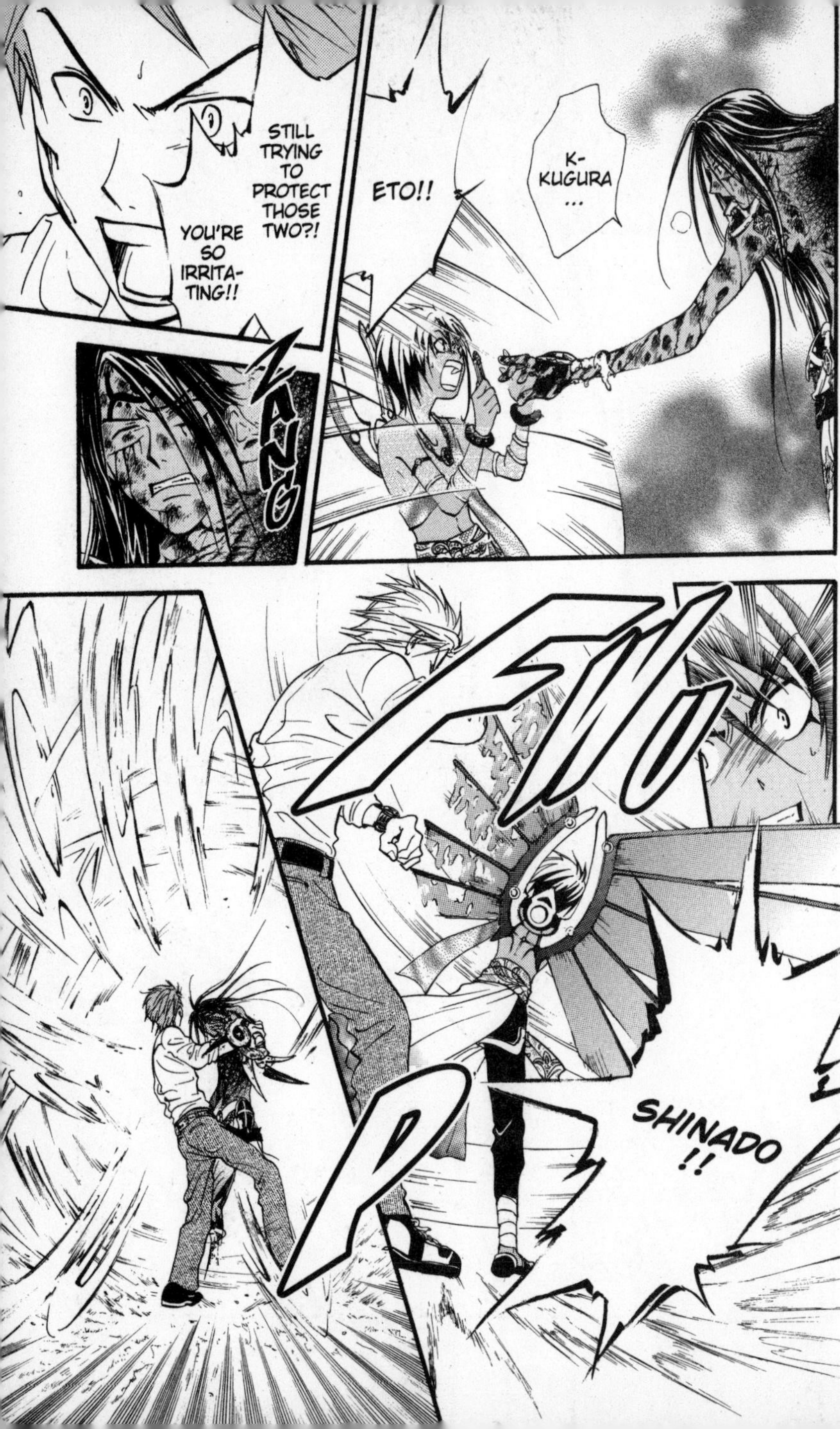
K-KUGURA...
ETO!!
STILL TRYING TO PROTECT THOSE TWO?!
YOU'RE SO IRRITA-TING!!
ZANG
SHINADO!!

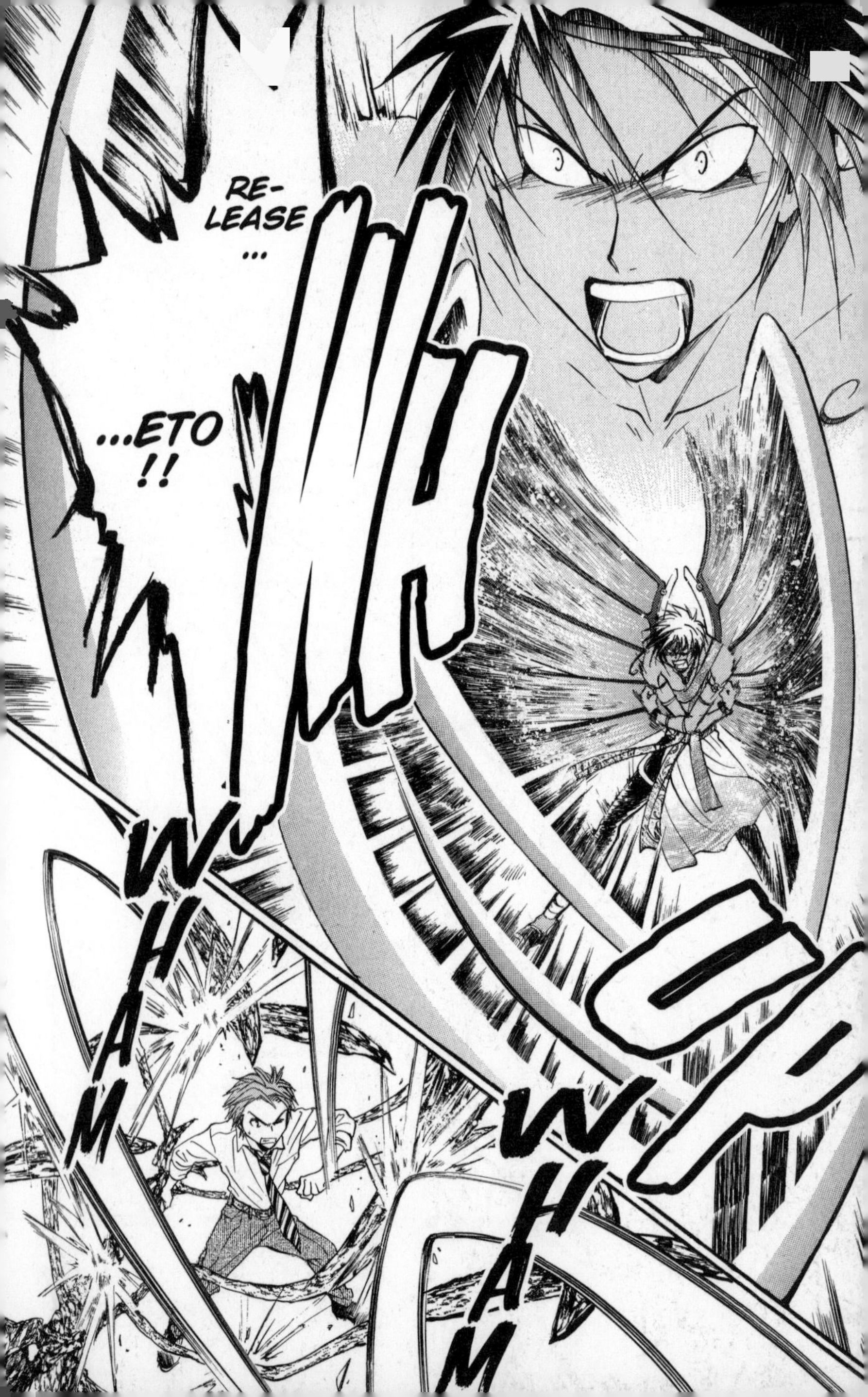
RE-
LEASE
...
...ETO
!!
WHAM
WHAM

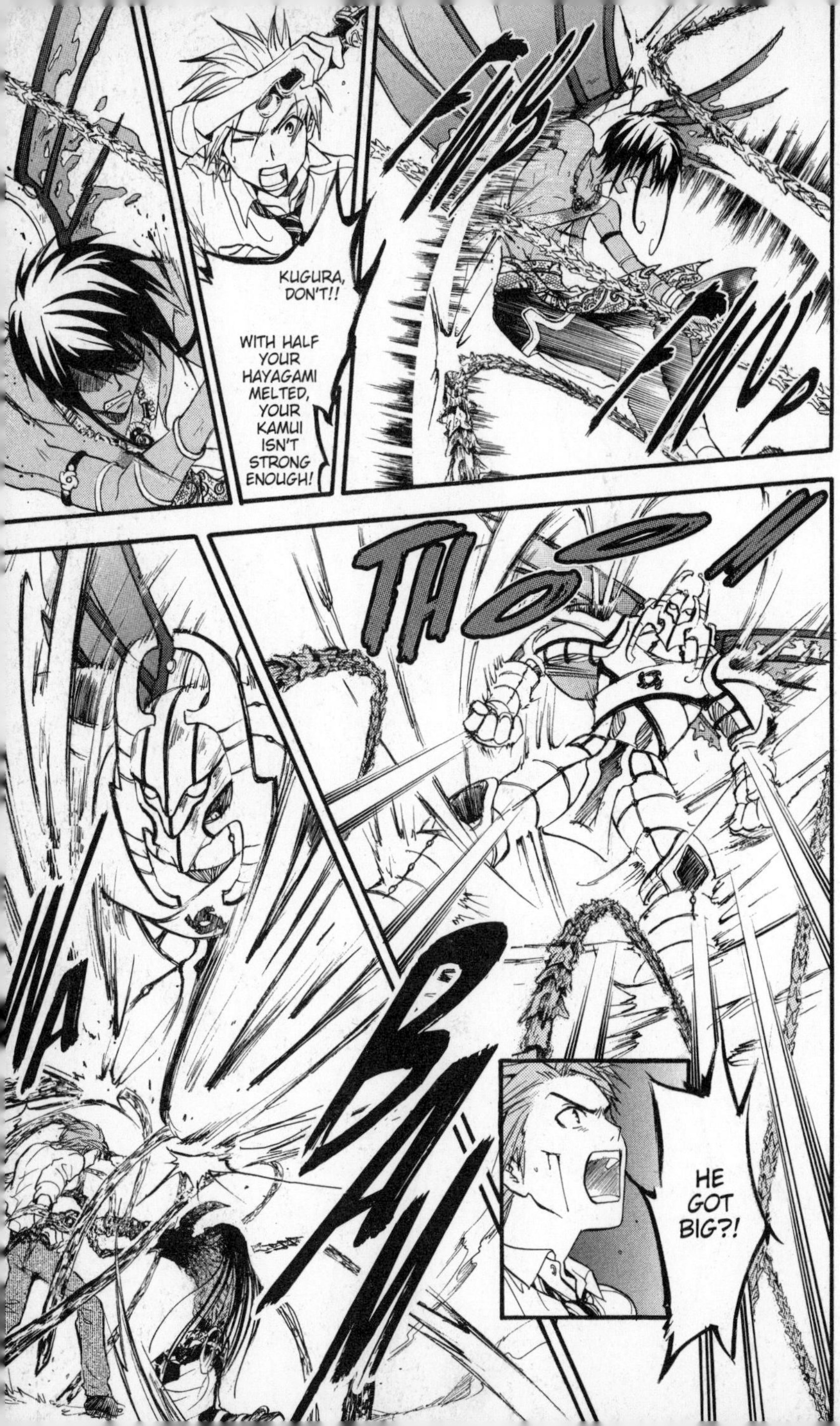
KUGURA, DON'T!!
WITH HALF YOUR HAYAGAMI MELTED, YOUR KAMUI ISN'T STRONG ENOUGH!
THOOM
HE GOT BIG?!

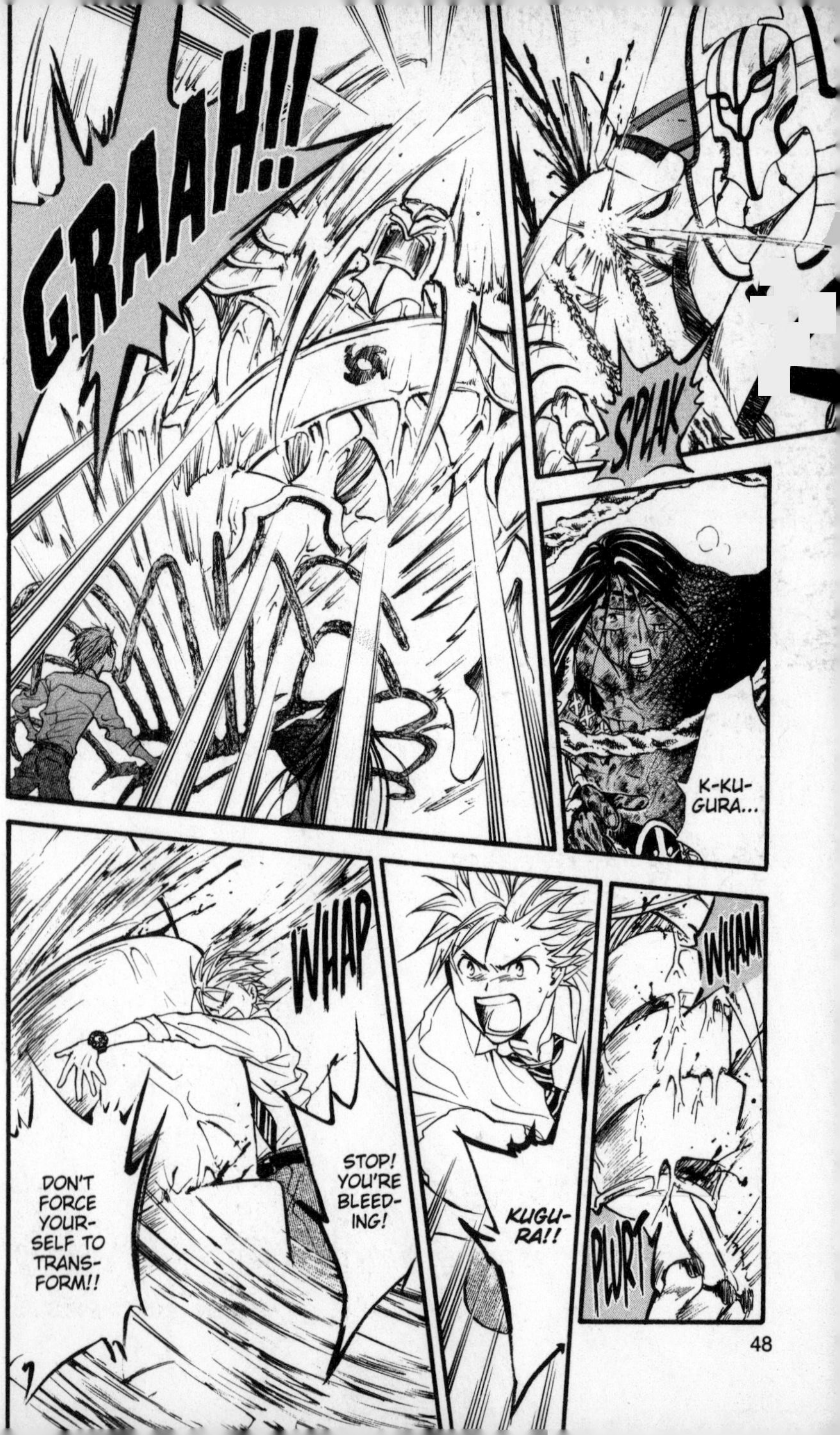
SPLAK
K-KU-GURA...
GRAAH!!
WHAM
PLURTY
KUGU-RA!!
WHAP
STOP! YOU'RE BLEEDING!
DON'T FORCE YOURSELF TO TRANSFORM!!

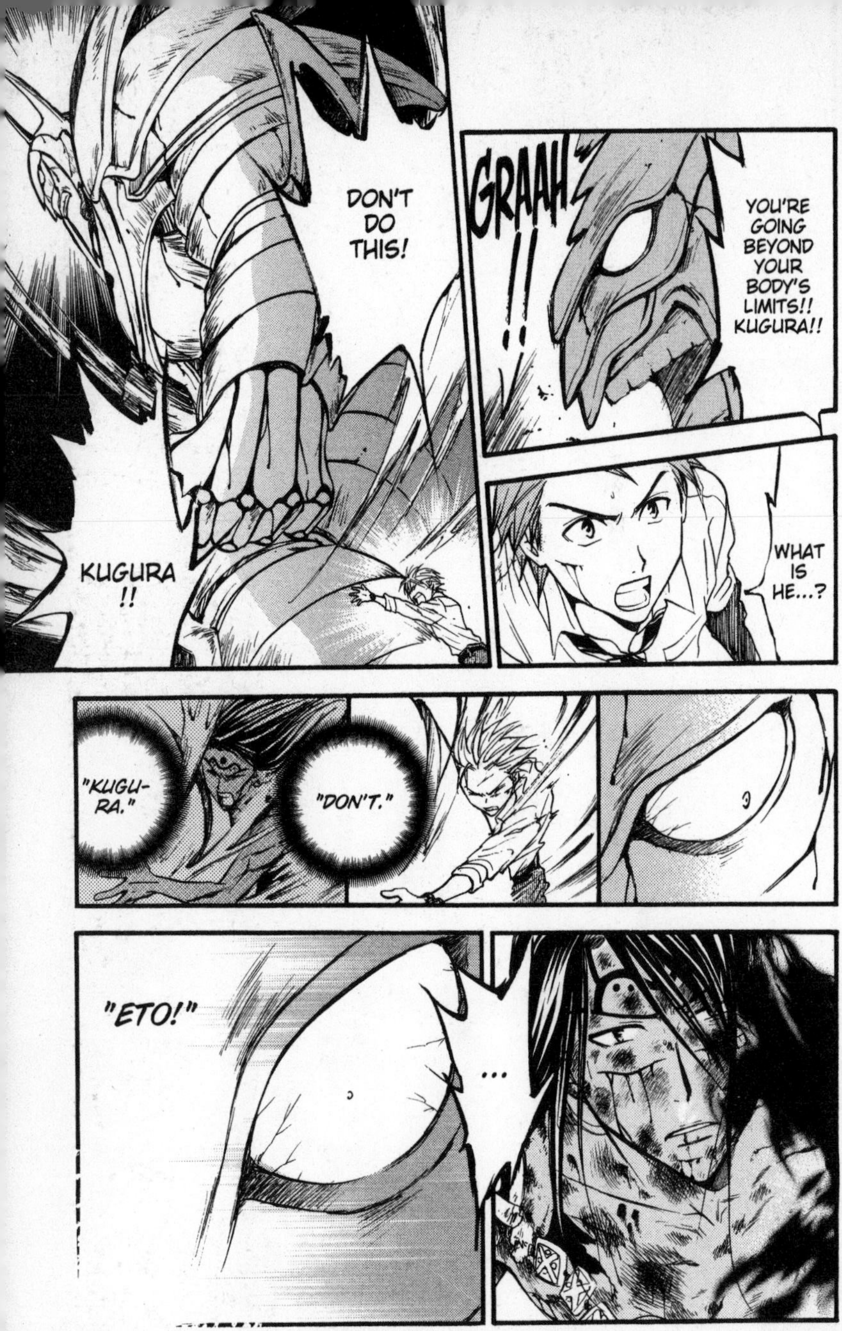
YOU'RE GOING BEYOND YOUR BODY'S LIMITS!! KUGURA!!
GRAAH!!
WHAT IS HE...?
DON'T DO THIS!
KUGURA!!
"DON'T."
"KUGU-RA."
...
"ETO!"

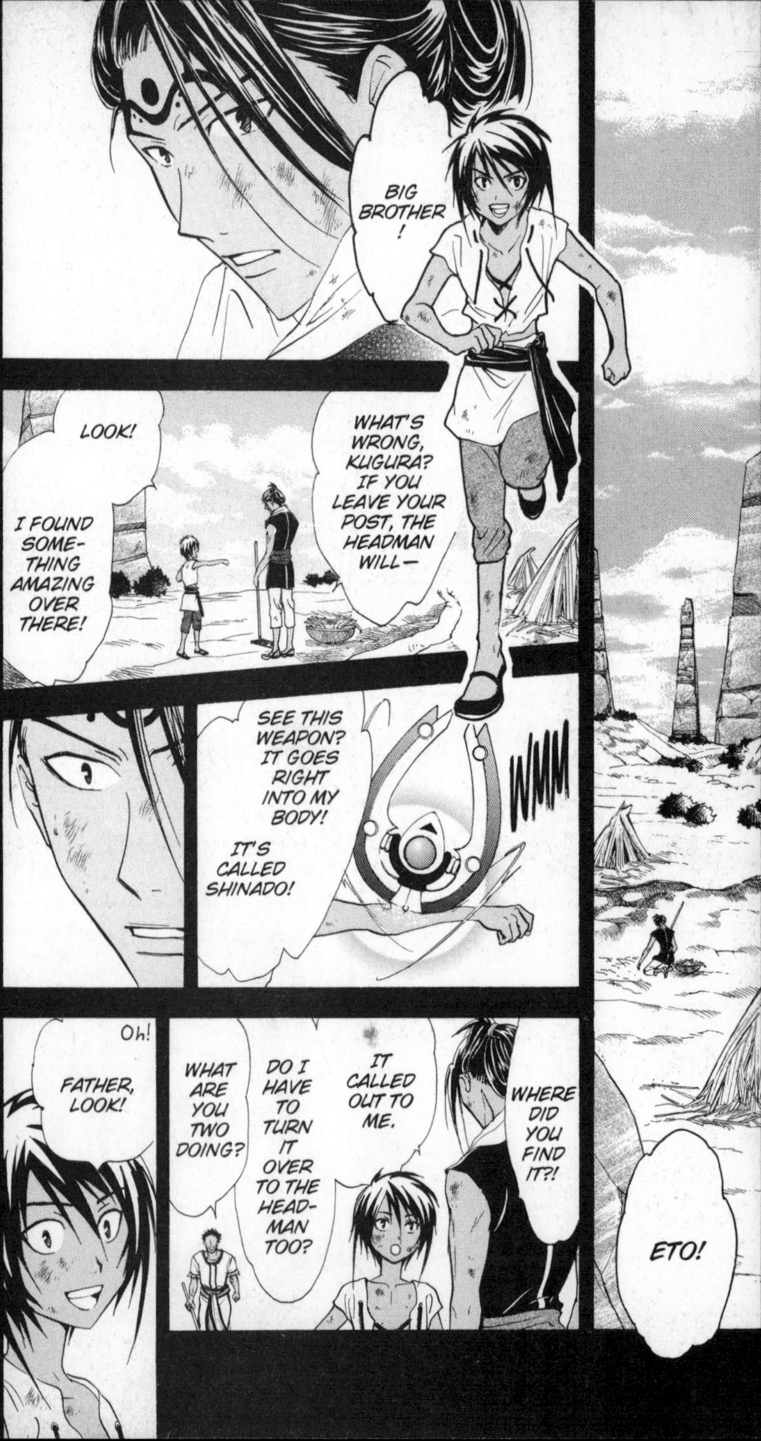
ETO!
BIG BROTHER!
WHAT'S WRONG, KUGURA? IF YOU LEAVE YOUR POST, THE HEADMAN WILL—
LOOK!
I FOUND SOMETHING AMAZING OVER THERE!
WMM
SEE THIS WEAPON? IT GOES RIGHT INTO MY BODY!
IT'S CALLED SHINADO!
WHERE DID YOU FIND IT?!
IT CALLED OUT TO ME.
DO I HAVE TO TURN IT OVER TO THE HEADMAN TOO?
WHAT ARE YOU TWO DOING?
Oh!
FATHER, LOOK!

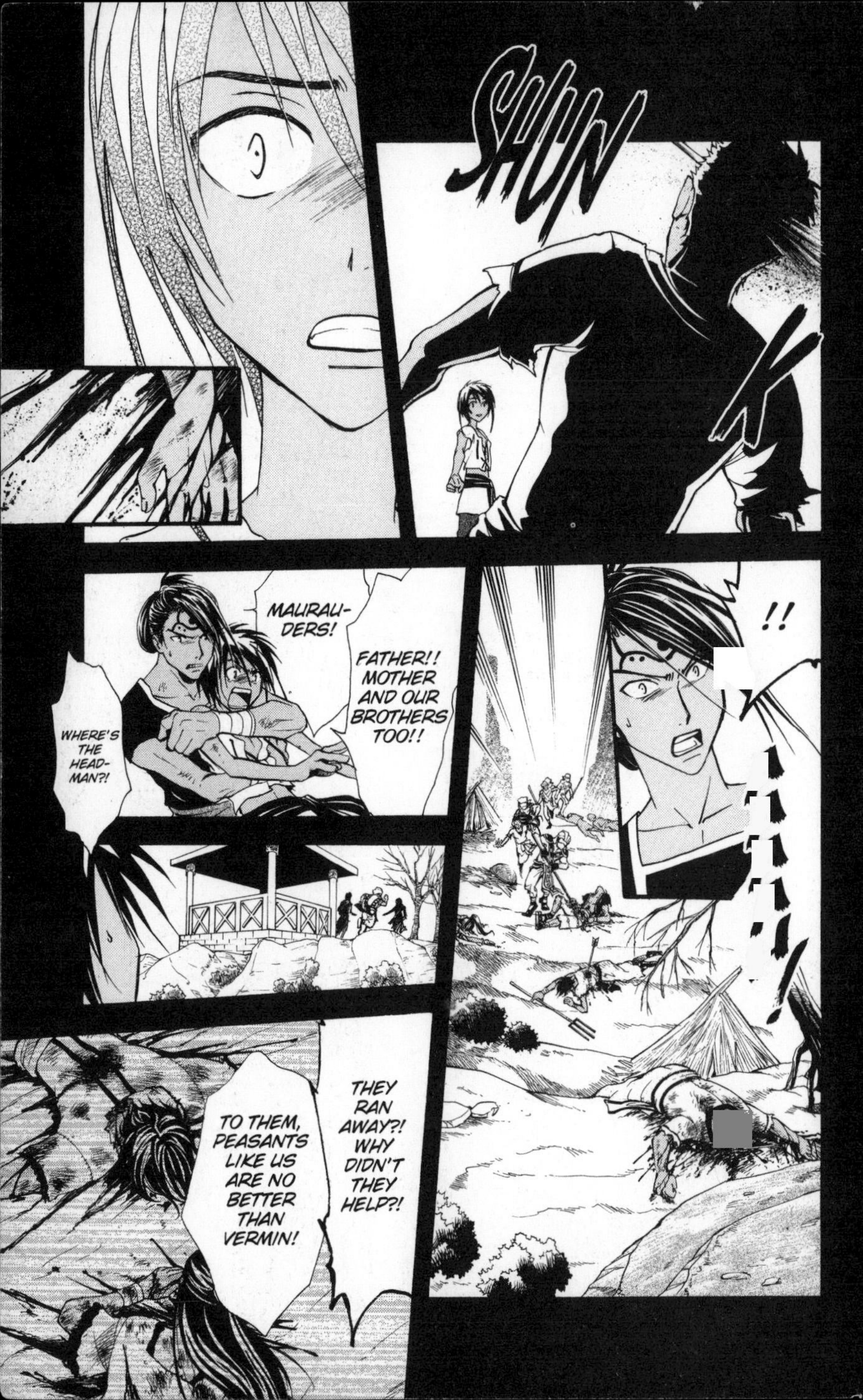
SHUN
!!
MAURAU-DERS!
FATHER!! MOTHER AND OUR BROTHERS TOO!!
WHERE'S THE HEAD-MAN?!
THEY RAN AWAY?! WHY DIDN'T THEY HELP?!
TO THEM, PEASANTS LIKE US ARE NO BETTER THAN VERMIN!

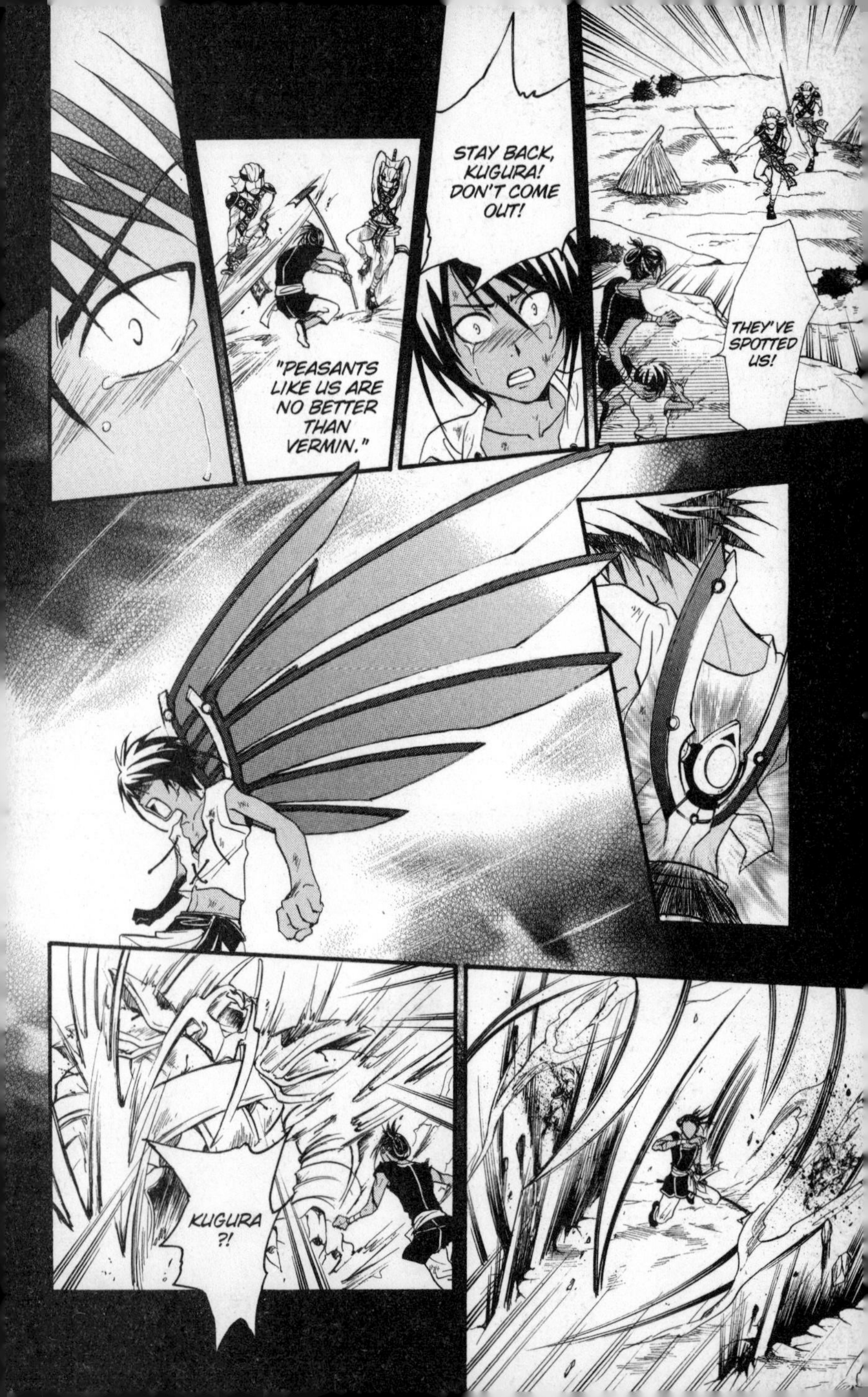
THEY'VE SPOTTED US!
STAY BACK, KUGURA! DON'T COME OUT!
"PEASANTS LIKE US ARE NO BETTER THAN VERMIN."
KUGURA ?!

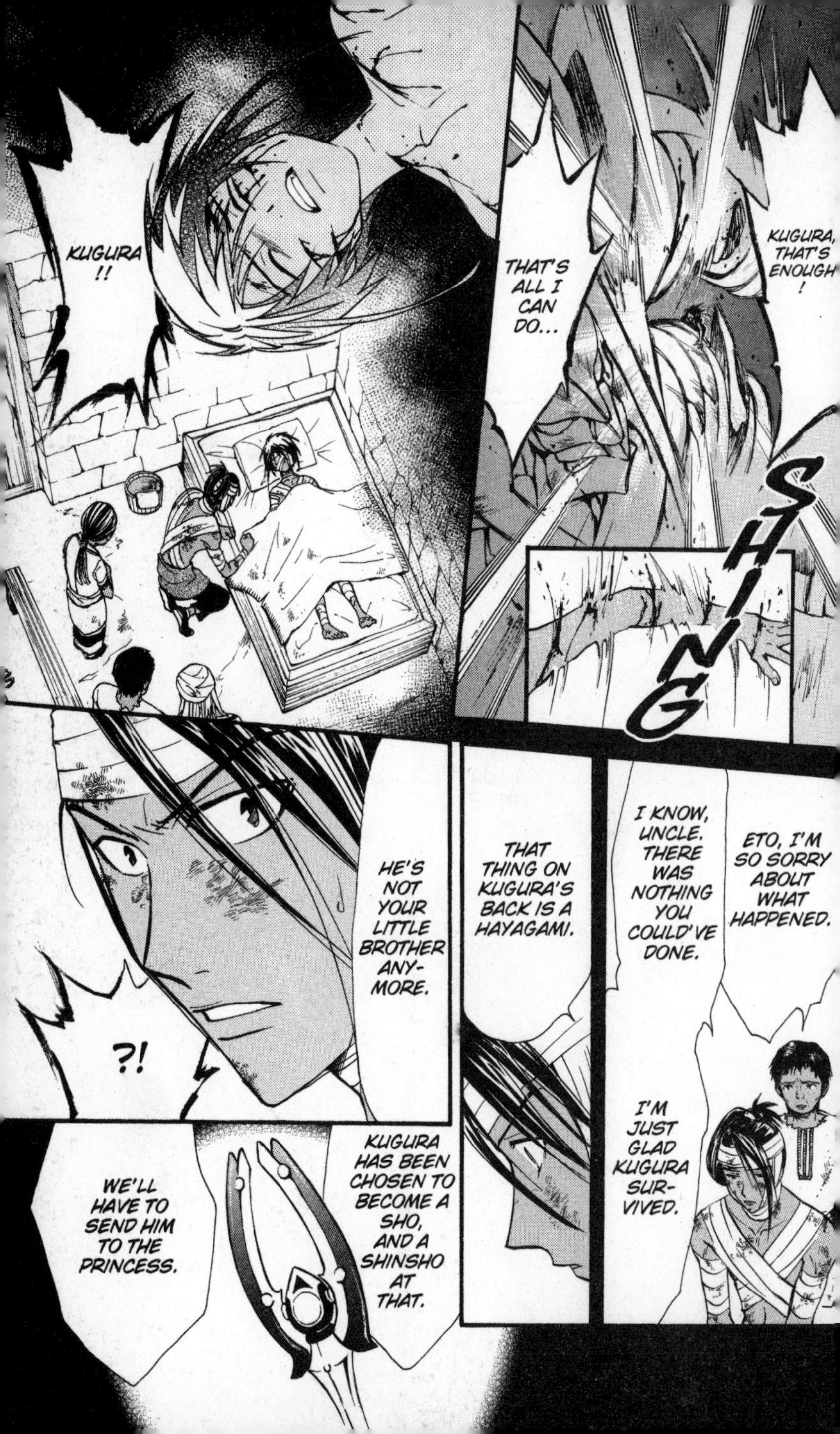
KUGURA, THAT'S ENOUGH!
THAT'S ALL I CAN DO...
SHING
KUGURA!!
ETO, I'M SO SORRY ABOUT WHAT HAPPENED.
I KNOW, UNCLE. THERE WAS NOTHING YOU COULD'VE DONE.
I'M JUST GLAD KUGURA SURVIVED.
THAT THING ON KUGURA'S BACK IS A HAYAGAMI.
HE'S NOT YOUR LITTLE BROTHER ANYMORE.
?!
KUGURA HAS BEEN CHOSEN TO BECOME A SHO, AND A SHINSHO AT THAT.
WE'LL HAVE TO SEND HIM TO THE PRINCESS.

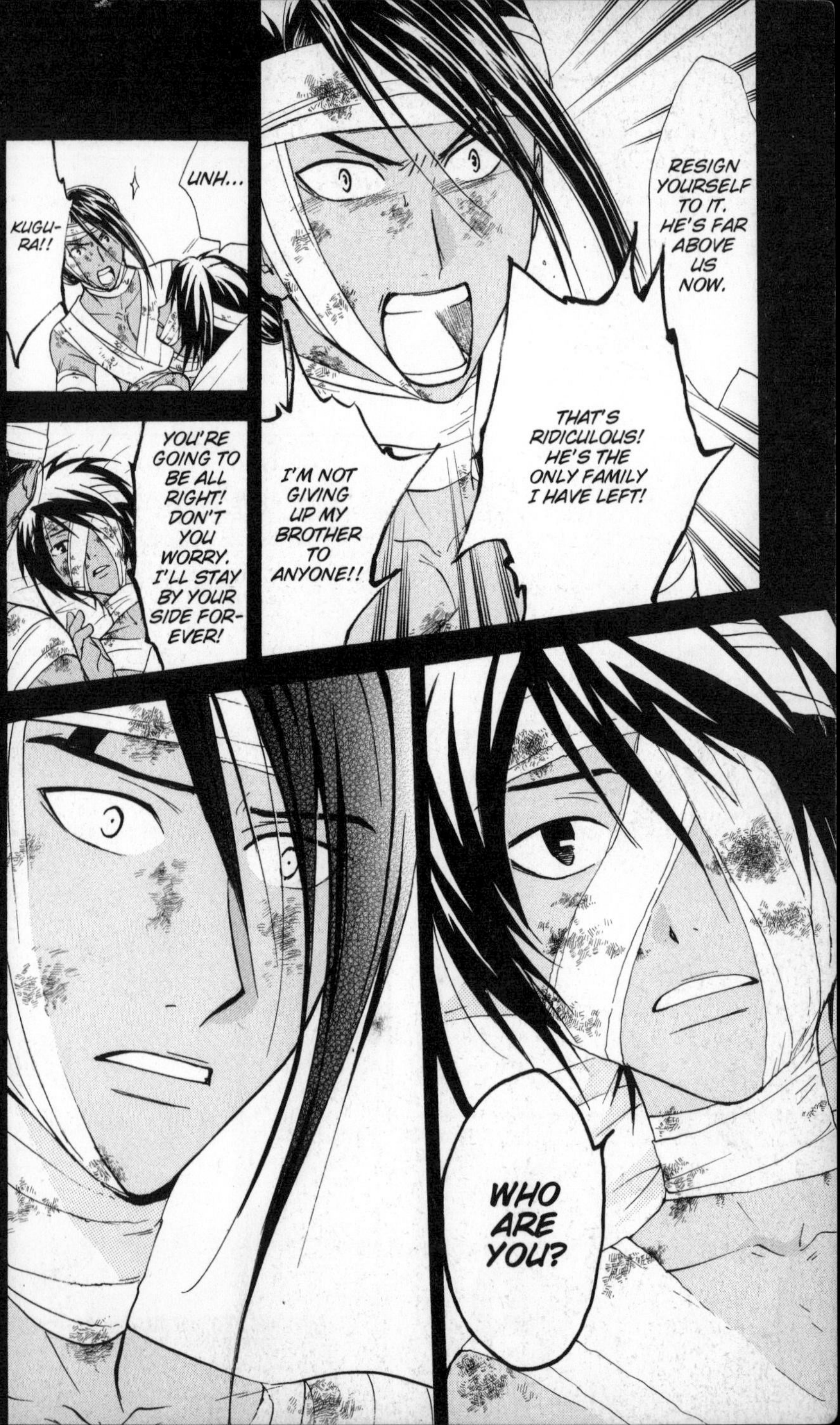
RESIGN YOURSELF TO IT. HE'S FAR ABOVE US NOW.
THAT'S RIDICULOUS! HE'S THE ONLY FAMILY I HAVE LEFT!
I'M NOT GIVING UP MY BROTHER TO ANYONE!!
UNH...
KUGU-RA!!
YOU'RE GOING TO BE ALL RIGHT! DON'T YOU WORRY. I'LL STAY BY YOUR SIDE FOR-EVER!
WHO ARE YOU?

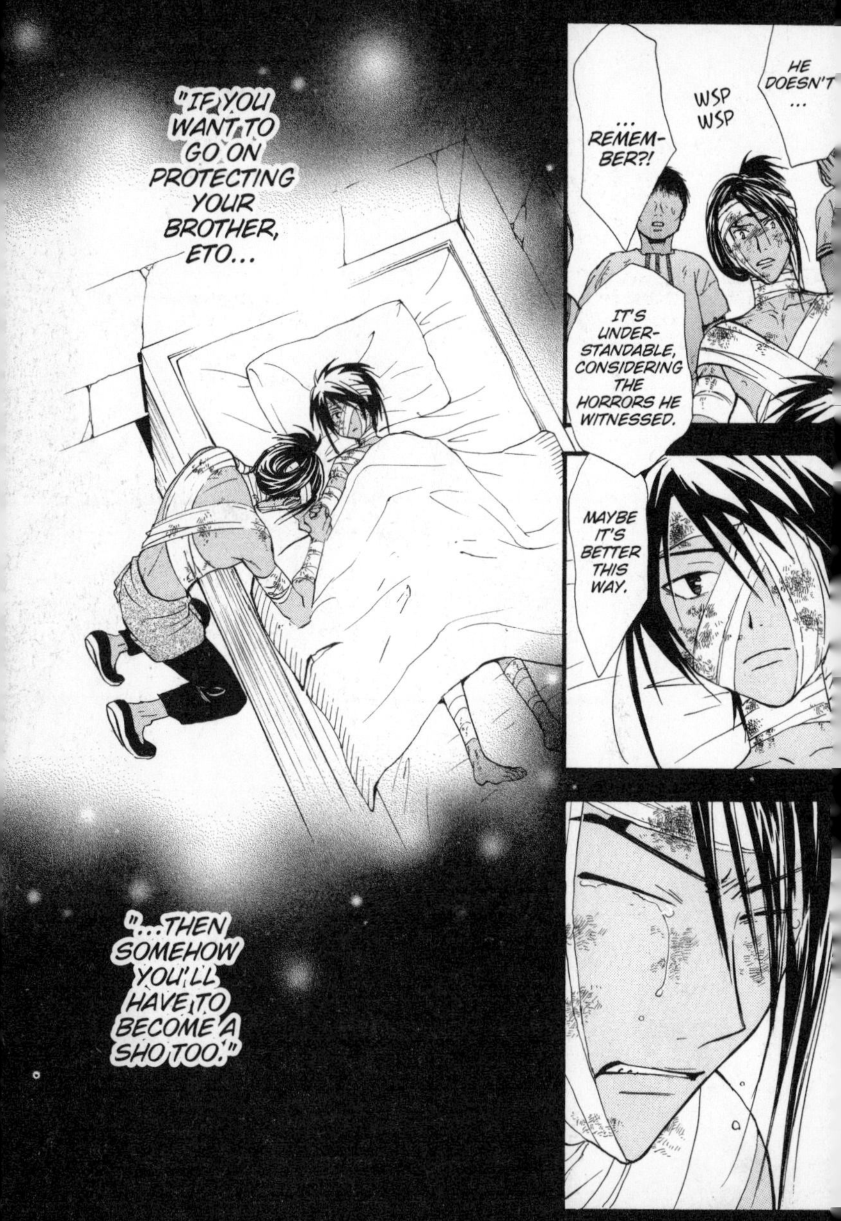
HE DOESN'T ...
WSP WSP
... REMEM-BER?!
IT'S UNDER-STANDABLE, CONSIDERING THE HORRORS HE WITNESSED.
MAYBE IT'S BETTER THIS WAY.
"IF YOU WANT TO GO ON PROTECTING YOUR BROTHER, ETO...
"...THEN SOMEHOW YOU'LL HAVE TO BECOME A SHO TOO."

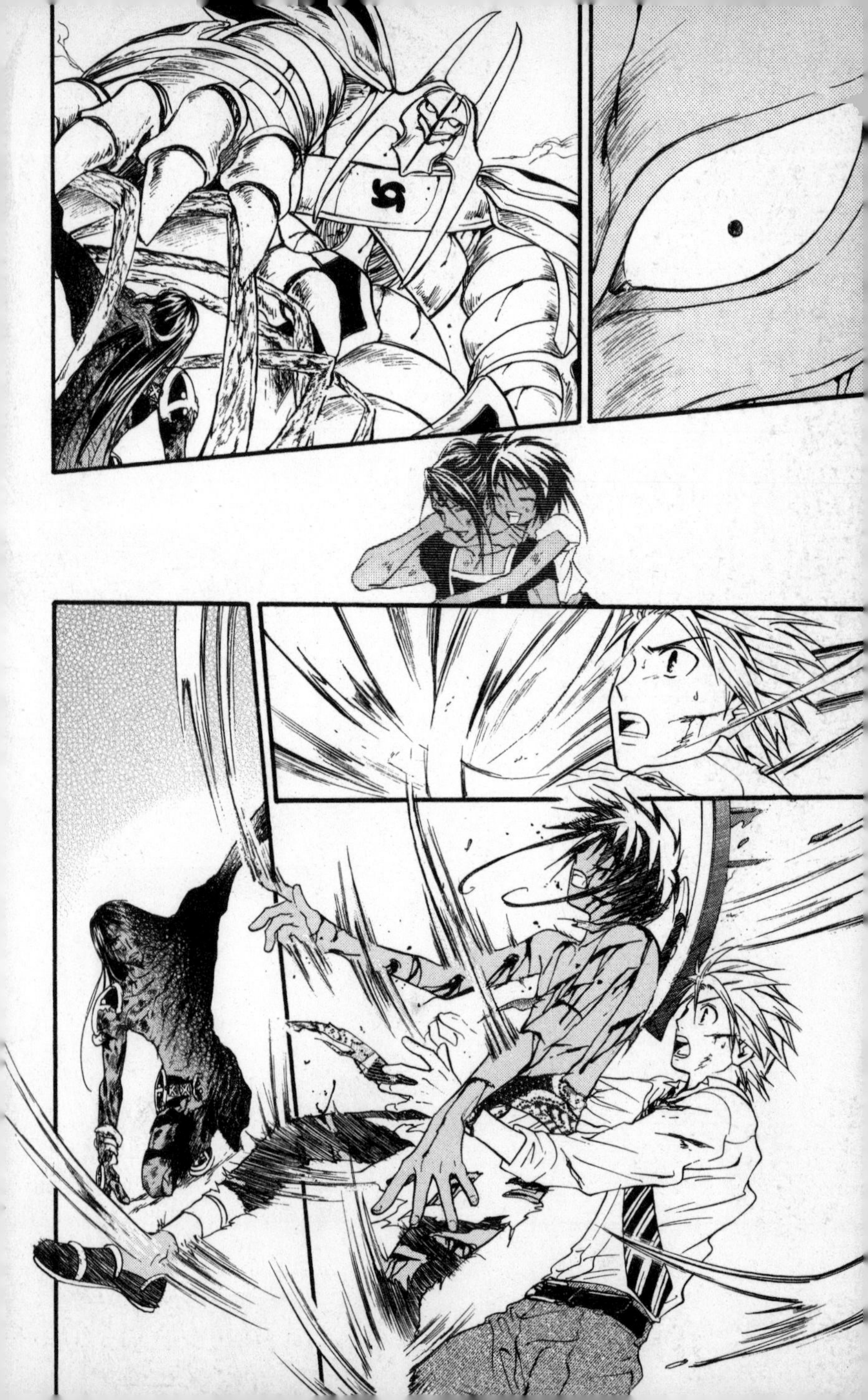

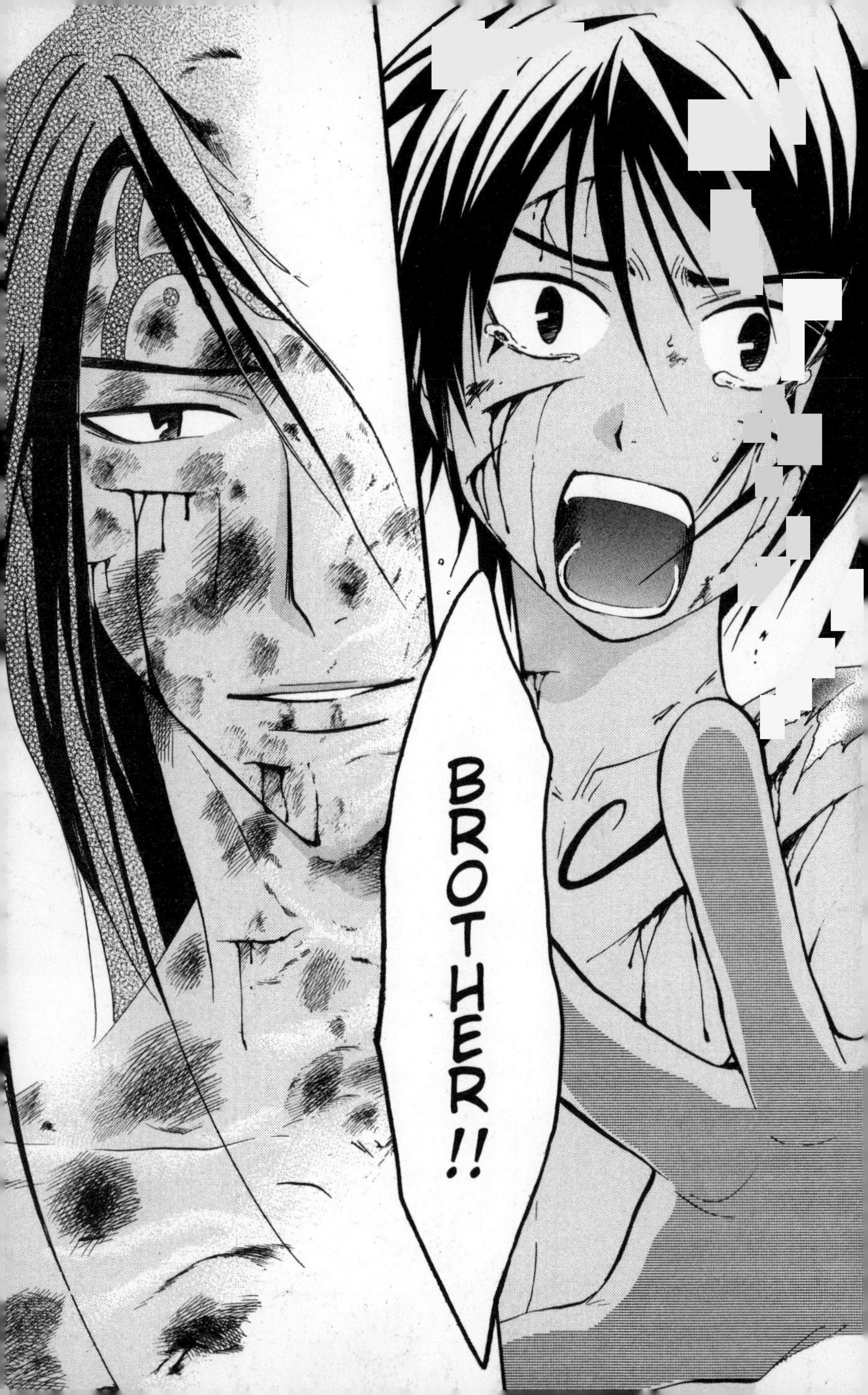
BROTHER!!

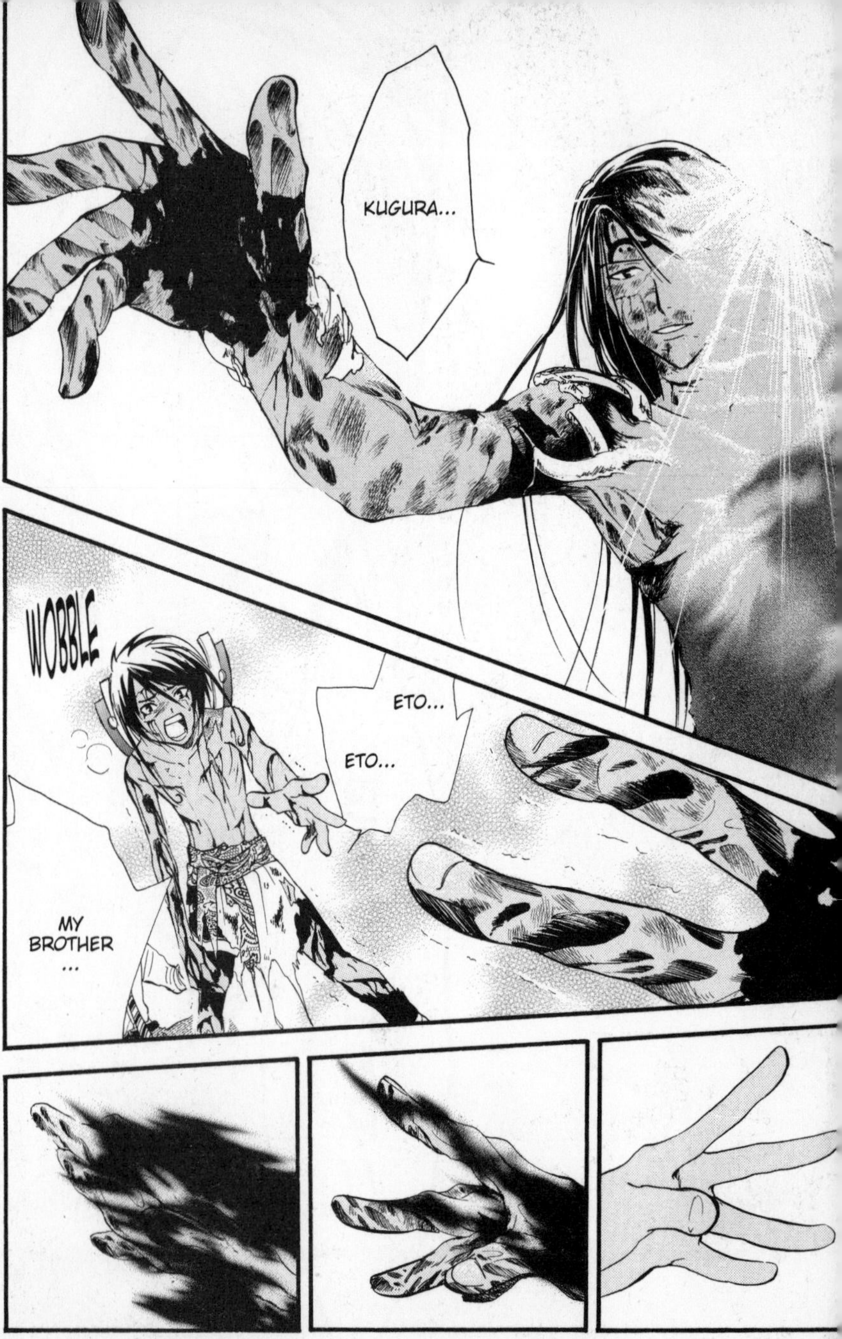
KUGURA...
ETO...
ETO...
WOBBLE
MY BROTHER ...

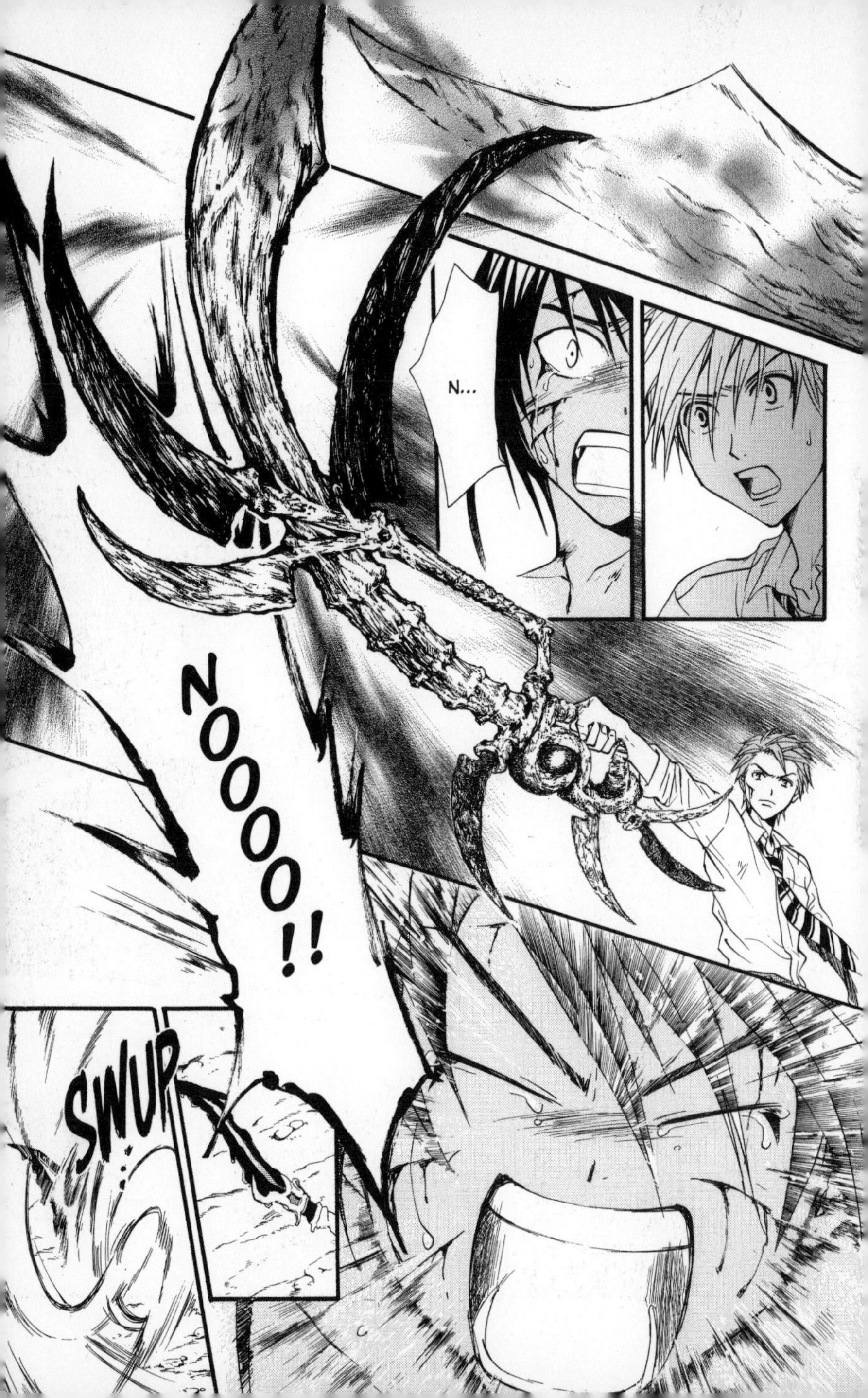
N...
NOOOOO!!
SWUP

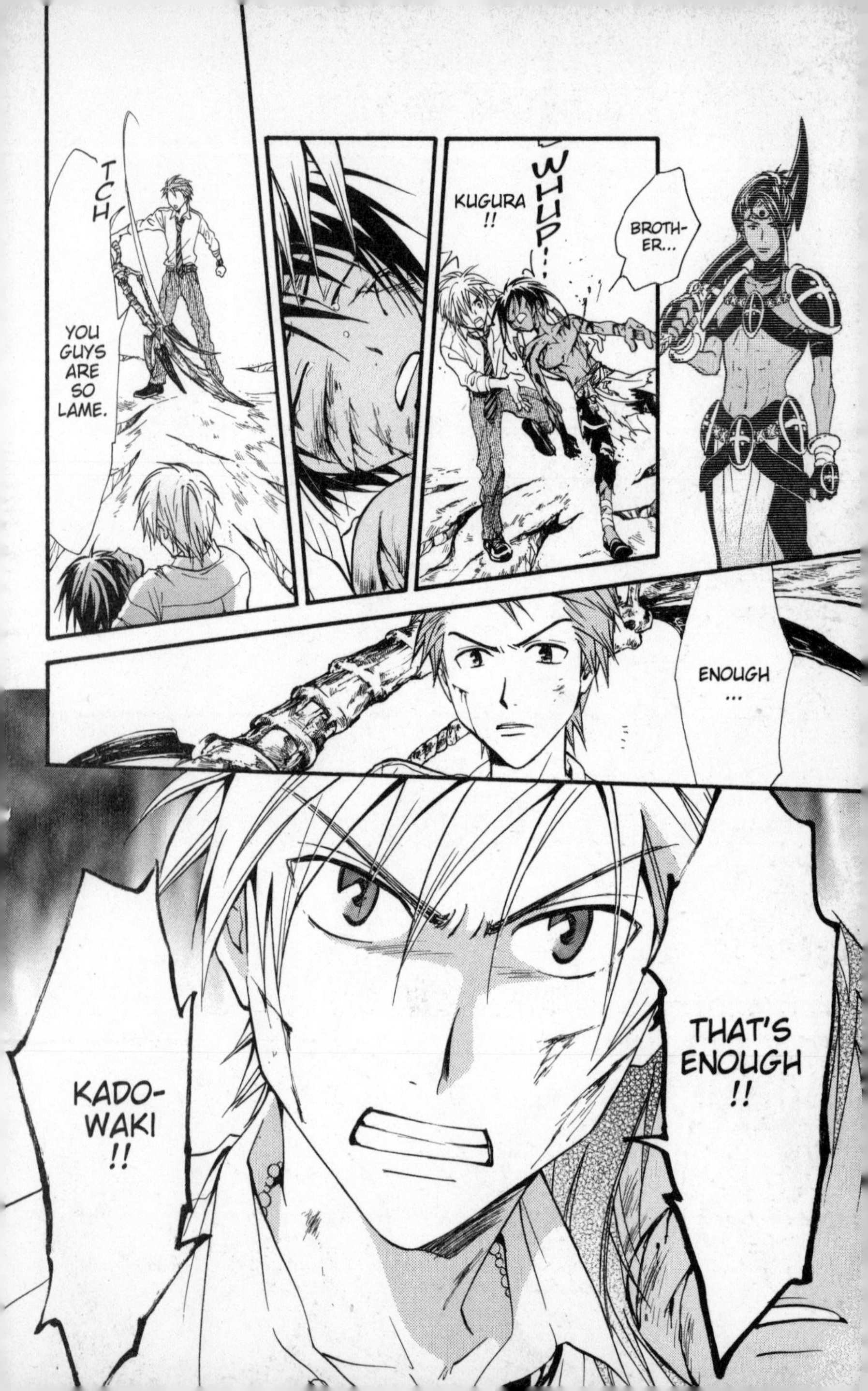

BROTH-ER...
WHUP!!
KUGURA !!
TCH
YOU GUYS ARE SO LAME.
ENOUGH ...
THAT'S ENOUGH !!
KADO-WAKI !!

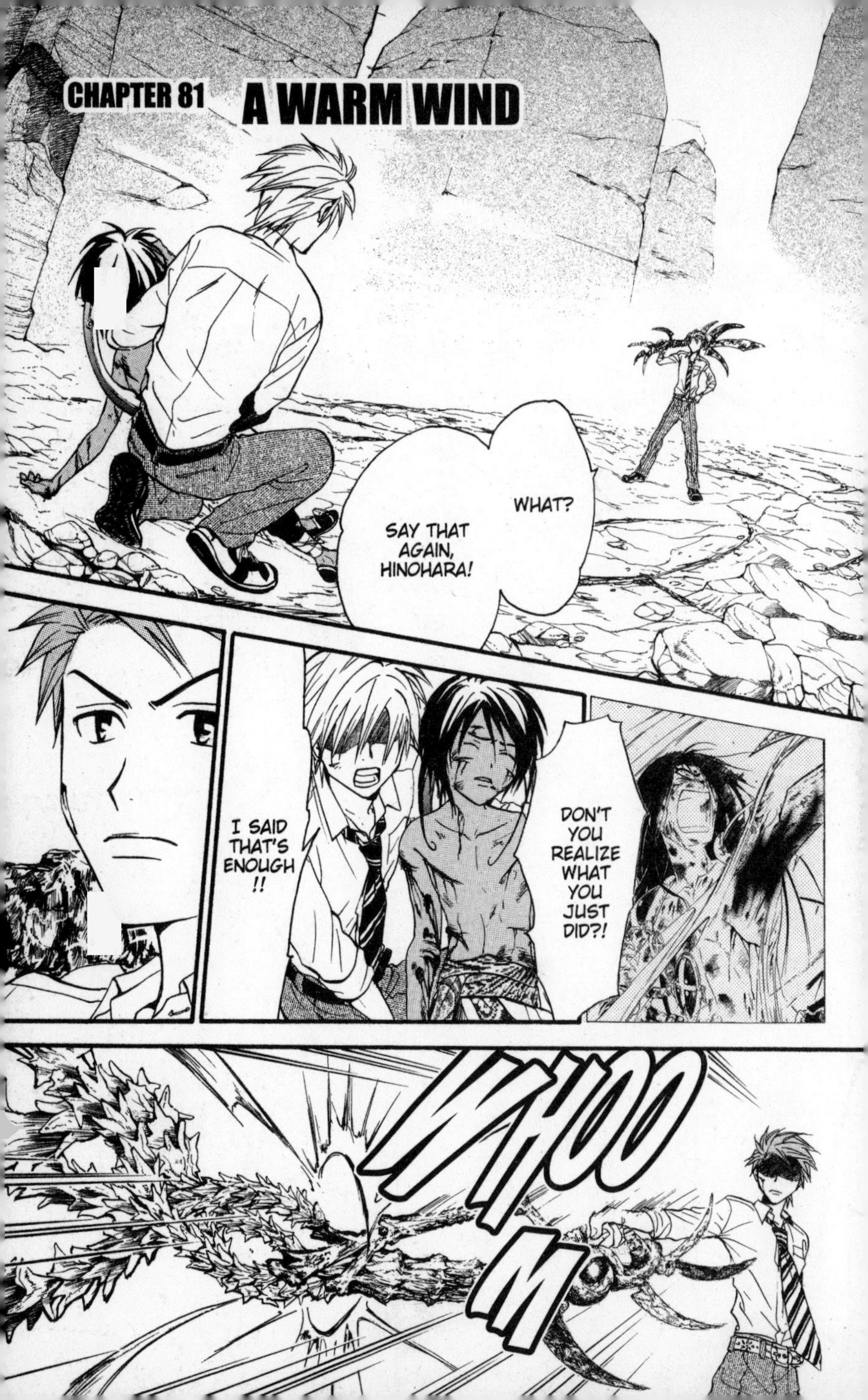
CHAPTER 81 A WARM WIND
WHAT? SAY THAT AGAIN, HINOHARA!
DON'T YOU REALIZE WHAT YOU JUST DID?!
I SAID THAT'S ENOUGH!!
WHOOM

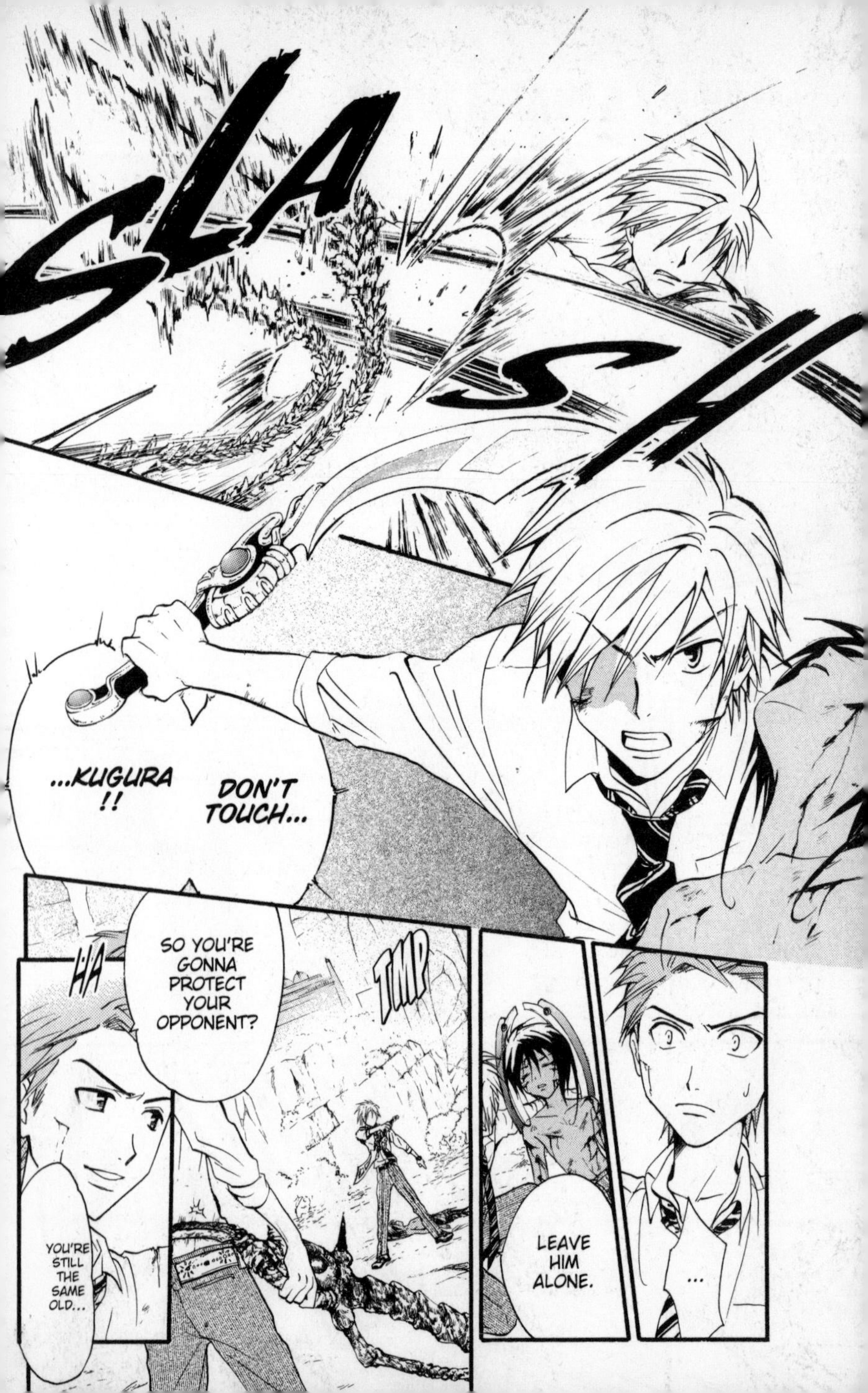
SLASH
DON'T TOUCH...
...KUGURA !!
...
LEAVE HIM ALONE.
TMP
SO YOU'RE GONNA PROTECT YOUR OPPONENT?
HA
YOU'RE STILL THE SAME OLD...

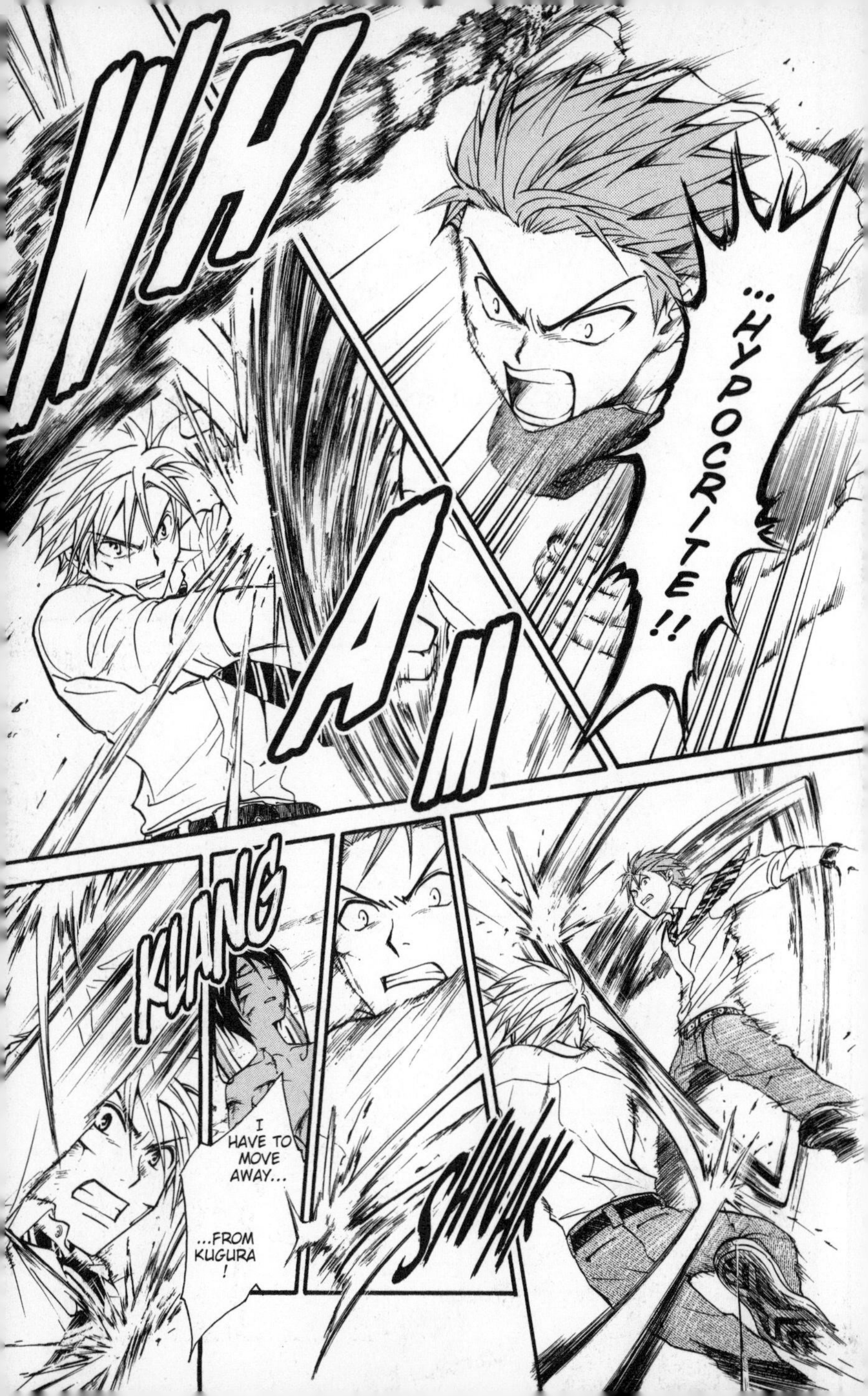
...HYPOCRITE!!
WHAM
KLANG
I HAVE TO MOVE AWAY...
...FROM KUGURA!
SCHWAK

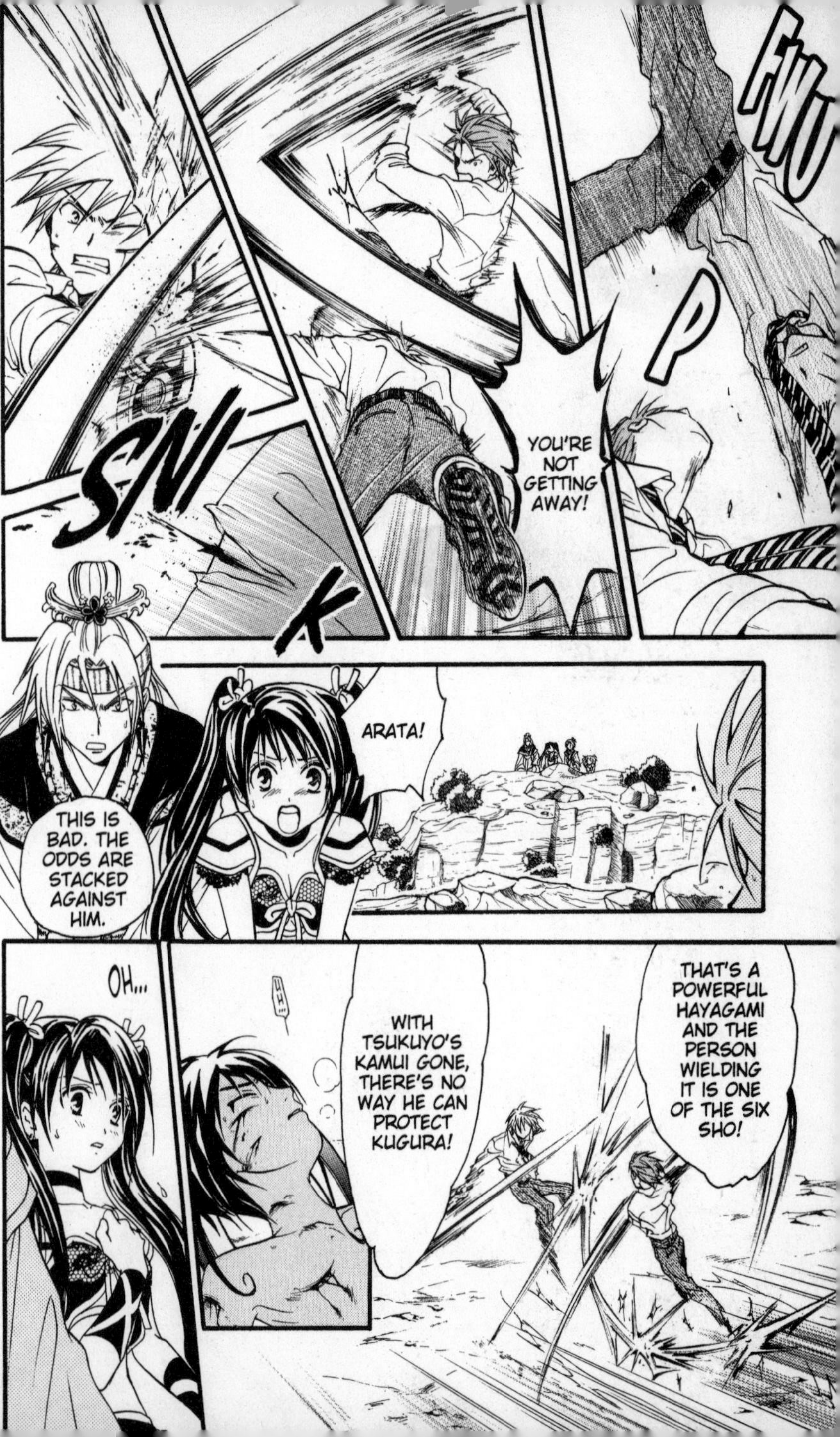
FWU
P
YOU'RE NOT GETTING AWAY!
SNI
K
ARATA!
THIS IS BAD. THE ODDS ARE STACKED AGAINST HIM.
THAT'S A POWERFUL HAYAGAMI AND THE PERSON WIELDING IT IS ONE OF THE SIX SHO!
WITH TSUKUYO'S KAMUI GONE, THERE'S NO WAY HE CAN PROTECT KUGURA!
OH...

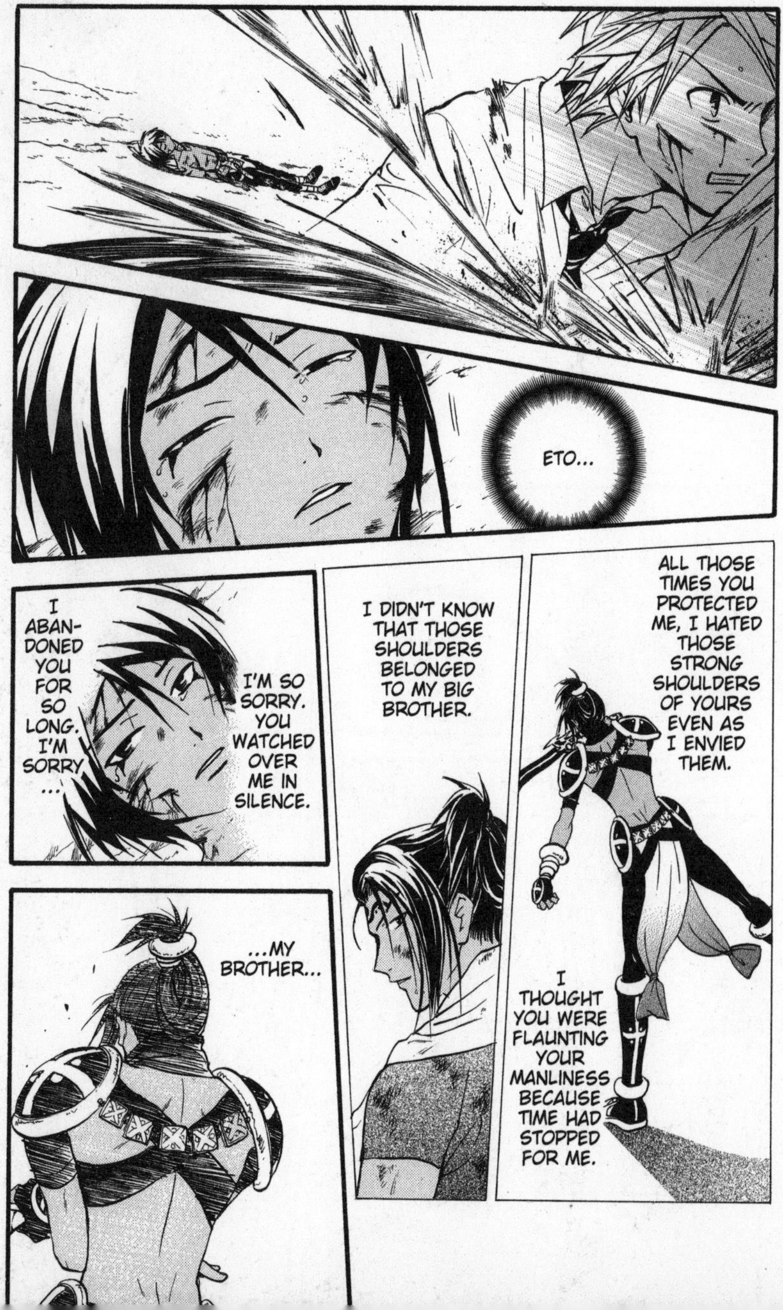
ETO...
ALL THOSE TIMES YOU PROTECTED ME, I HATED THOSE STRONG SHOULDERS OF YOURS EVEN AS I ENVIED THEM.
I THOUGHT YOU WERE FLAUNTING YOUR MANLINESS BECAUSE TIME HAD STOPPED FOR ME.
I DIDN'T KNOW THAT THOSE SHOULDERS BELONGED TO MY BIG BROTHER.
I'M SO SORRY. YOU WATCHED OVER ME IN SILENCE.
I ABAN-DONED YOU FOR SO LONG. I'M SORRY...
...MY BROTHER...

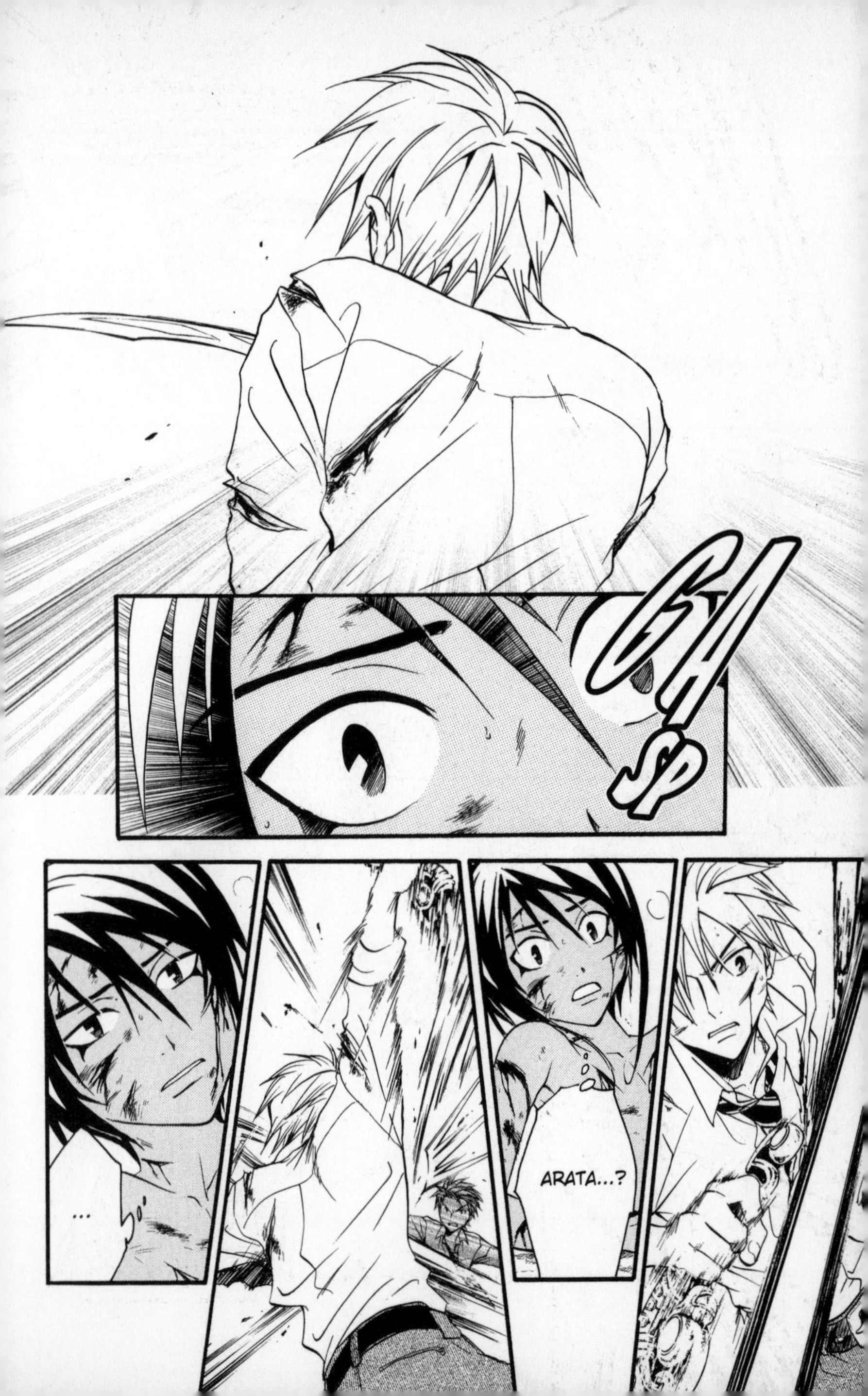
GASP
ARATA...?
...

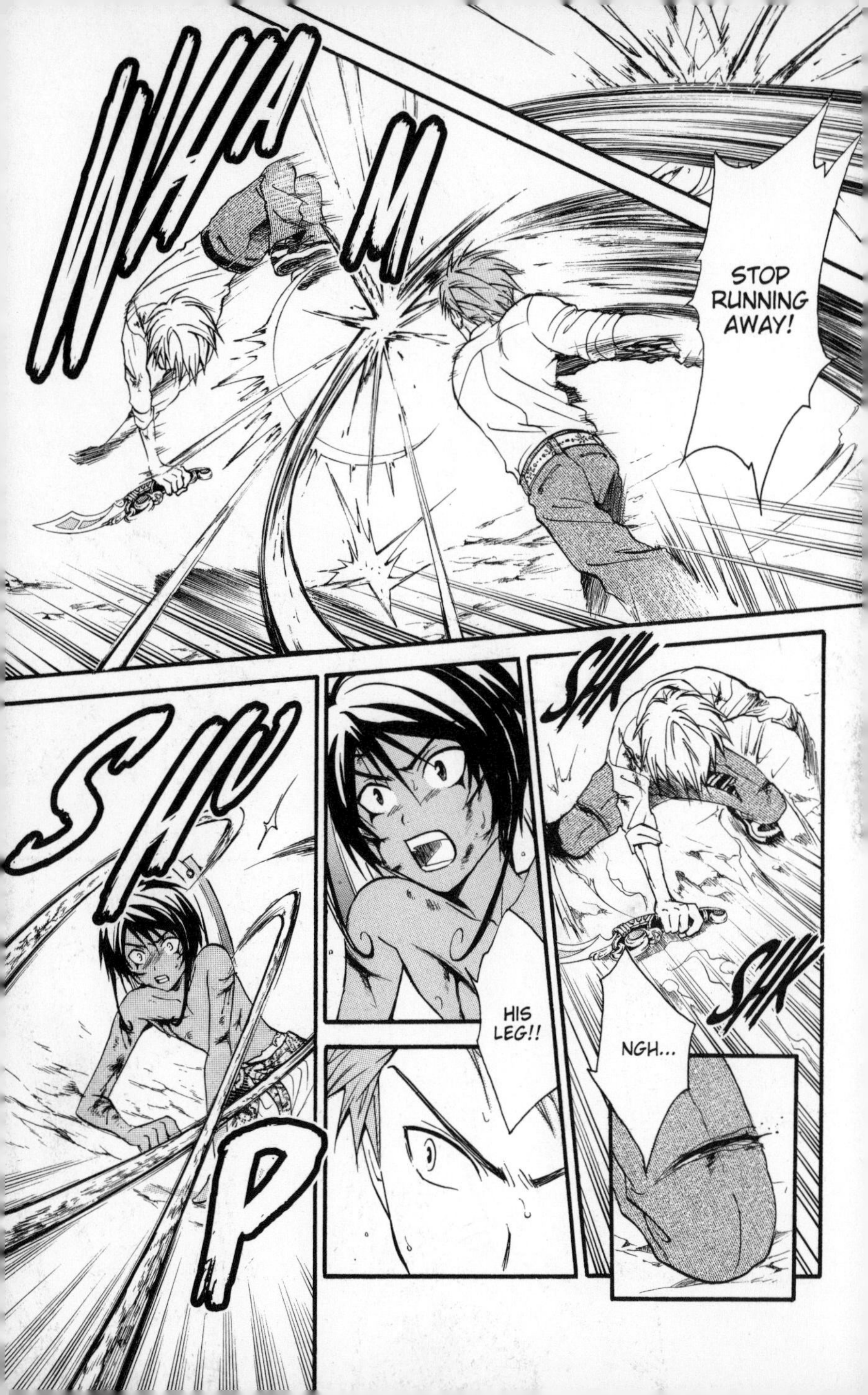
STOP RUNNING AWAY!
SHK
SHK
NGH...
HIS LEG!!

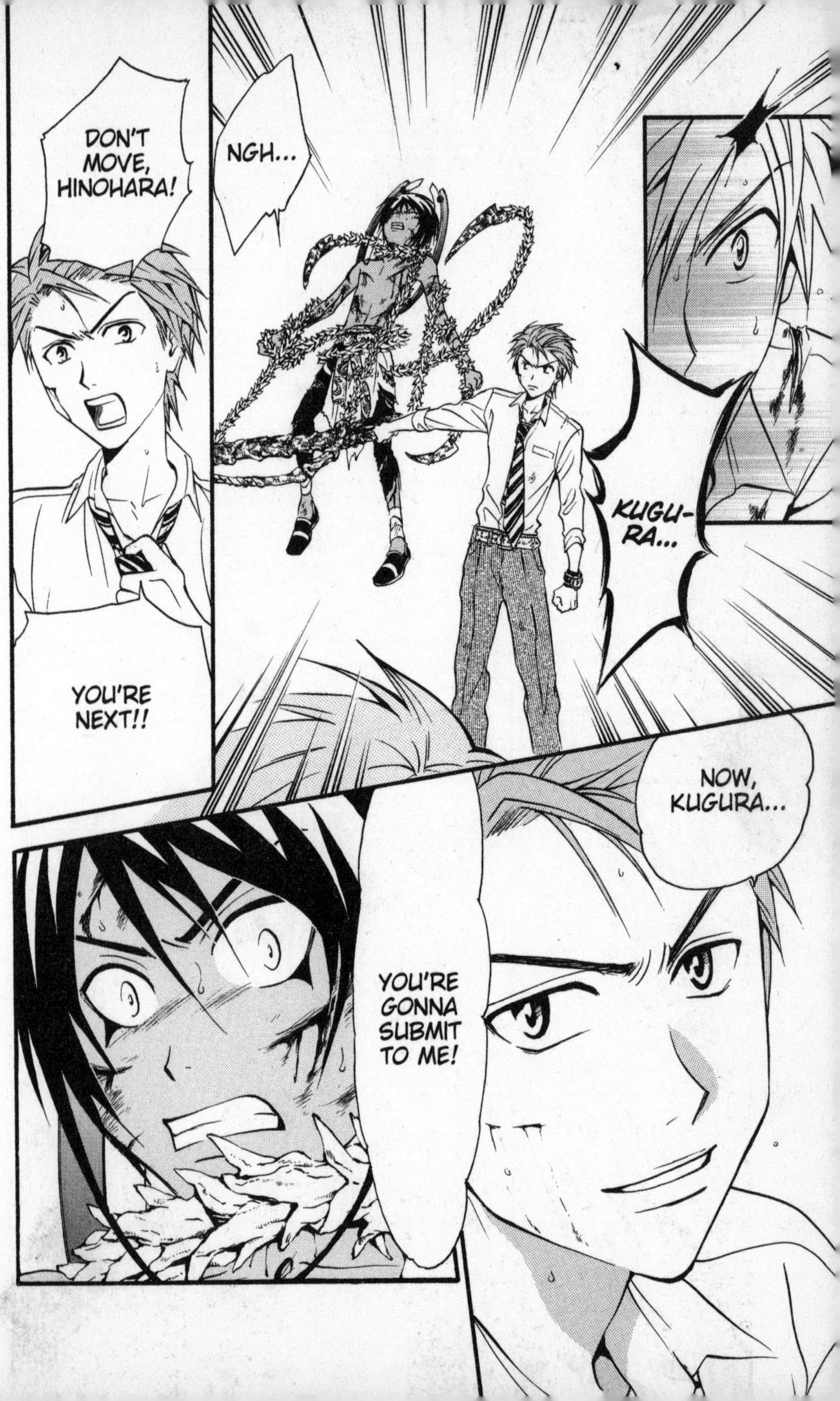
KUGU-RA...
NGH...
DON'T MOVE, HINOHARA!
YOU'RE NEXT!!
NOW, KUGURA...
YOU'RE GONNA SUBMIT TO ME!

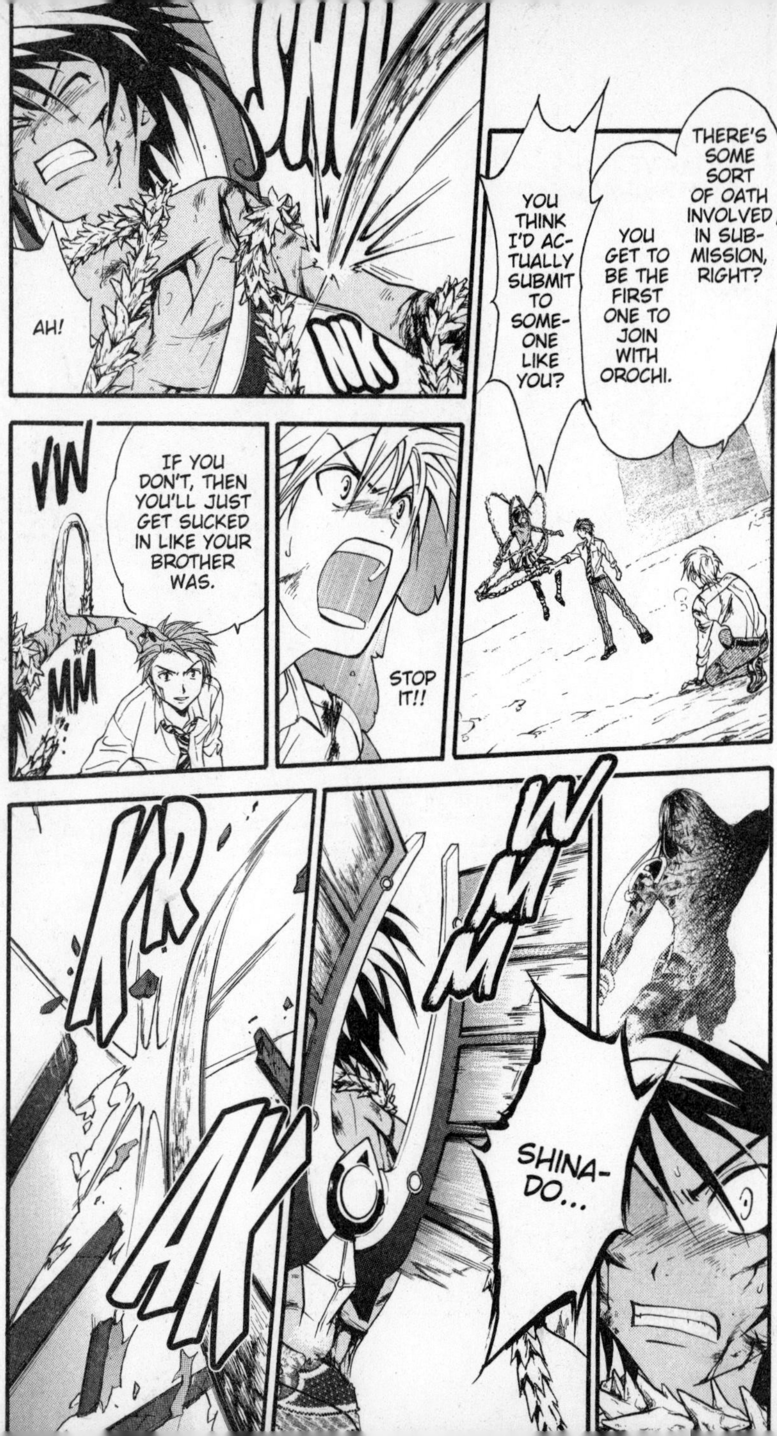
THERE'S SOME SORT OF OATH INVOLVED IN SUB-MISSION, RIGHT?
YOU GET TO BE THE FIRST ONE TO JOIN WITH OROCHI.
YOU THINK I'D AC-TUALLY SUBMIT TO SOME-ONE LIKE YOU?
AH!
NK
STOP IT!!
VW
IF YOU DON'T, THEN YOU'LL JUST GET SUCKED IN LIKE YOUR BROTHER WAS.
MM
SHINA-DO...

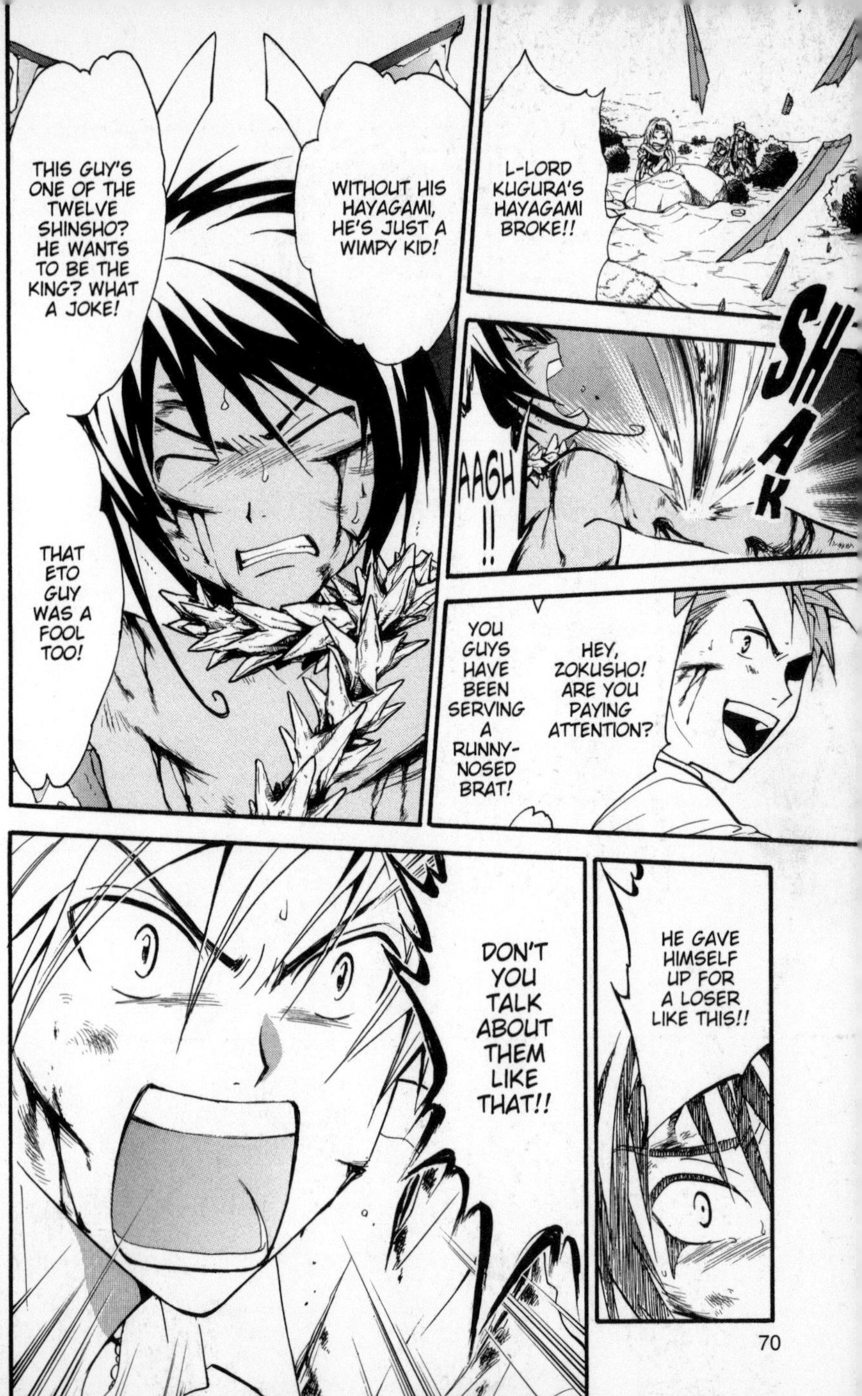
L-LORD KUGURA'S HAYAGAMI BROKE!!
SHAK
AAGH!!
HEY, ZOKUSHO! ARE YOU PAYING ATTENTION?
YOU GUYS HAVE BEEN SERVING A RUNNY-NOSED BRAT!
WITHOUT HIS HAYAGAMI, HE'S JUST A WIMPY KID!
THIS GUY'S ONE OF THE TWELVE SHINSHO? HE WANTS TO BE THE KING? WHAT A JOKE!
THAT ETO GUY WAS A FOOL TOO!
HE GAVE HIMSELF UP FOR A LOSER LIKE THIS!!
DON'T YOU TALK ABOUT THEM LIKE THAT!!

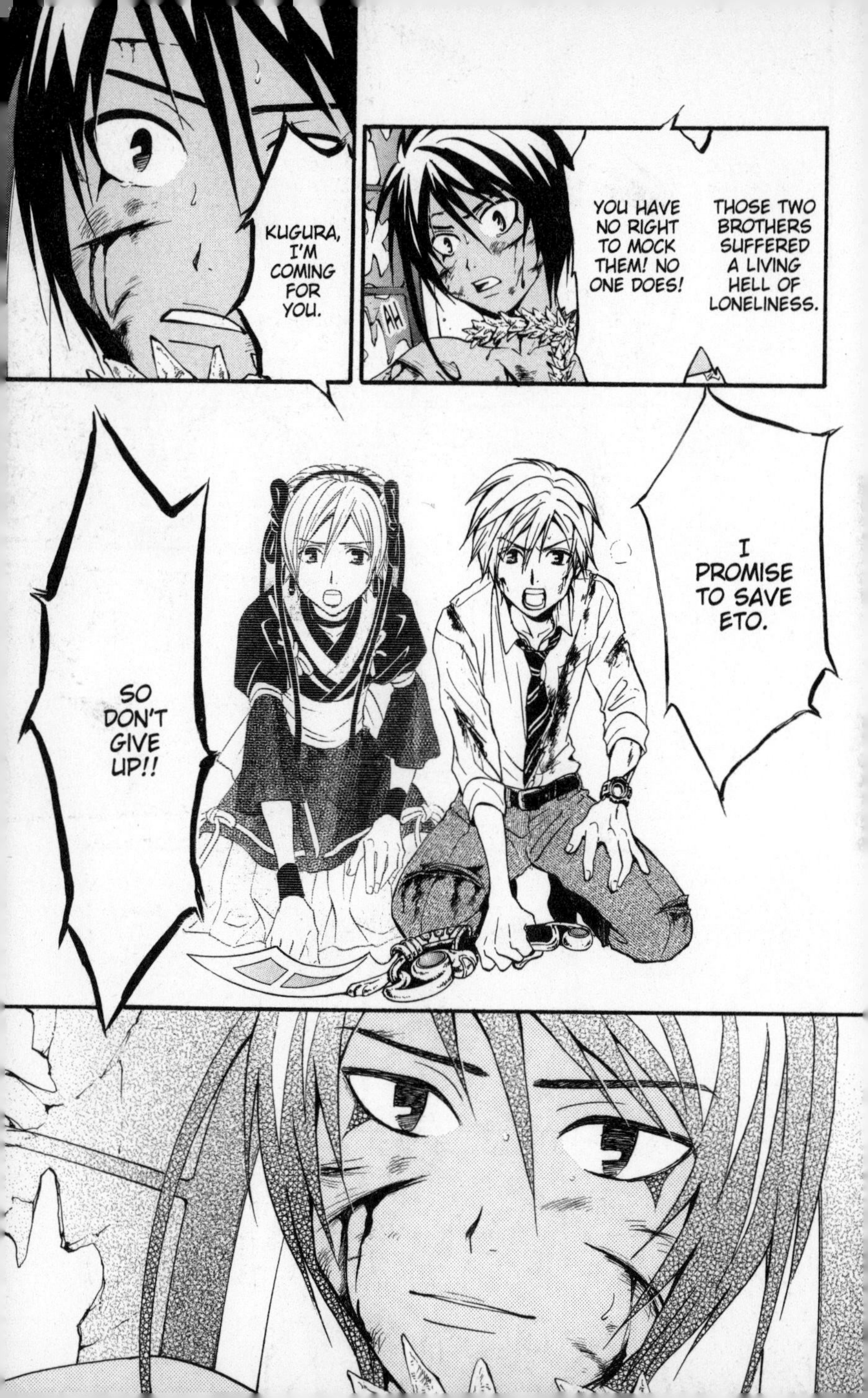
THOSE TWO BROTHERS SUFFERED A LIVING HELL OF LONELINESS.
YOU HAVE NO RIGHT TO MOCK THEM! NO ONE DOES!
AH
KUGURA, I'M COMING FOR YOU.
I PROMISE TO SAVE ETO.
SO DON'T GIVE UP!!

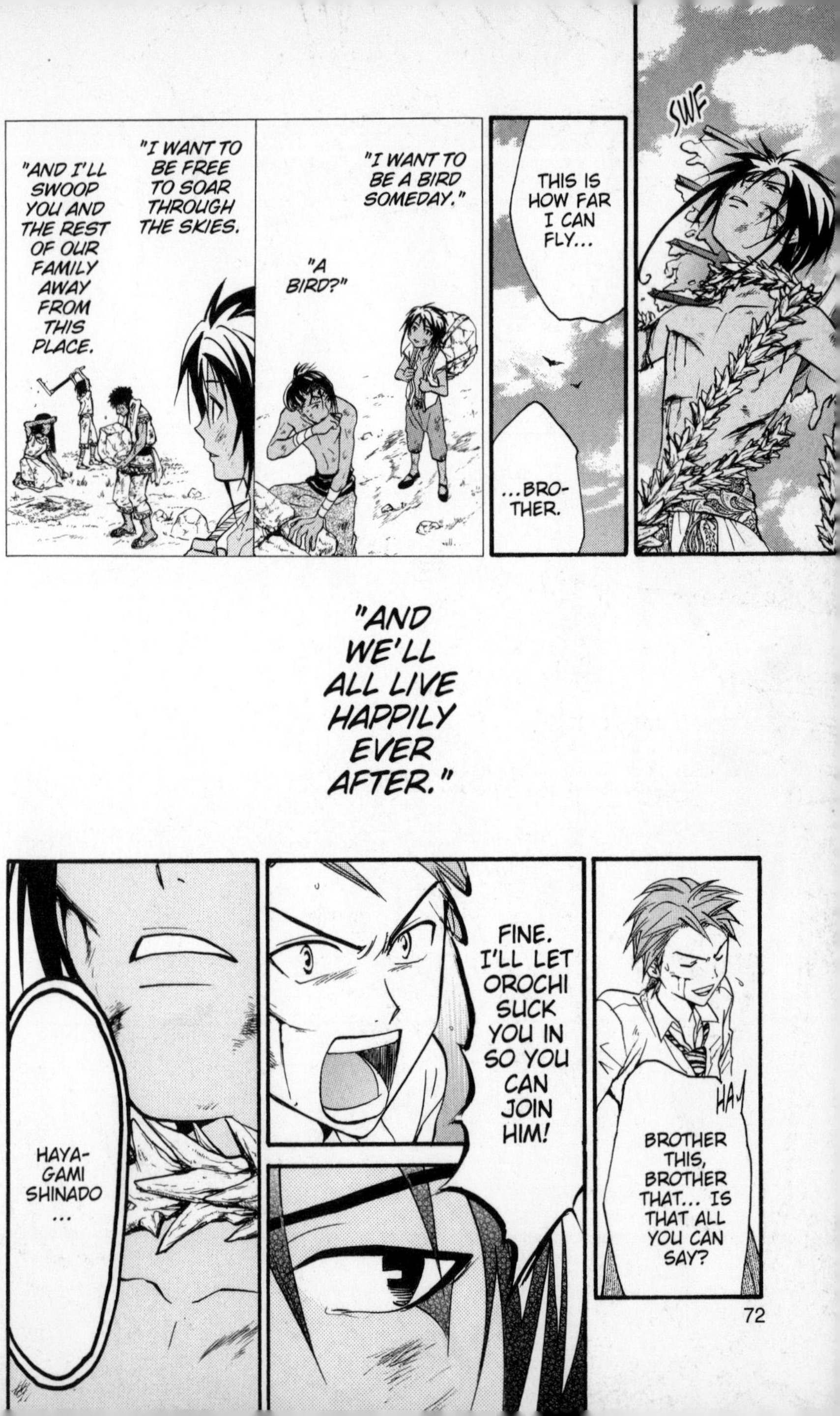
SWF
THIS IS HOW FAR I CAN FLY...
...BROTHER.
"I WANT TO BE A BIRD SOMEDAY."
"A BIRD?"
"I WANT TO BE FREE TO SOAR THROUGH THE SKIES.
"AND I'LL SWOOP YOU AND THE REST OF OUR FAMILY AWAY FROM THIS PLACE.
"AND WE'LL ALL LIVE HAPPILY EVER AFTER."
HAH
BROTHER THIS, BROTHER THAT... IS THAT ALL YOU CAN SAY?
FINE. I'LL LET OROCHI SUCK YOU IN SO YOU CAN JOIN HIM!
HAYA-GAMI SHINADO ...

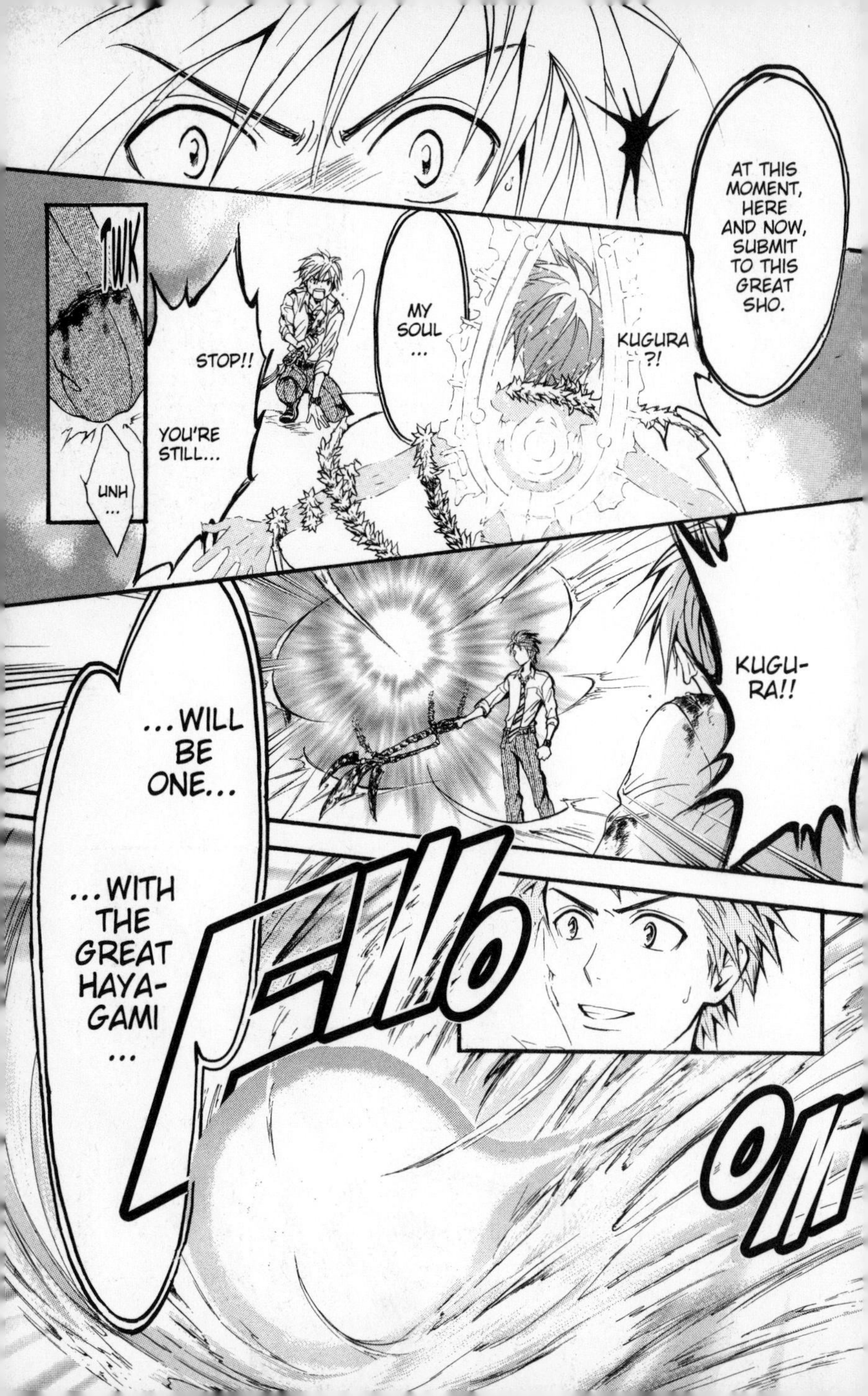
AT THIS MOMENT, HERE AND NOW, SUBMIT TO THIS GREAT SHO.
KUGURA ?!
MY SOUL ...
STOP!!
YOU'RE STILL...
TWK
UNH ...
KUGU-RA!!
...WILL BE ONE...
...WITH THE GREAT HAYA-GAMI ...

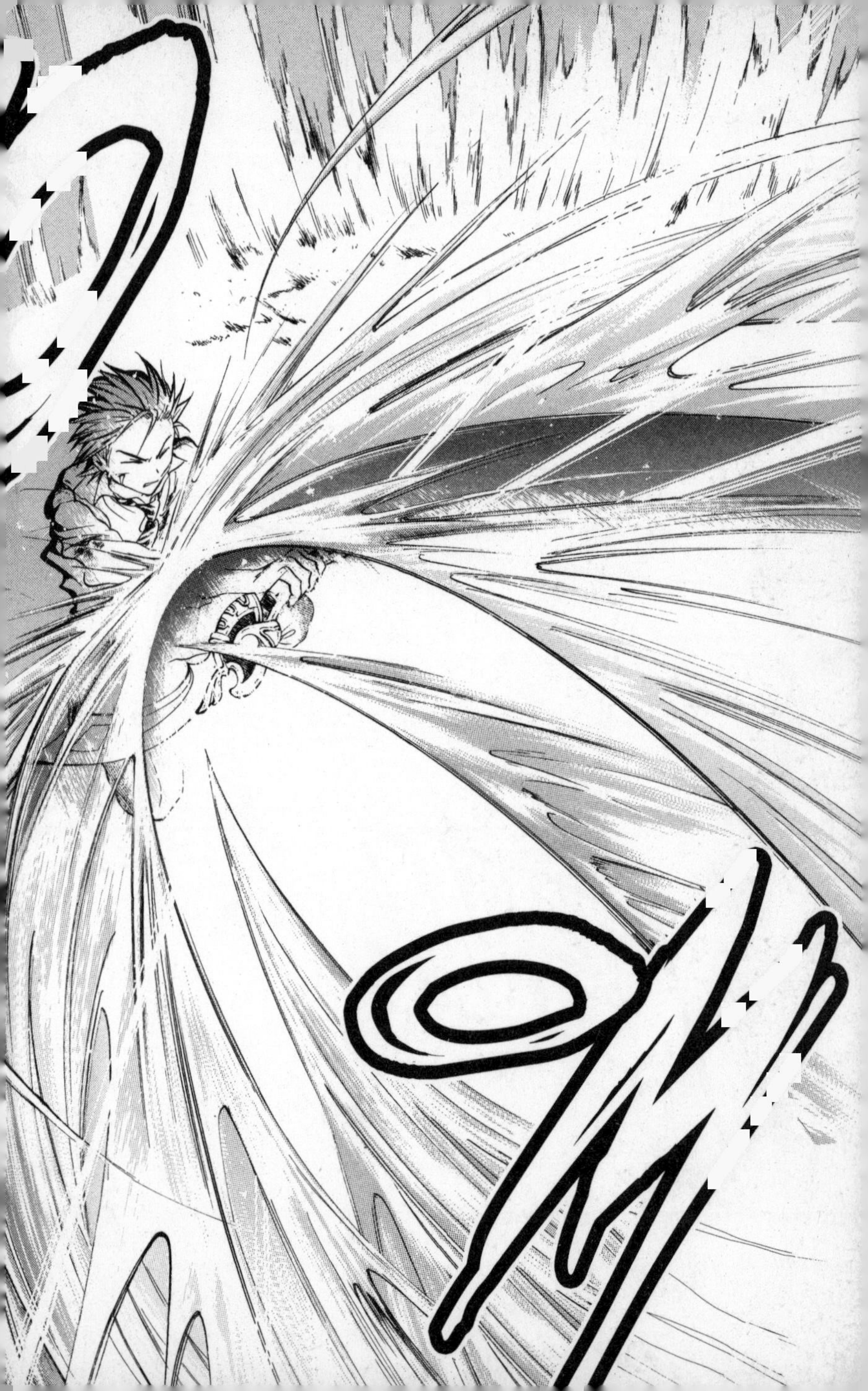

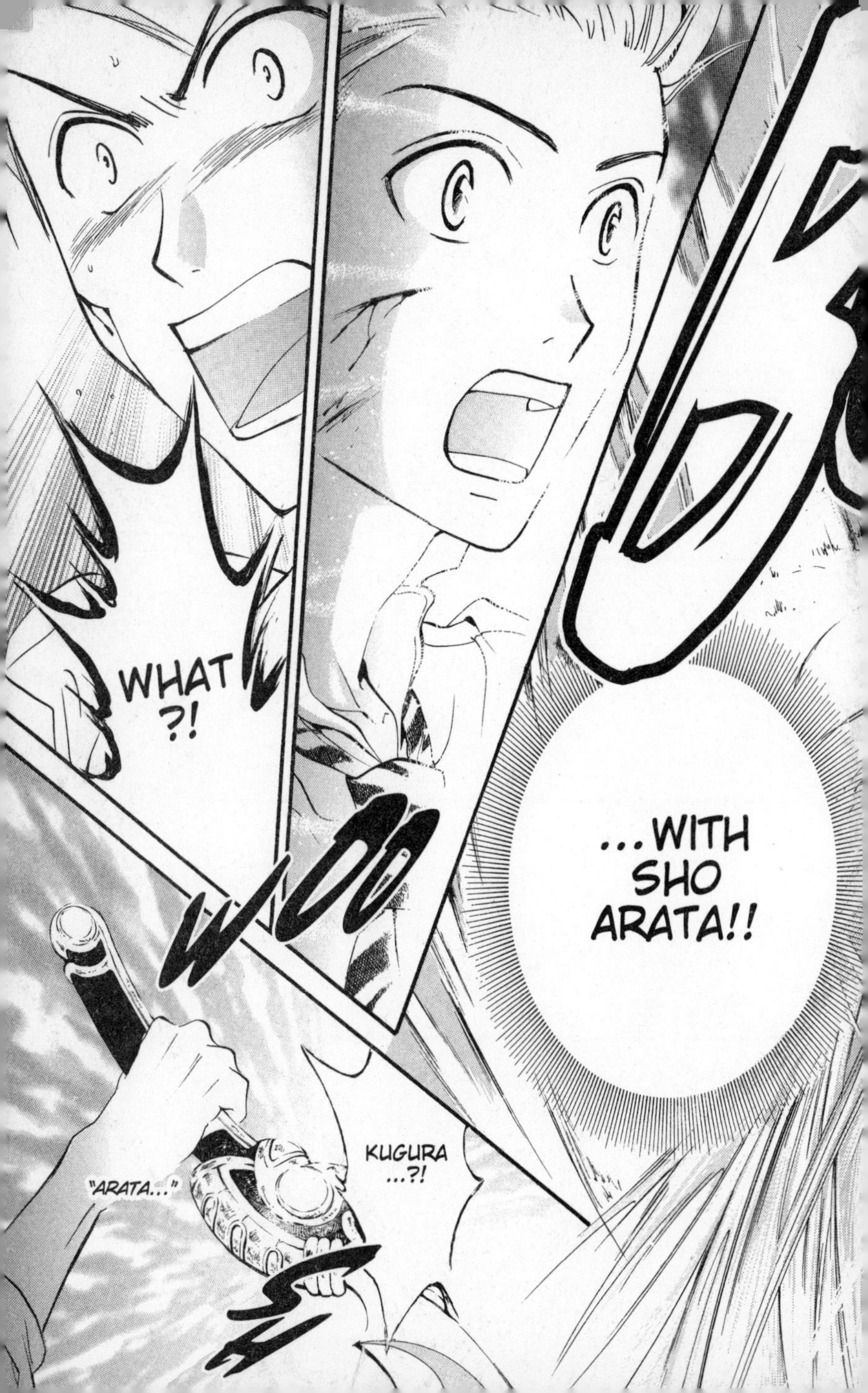
...WITH SHO ARATA!!
WHAT ?!
KUGURA ...?!
"ARATA..."

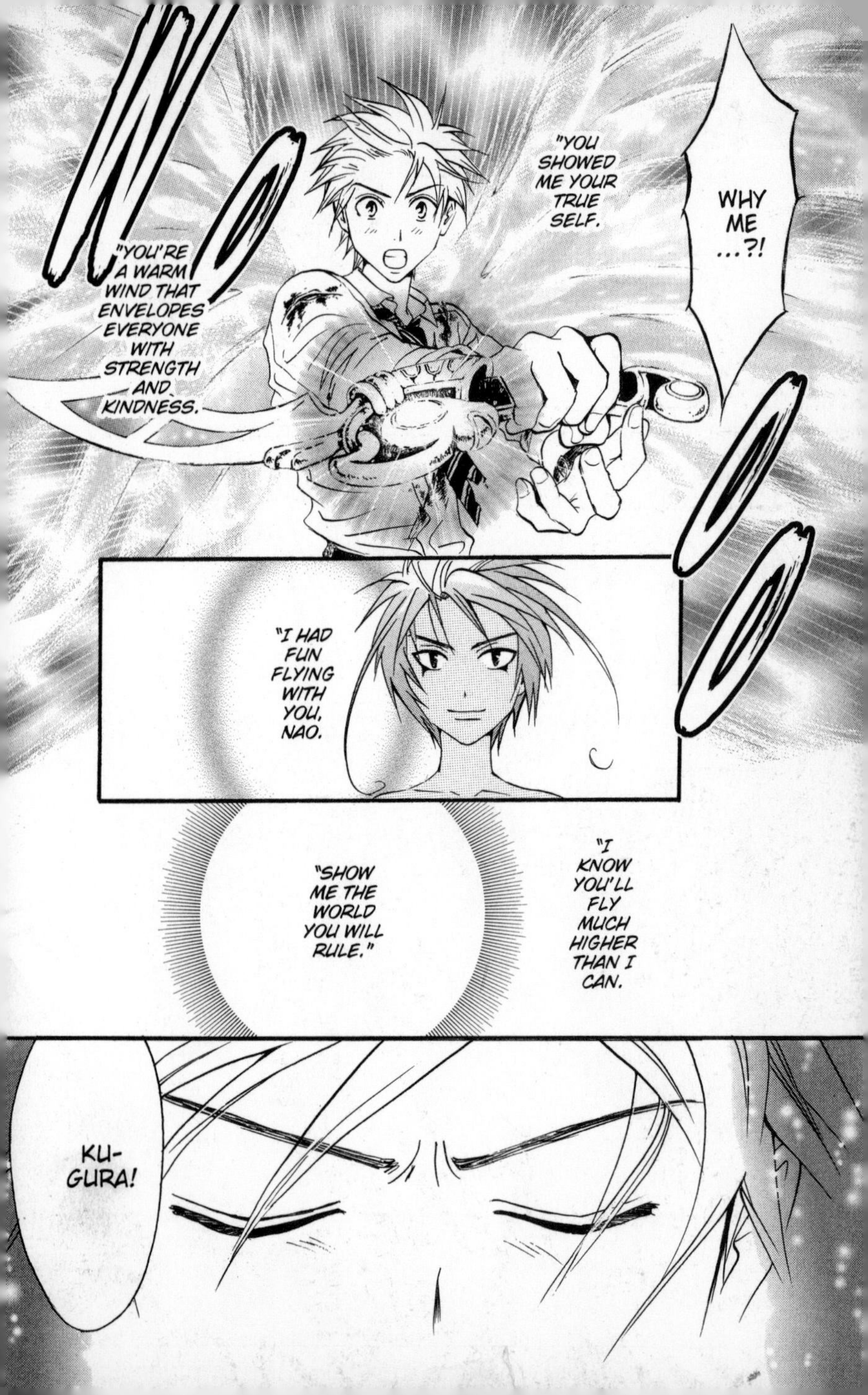
WHY ME ...?!
"YOU SHOWED ME YOUR TRUE SELF.
"YOU'RE A WARM WIND THAT ENVELOPES EVERYONE WITH STRENGTH AND KINDNESS.
NOOOO
"I HAD FUN FLYING WITH YOU, NAO.
"I KNOW YOU'LL FLY MUCH HIGHER THAN I CAN.
"SHOW ME THE WORLD YOU WILL RULE."
KU-GURA!

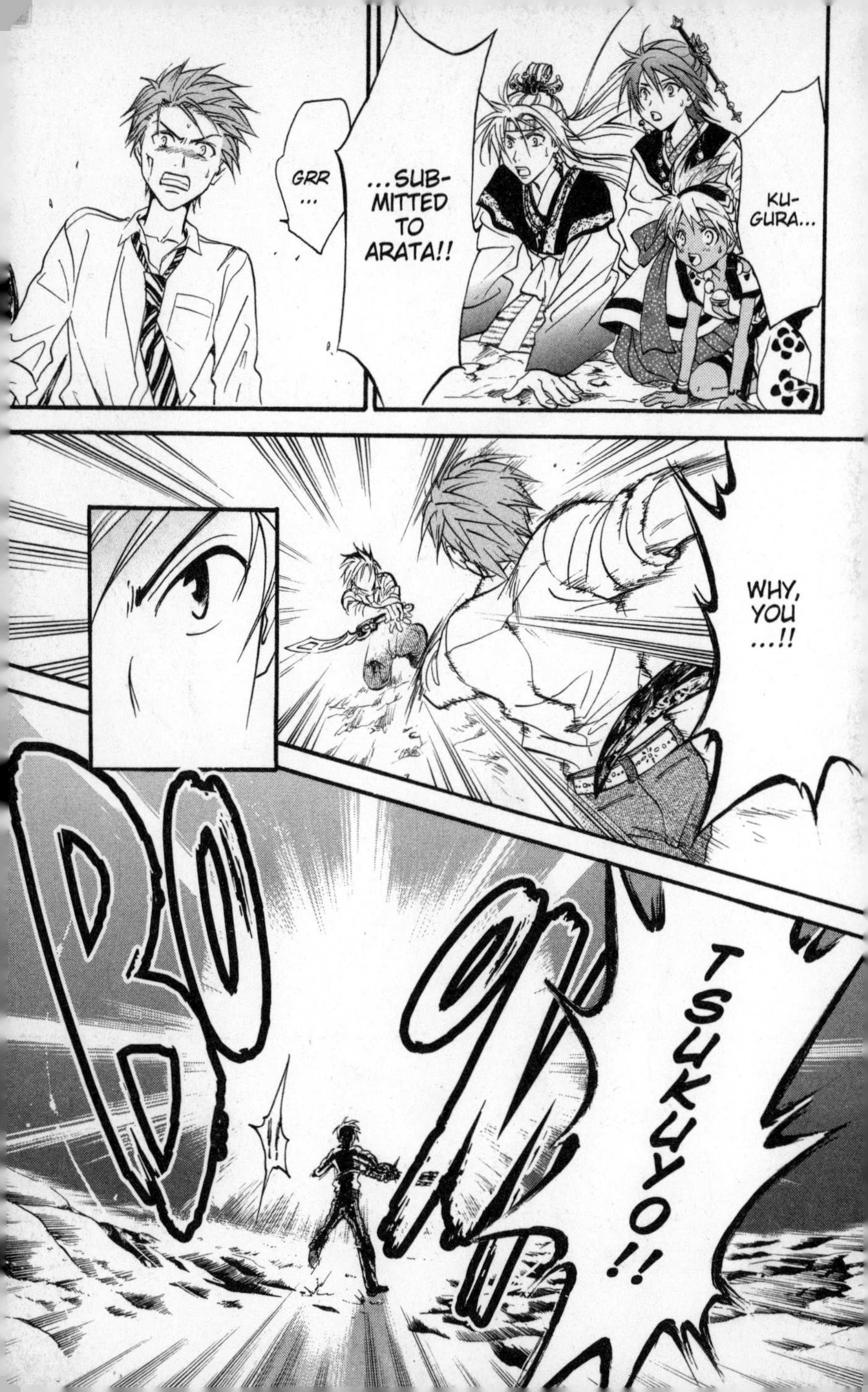
KU-
GURA...
...SUB-
MITTED
TO
ARATA!!
GRR
...
WHY,
YOU
...!!
TSUKUYO!!

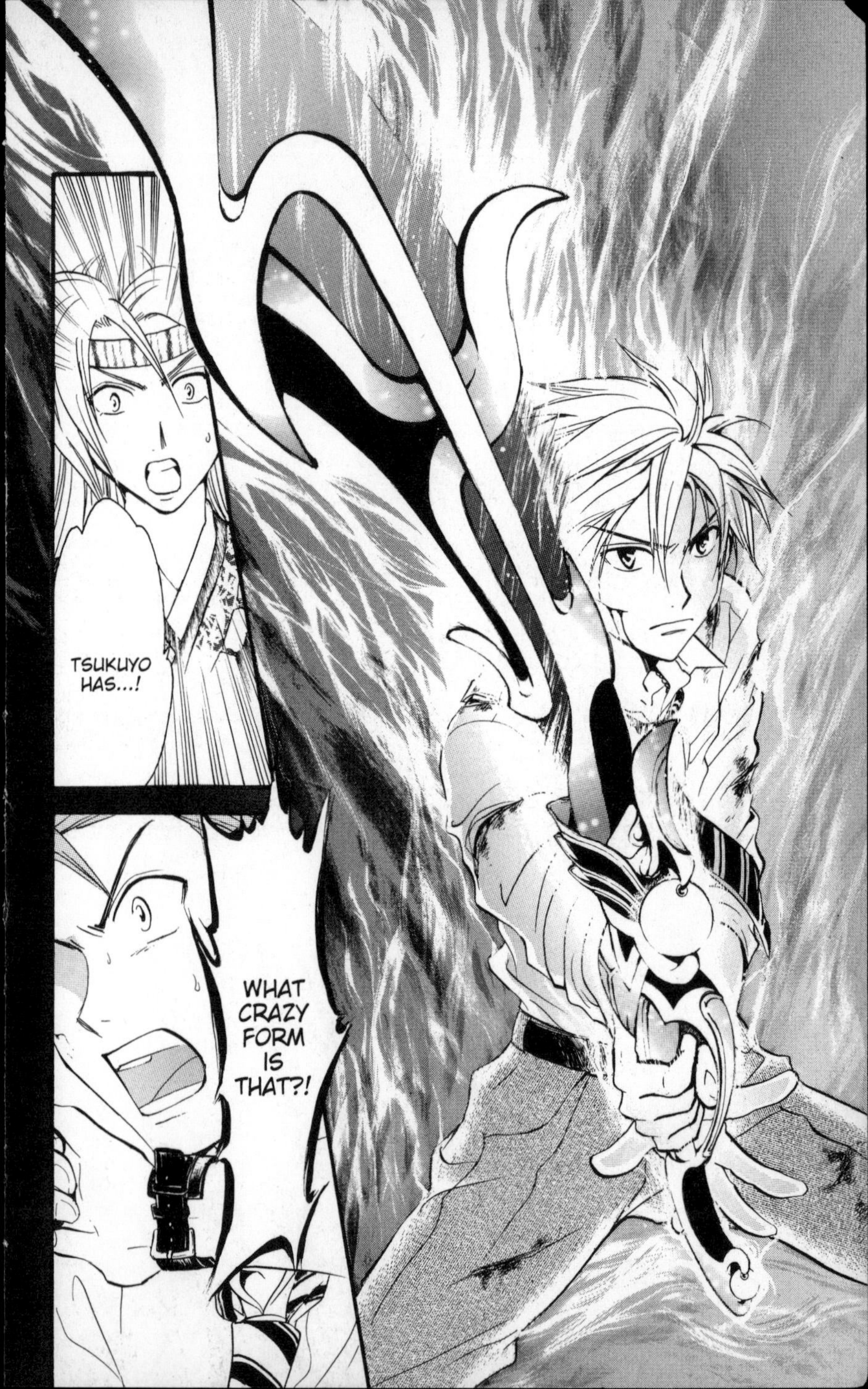
TSUKUYO HAS...!
WHAT CRAZY FORM IS THAT?!

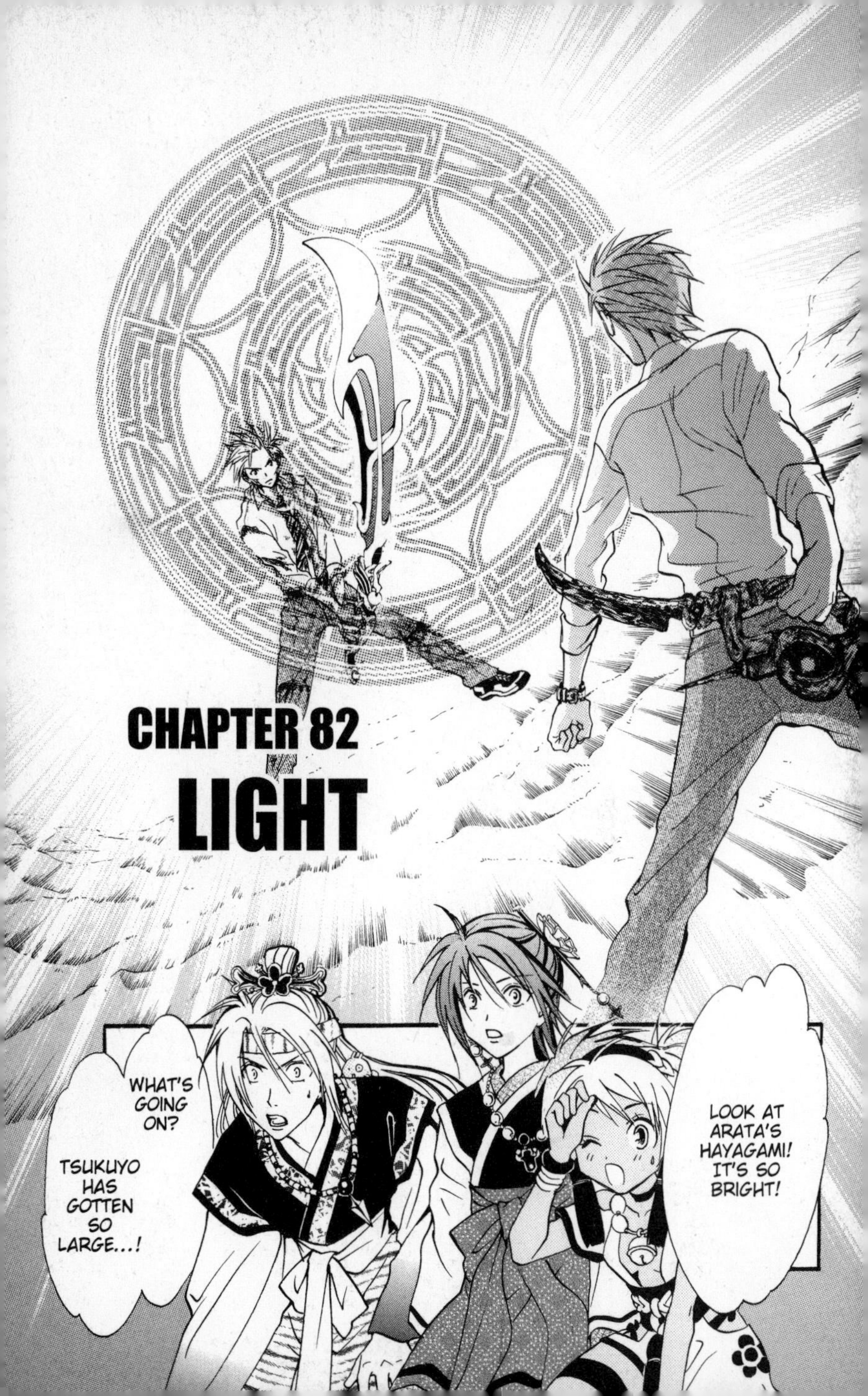
CHAPTER 82
LIGHT
LOOK AT ARATA'S HAYAGAMI! IT'S SO BRIGHT!
WHAT'S GOING ON?
TSUKUYO HAS GOTTEN SO LARGE...!

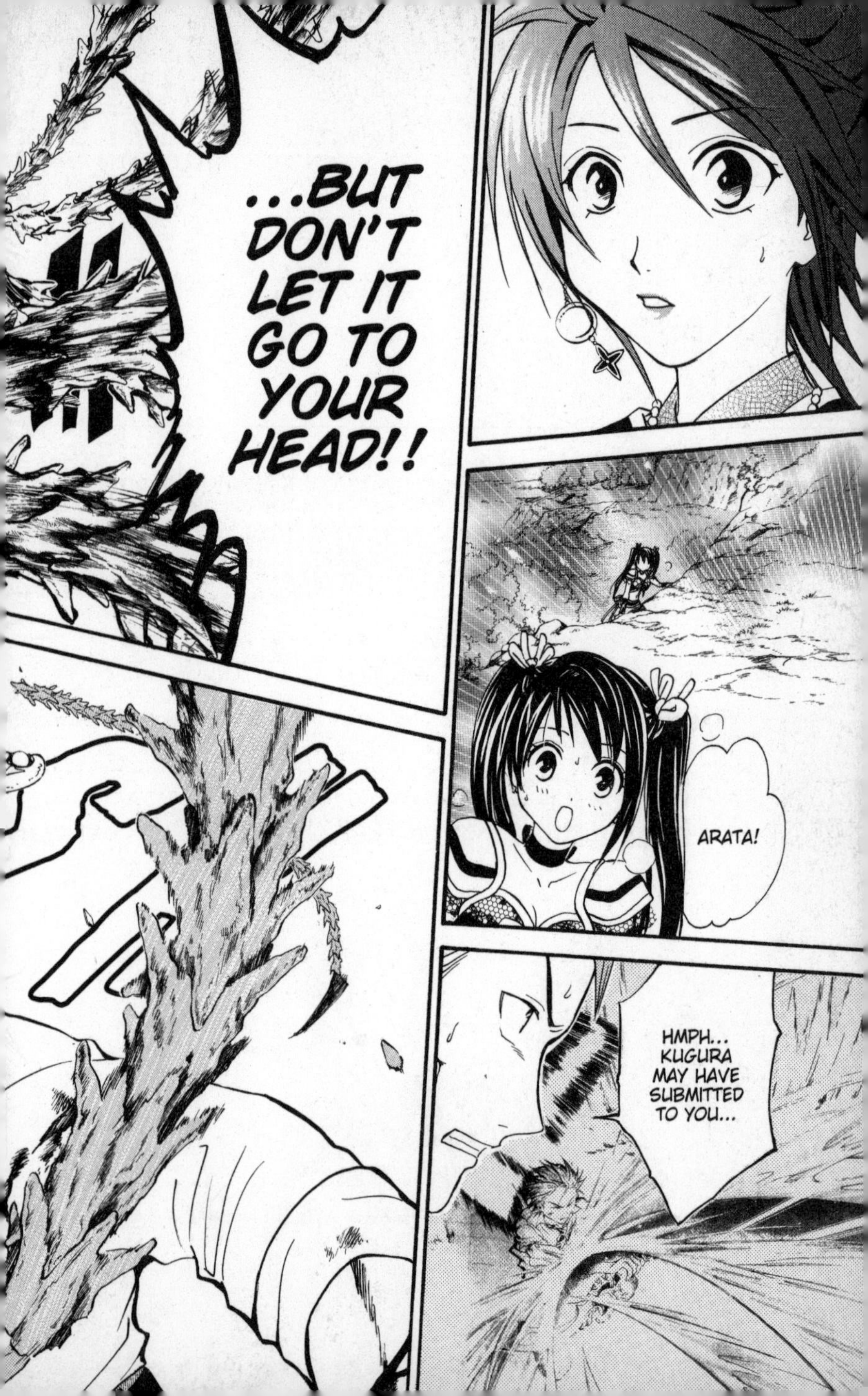
...BUT DON'T LET IT GO TO YOUR HEAD!!
ARATA!
HMPH... KUGURA MAY HAVE SUBMITTED TO YOU...

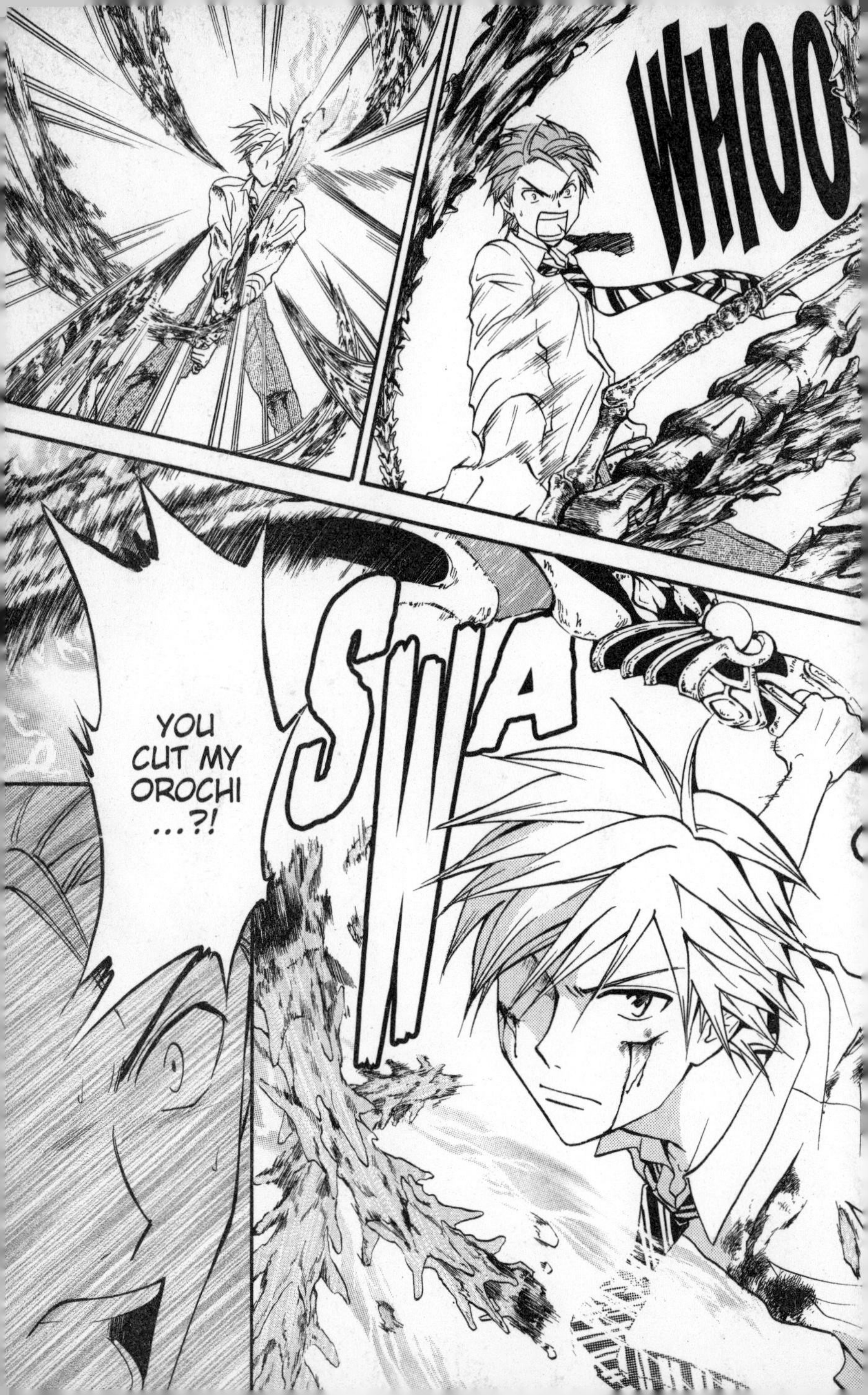
WHOO
SHA
YOU CUT MY OROCHI ...?!

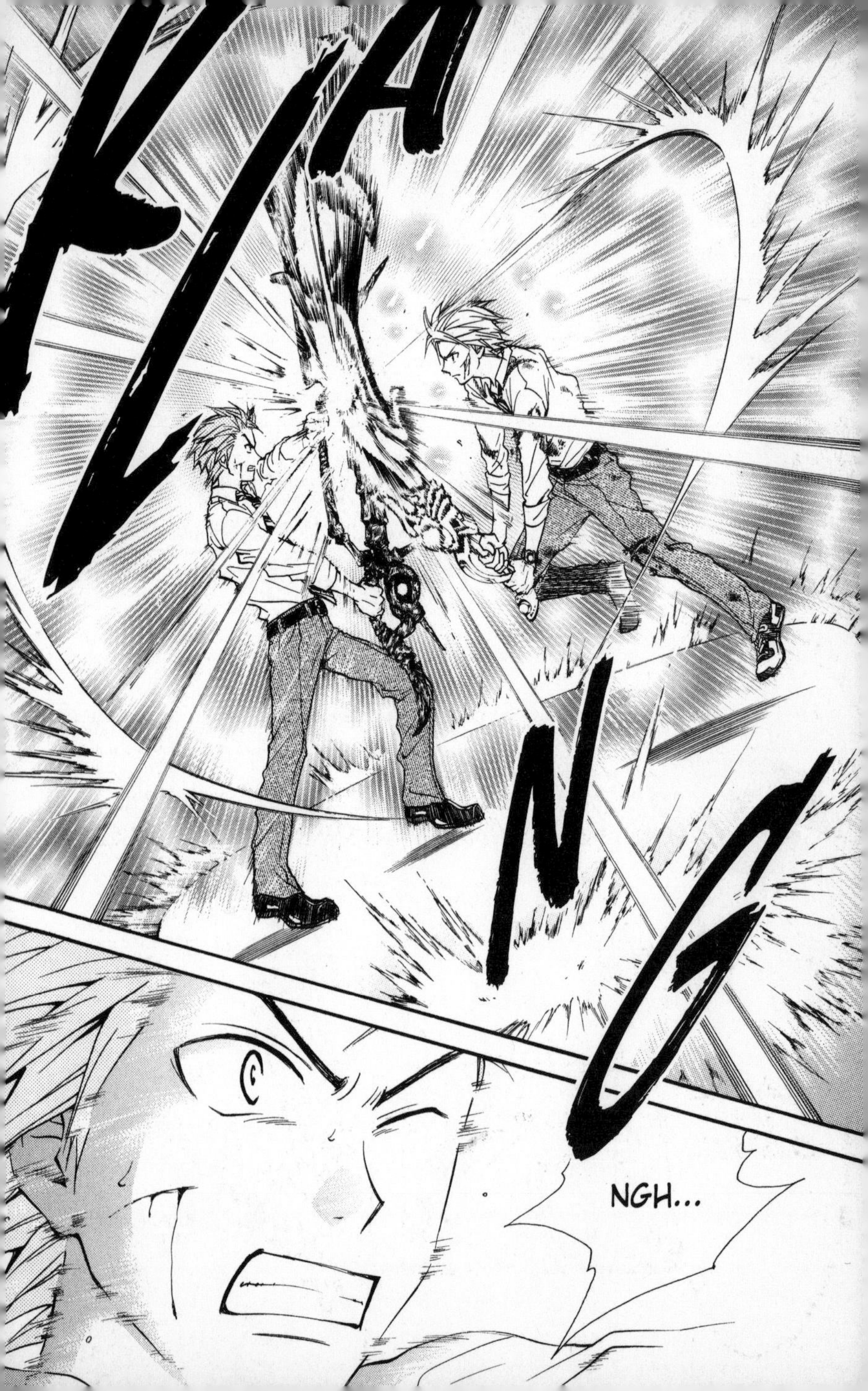
KLANG
NGH...

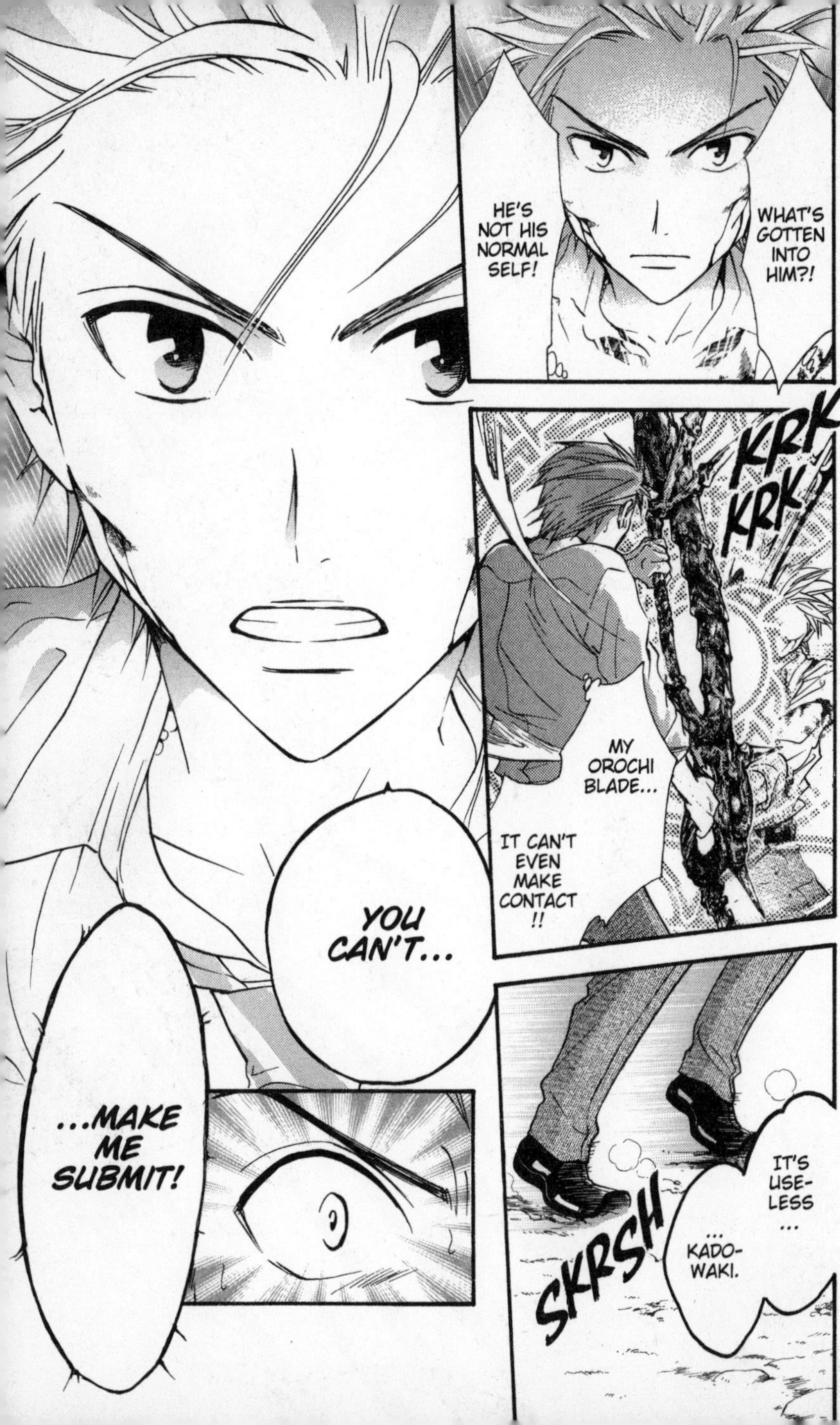
WHAT'S GOTTEN INTO HIM?!
HE'S NOT HIS NORMAL SELF!
KRK KRK
MY OROCHI BLADE...
IT CAN'T EVEN MAKE CONTACT!!
SKRSH
IT'S USELESS... ...KADOWAKI.
YOU CAN'T...
...MAKE ME SUBMIT!

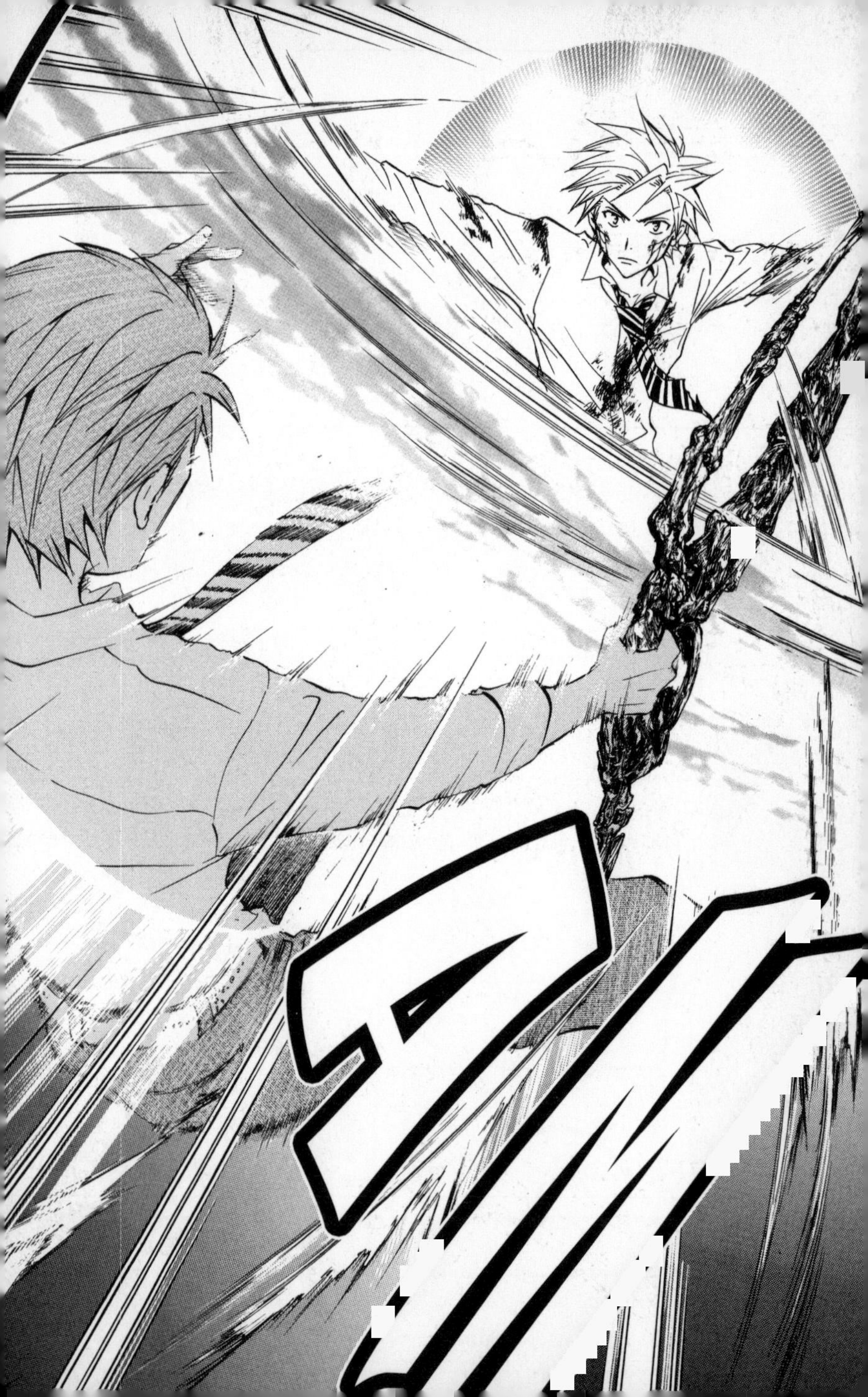

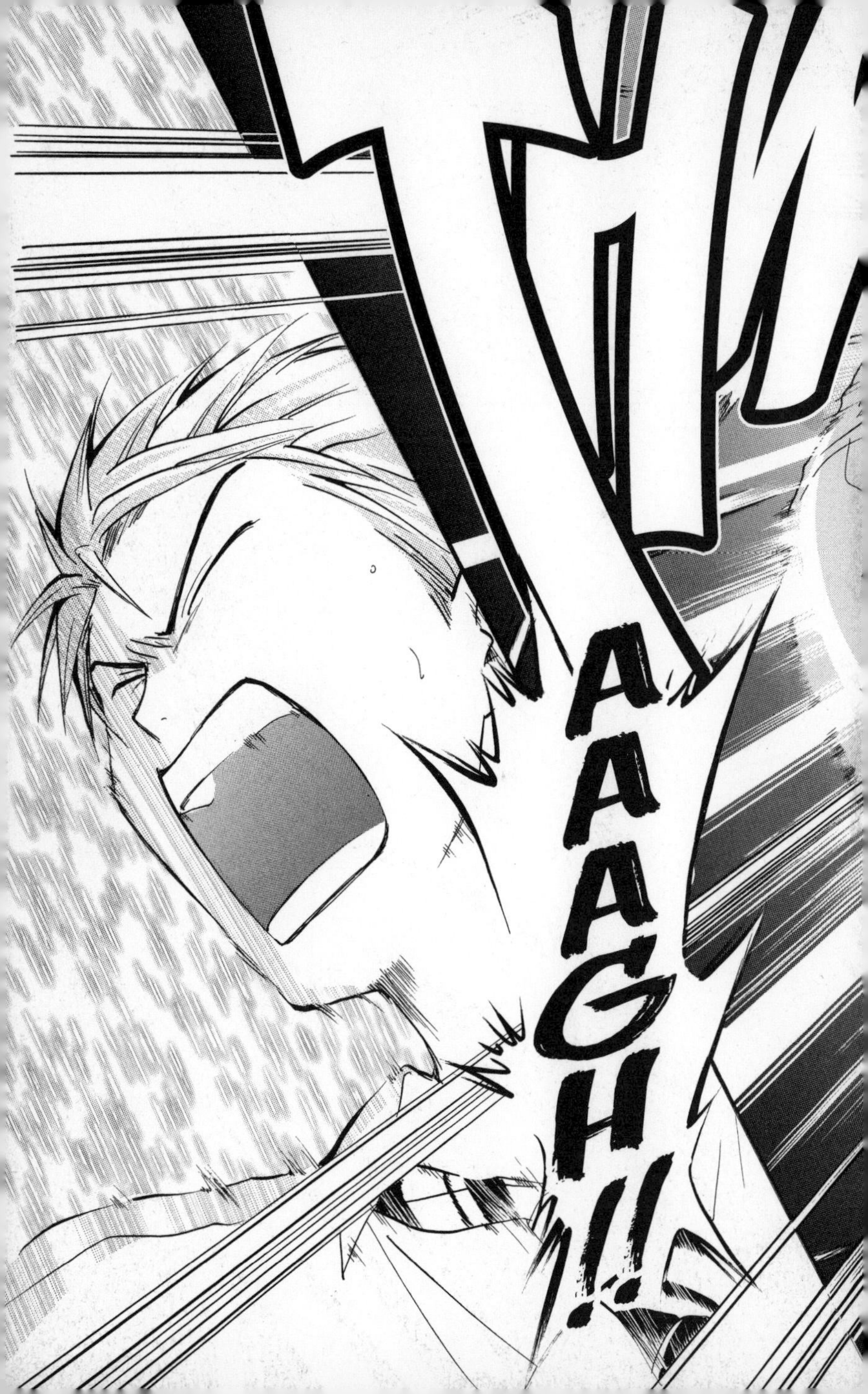
AAAGH!!

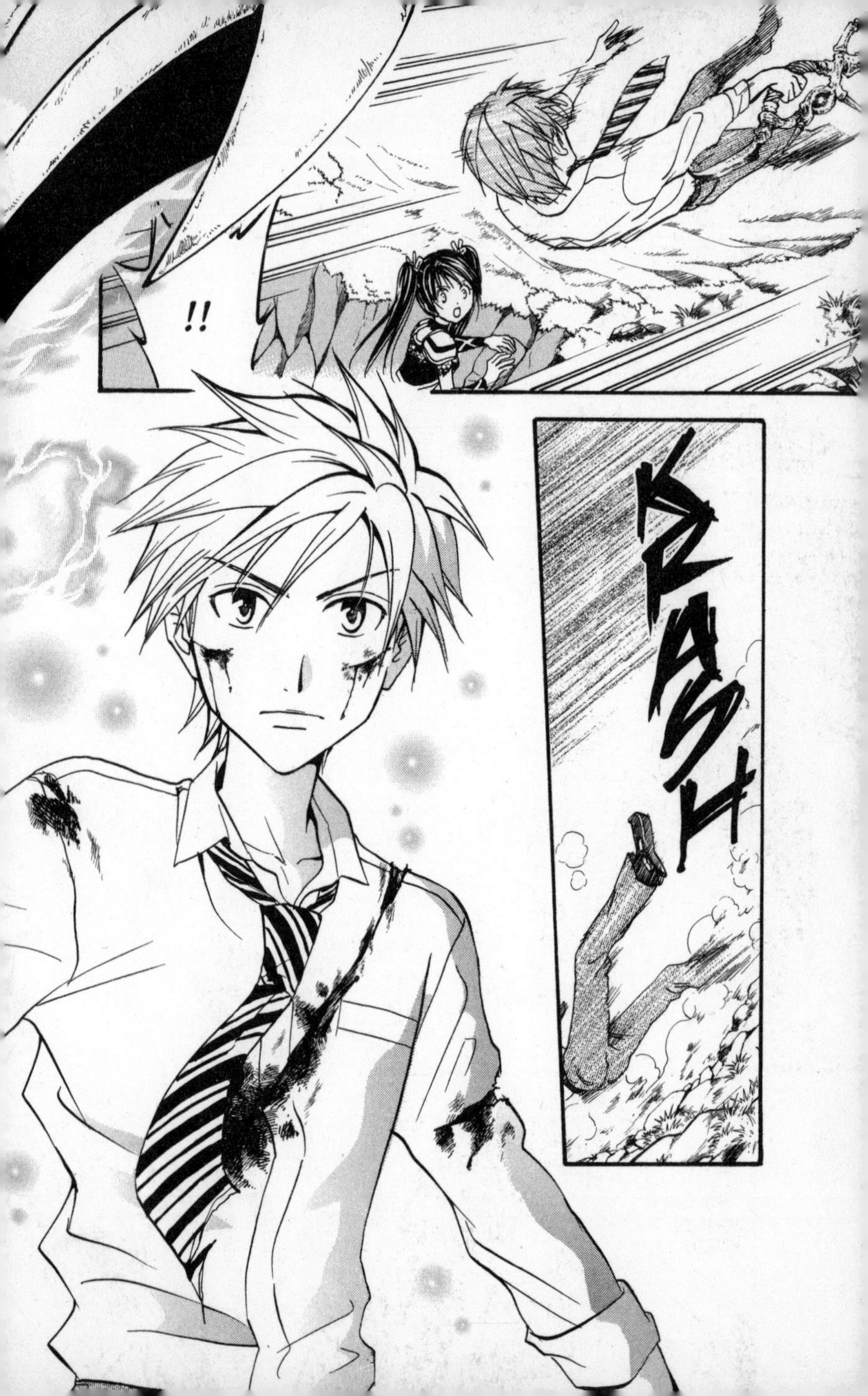
!!
KRASH

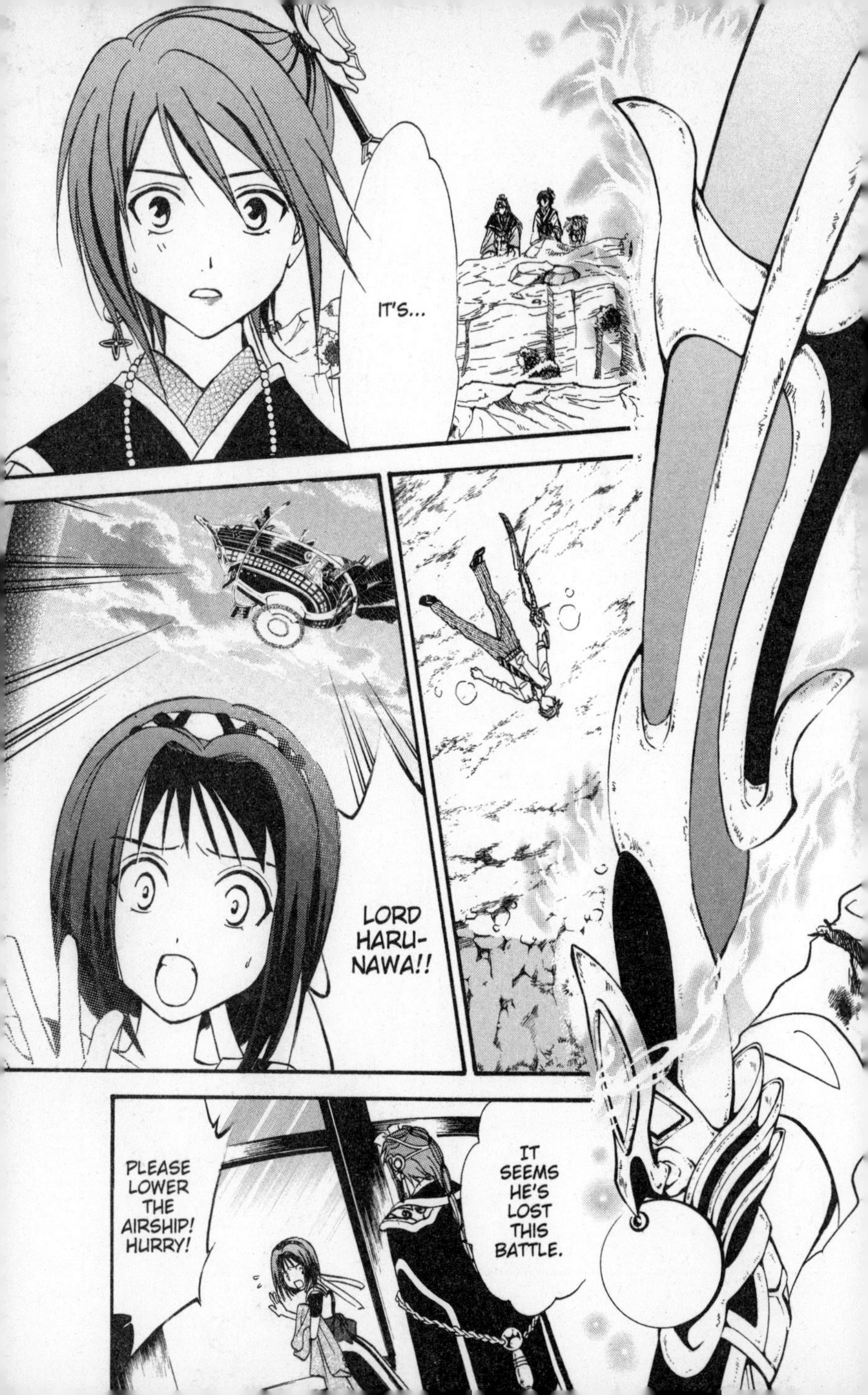
IT'S...
LORD HARU-NAWA!!
IT SEEMS HE'S LOST THIS BATTLE.
PLEASE LOWER THE AIRSHIP! HURRY!

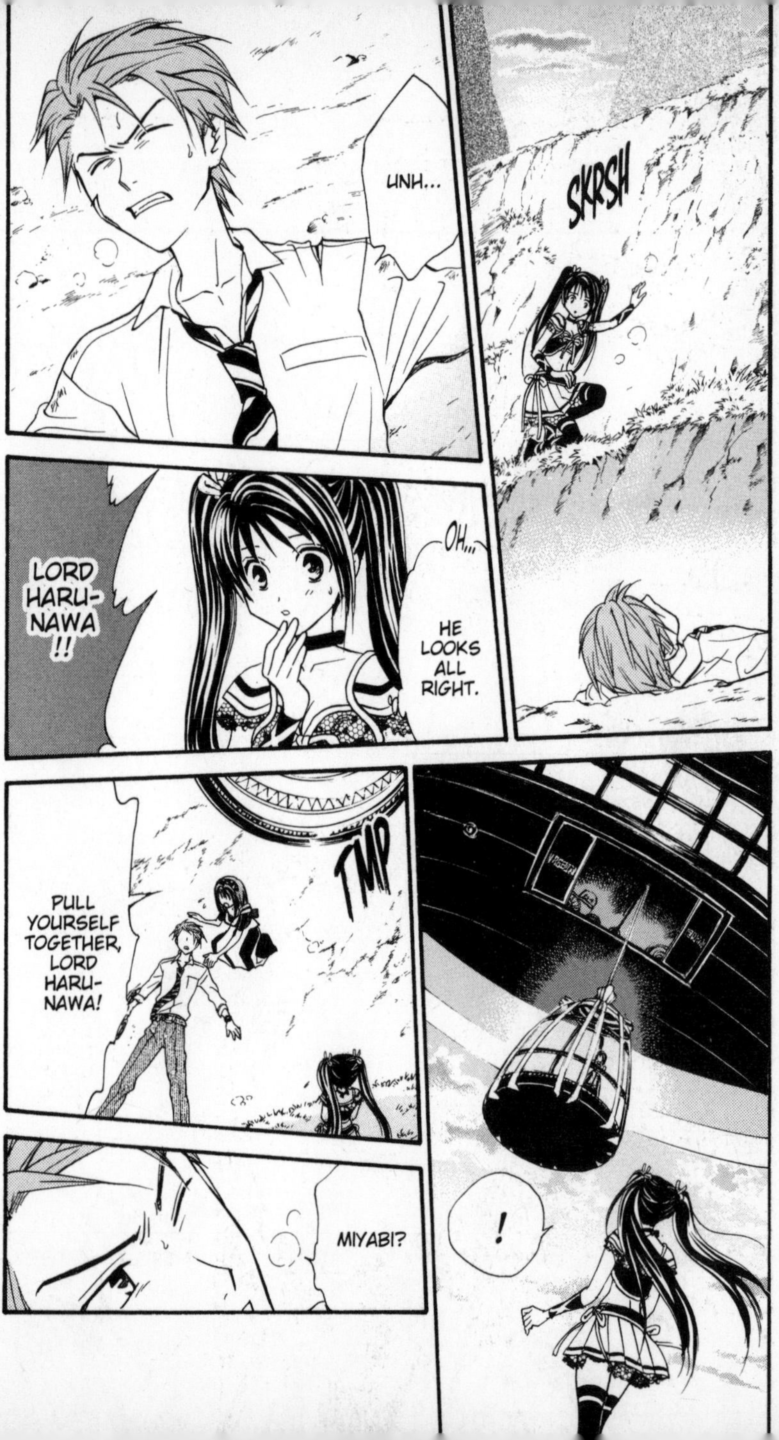
SKRSH
UNH...
OH...
HE LOOKS ALL RIGHT.
LORD HARU-NAWA!!
!
TMP
PULL YOURSELF TOGETHER, LORD HARU-NAWA!
MIYABI?

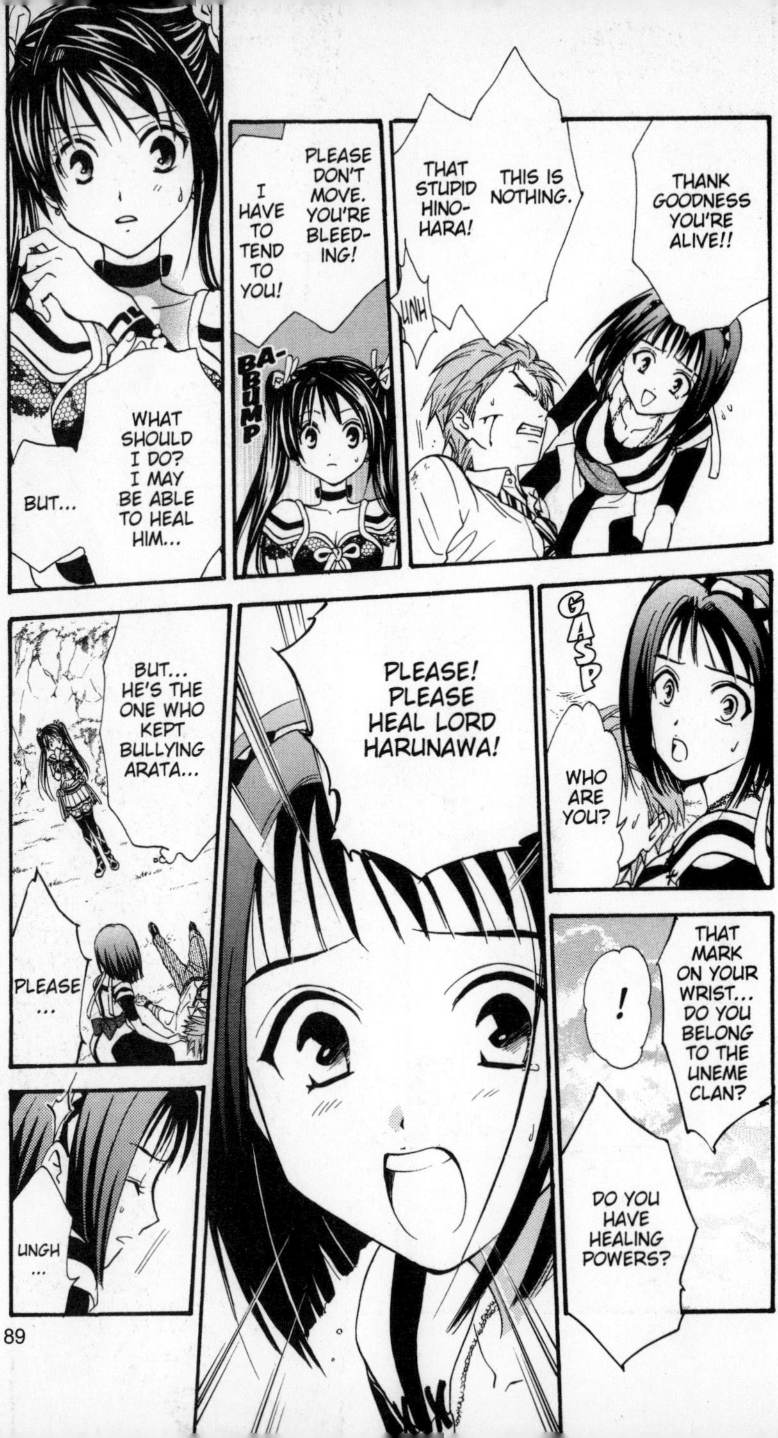
THANK GOODNESS YOU'RE ALIVE!!
THIS IS NOTHING.
THAT STUPID HINO-HARA!
UNH
PLEASE DON'T MOVE. YOU'RE BLEED-ING!
I HAVE TO TEND TO YOU!
BA-BUMP
WHAT SHOULD I DO? I MAY BE ABLE TO HEAL HIM...
BUT...
GASP
WHO ARE YOU?
THAT MARK ON YOUR WRIST... DO YOU BELONG TO THE UNEME CLAN?
!
DO YOU HAVE HEALING POWERS?
PLEASE! PLEASE HEAL LORD HARUNAWA!
BUT... HE'S THE ONE WHO KEPT BULLYING ARATA...
PLEASE...
UNGH...

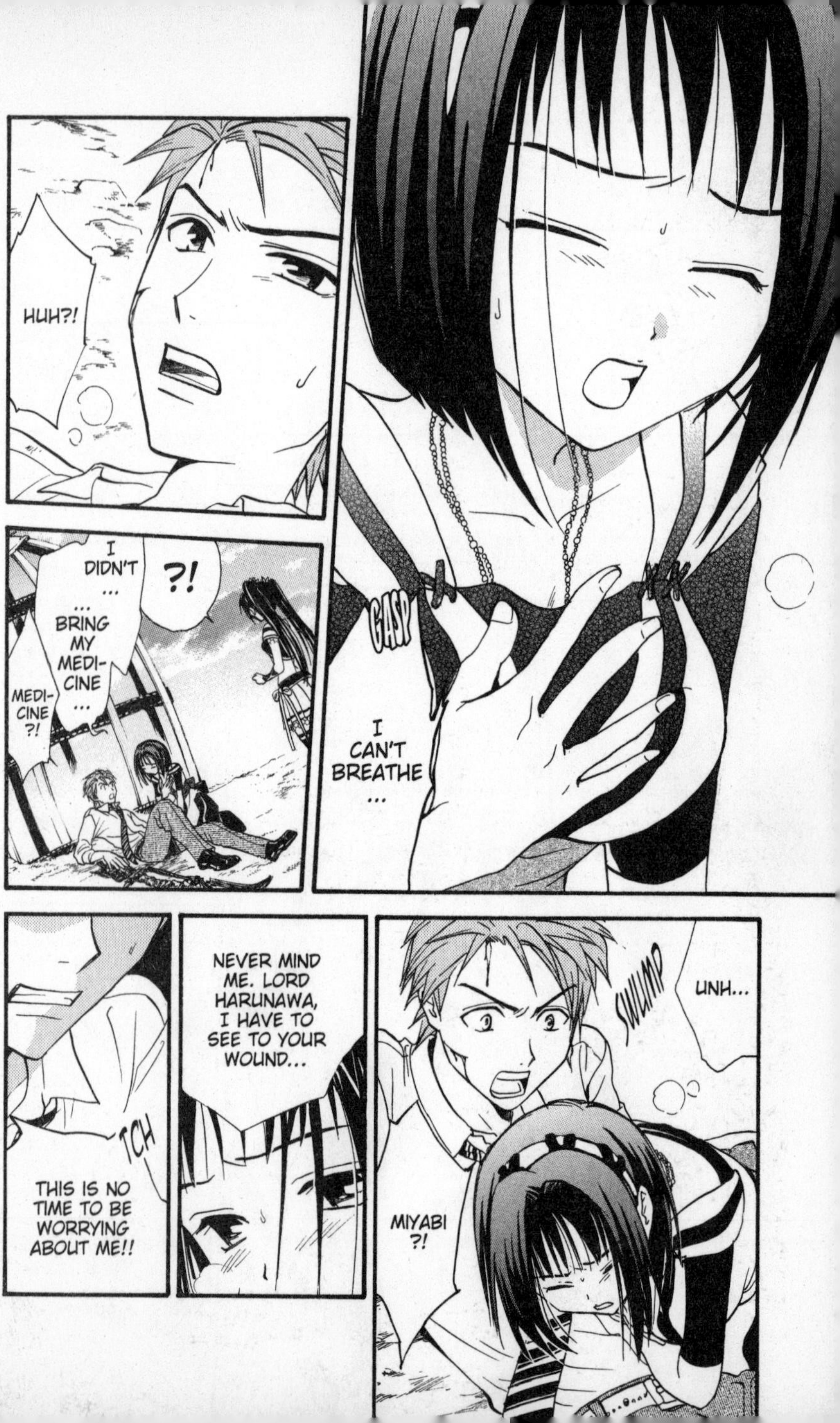
GASP
I CAN'T BREATHE ...
HUH?!
?!
I DIDN'T ... ... BRING MY MEDICINE ...
MEDICINE ?!
UNH...
SWUMP
MIYABI ?!
NEVER MIND ME. LORD HARUNAWA, I HAVE TO SEE TO YOUR WOUND...
TCH
THIS IS NO TIME TO BE WORRYING ABOUT ME!!

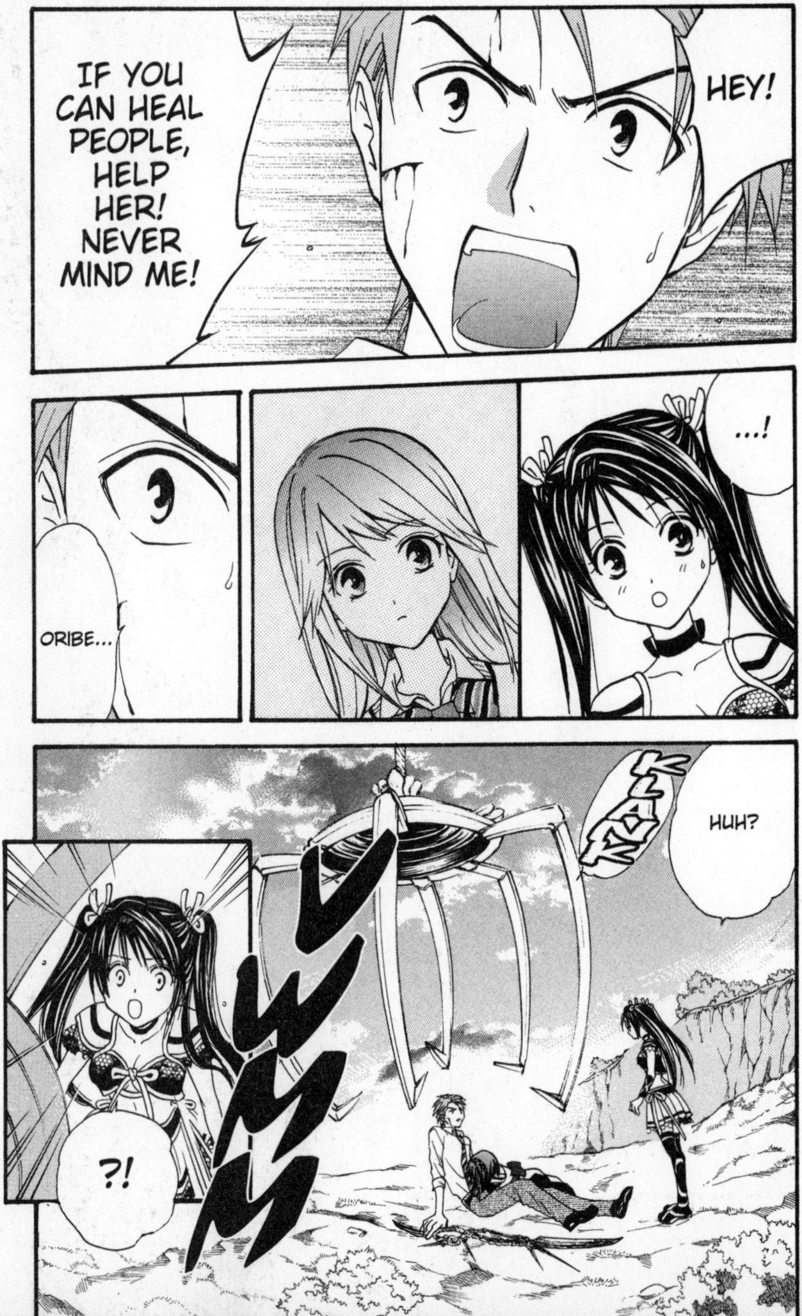
HEY!
IF YOU CAN HEAL PEOPLE, HELP HER! NEVER MIND ME!
...!
ORIBE...
HUH?
KLANK
?!

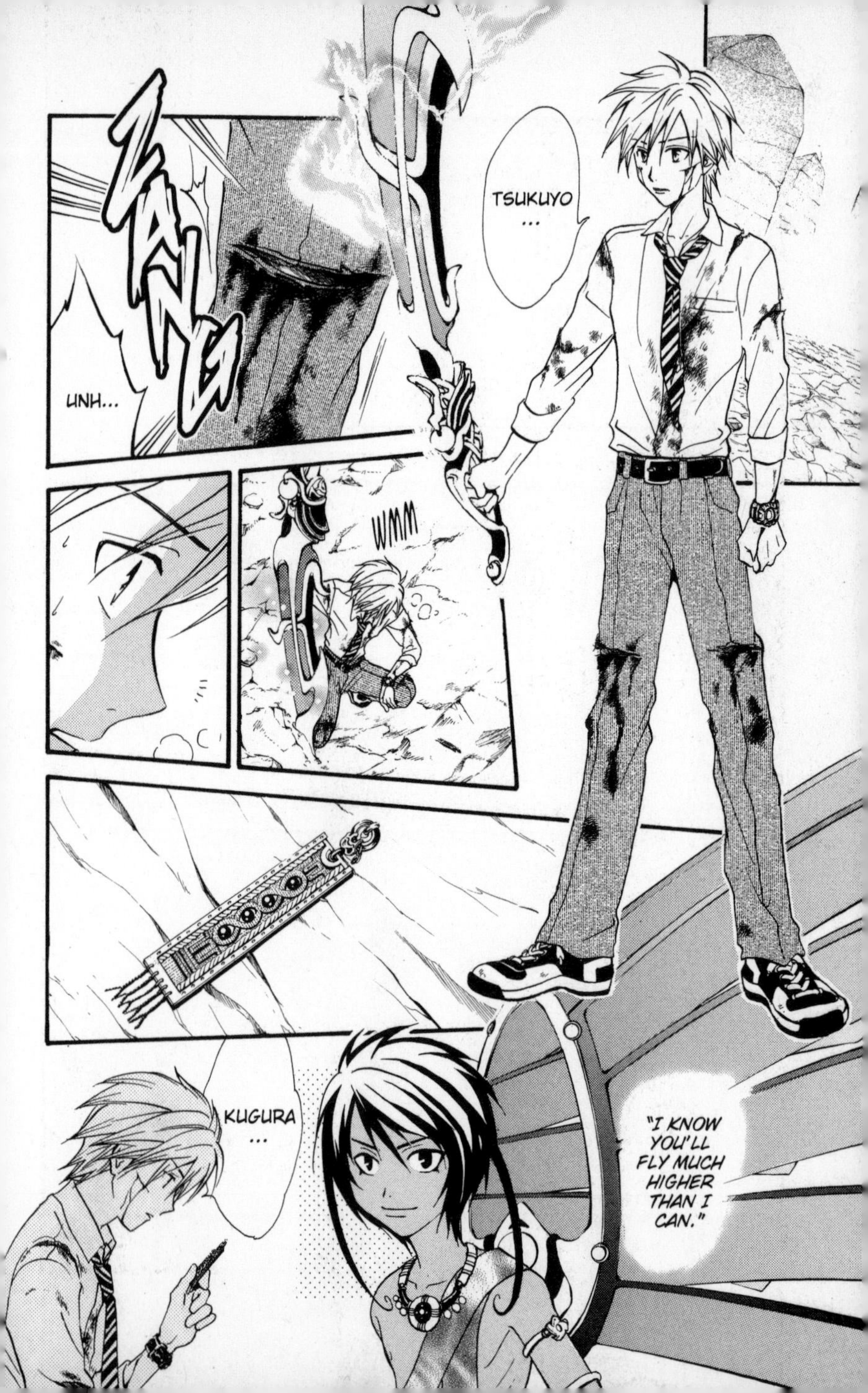
TSUKUYO ...
ZANG
UNH...
WMM
"I KNOW YOU'LL FLY MUCH HIGHER THAN I CAN."
KUGURA ...

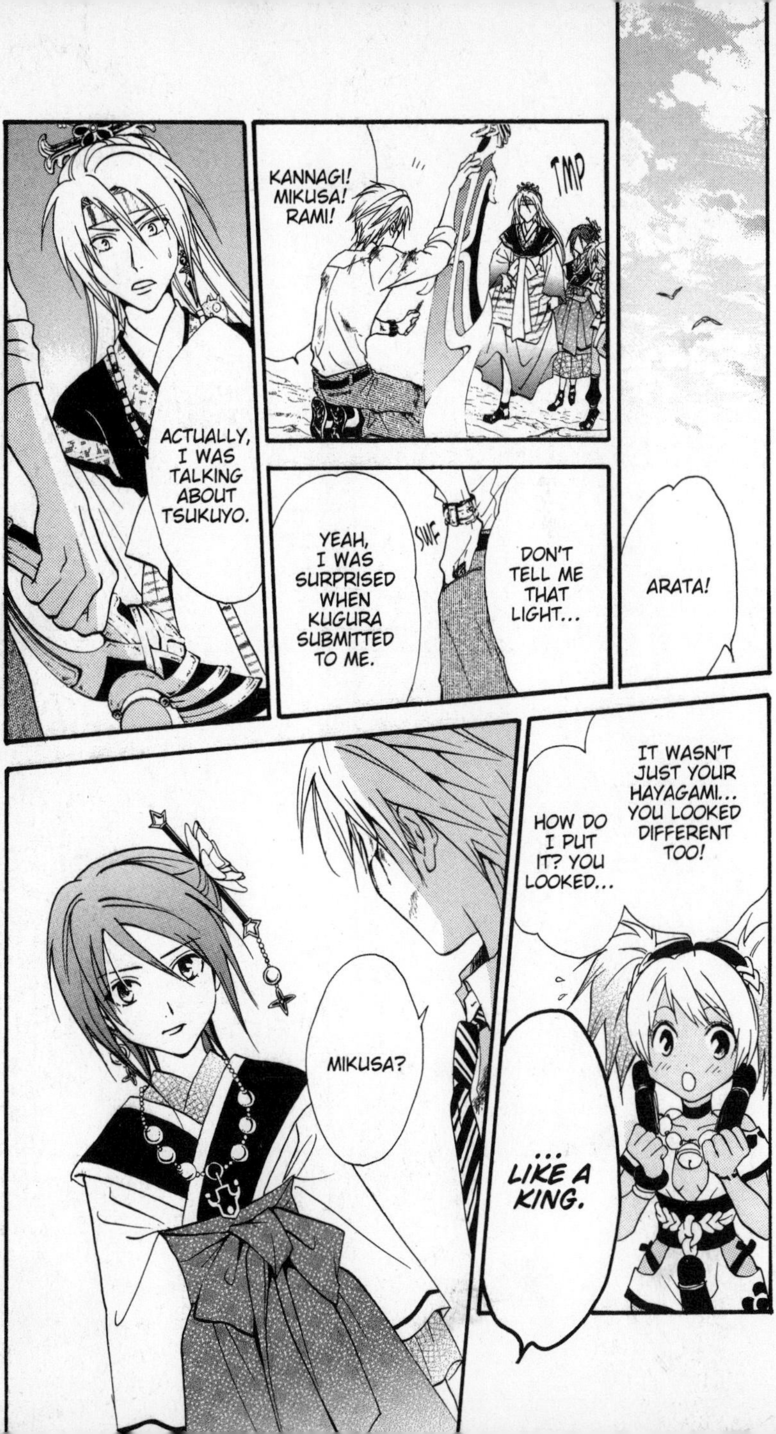
ARATA!
KANNAGI! MIKUSA! RAMI!
TMP
DON'T TELL ME THAT LIGHT...
SWF
YEAH, I WAS SURPRISED WHEN KUGURA SUBMITTED TO ME.
ACTUALLY, I WAS TALKING ABOUT TSUKUYO.
IT WASN'T JUST YOUR HAYAGAMI... YOU LOOKED DIFFERENT TOO!
HOW DO I PUT IT? YOU LOOKED...
...LIKE A KING.
MIKUSA?

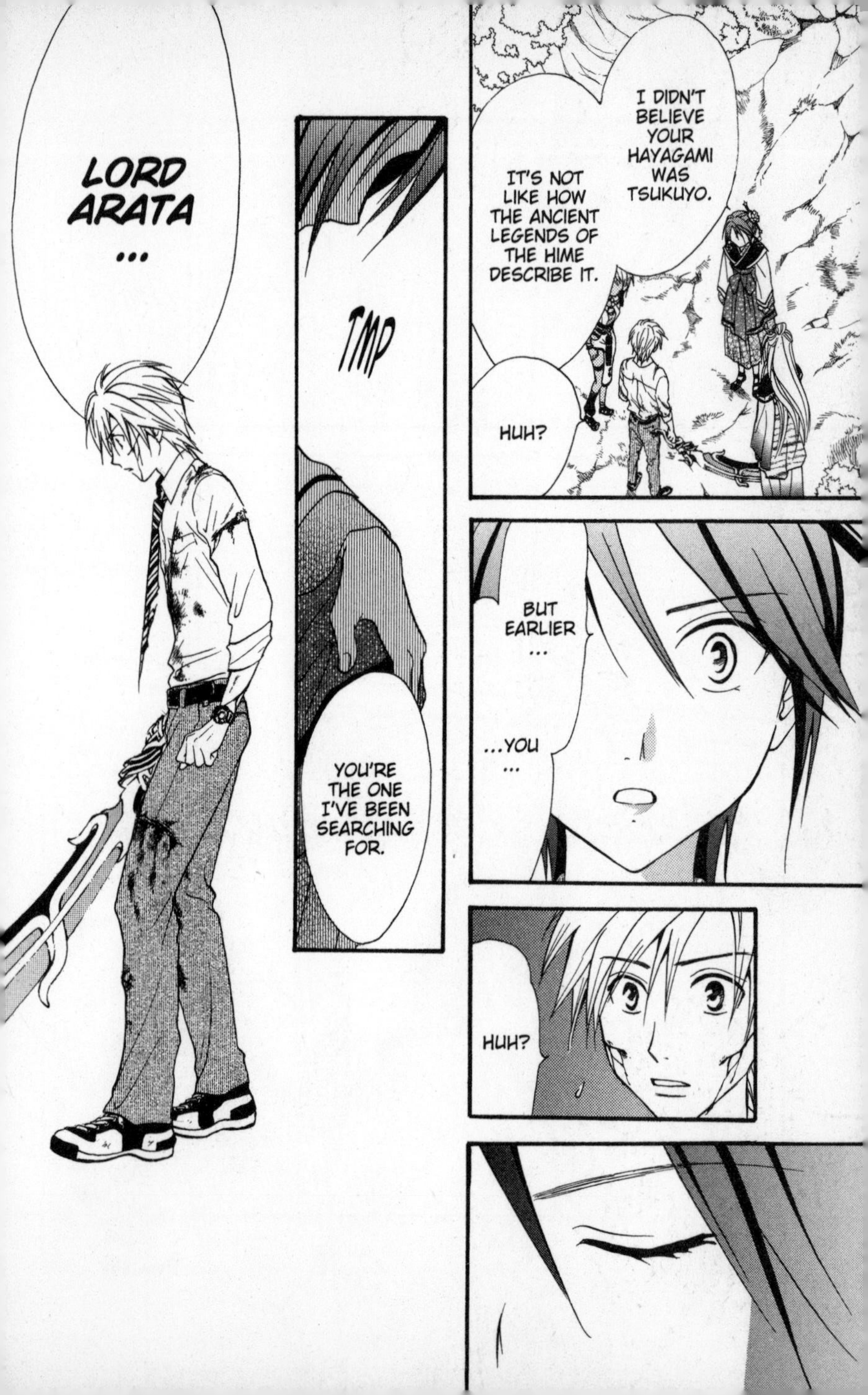
I DIDN'T BELIEVE YOUR HAYAGAMI WAS TSUKUYO.
IT'S NOT LIKE HOW THE ANCIENT LEGENDS OF THE HIME DESCRIBE IT.
HUH?
BUT EARLIER ...
...YOU ...
HUH?
TMP
YOU'RE THE ONE I'VE BEEN SEARCHING FOR.
LORD ARATA ...

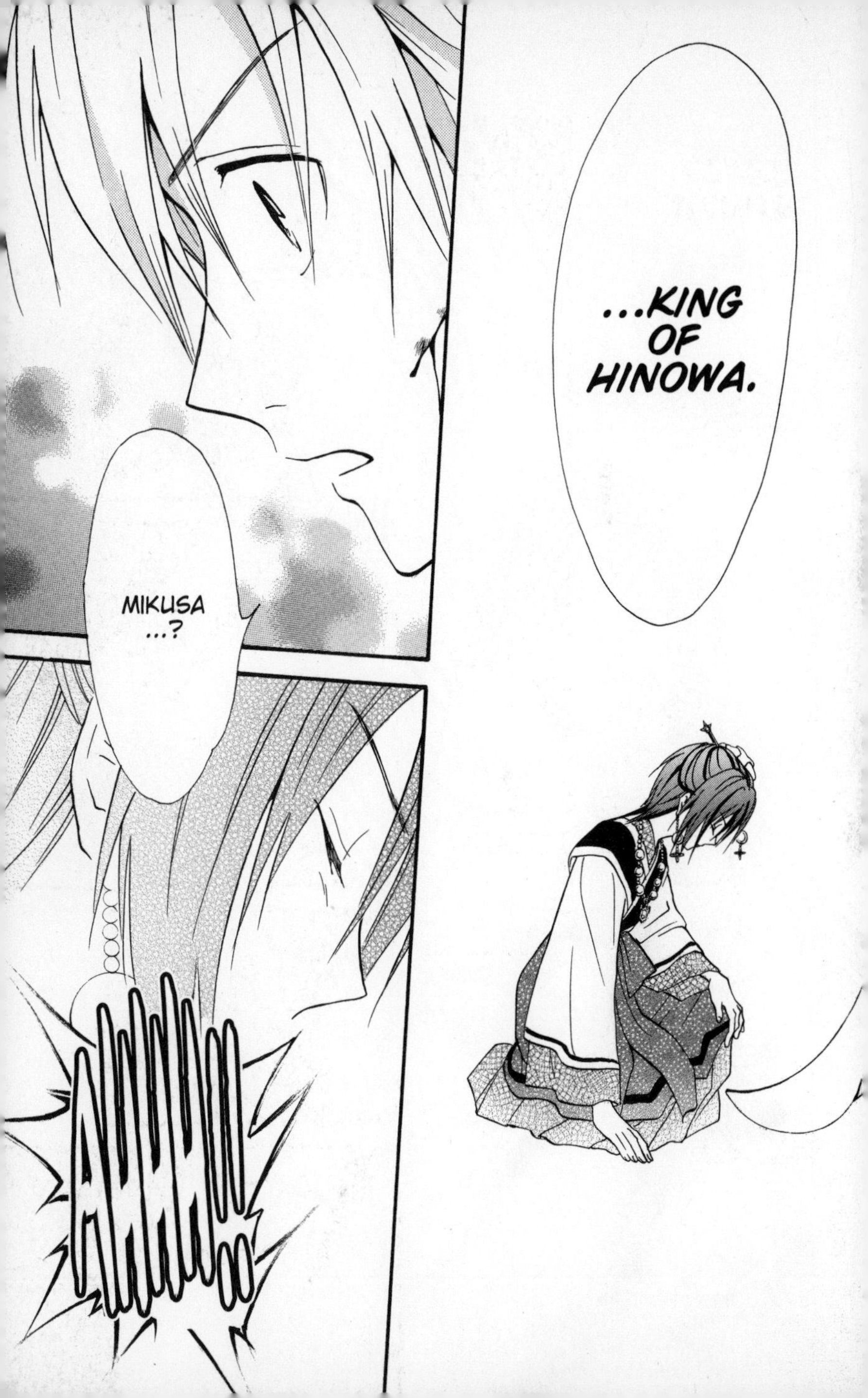
...KING OF HINOWA.
MIKUSA ...?
AHH!!

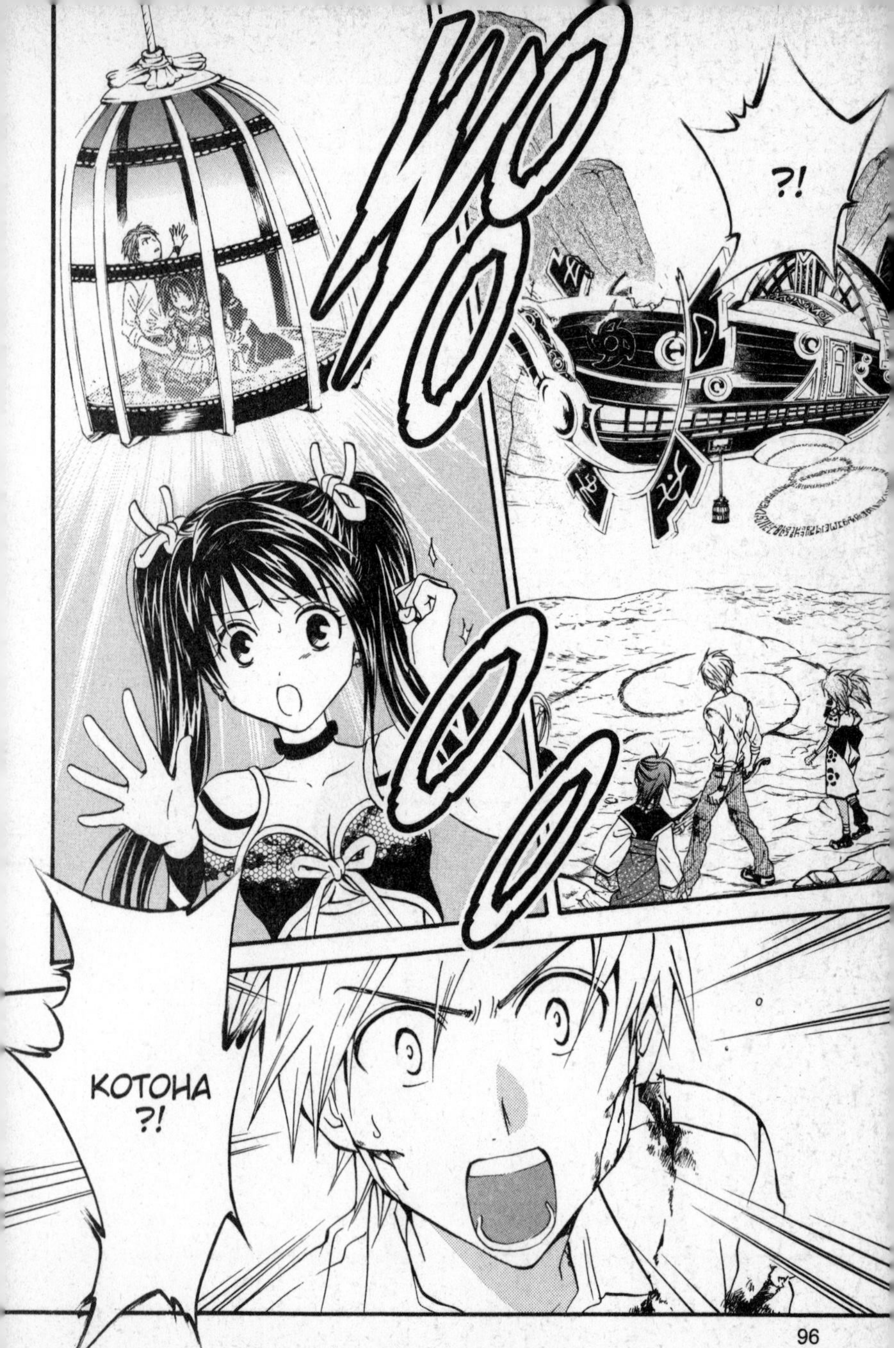
?!
KOTOHA ?!

Arata
THE LEGEND

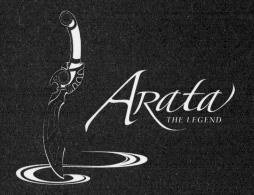

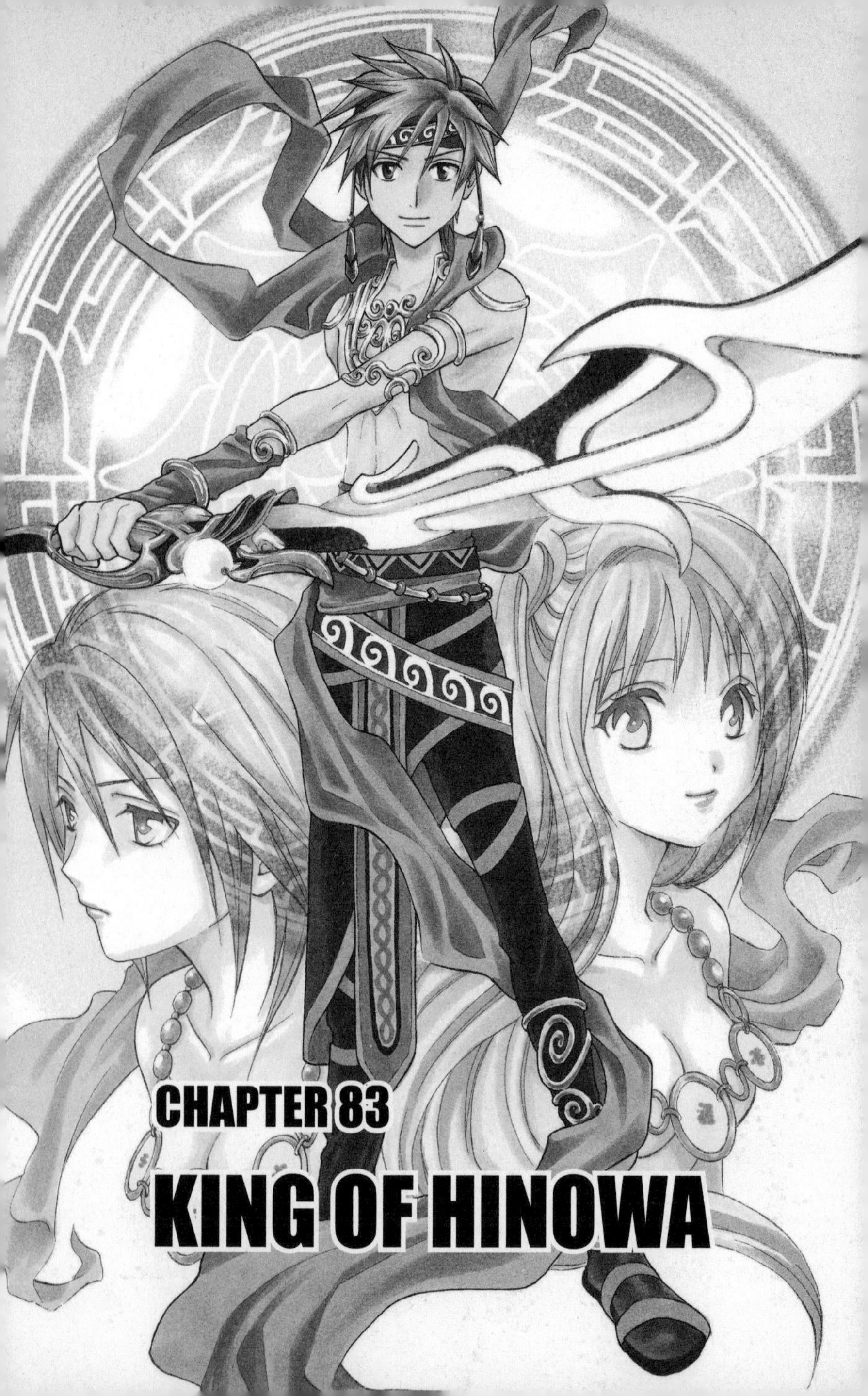
CHAPTER 83
KING OF HINOWA

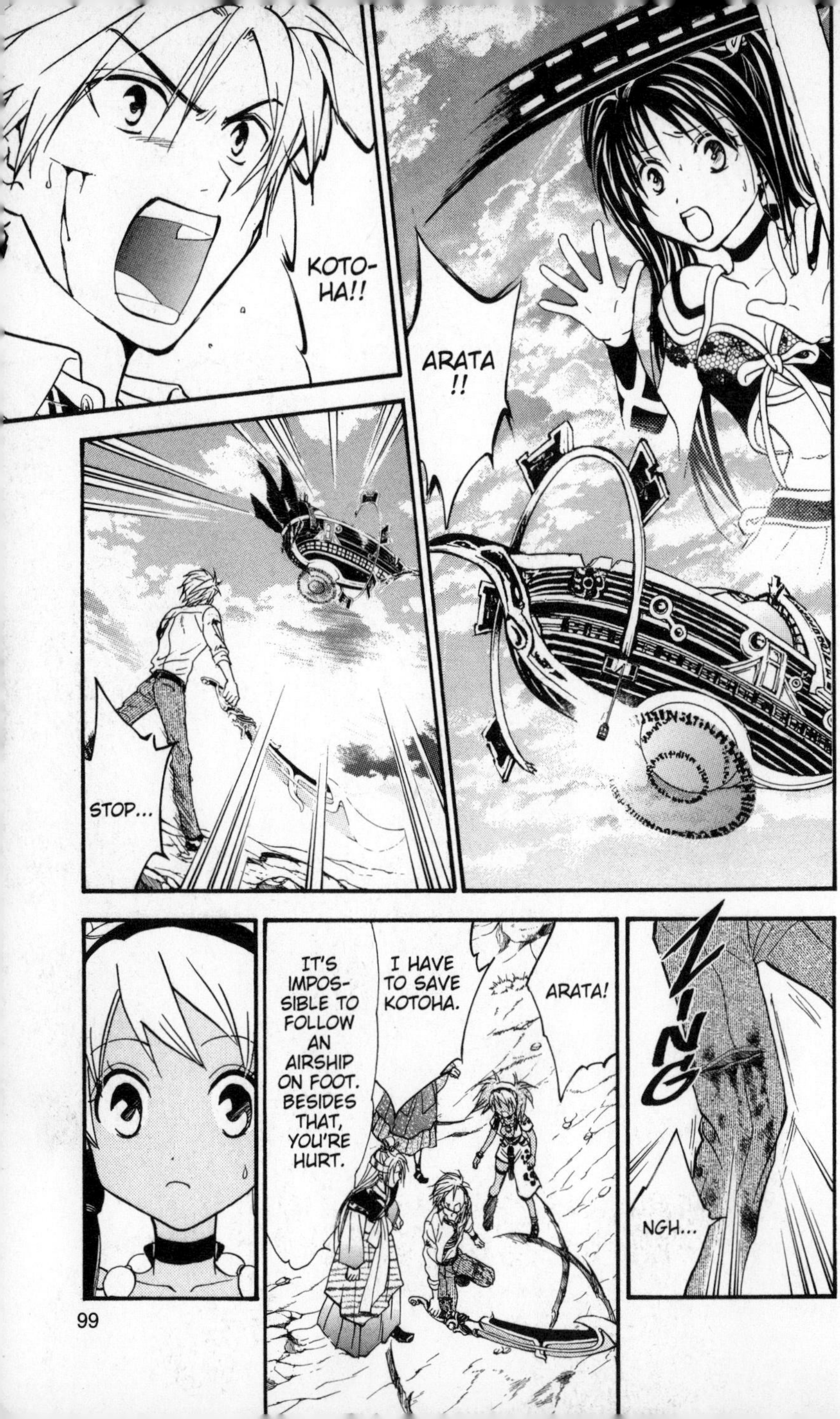
ARATA !!
KOTO-HA!!
STOP...
NGH...
ARATA!
I HAVE TO SAVE KOTOHA.
IT'S IMPOSSIBLE TO FOLLOW AN AIRSHIP ON FOOT. BESIDES THAT, YOU'RE HURT.

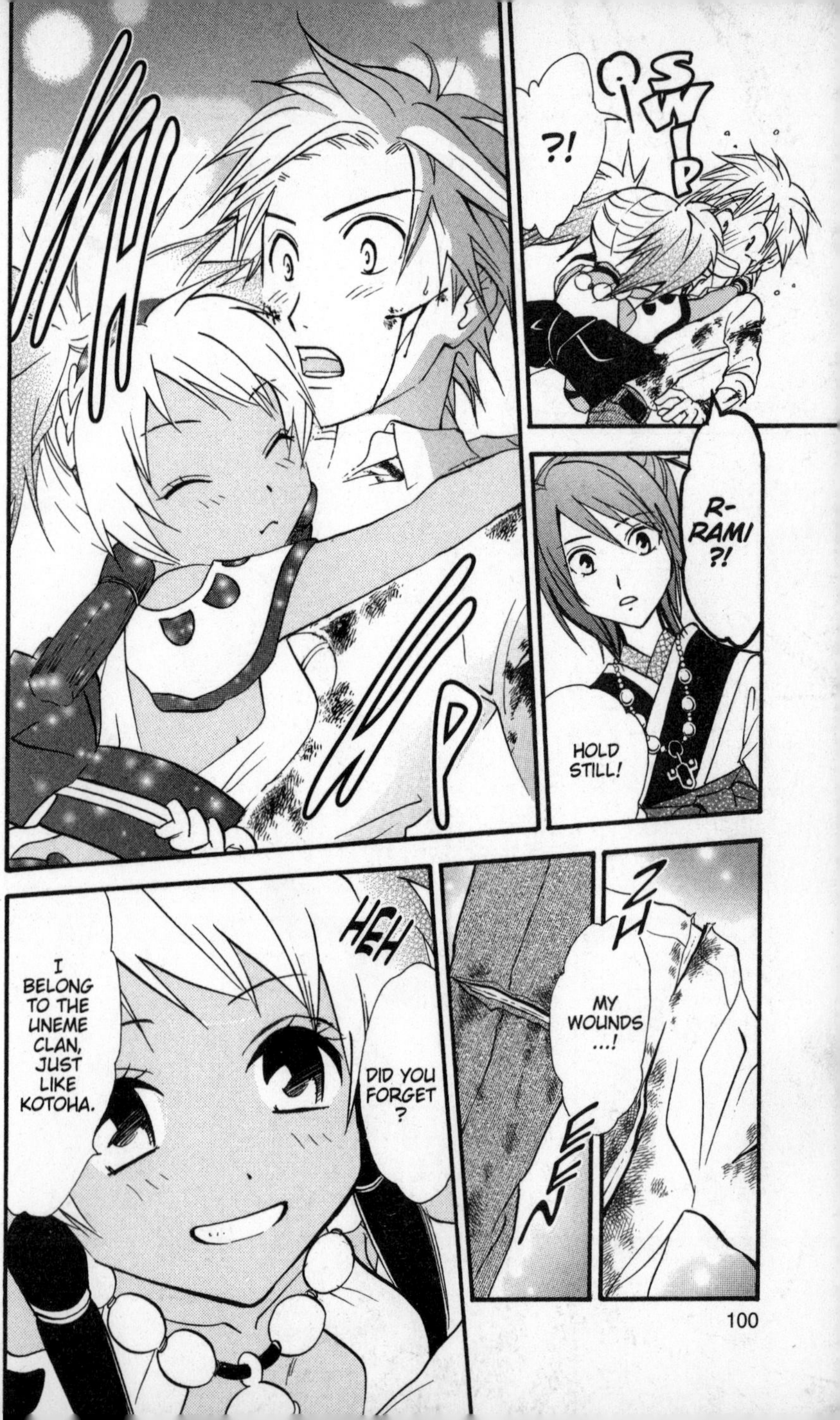
SWIP
?!
R-RAMI?!
HOLD STILL!
MY WOUNDS...!
HEH
DID YOU FORGET?
I BELONG TO THE UNEME CLAN, JUST LIKE KOTOHA.

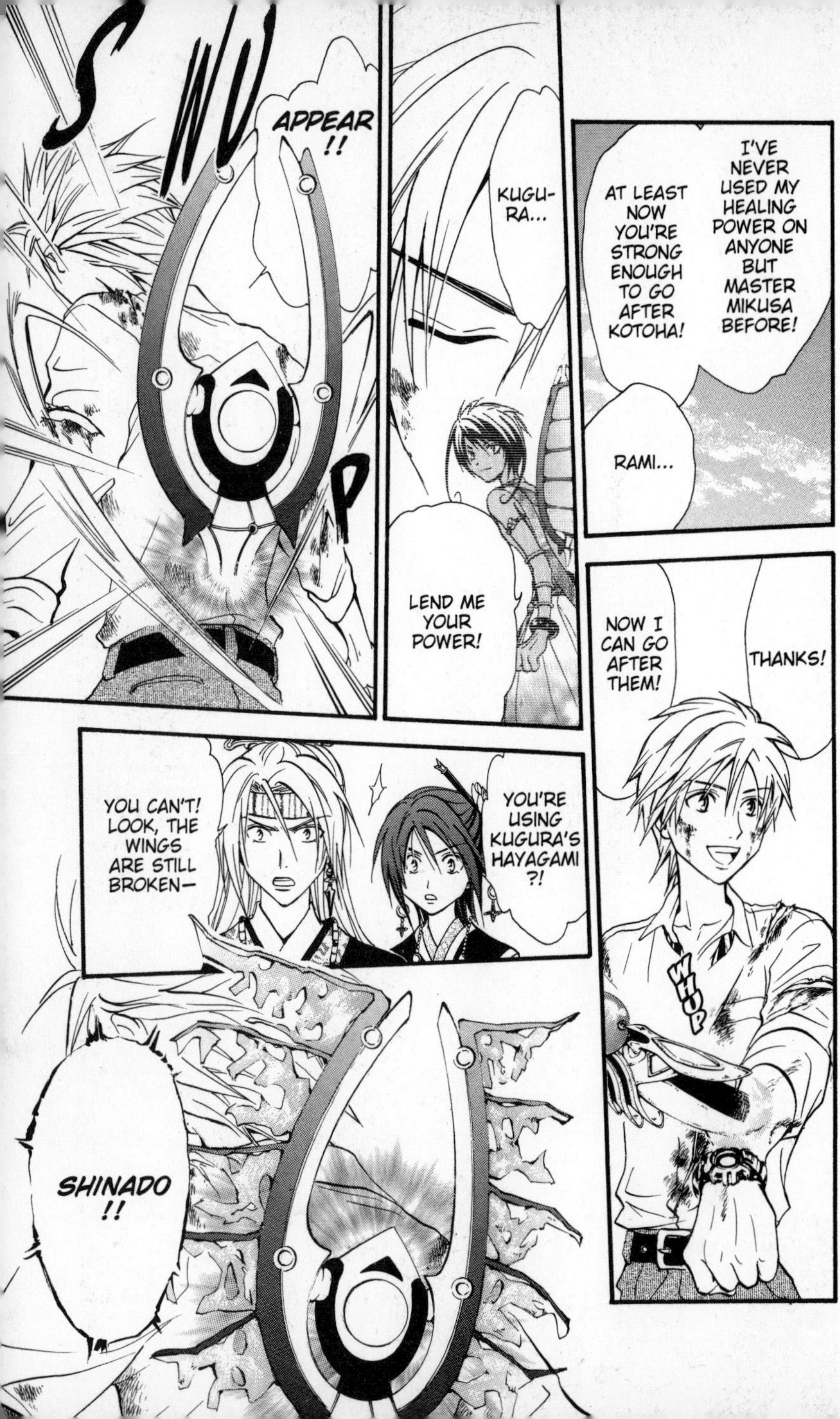
I'VE NEVER USED MY HEALING POWER ON ANYONE BUT MASTER MIKUSA BEFORE!
AT LEAST NOW YOU'RE STRONG ENOUGH TO GO AFTER KOTOHA!
RAMI...
KUGU-RA...
LEND ME YOUR POWER!
SWOOP
APPEAR!!
THANKS!
NOW I CAN GO AFTER THEM!
WHUP
YOU'RE USING KUGURA'S HAYAGAMI?!
YOU CAN'T! LOOK, THE WINGS ARE STILL BROKEN—
SHINADO!!

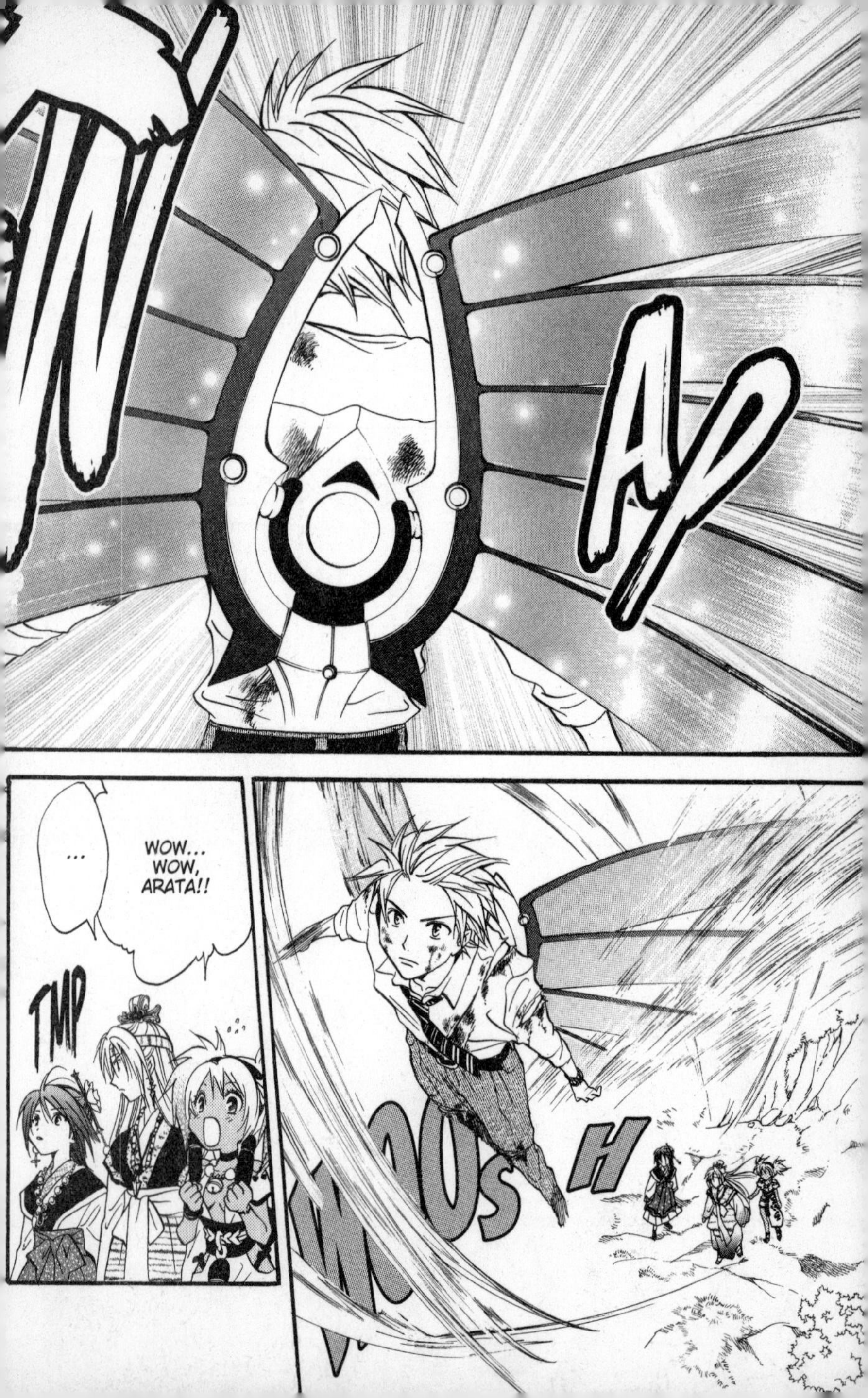

WAP
WHOOSH
WOW... WOW, ARATA!!
...
TMP

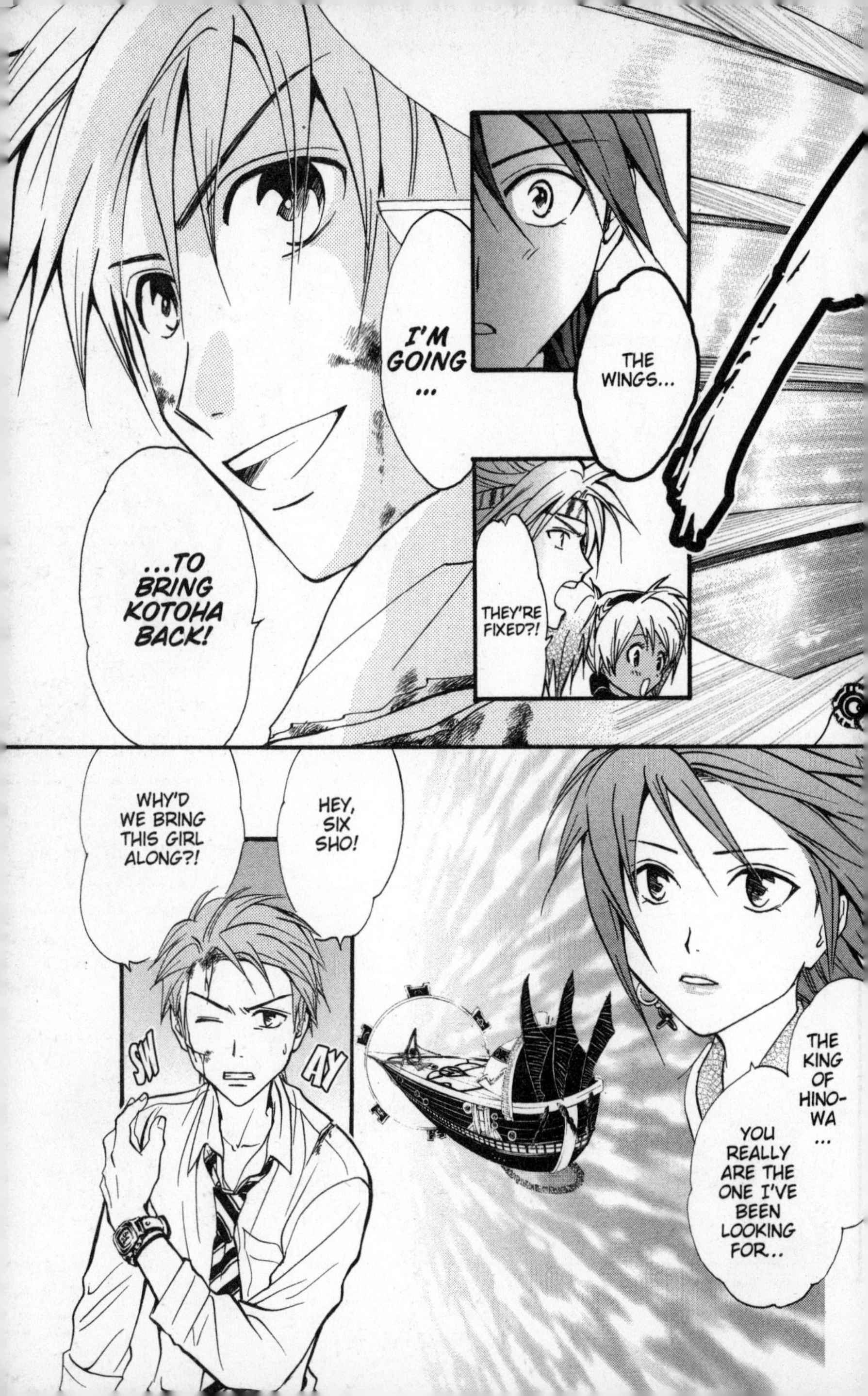
THE WINGS...
THEY'RE FIXED?!
I'M GOING...
...TO BRING KOTOHA BACK!
THE KING OF HINO-WA...
YOU REALLY ARE THE ONE I'VE BEEN LOOKING FOR..
HEY, SIX SHO!
WHY'D WE BRING THIS GIRL ALONG?!
SWAY

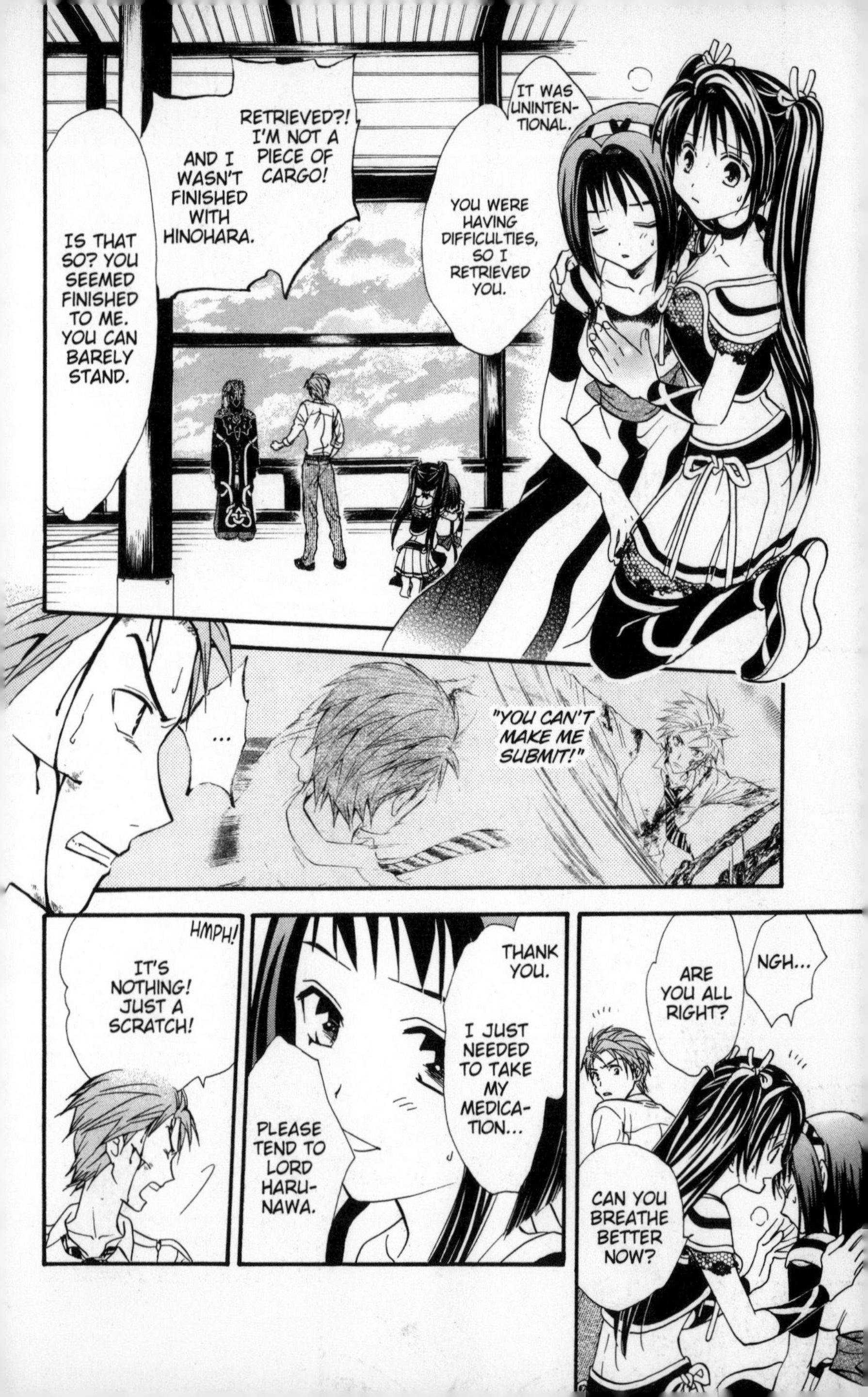
IT WAS UNINTEN-TIONAL.
YOU WERE HAVING DIFFICULTIES, SO I RETRIEVED YOU.
RETRIEVED?! I'M NOT A PIECE OF CARGO!
AND I WASN'T FINISHED WITH HINOHARA.
IS THAT SO? YOU SEEMED FINISHED TO ME. YOU CAN BARELY STAND.
"YOU CAN'T MAKE ME SUBMIT!"
...
NGH...
ARE YOU ALL RIGHT?
CAN YOU BREATHE BETTER NOW?
THANK YOU.
I JUST NEEDED TO TAKE MY MEDICA-TION...
PLEASE TEND TO LORD HARU-NAWA.
HMPH!
IT'S NOTHING! JUST A SCRATCH!

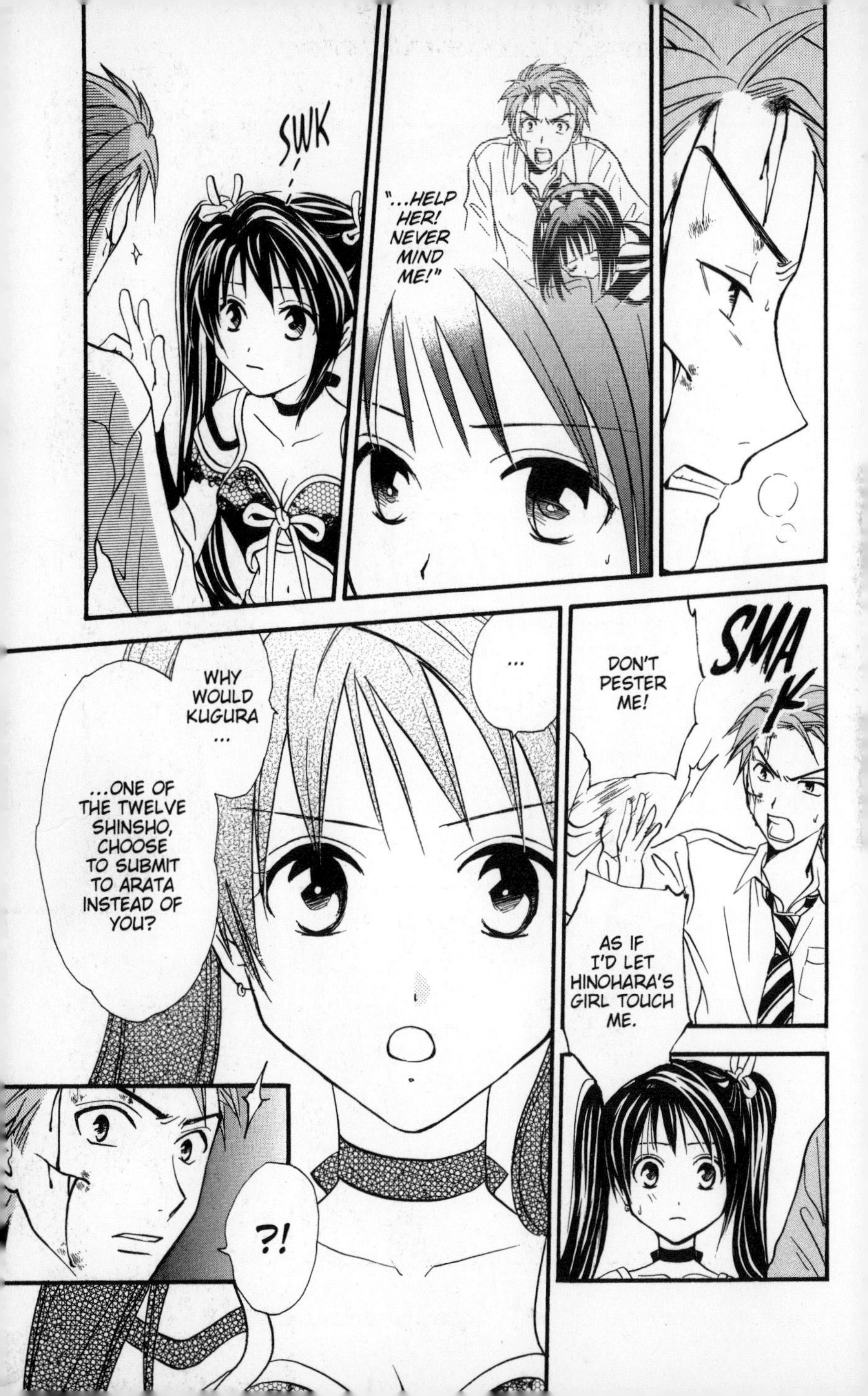
"...HELP HER! NEVER MIND ME!"
SWK
SMAK
DON'T PESTER ME!
AS IF I'D LET HINOHARA'S GIRL TOUCH ME.
...
WHY WOULD KUGURA ...
...ONE OF THE TWELVE SHINSHO, CHOOSE TO SUBMIT TO ARATA INSTEAD OF YOU?
?!

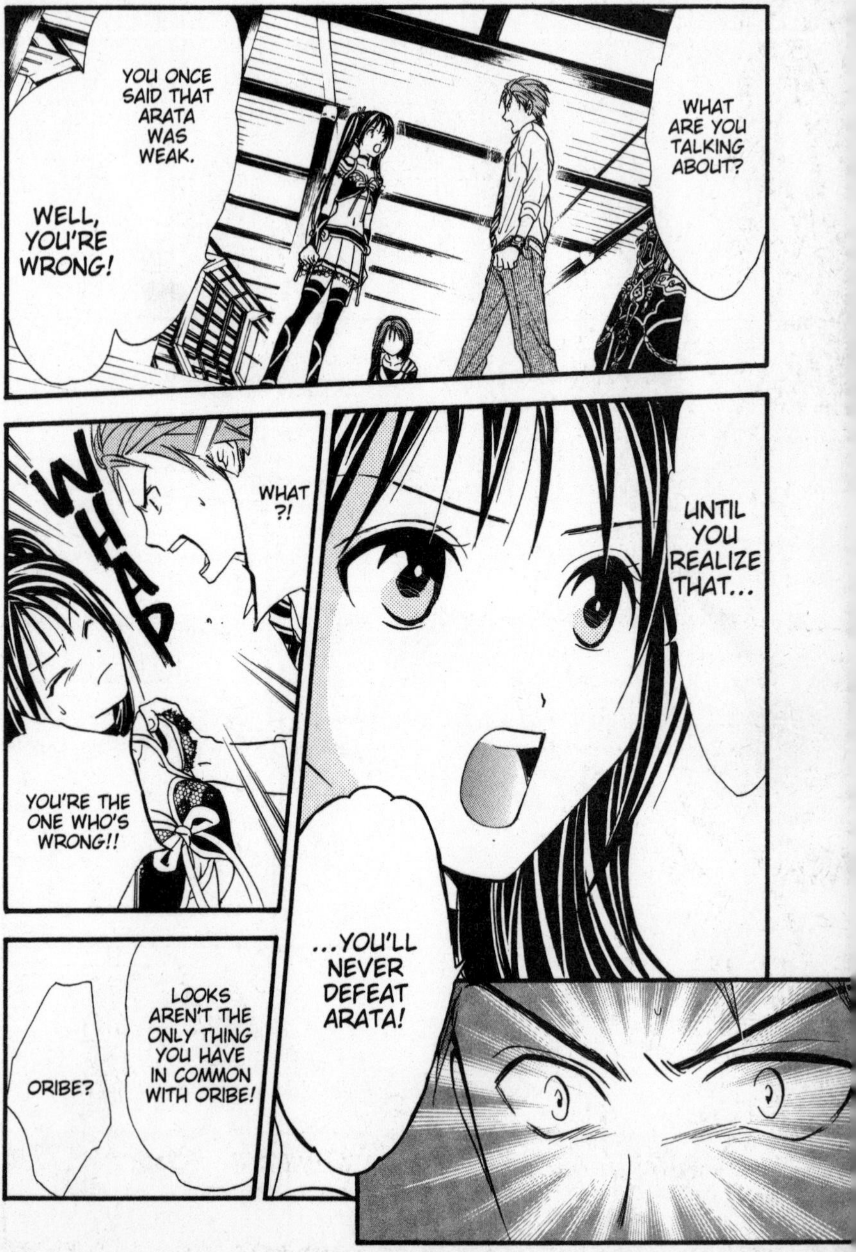
WHAT ARE YOU TALKING ABOUT?
YOU ONCE SAID THAT ARATA WAS WEAK.
WELL, YOU'RE WRONG!
UNTIL YOU REALIZE THAT...
...YOU'LL NEVER DEFEAT ARATA!
WHAT?!
WHAP
YOU'RE THE ONE WHO'S WRONG!!
LOOKS AREN'T THE ONLY THING YOU HAVE IN COMMON WITH ORIBE!
ORIBE?

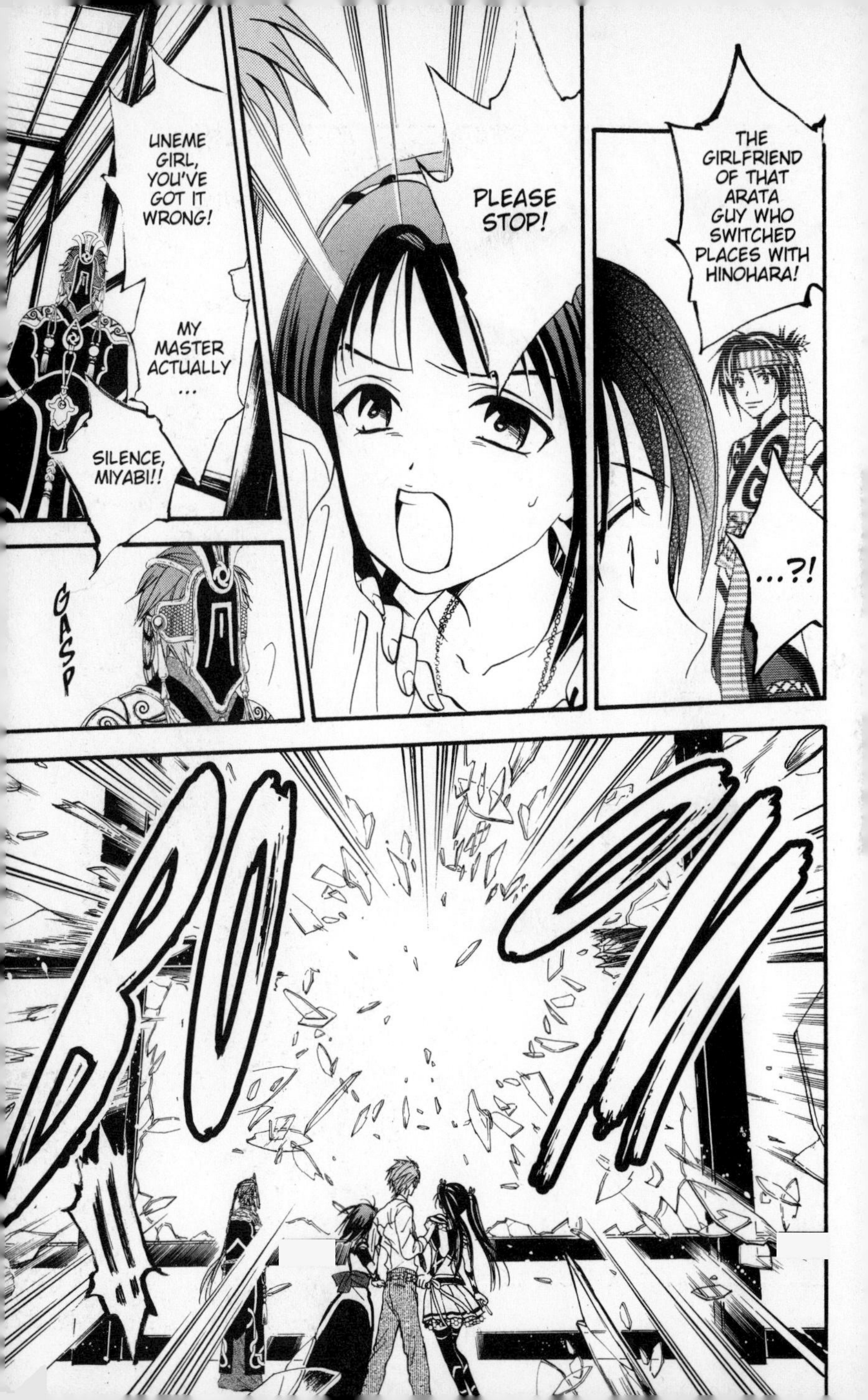
THE GIRLFRIEND OF THAT ARATA GUY WHO SWITCHED PLACES WITH HINOHARA!
...?!
PLEASE STOP!
UNEME GIRL, YOU'VE GOT IT WRONG!
MY MASTER ACTUALLY ...
SILENCE, MIYABI!!
GASP
BOOM

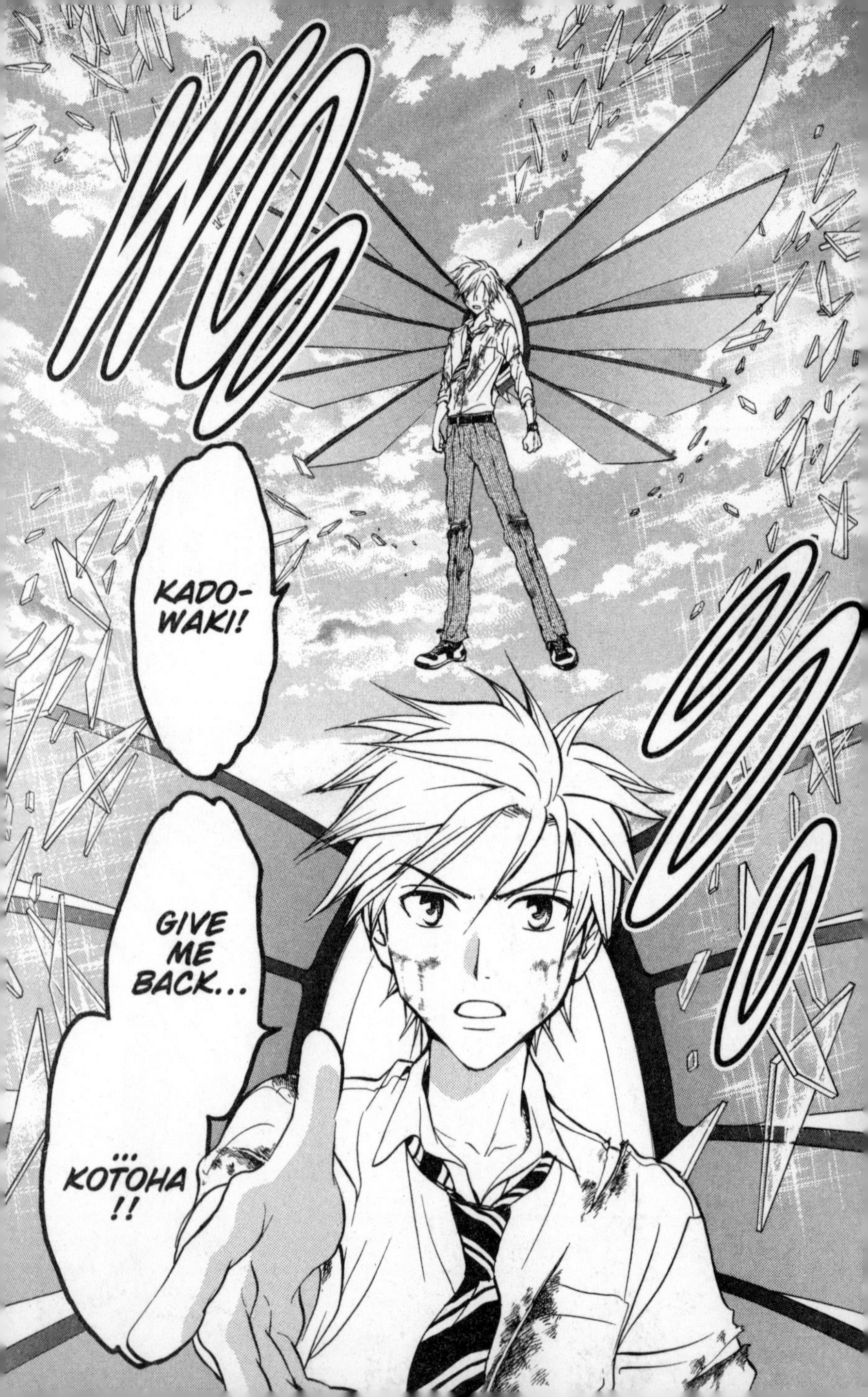
WHOOSH
KADO-WAKI!
GIVE ME BACK...
...KOTOHA!!

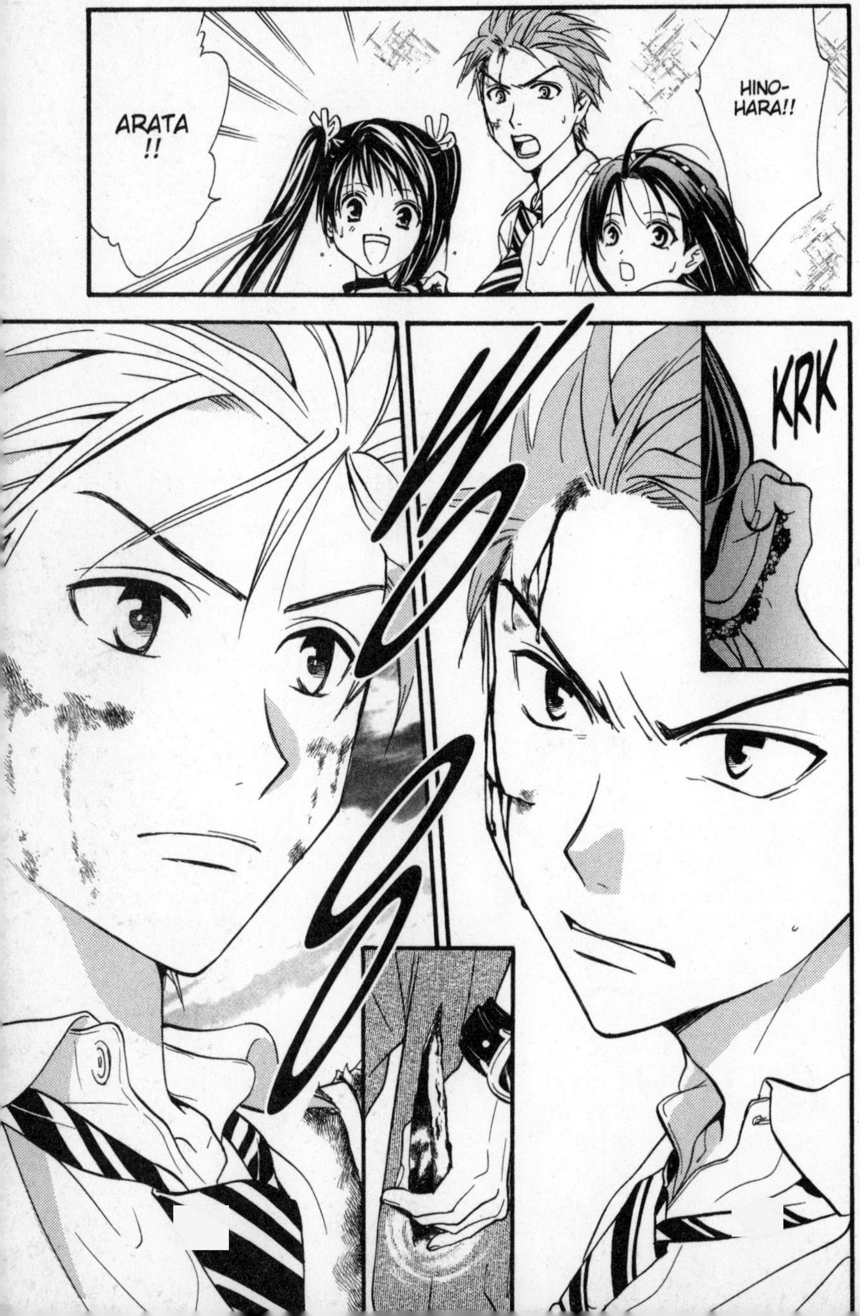
HINO-HARA!!
ARATA !!
KRK

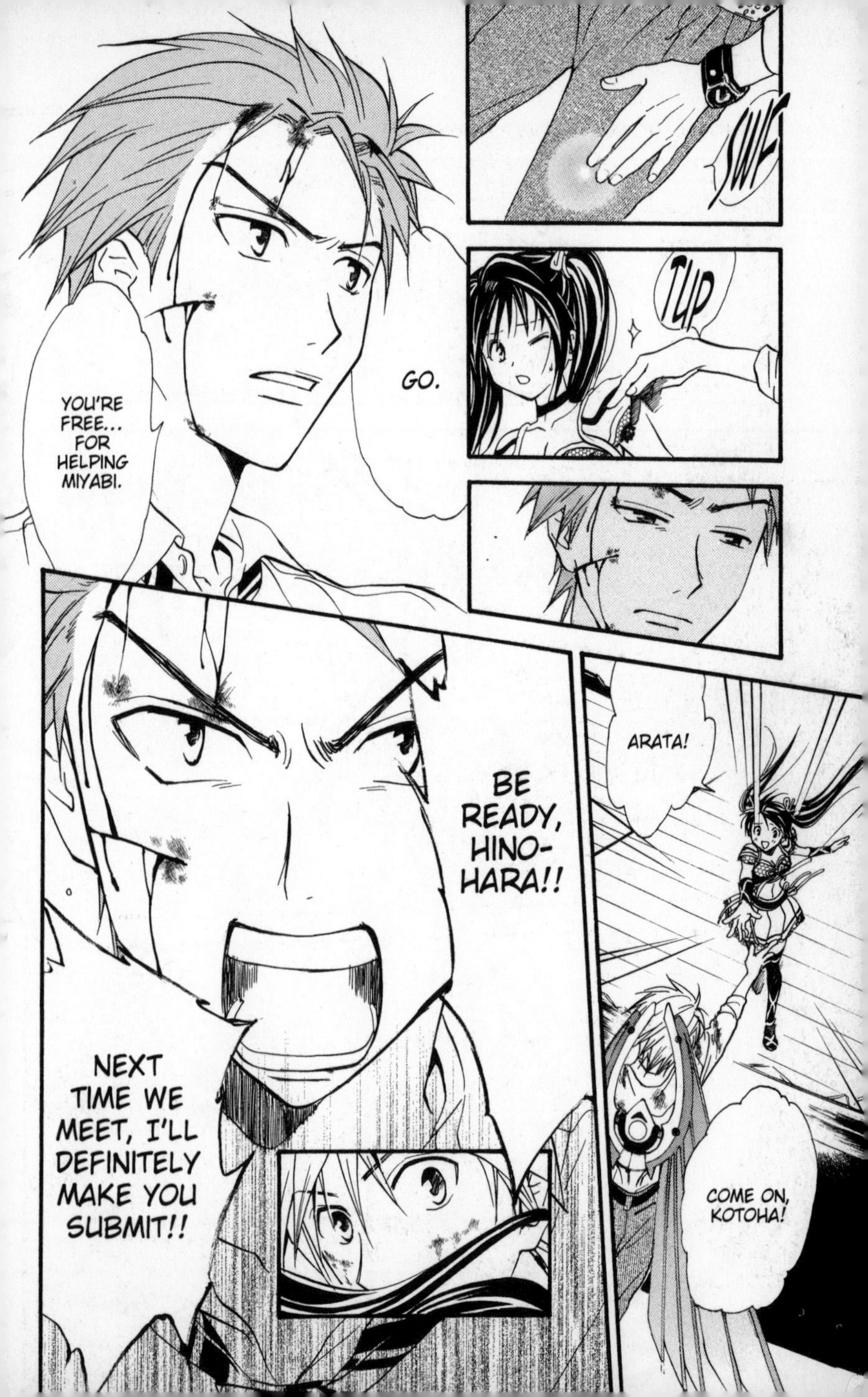
SWF
TUP
GO.
YOU'RE FREE... FOR HELPING MIYABI.
ARATA!
COME ON, KOTOHA!
BE READY, HINO-HARA!!
NEXT TIME WE MEET, I'LL DEFINITELY MAKE YOU SUBMIT!!

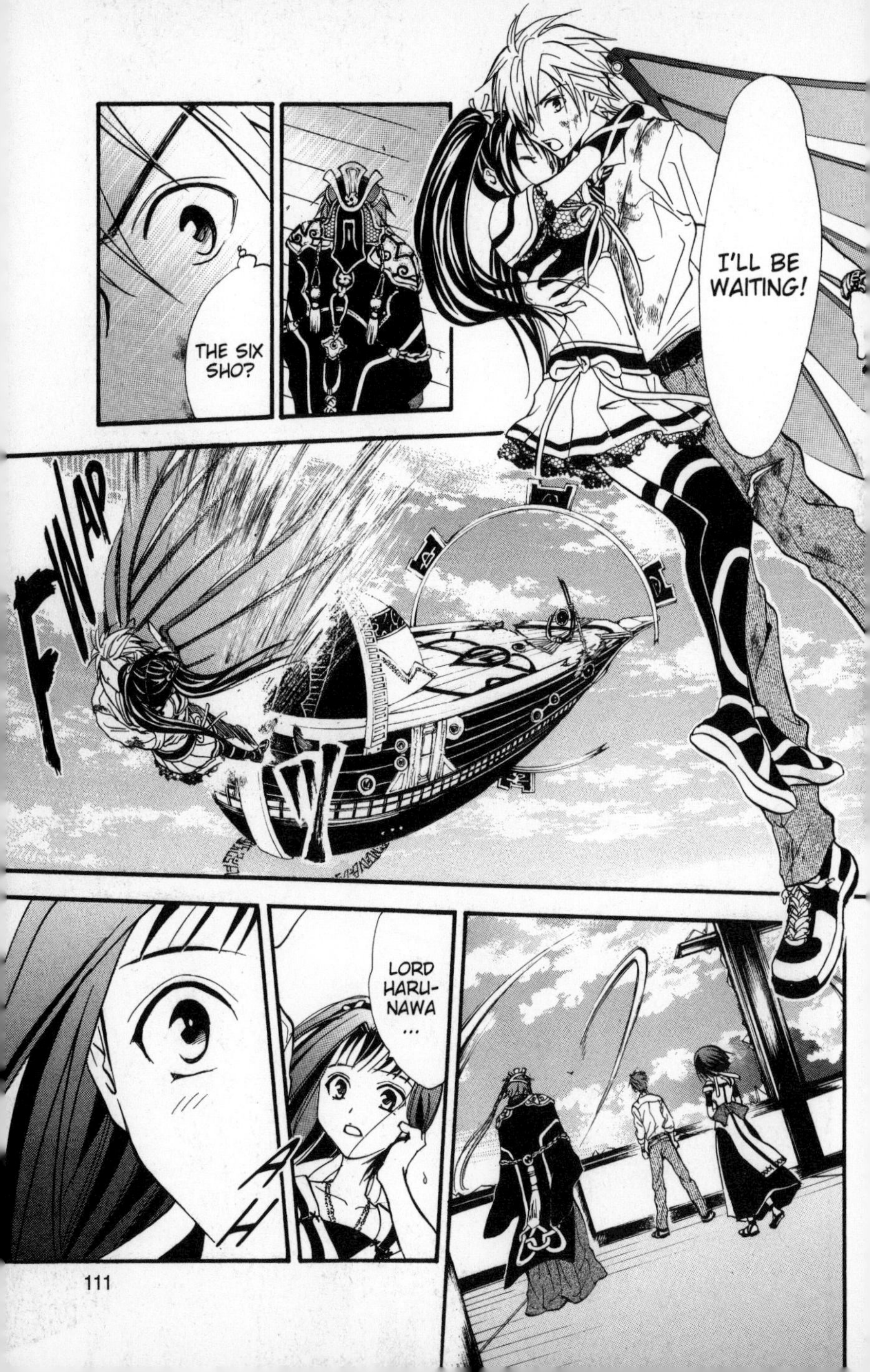
I'LL BE WAITING!
THE SIX SHO?
FWAP
LORD HARU-NAWA ...
AH

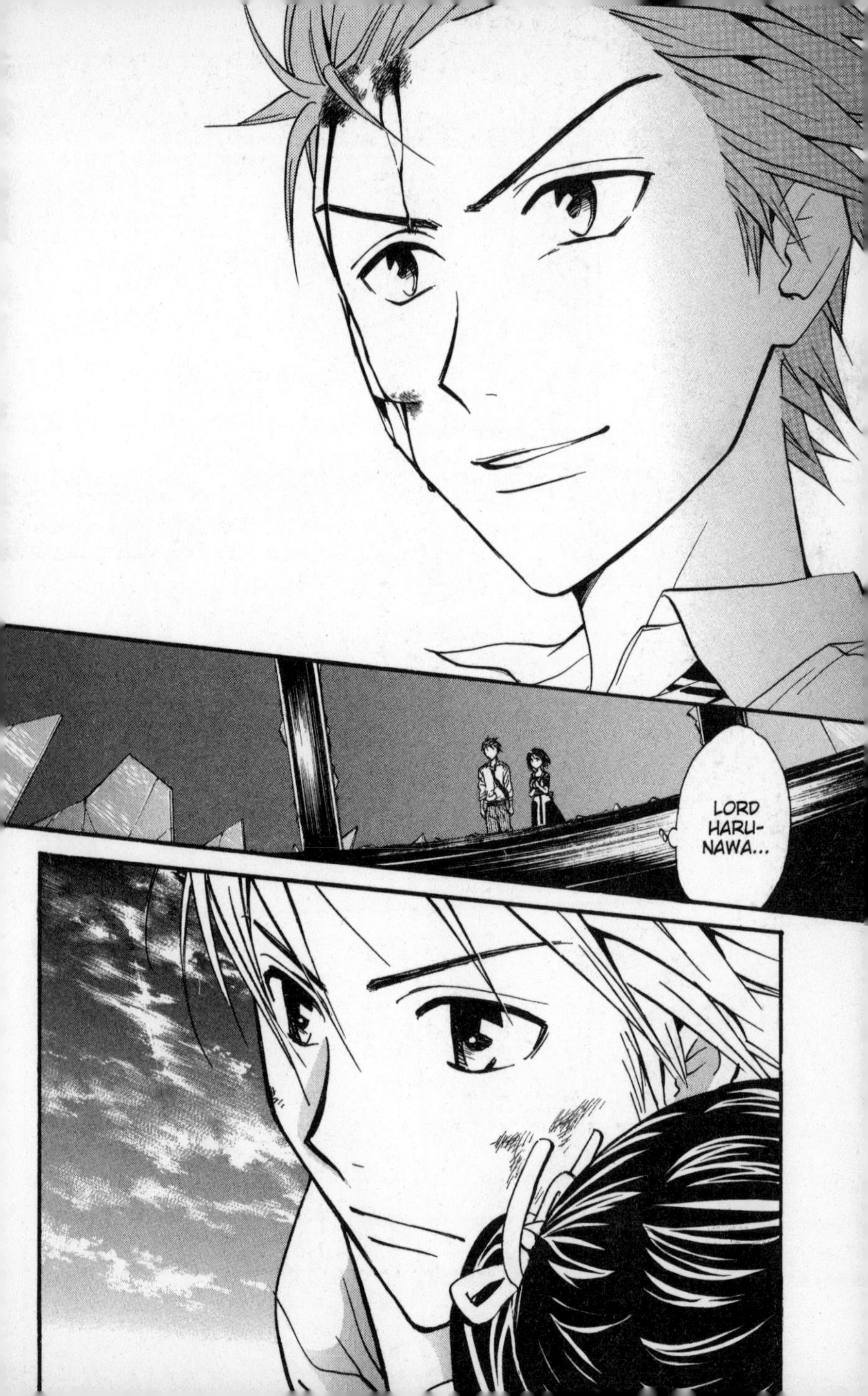
LORD HARU-NAWA...

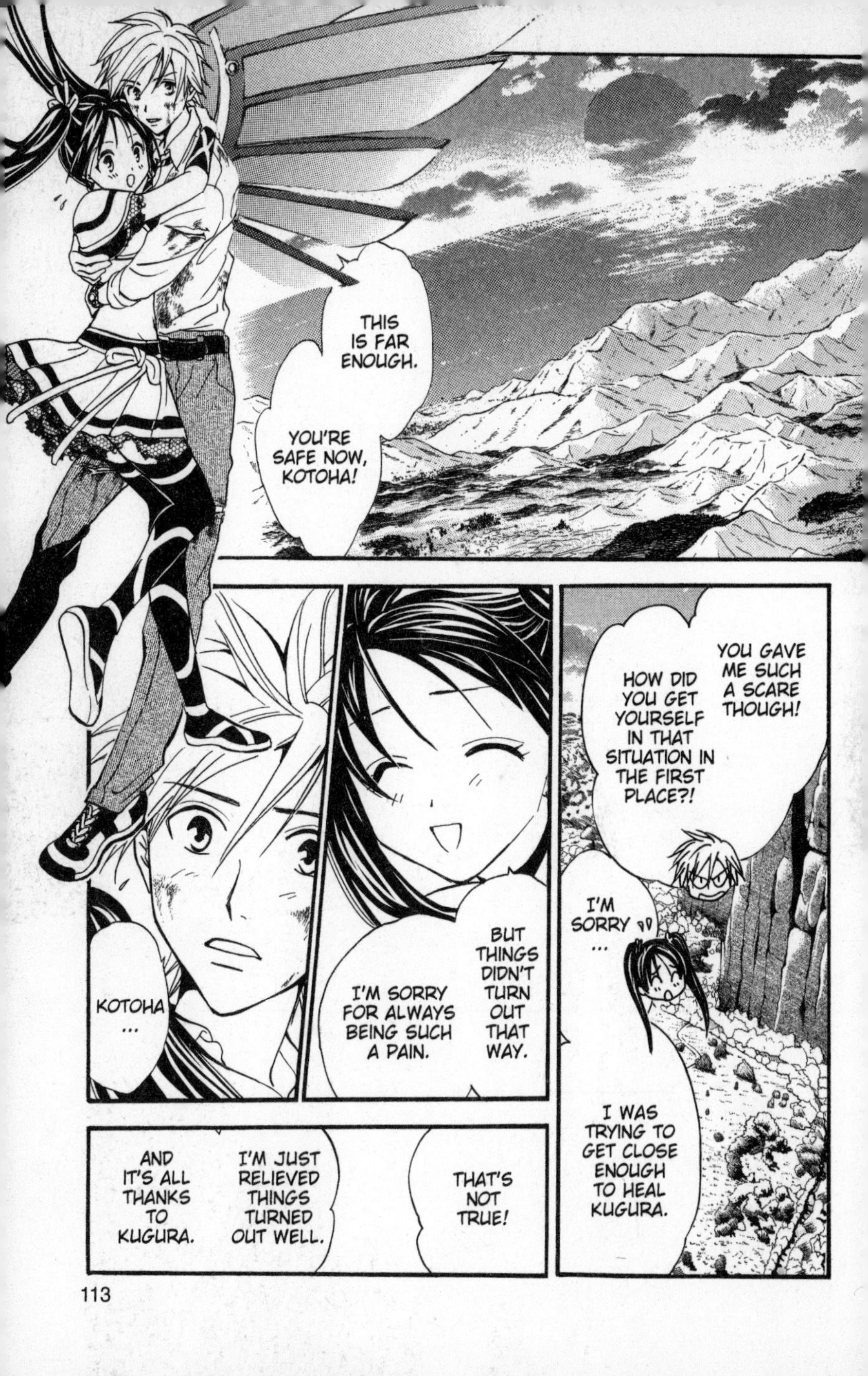
THIS IS FAR ENOUGH.
YOU'RE SAFE NOW, KOTOHA!
YOU GAVE ME SUCH A SCARE THOUGH!
HOW DID YOU GET YOURSELF IN THAT SITUATION IN THE FIRST PLACE?!
I'M SORRY ...
I WAS TRYING TO GET CLOSE ENOUGH TO HEAL KUGURA.
BUT THINGS DIDN'T TURN OUT THAT WAY.
I'M SORRY FOR ALWAYS BEING SUCH A PAIN.
KOTOHA ...
THAT'S NOT TRUE!
I'M JUST RELIEVED THINGS TURNED OUT WELL.
AND IT'S ALL THANKS TO KUGURA.

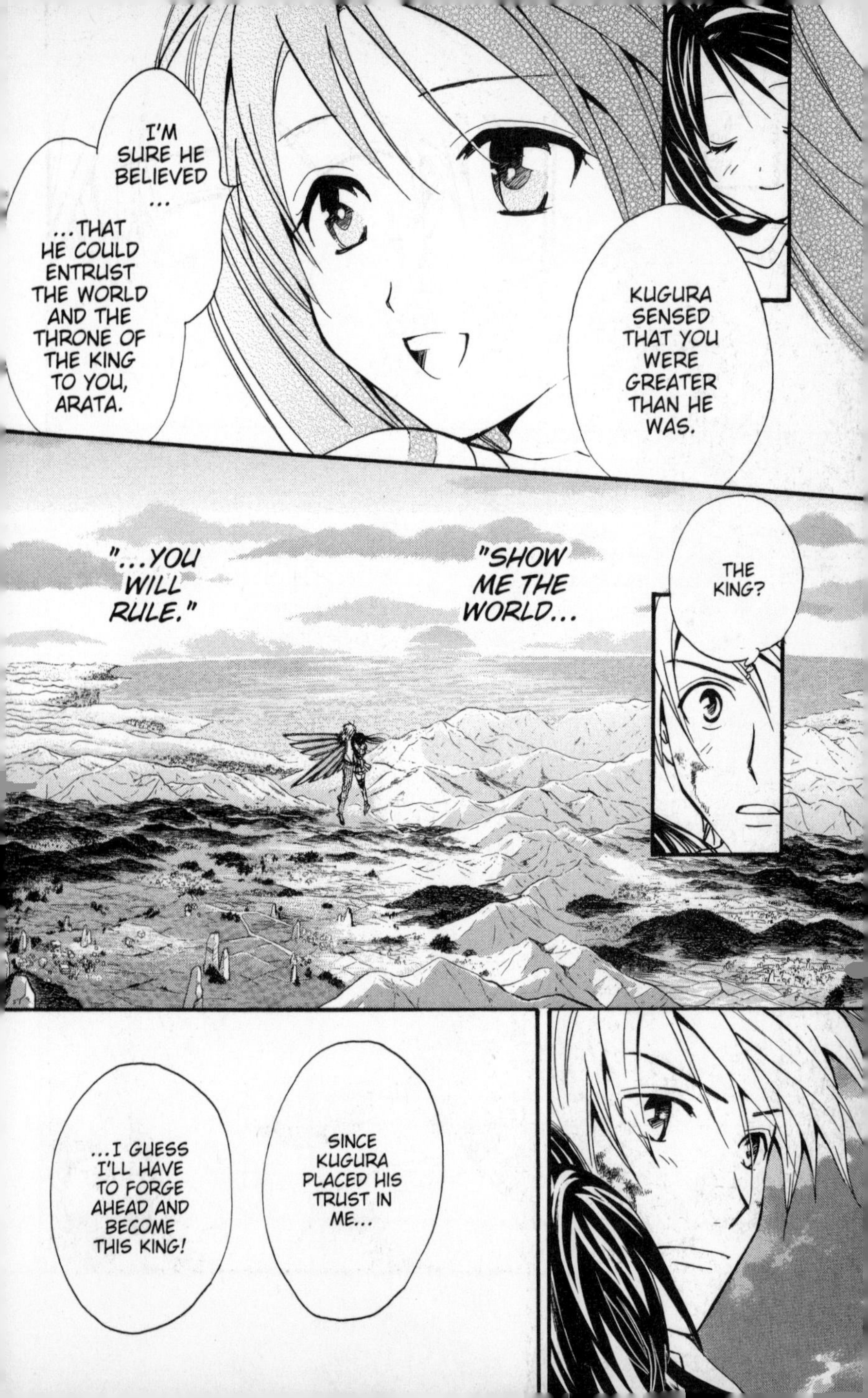
KUGURA SENSED THAT YOU WERE GREATER THAN HE WAS.
I'M SURE HE BELIEVED...
...THAT HE COULD ENTRUST THE WORLD AND THE THRONE OF THE KING TO YOU, ARATA.
THE KING?
"SHOW ME THE WORLD...
"...YOU WILL RULE."
SINCE KUGURA PLACED HIS TRUST IN ME...
...I GUESS I'LL HAVE TO FORGE AHEAD AND BECOME THIS KING!

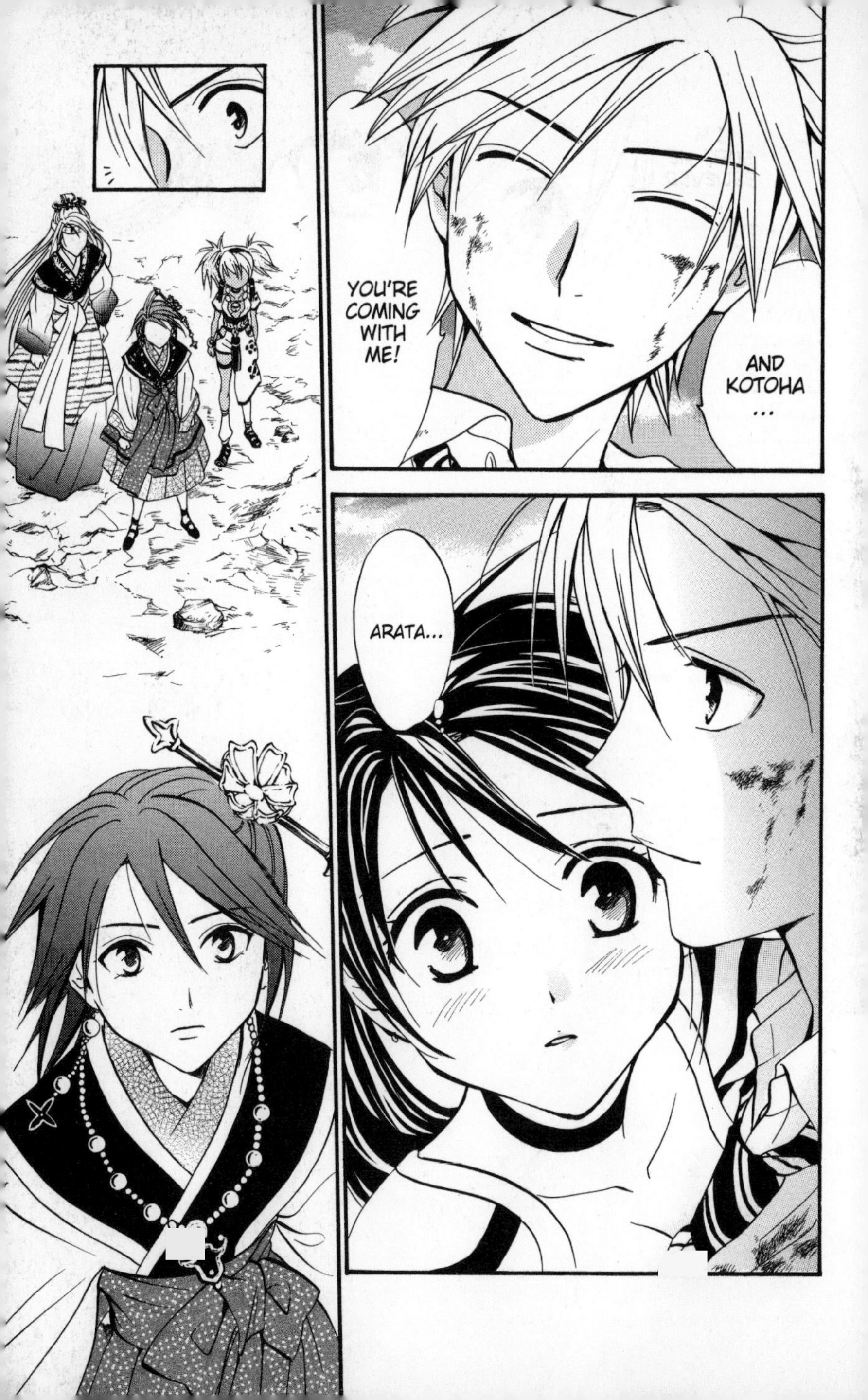
AND KOTOHA ...
YOU'RE COMING WITH ME!
ARATA...

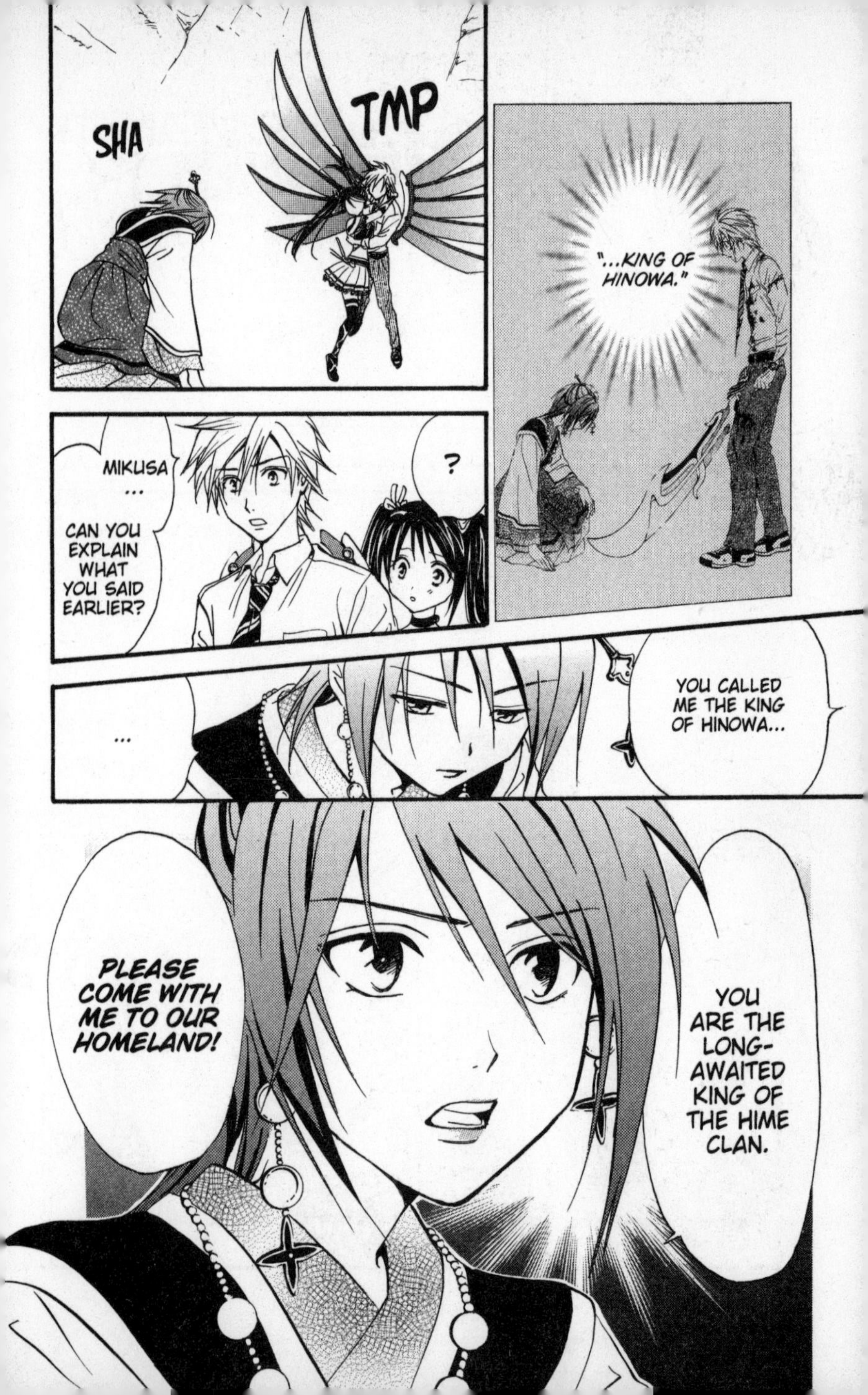
"...KING OF HINOWA."
TMP
SHA
?
MIKUSA ...
CAN YOU EXPLAIN WHAT YOU SAID EARLIER?
YOU CALLED ME THE KING OF HINOWA...
...
YOU ARE THE LONG-AWAITED KING OF THE HIME CLAN.
PLEASE COME WITH ME TO OUR HOMELAND!

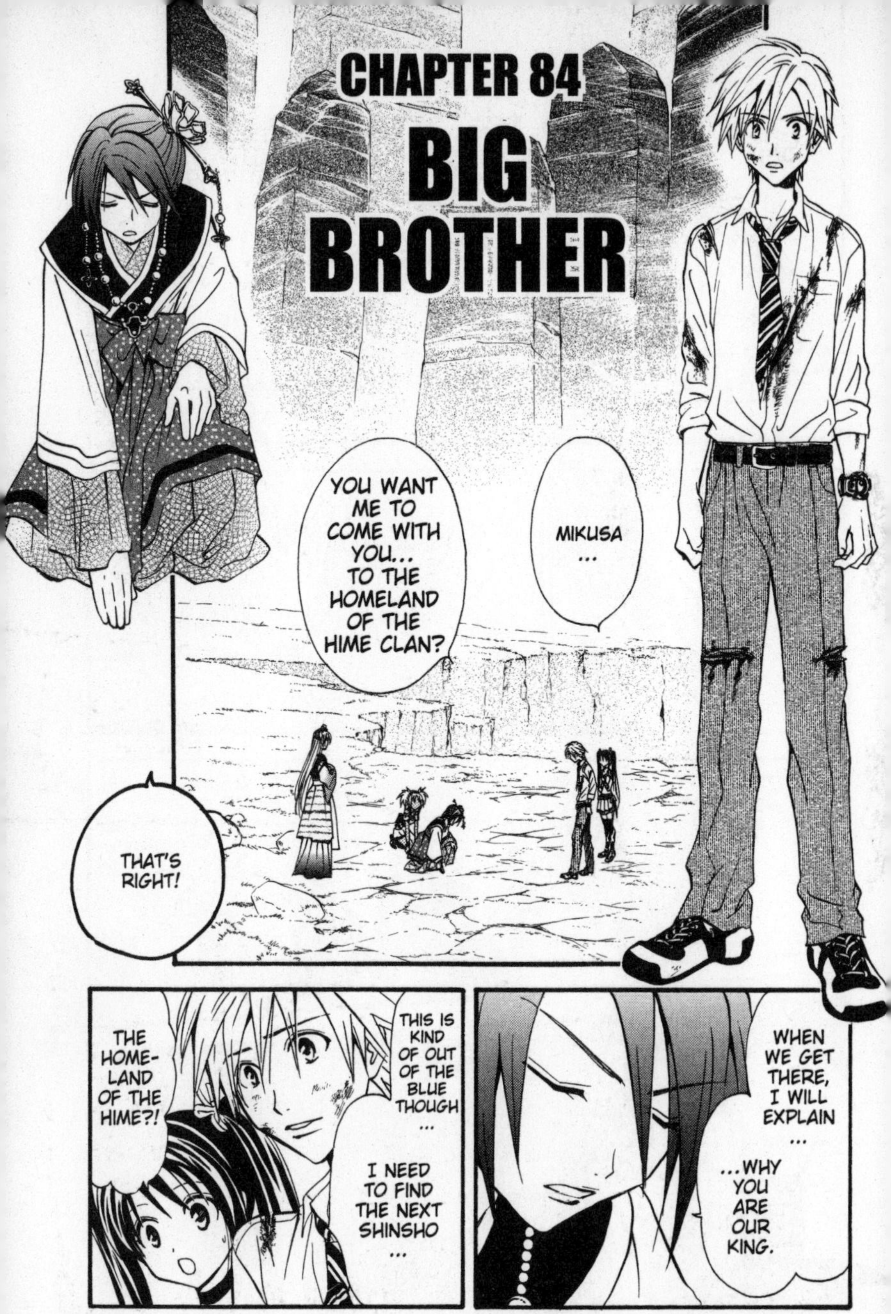
CHAPTER 84
BIG BROTHER
MIKUSA ...
YOU WANT ME TO COME WITH YOU... TO THE HOMELAND OF THE HIME CLAN?
THAT'S RIGHT!
WHEN WE GET THERE, I WILL EXPLAIN ...
...WHY YOU ARE OUR KING.
THIS IS KIND OF OUT OF THE BLUE THOUGH ...
I NEED TO FIND THE NEXT SHINSHO ...
THE HOME-LAND OF THE HIME?!

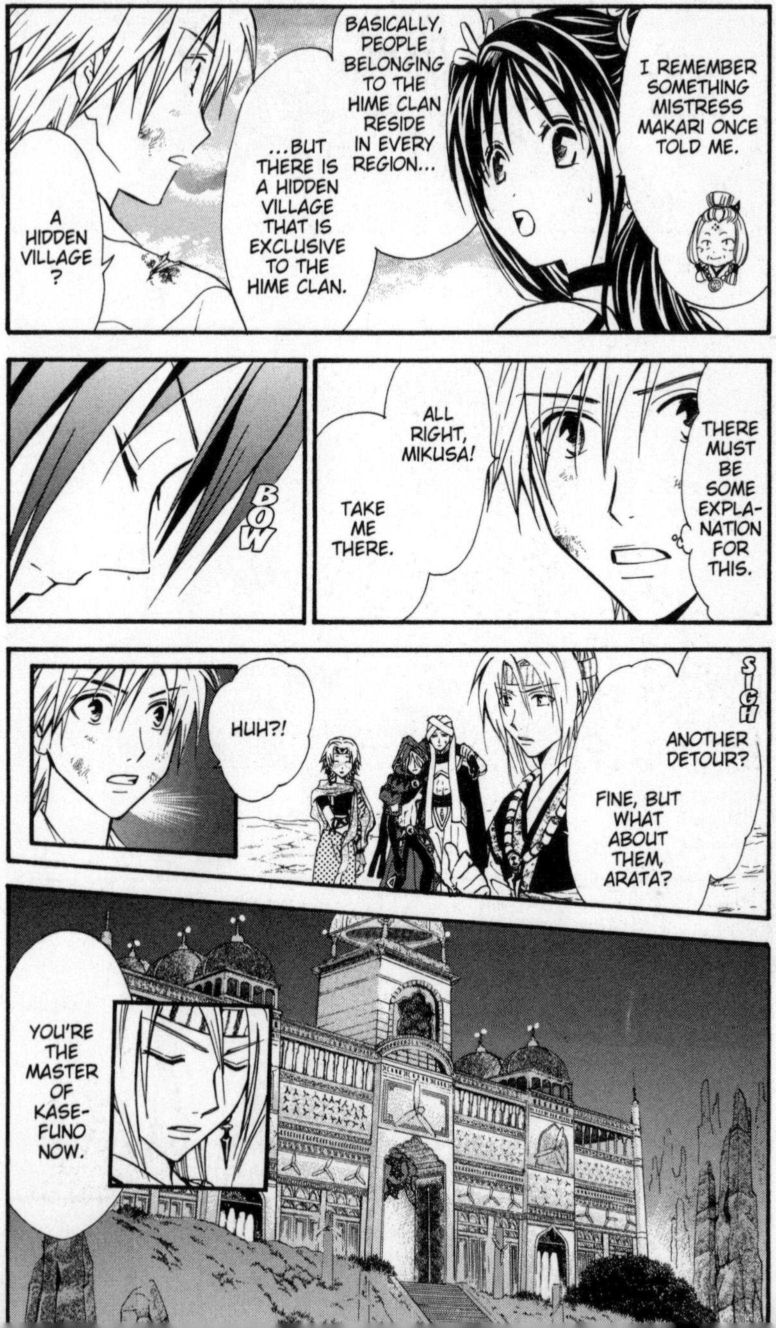
I REMEMBER SOMETHING MISTRESS MAKARI ONCE TOLD ME.
BASICALLY, PEOPLE BELONGING TO THE HIME CLAN RESIDE IN EVERY REGION...
...BUT THERE IS A HIDDEN VILLAGE THAT IS EXCLUSIVE TO THE HIME CLAN.
A HIDDEN VILLAGE?
THERE MUST BE SOME EXPLANATION FOR THIS.
ALL RIGHT, MIKUSA!
TAKE ME THERE.
BOW
SIGH
ANOTHER DETOUR?
FINE, BUT WHAT ABOUT THEM, ARATA?
HUH?!
YOU'RE THE MASTER OF KASE-FUNO NOW.

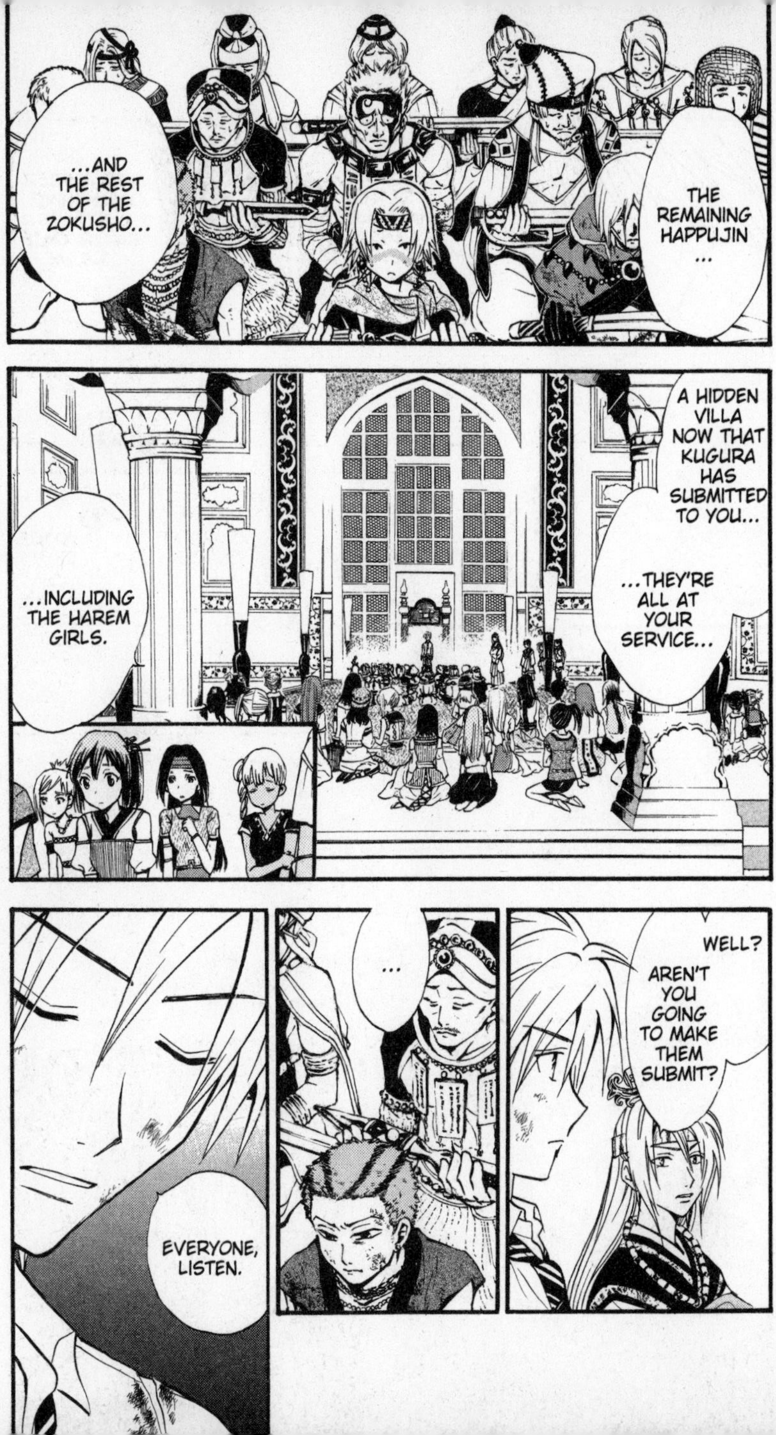
THE REMAINING HAPPUJIN ...
...AND THE REST OF THE ZOKUSHO...
A HIDDEN VILLA NOW THAT KUGURA HAS SUBMITTED TO YOU...
...THEY'RE ALL AT YOUR SERVICE...
...INCLUDING THE HAREM GIRLS.
WELL?
AREN'T YOU GOING TO MAKE THEM SUBMIT?
...
EVERYONE, LISTEN.

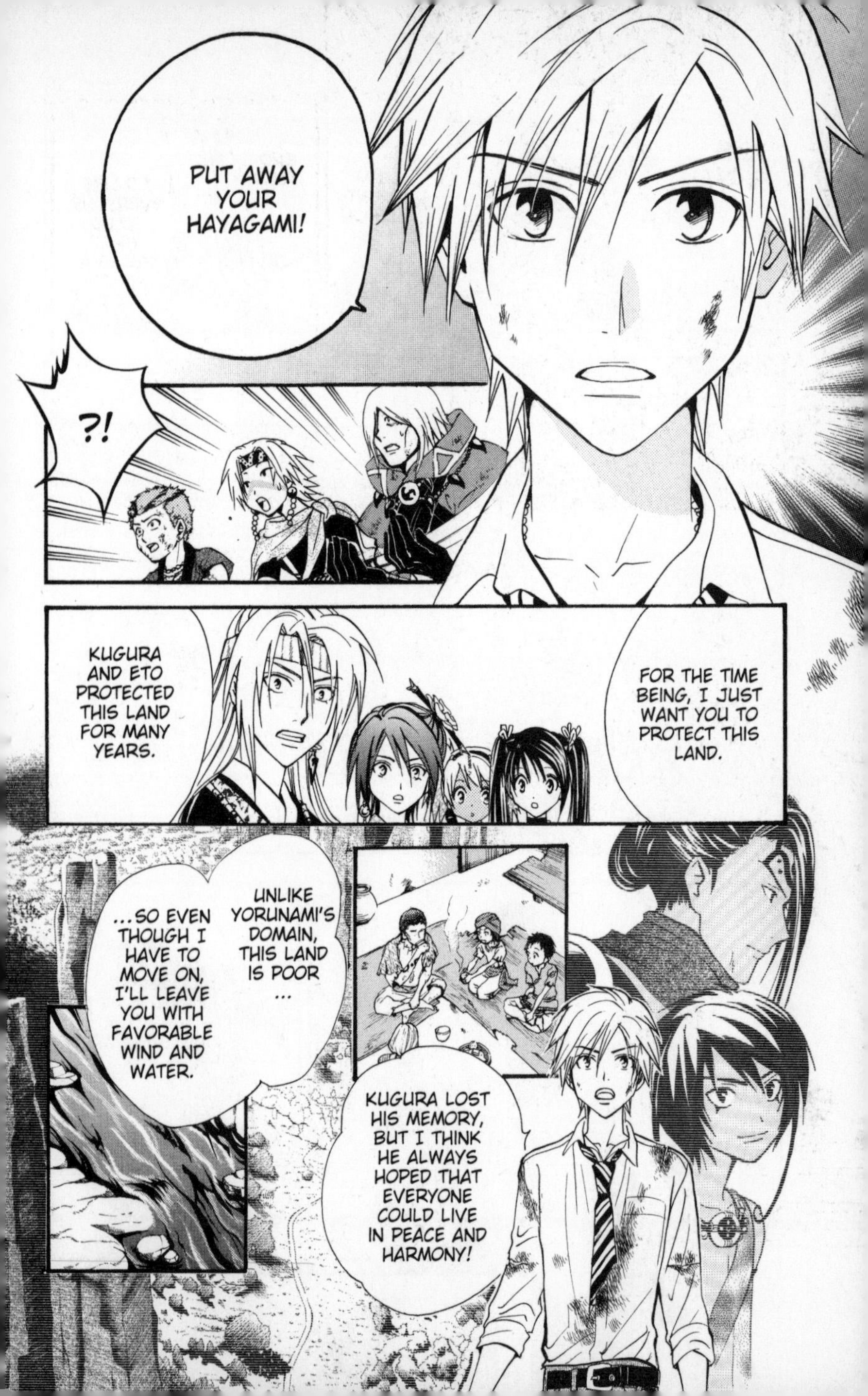
PUT AWAY YOUR HAYAGAMI!
?!
FOR THE TIME BEING, I JUST WANT YOU TO PROTECT THIS LAND.
KUGURA AND ETO PROTECTED THIS LAND FOR MANY YEARS.
KUGURA LOST HIS MEMORY, BUT I THINK HE ALWAYS HOPED THAT EVERYONE COULD LIVE IN PEACE AND HARMONY!
UNLIKE YORUNAMI'S DOMAIN, THIS LAND IS POOR ...
...SO EVEN THOUGH I HAVE TO MOVE ON, I'LL LEAVE YOU WITH FAVORABLE WIND AND WATER.

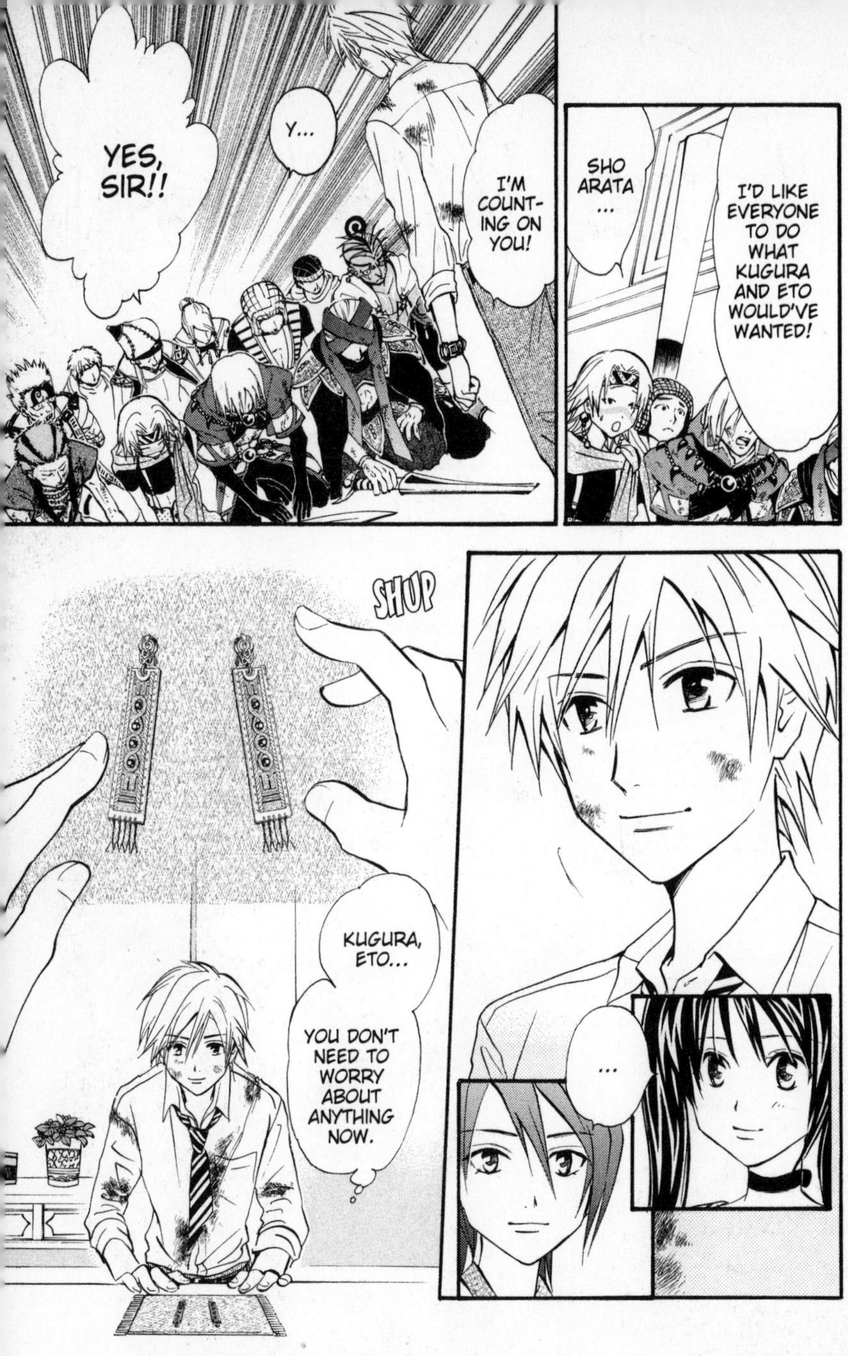
I'D LIKE EVERYONE TO DO WHAT KUGURA AND ETO WOULD'VE WANTED!
SHO ARATA ...
I'M COUNTING ON YOU!
Y...
YES, SIR!!
...
SHUP
KUGURA, ETO...
YOU DON'T NEED TO WORRY ABOUT ANYTHING NOW.

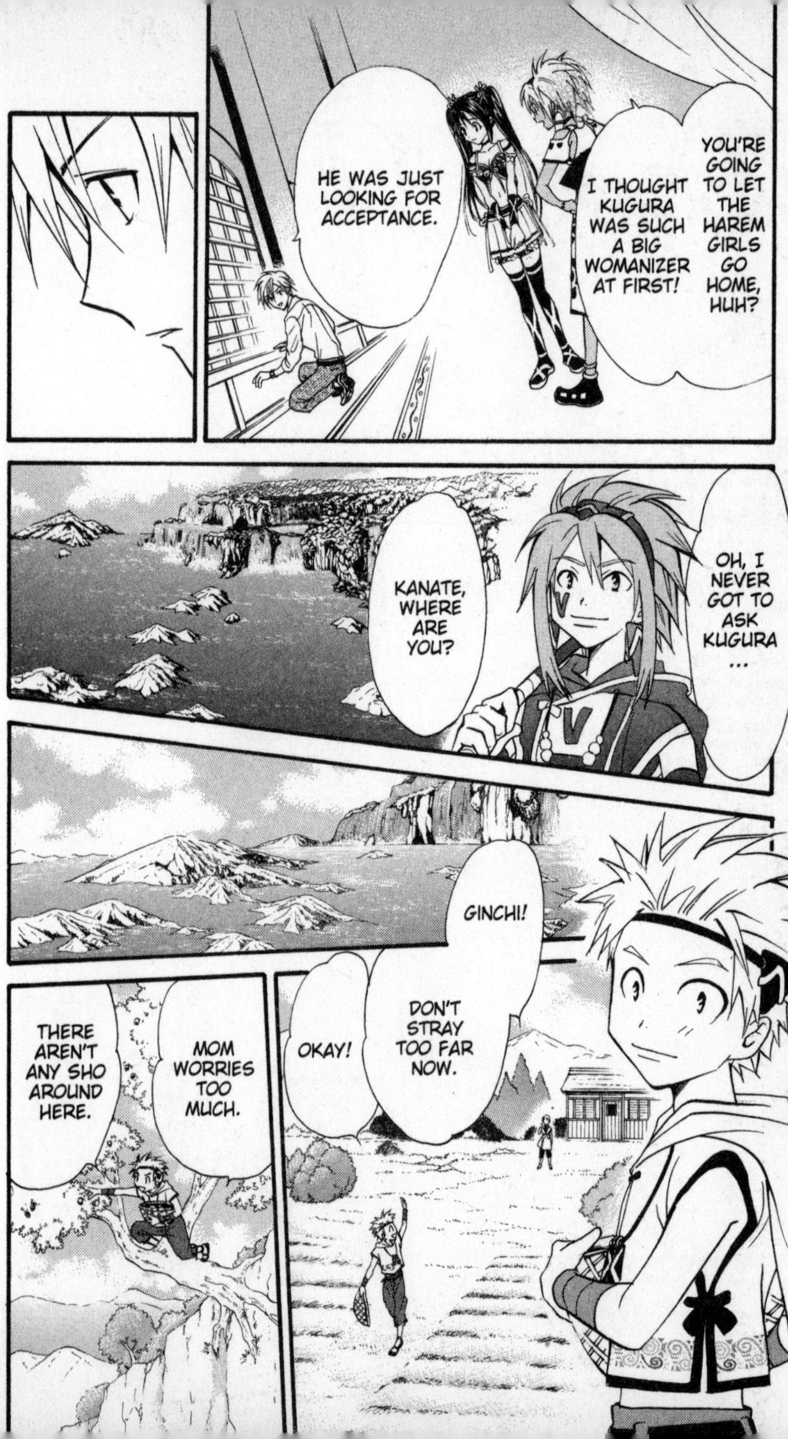
YOU'RE GOING TO LET THE HAREM GIRLS GO HOME, HUH?
I THOUGHT KUGURA WAS SUCH A BIG WOMANIZER AT FIRST!
HE WAS JUST LOOKING FOR ACCEPTANCE.
OH, I NEVER GOT TO ASK KUGURA...
KANATE, WHERE ARE YOU?
GINCHI!
DON'T STRAY TOO FAR NOW.
OKAY!
MOM WORRIES TOO MUCH.
THERE AREN'T ANY SHO AROUND HERE.

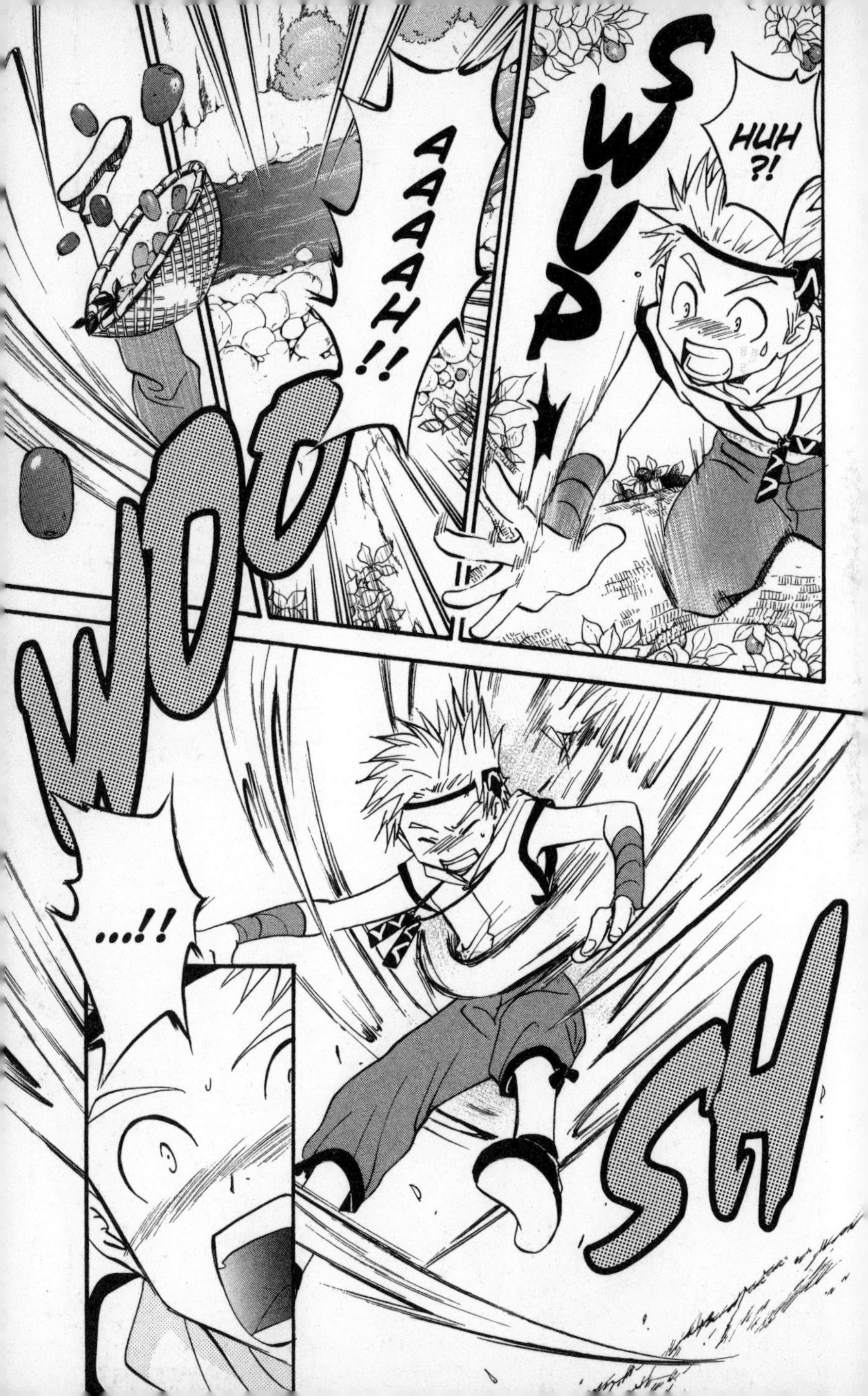
HUH ?!
SWUP
AAAAAH!!
WOOO
SH
...!!

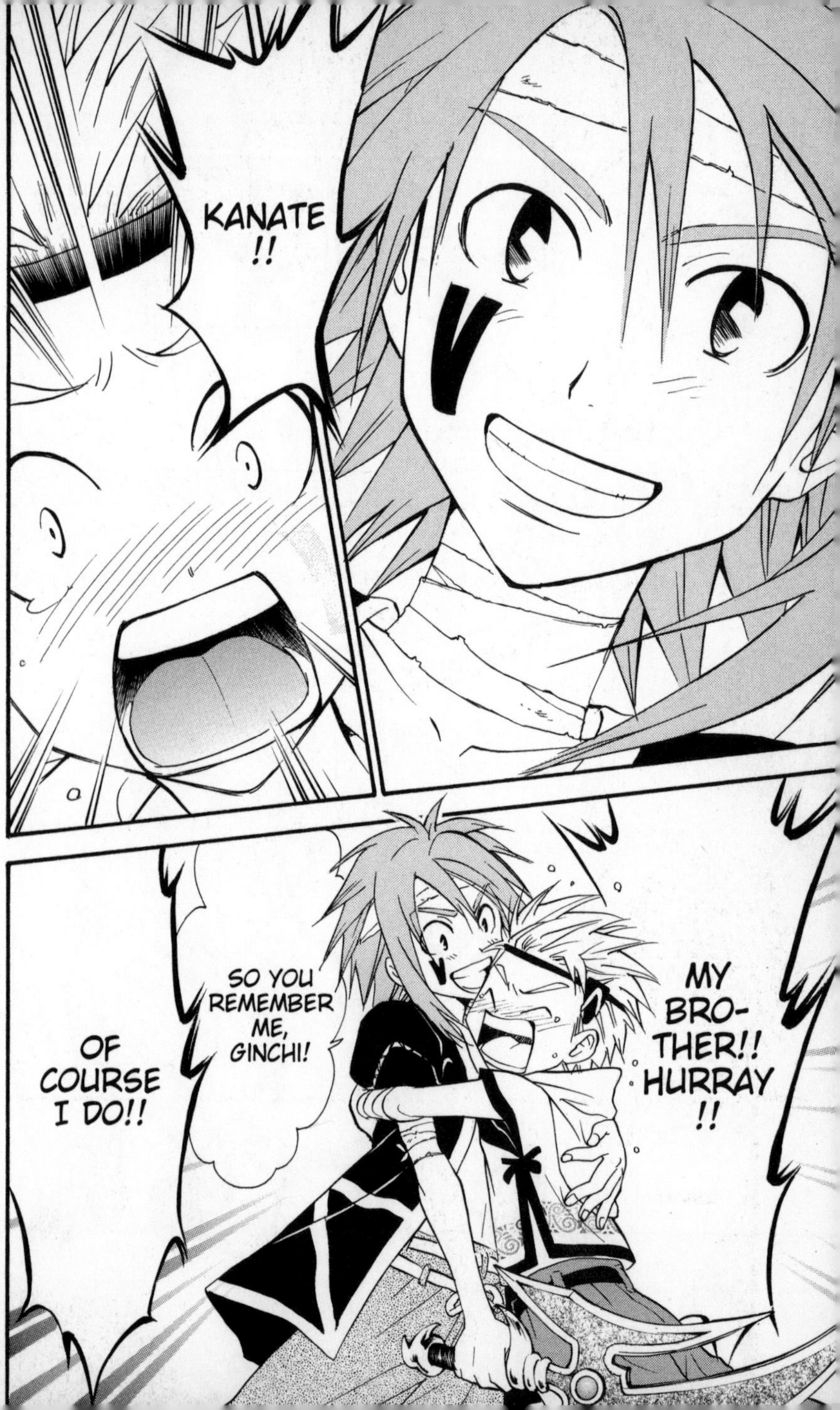
KANATE !!
MY BROTHER!! HURRAY !!
SO YOU REMEMBER ME, GINCHI!
OF COURSE I DO!!

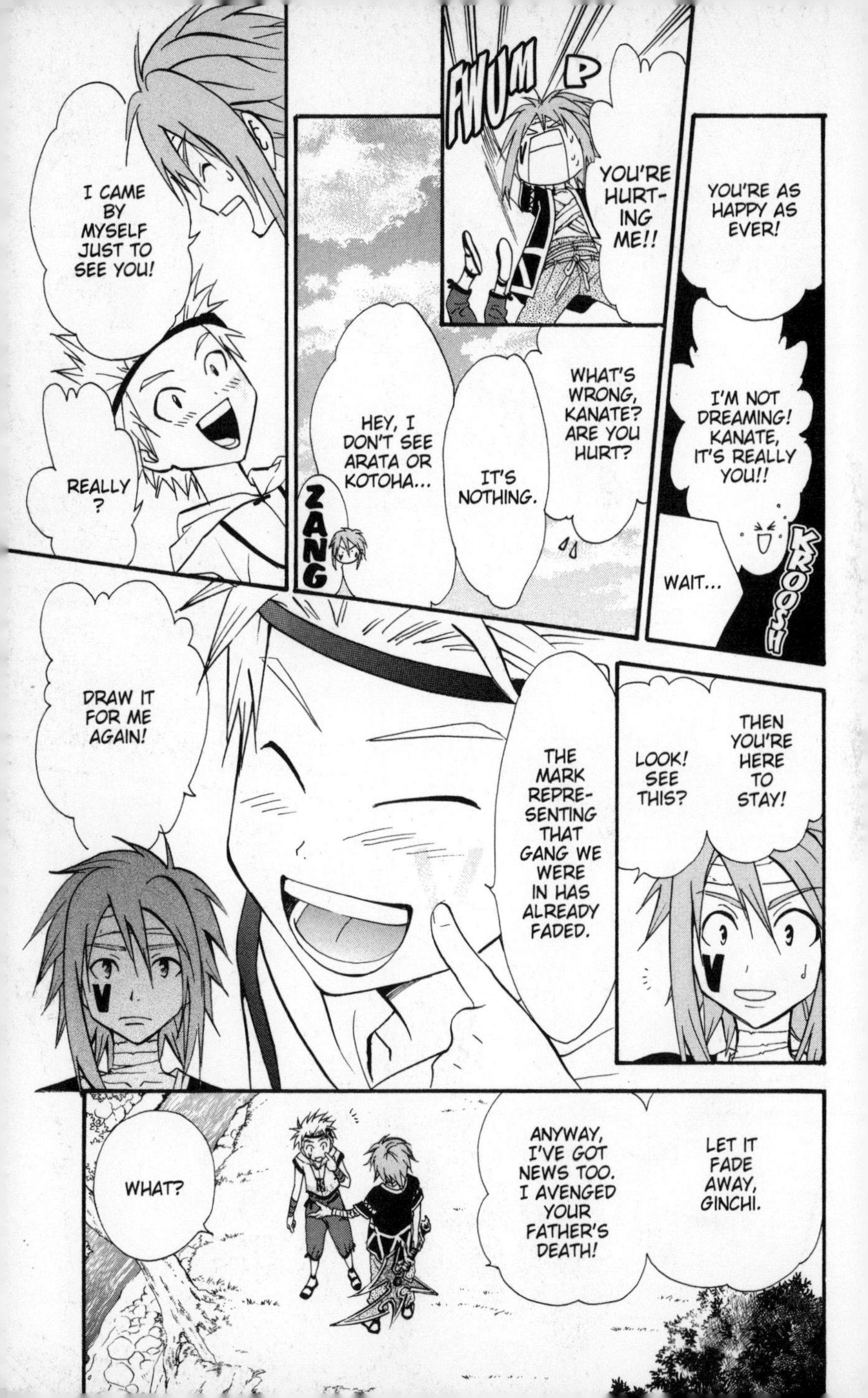
YOU'RE AS HAPPY AS EVER!
I'M NOT DREAMING! KANATE, IT'S REALLY YOU!!
KROOSH
WAIT...
FWUMP
YOU'RE HURTING ME!!
WHAT'S WRONG, KANATE? ARE YOU HURT?
IT'S NOTHING.
HEY, I DON'T SEE ARATA OR KOTOHA...
ZANG
I CAME BY MYSELF JUST TO SEE YOU!
REALLY?
THEN YOU'RE HERE TO STAY!
LOOK! SEE THIS?
THE MARK REPRESENTING THAT GANG WE WERE IN HAS ALREADY FADED.
DRAW IT FOR ME AGAIN!
LET IT FADE AWAY, GINCHI.
ANYWAY, I'VE GOT NEWS TOO. I AVENGED YOUR FATHER'S DEATH!
WHAT?

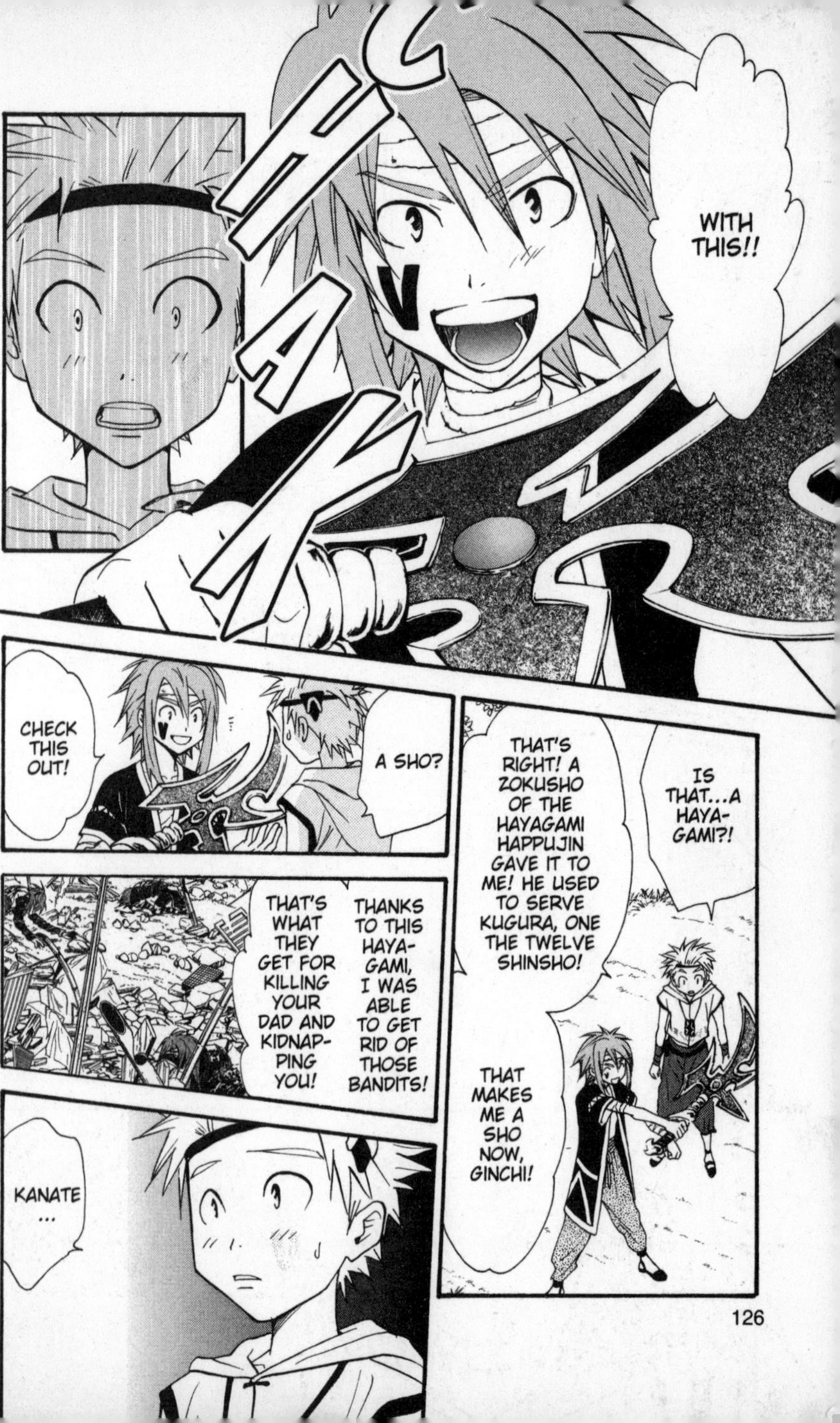

WITH THIS!!
CHAK
IS THAT...A HAYA-GAMI?!
THAT'S RIGHT! A ZOKUSHO OF THE HAYAGAMI HAPPUJIN GAVE IT TO ME! HE USED TO SERVE KUGURA, ONE THE TWELVE SHINSHO!
THAT MAKES ME A SHO NOW, GINCHI!
A SHO?
CHECK THIS OUT!
THANKS TO THIS HAYA-GAMI, I WAS ABLE TO GET RID OF THOSE BANDITS!
THAT'S WHAT THEY GET FOR KILLING YOUR DAD AND KIDNAP-PING YOU!
KANATE ...

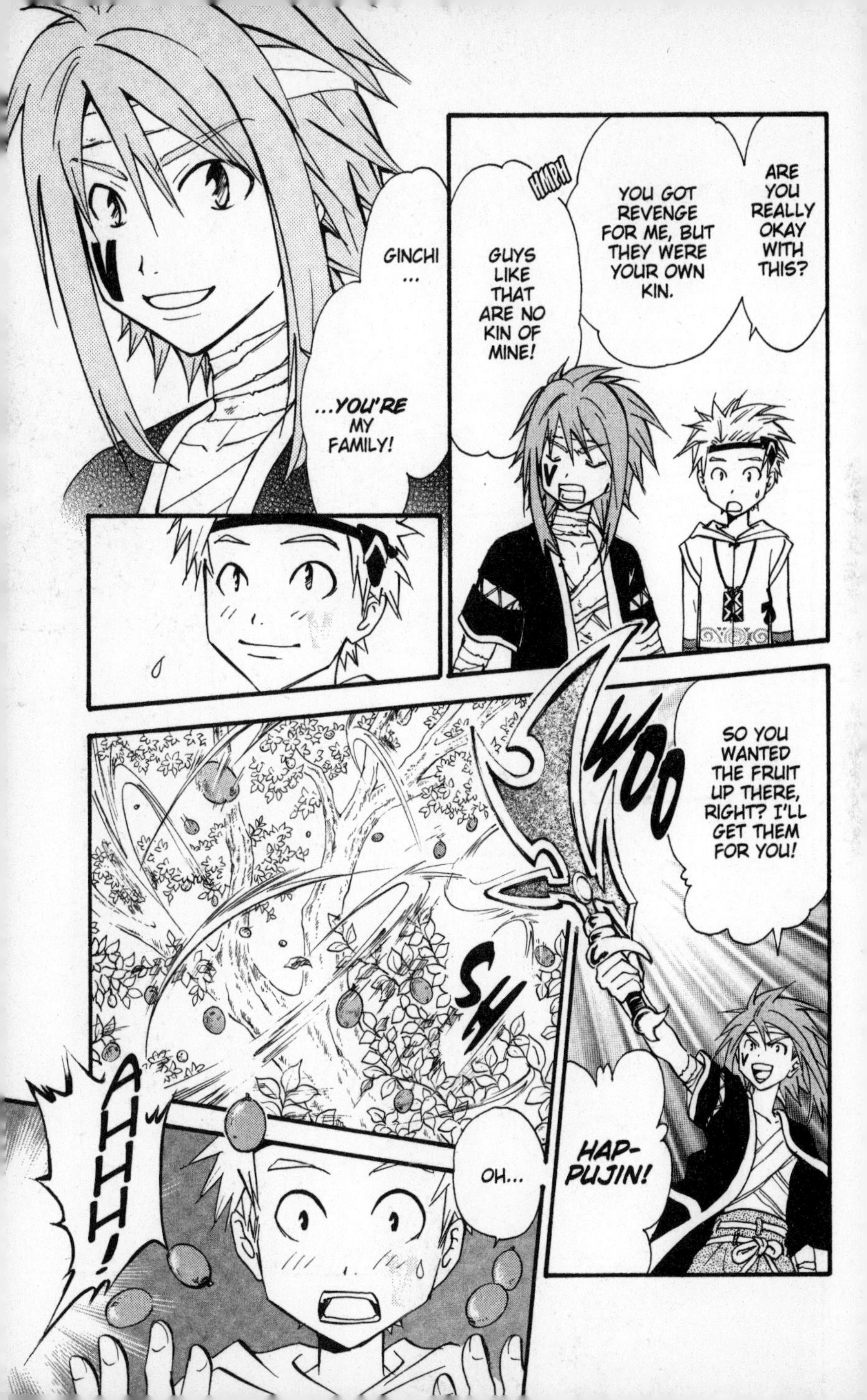
ARE YOU REALLY OKAY WITH THIS?
YOU GOT REVENGE FOR ME, BUT THEY WERE YOUR OWN KIN.
HMPH
GUYS LIKE THAT ARE NO KIN OF MINE!
GINCHI ...
...YOU'RE MY FAMILY!
SO YOU WANTED THE FRUIT UP THERE, RIGHT? I'LL GET THEM FOR YOU!
WOO
SH
HAP-PUJIN!
OH...
AHHH!

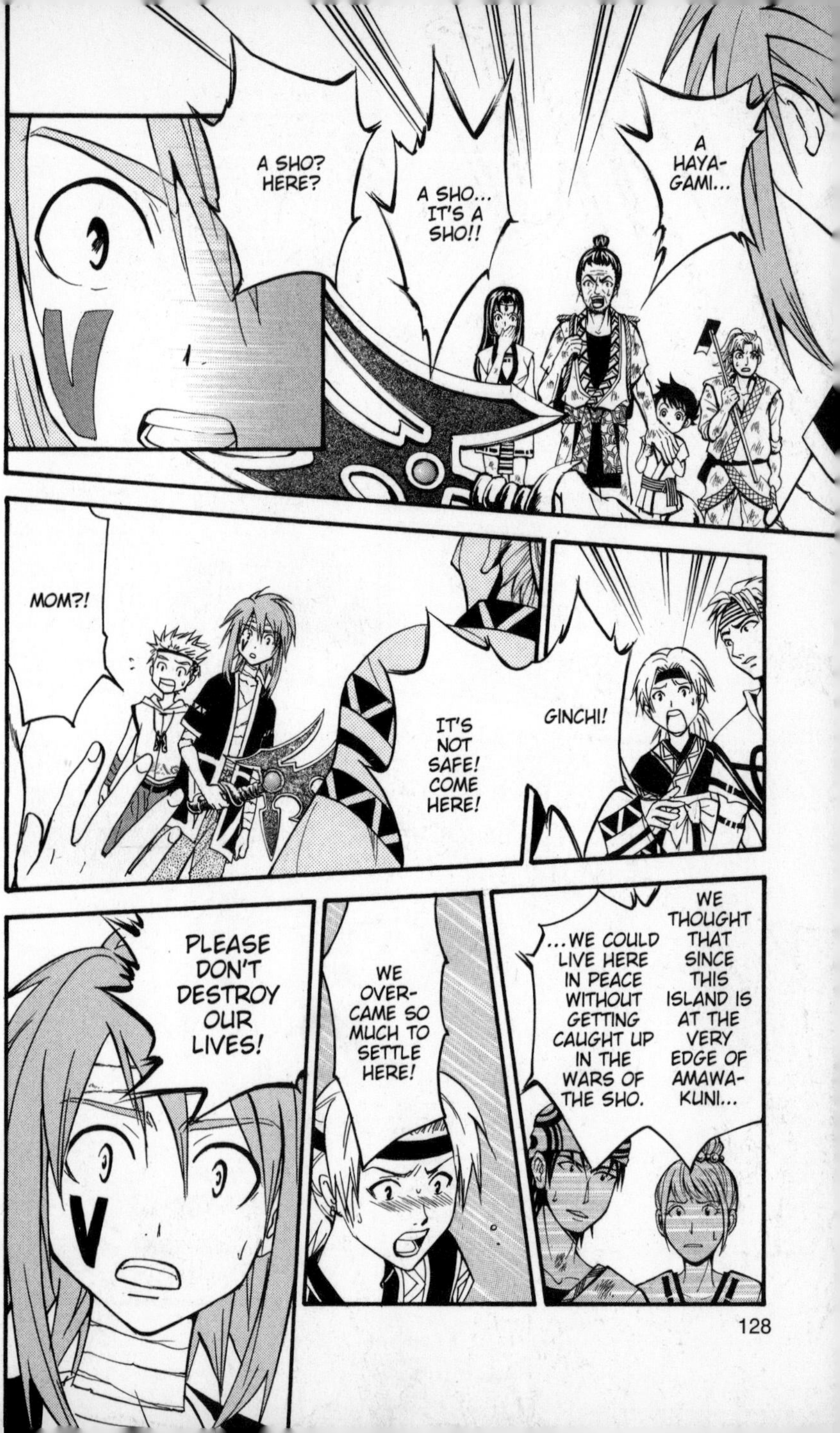
A HAYA-GAMI...
A SHO... IT'S A SHO!!
A SHO? HERE?
GINCHI!
IT'S NOT SAFE! COME HERE!
MOM?!
WE THOUGHT THAT SINCE THIS ISLAND IS AT THE VERY EDGE OF AMAWA-KUNI...
...WE COULD LIVE HERE IN PEACE WITHOUT GETTING CAUGHT UP IN THE WARS OF THE SHO.
WE OVER-CAME SO MUCH TO SETTLE HERE!
PLEASE DON'T DESTROY OUR LIVES!

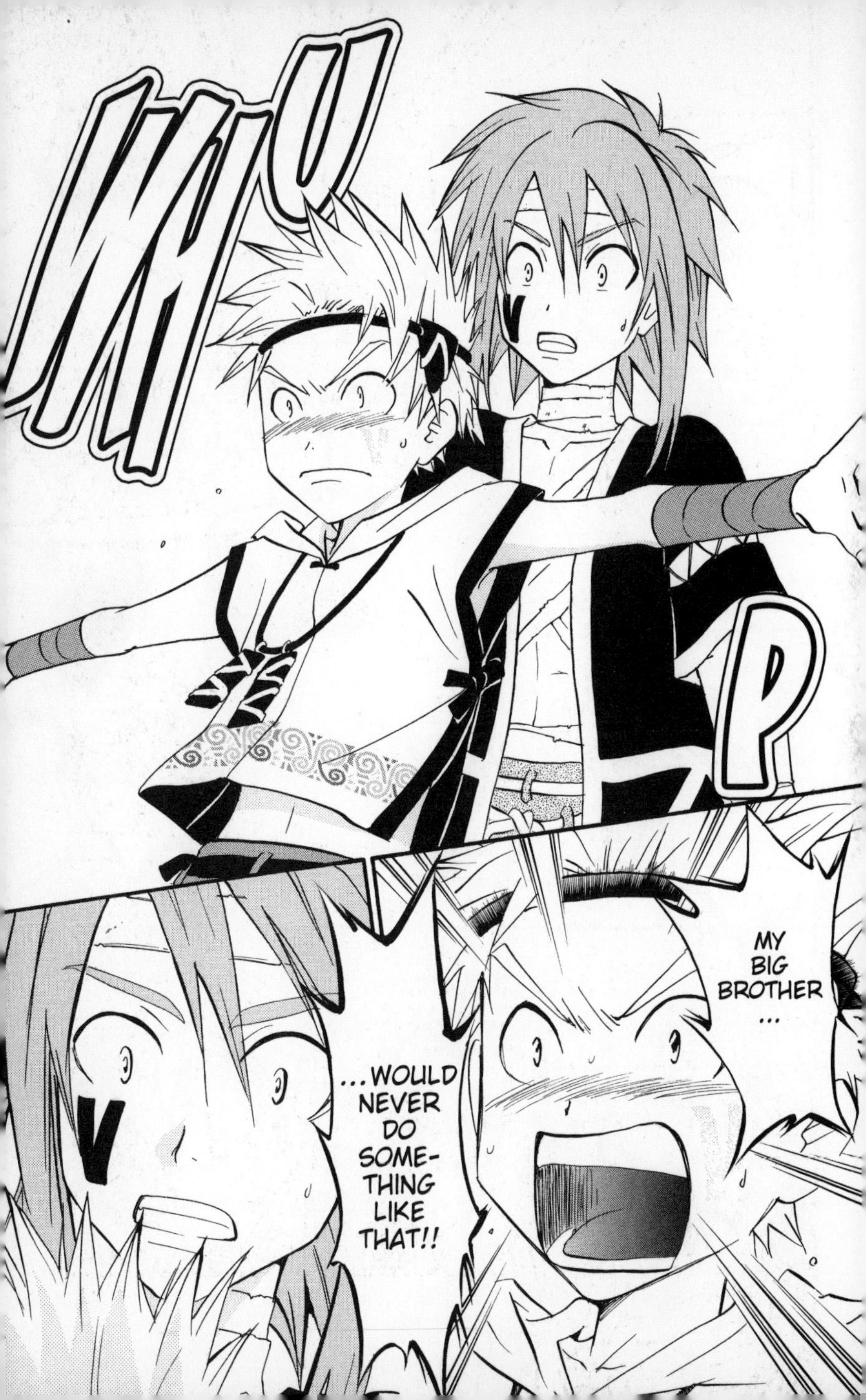
MY BIG BROTHER ...
...WOULD NEVER DO SOME-THING LIKE THAT!!

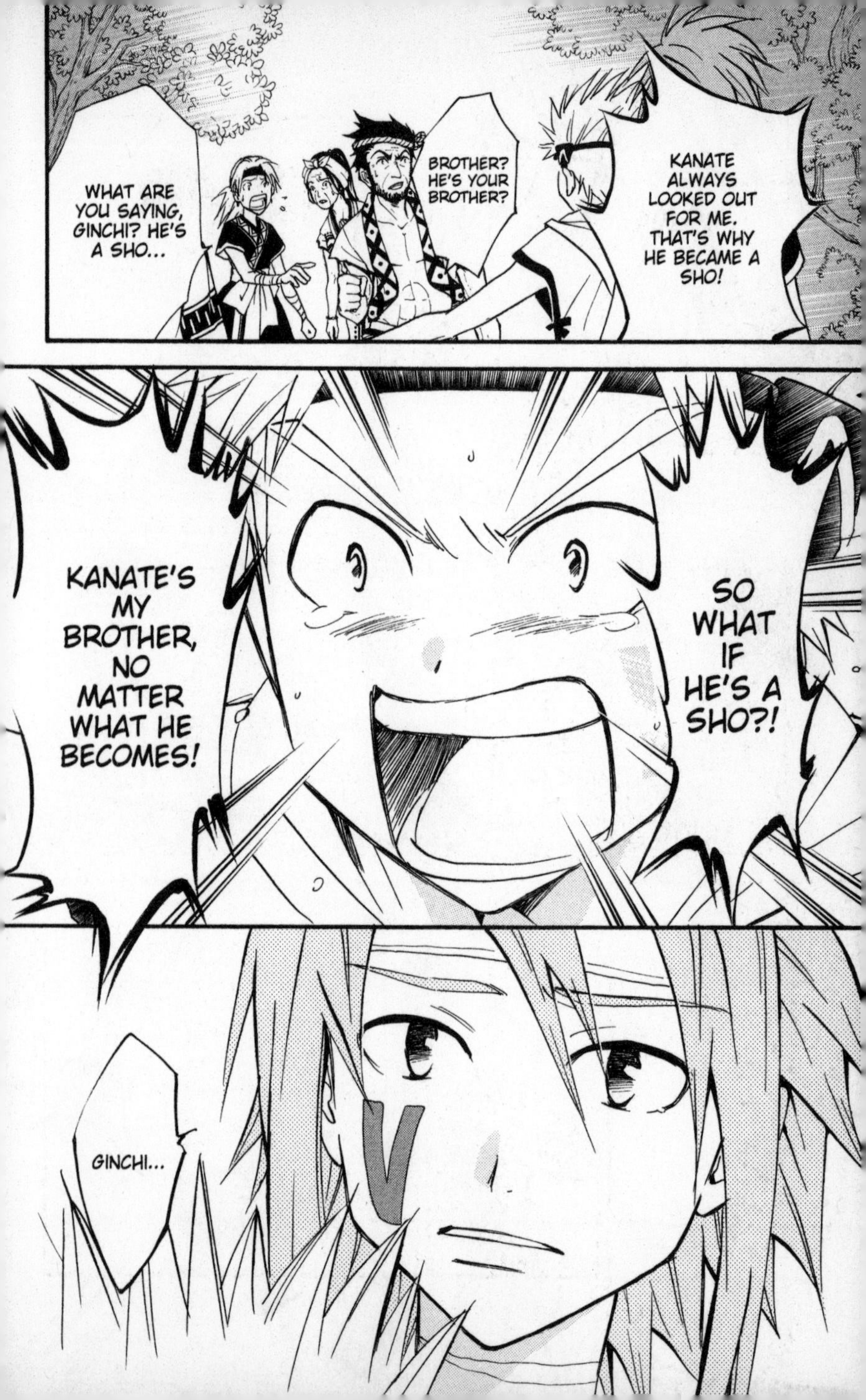
KANATE ALWAYS LOOKED OUT FOR ME. THAT'S WHY HE BECAME A SHO!
BROTHER? HE'S YOUR BROTHER?
WHAT ARE YOU SAYING, GINCHI? HE'S A SHO...
SO WHAT IF HE'S A SHO?!
KANATE'S MY BROTHER, NO MATTER WHAT HE BECOMES!
GINCHI...

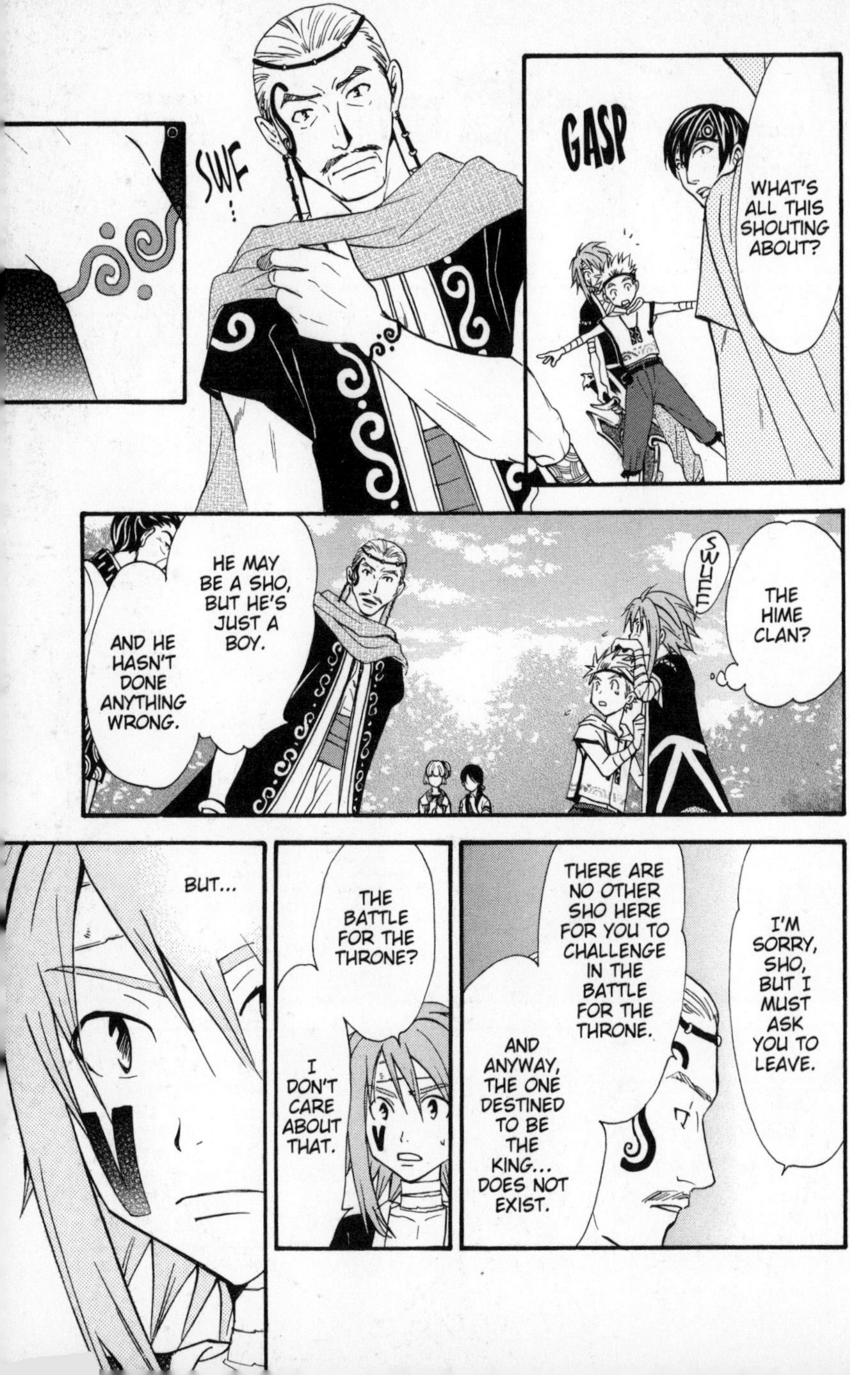
GASP
WHAT'S ALL THIS SHOUTING ABOUT?
SWF
...
THE HIME CLAN?
SWUFF
HE MAY BE A SHO, BUT HE'S JUST A BOY.
AND HE HASN'T DONE ANYTHING WRONG.
I'M SORRY, SHO, BUT I MUST ASK YOU TO LEAVE.
THERE ARE NO OTHER SHO HERE FOR YOU TO CHALLENGE IN THE BATTLE FOR THE THRONE.
AND ANYWAY, THE ONE DESTINED TO BE THE KING... DOES NOT EXIST.
THE BATTLE FOR THE THRONE?
I DON'T CARE ABOUT THAT.
BUT...

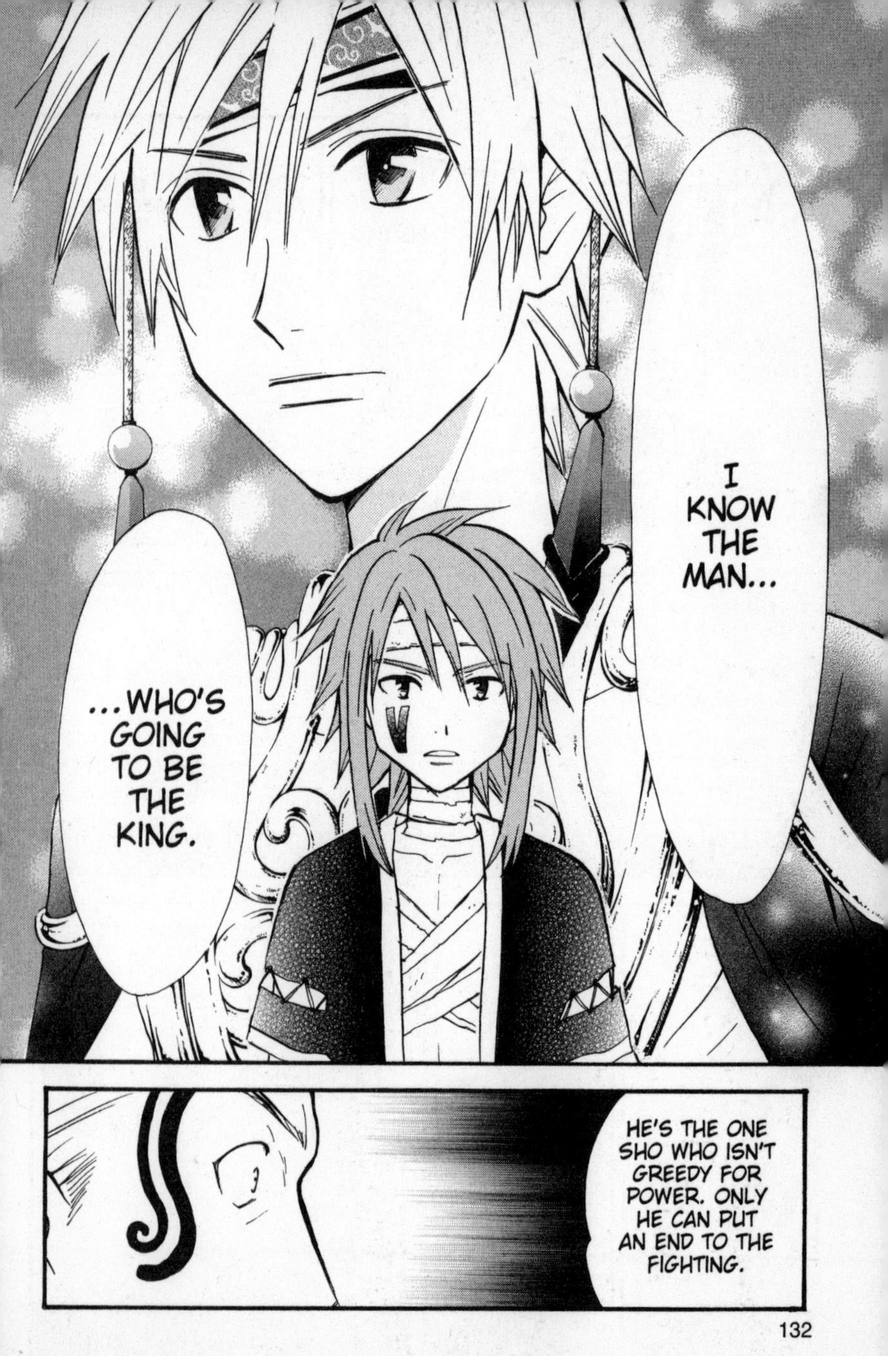
I KNOW THE MAN...
...WHO'S GOING TO BE THE KING.
HE'S THE ONE SHO WHO ISN'T GREEDY FOR POWER. ONLY HE CAN PUT AN END TO THE FIGHTING.

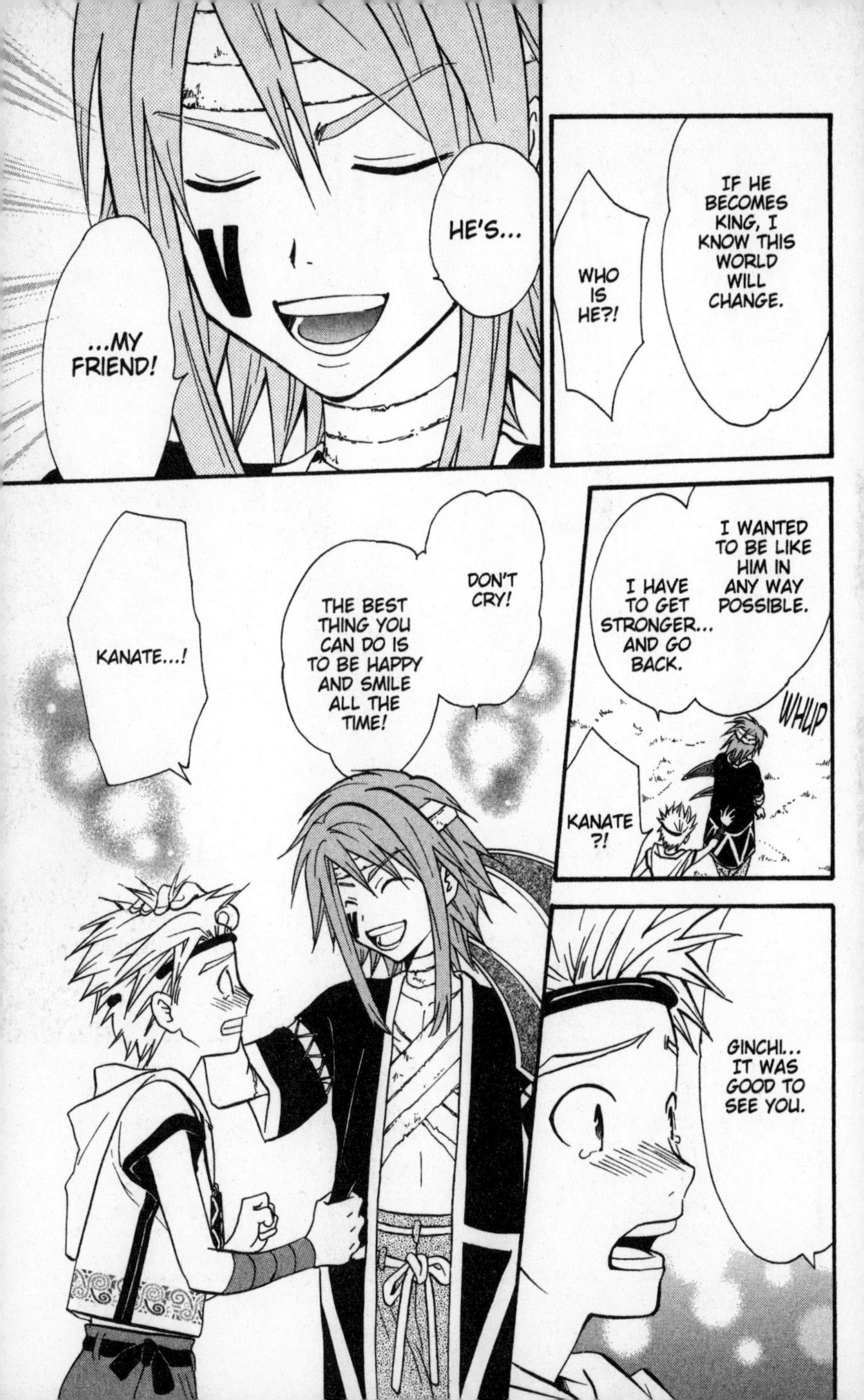
IF HE BECOMES KING, I KNOW THIS WORLD WILL CHANGE.
WHO IS HE?!
HE'S...
...MY FRIEND!
I WANTED TO BE LIKE HIM IN ANY WAY POSSIBLE.
I HAVE TO GET STRONGER... AND GO BACK.
WHUP
KANATE?!
GINCHI... IT WAS GOOD TO SEE YOU.
DON'T CRY!
THE BEST THING YOU CAN DO IS TO BE HAPPY AND SMILE ALL THE TIME!
KANATE...!

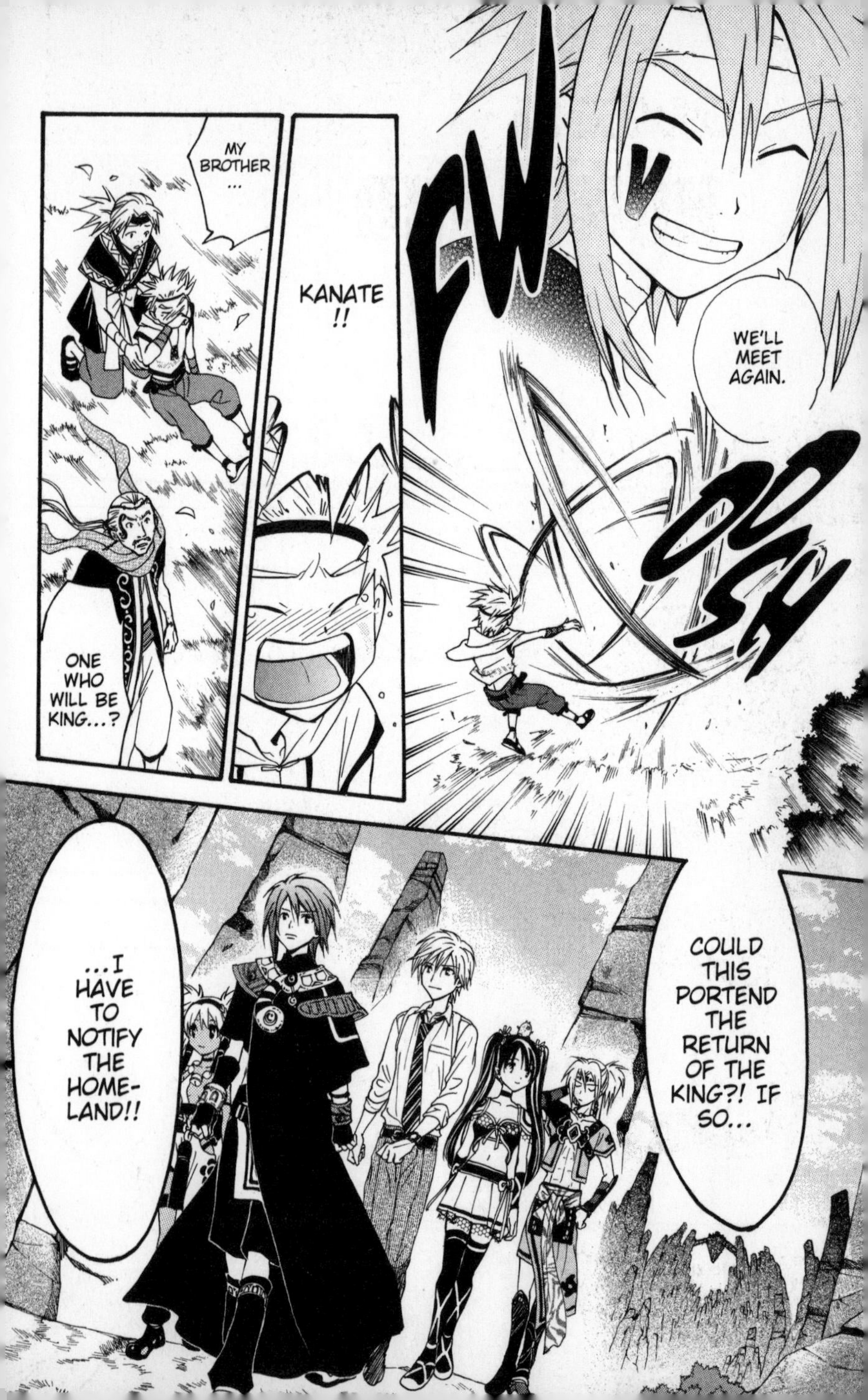
WE'LL MEET AGAIN.
FW
OOSH
KANATE !!
MY BROTHER ...
ONE WHO WILL BE KING...?
COULD THIS PORTEND THE RETURN OF THE KING?! IF SO...
...I HAVE TO NOTIFY THE HOME-LAND!!

CHAPTER 85
HOMELAND

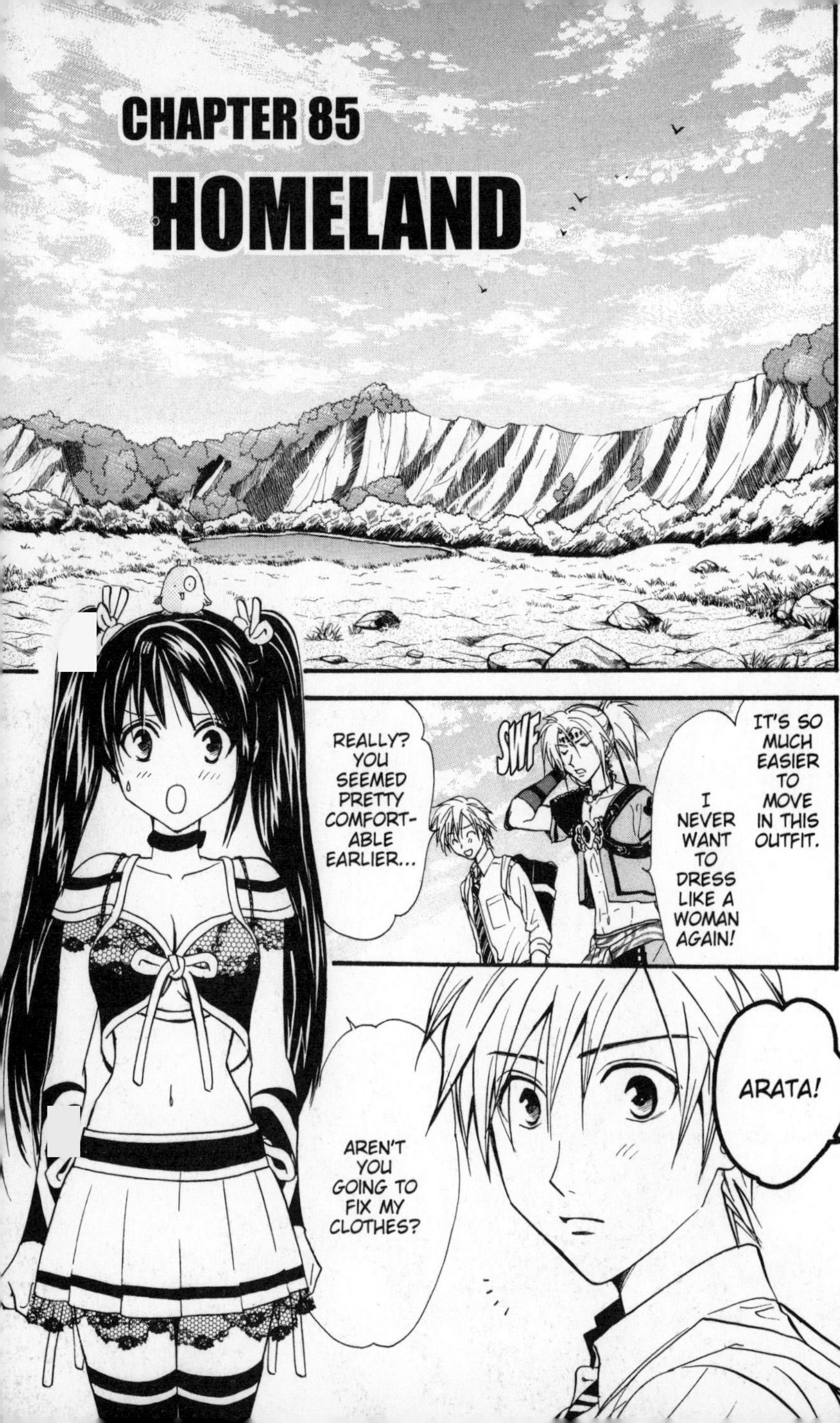

IT'S SO MUCH EASIER TO MOVE IN THIS OUTFIT.
I NEVER WANT TO DRESS LIKE A WOMAN AGAIN!
SWF
REALLY? YOU SEEMED PRETTY COMFORT-ABLE EARLIER...
ARATA!
AREN'T YOU GOING TO FIX MY CLOTHES?

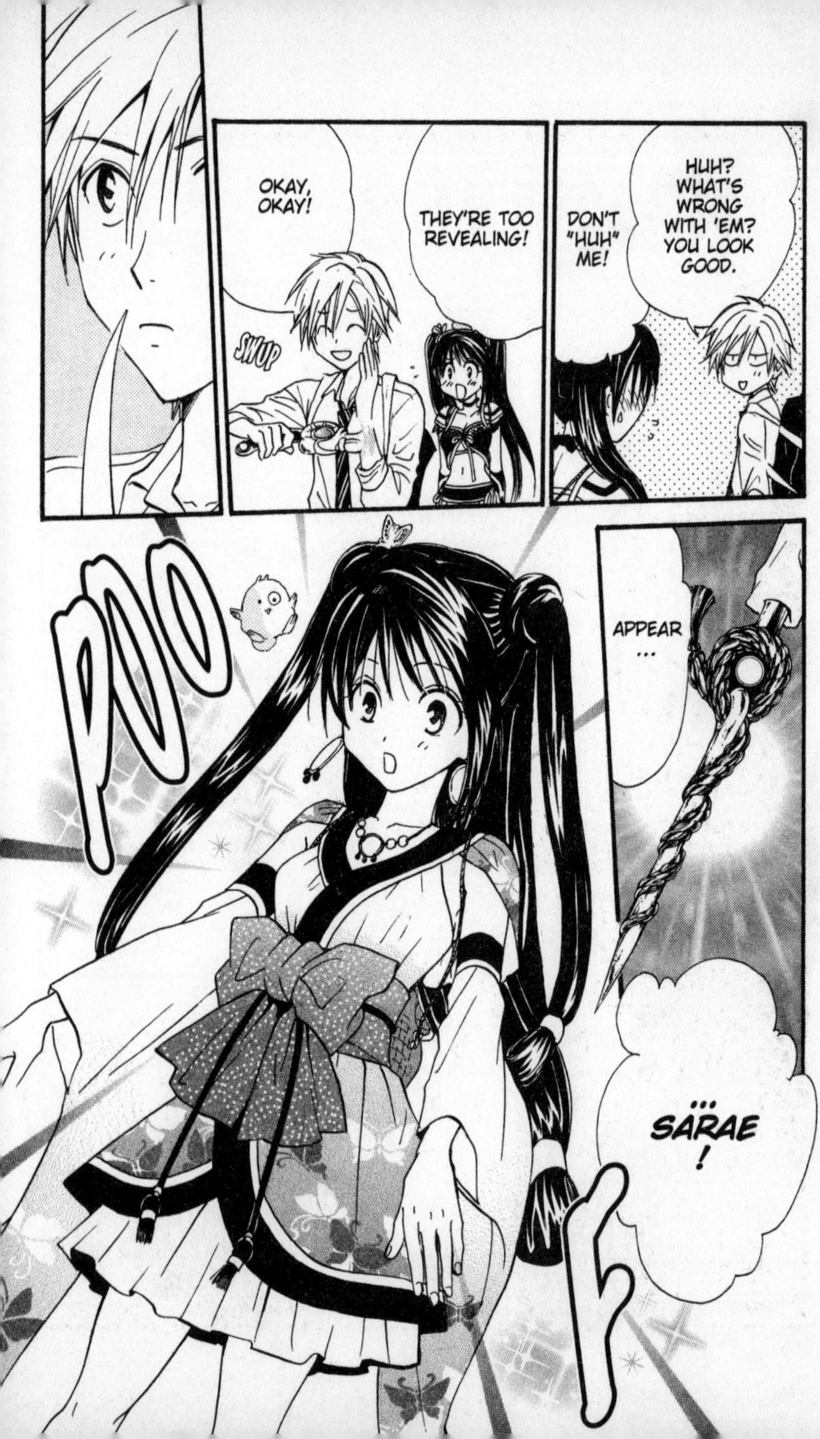
HUH? WHAT'S WRONG WITH 'EM? YOU LOOK GOOD.
DON'T "HUH" ME!
THEY'RE TOO REVEALING!
OKAY, OKAY!
SWUP
APPEAR ...
... SÄRAE!
POO

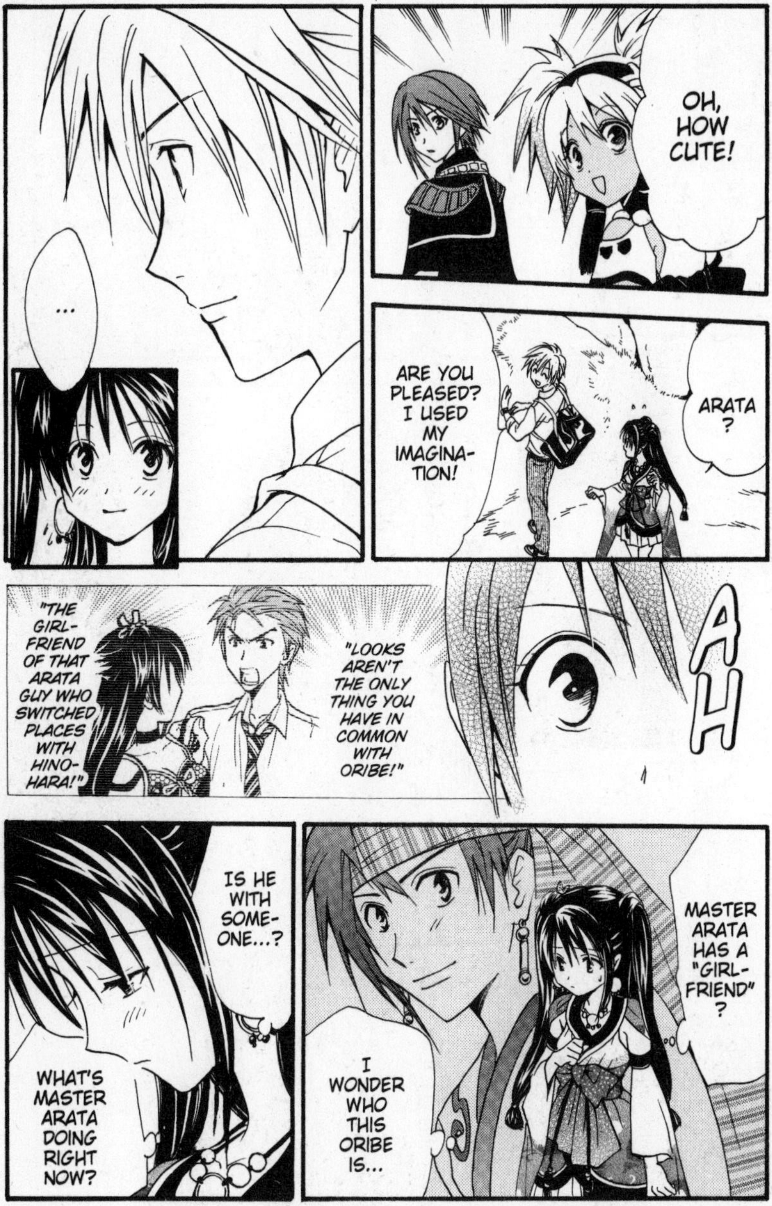
OH, HOW CUTE!
ARATA?
ARE YOU PLEASED? I USED MY IMAGINATION!
...
AH
"LOOKS AREN'T THE ONLY THING YOU HAVE IN COMMON WITH ORIBE!"
"THE GIRLFRIEND OF THAT ARATA GUY WHO SWITCHED PLACES WITH HINOHARA!"
MASTER ARATA HAS A "GIRLFRIEND"?
I WONDER WHO THIS ORIBE IS...
IS HE WITH SOMEONE...?
WHAT'S MASTER ARATA DOING RIGHT NOW?

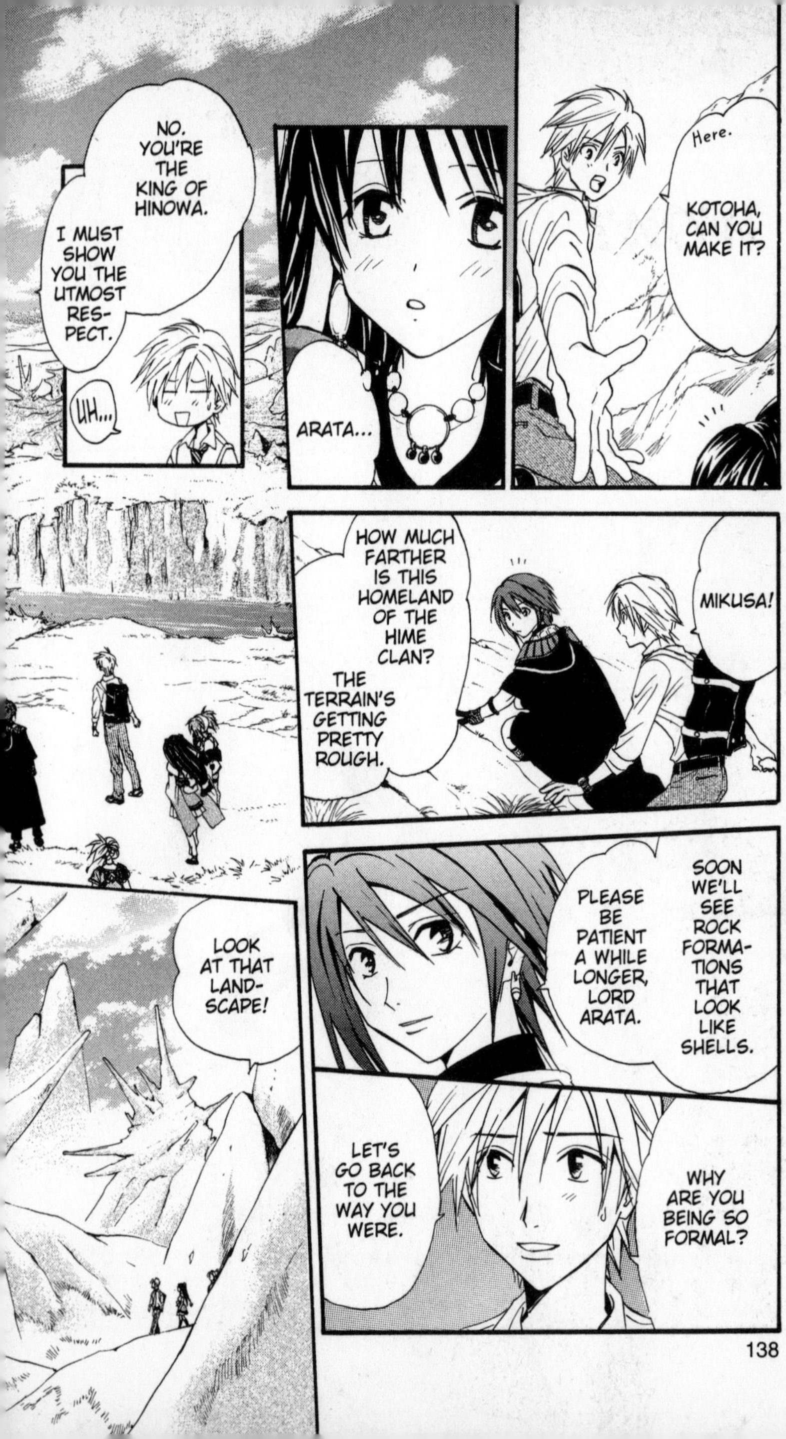
Here.
KOTOHA, CAN YOU MAKE IT?
ARATA...
NO. YOU'RE THE KING OF HINOWA.
I MUST SHOW YOU THE UTMOST RESPECT.
UH...
MIKUSA!
HOW MUCH FARTHER IS THIS HOMELAND OF THE HIME CLAN?
THE TERRAIN'S GETTING PRETTY ROUGH.
SOON WE'LL SEE ROCK FORMATIONS THAT LOOK LIKE SHELLS.
PLEASE BE PATIENT A WHILE LONGER, LORD ARATA.
WHY ARE YOU BEING SO FORMAL?
LET'S GO BACK TO THE WAY YOU WERE.
LOOK AT THAT LANDSCAPE!

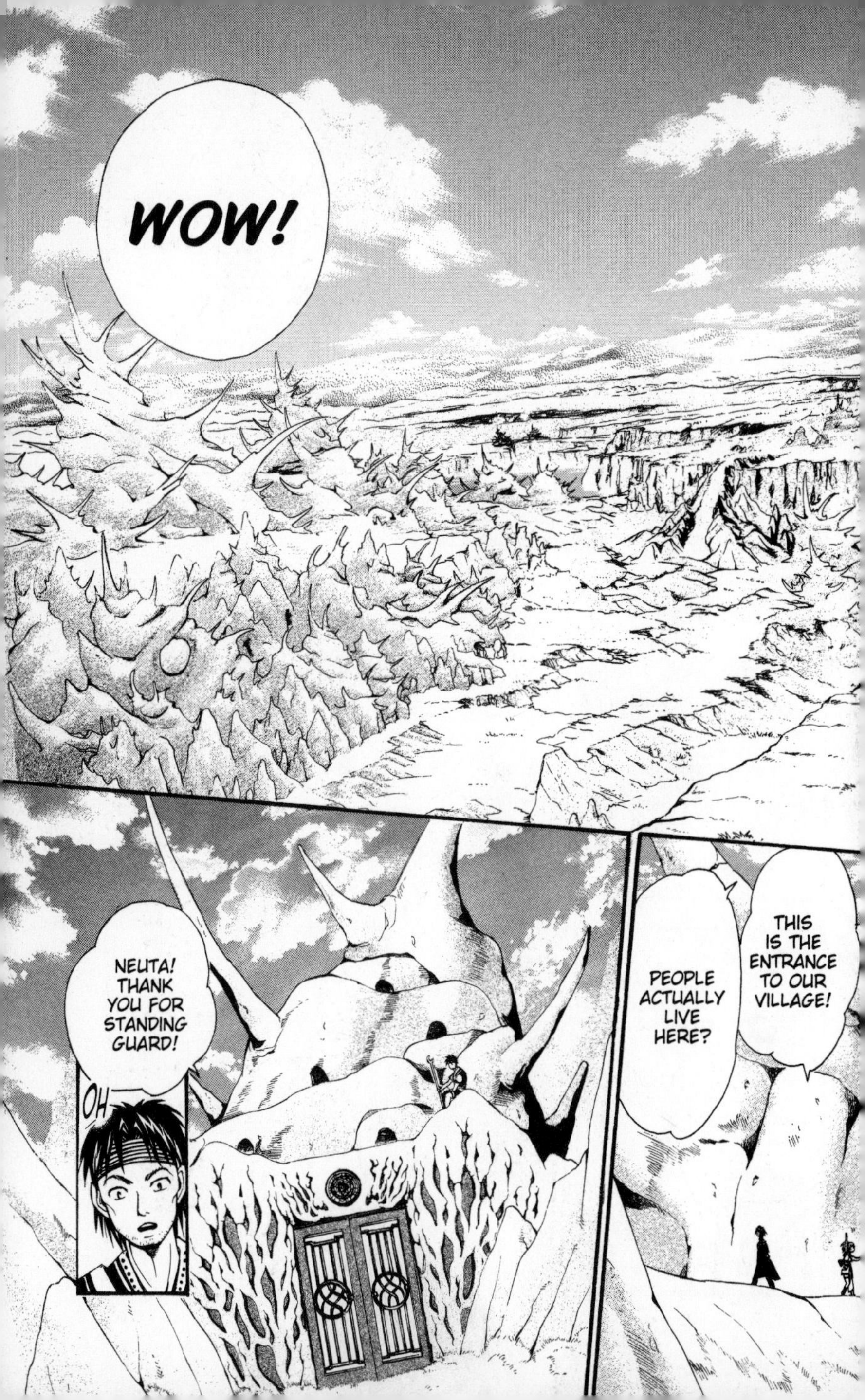
WOW!
THIS IS THE ENTRANCE TO OUR VILLAGE!
PEOPLE ACTUALLY LIVE HERE?
NEUTA! THANK YOU FOR STANDING GUARD!
OH

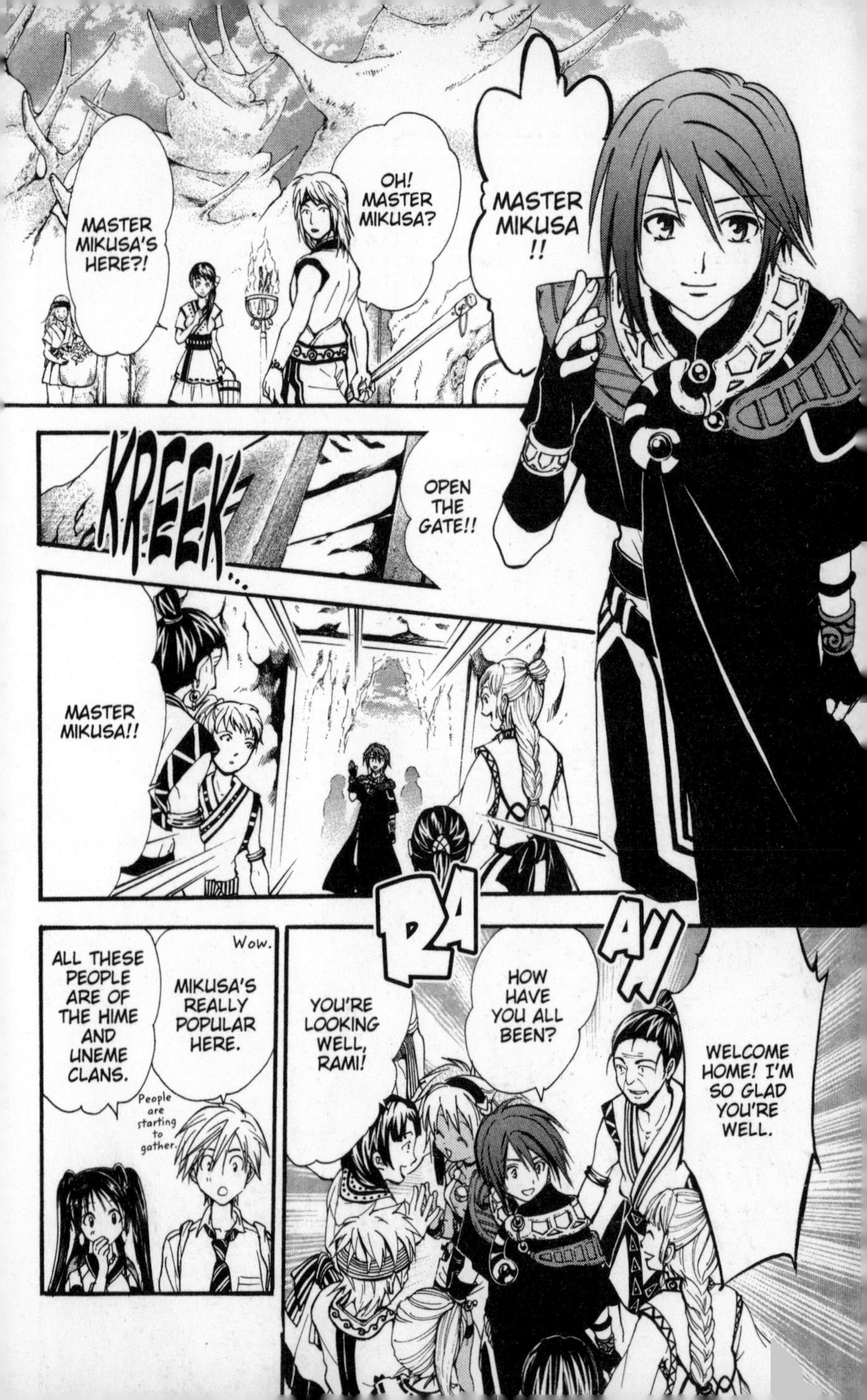
MASTER MIKUSA !!
OH! MASTER MIKUSA?
MASTER MIKUSA'S HERE?!
OPEN THE GATE!!
KREEK...
MASTER MIKUSA!!
RAAH
WELCOME HOME! I'M SO GLAD YOU'RE WELL.
HOW HAVE YOU ALL BEEN?
YOU'RE LOOKING WELL, RAMI!
Wow.
MIKUSA'S REALLY POPULAR HERE.
ALL THESE PEOPLE ARE OF THE HIME AND UNEME CLANS.
People are starting to gather.

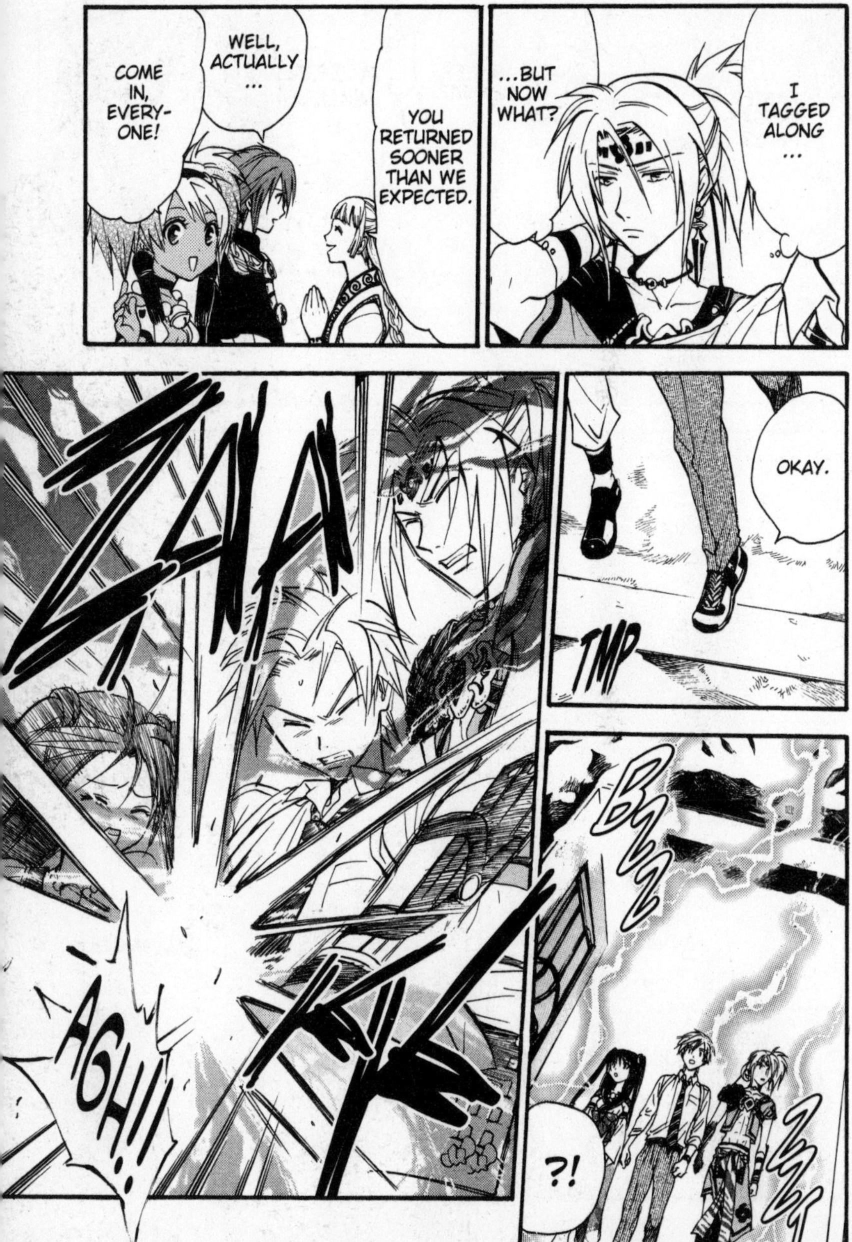
I TAGGED ALONG ...
...BUT NOW WHAT?
YOU RETURNED SOONER THAN WE EXPECTED.
WELL, ACTUALLY ...
COME IN, EVERY-ONE!
OKAY.
TMP
BZZ
?!
ZAP
AGH!!

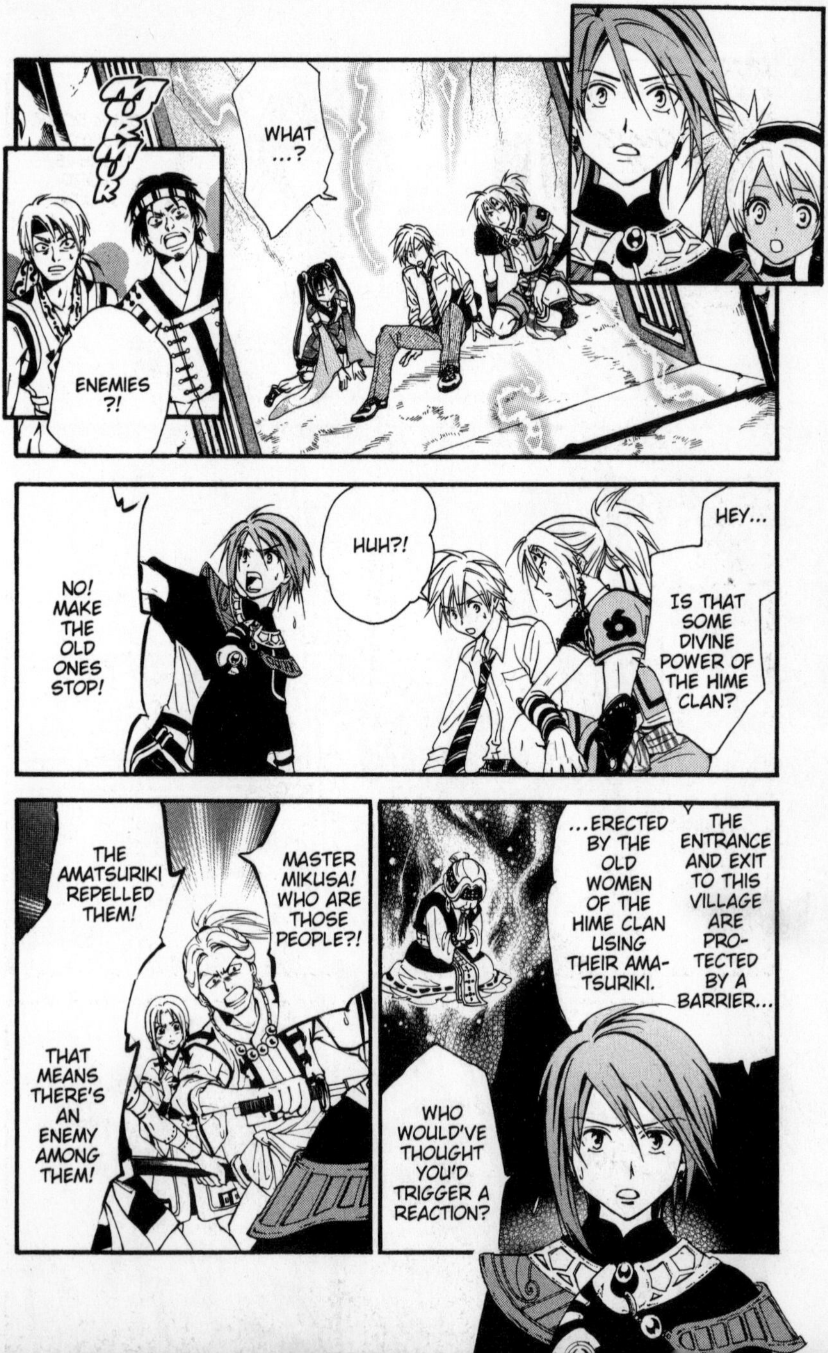
WHAT ...?
MURMUR
ENEMIES ?!
HEY...
IS THAT SOME DIVINE POWER OF THE HIME CLAN?
HUH?!
NO! MAKE THE OLD ONES STOP!
THE ENTRANCE AND EXIT TO THIS VILLAGE ARE PRO-TECTED BY A BARRIER...
...ERECTED BY THE OLD WOMEN OF THE HIME CLAN USING THEIR AMA-TSURIKI.
WHO WOULD'VE THOUGHT YOU'D TRIGGER A REACTION?
MASTER MIKUSA! WHO ARE THOSE PEOPLE?!
THE AMATSURIKI REPELLED THEM!
THAT MEANS THERE'S AN ENEMY AMONG THEM!

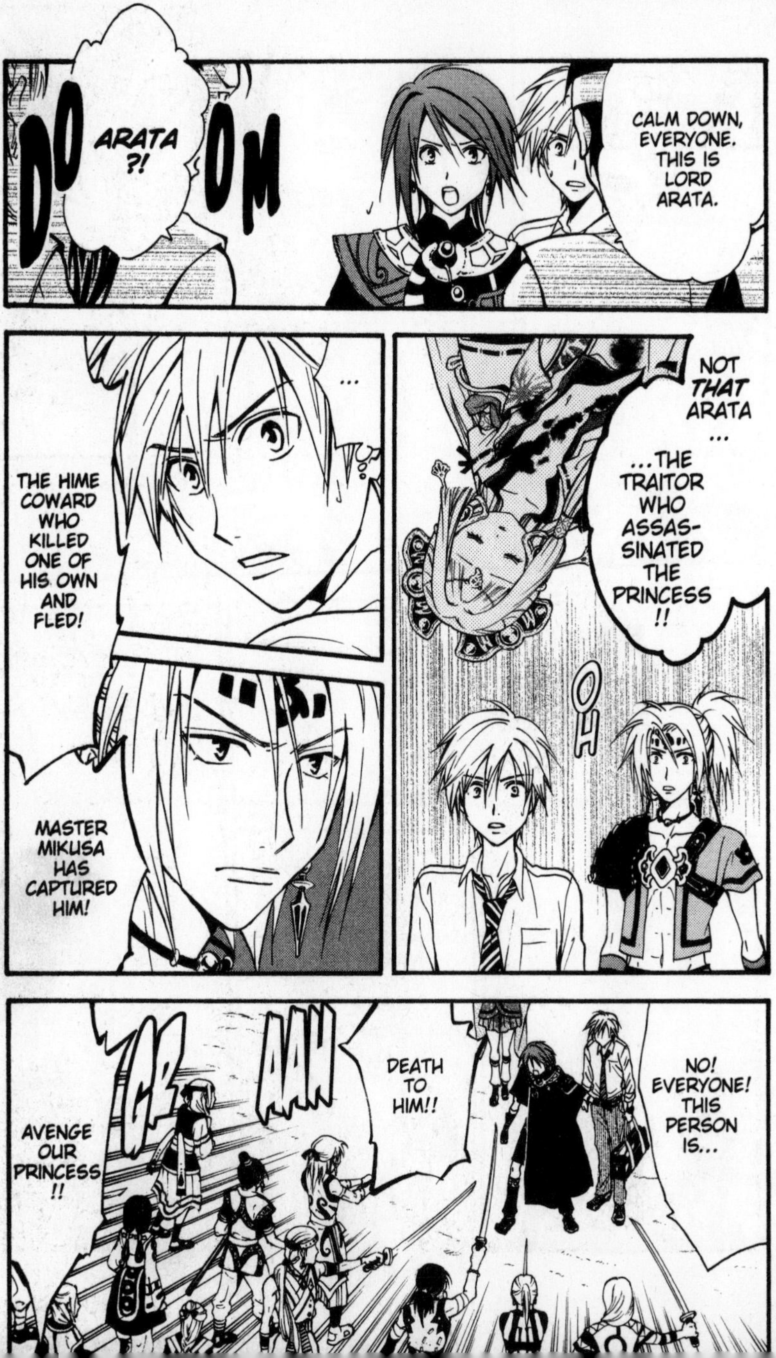
CALM DOWN, EVERYONE. THIS IS LORD ARATA.
ARATA ?!
DOOM
NOT THAT ARATA...
...THE TRAITOR WHO ASSAS-SINATED THE PRINCESS!!
OH
...
THE HIME COWARD WHO KILLED ONE OF HIS OWN AND FLED!
MASTER MIKUSA HAS CAPTURED HIM!
NO! EVERYONE! THIS PERSON IS...
DEATH TO HIM!!
CRAAH
AVENGE OUR PRINCESS!!

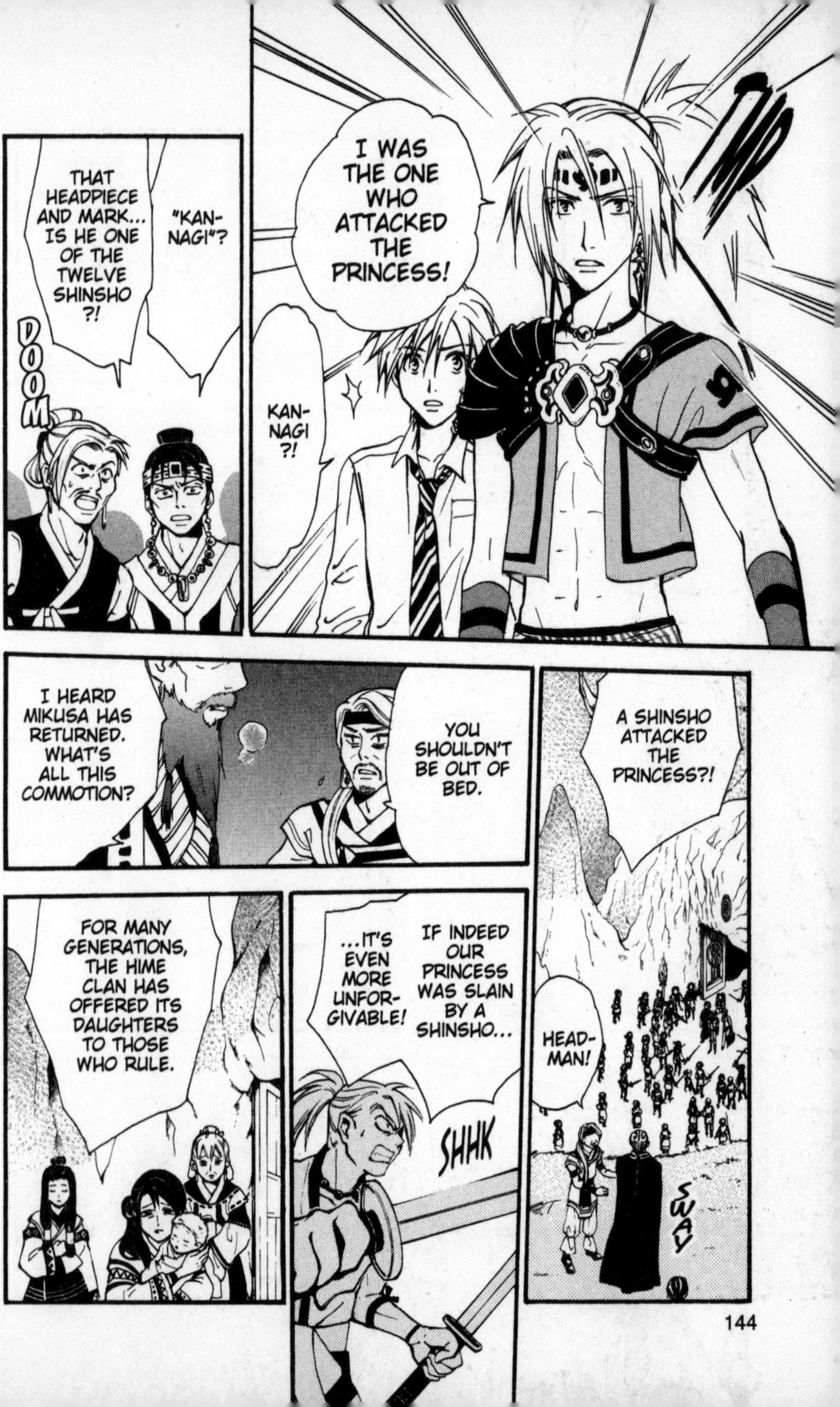

I WAS THE ONE WHO ATTACKED THE PRINCESS!
KAN-NAGI ?!
"KAN-NAGI"?
THAT HEADPIECE AND MARK... IS HE ONE OF THE TWELVE SHINSHO ?!
DOOM
A SHINSHO ATTACKED THE PRINCESS?!
HEAD-MAN!
SWAY
I HEARD MIKUSA HAS RETURNED. WHAT'S ALL THIS COMMOTION?
YOU SHOULDN'T BE OUT OF BED.
IF INDEED OUR PRINCESS WAS SLAIN BY A SHINSHO...
...IT'S EVEN MORE UNFORGIVABLE!
SHHK
FOR MANY GENERATIONS, THE HIME CLAN HAS OFFERED ITS DAUGHTERS TO THOSE WHO RULE.

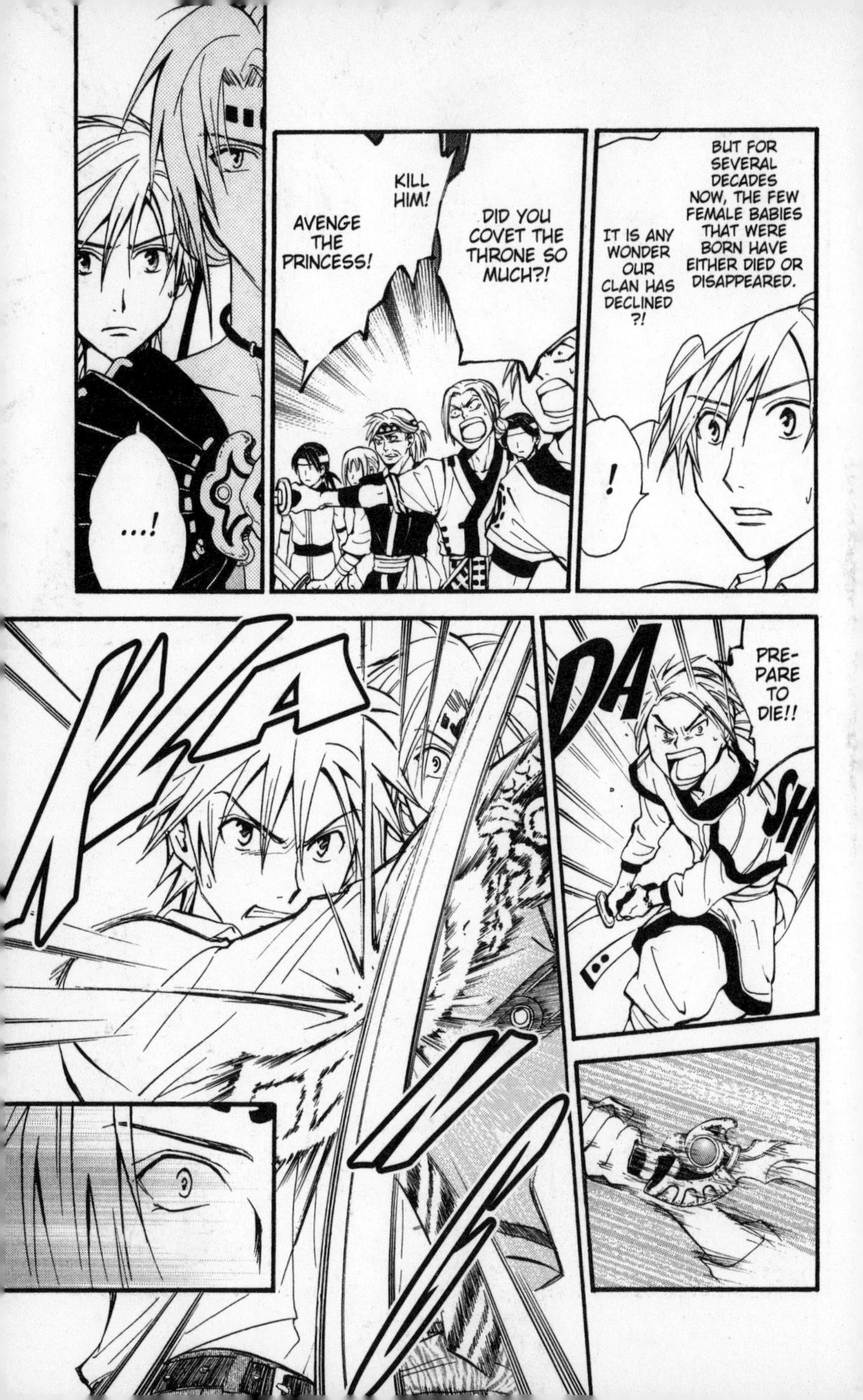
BUT FOR SEVERAL DECADES NOW, THE FEW FEMALE BABIES THAT WERE BORN HAVE EITHER DIED OR DISAPPEARED.
IT IS ANY WONDER OUR CLAN HAS DECLINED ?!
!
DID YOU COVET THE THRONE SO MUCH?!
KILL HIM!
AVENGE THE PRINCESS!
...!
PRE-PARE TO DIE!!
DA
SH
KA

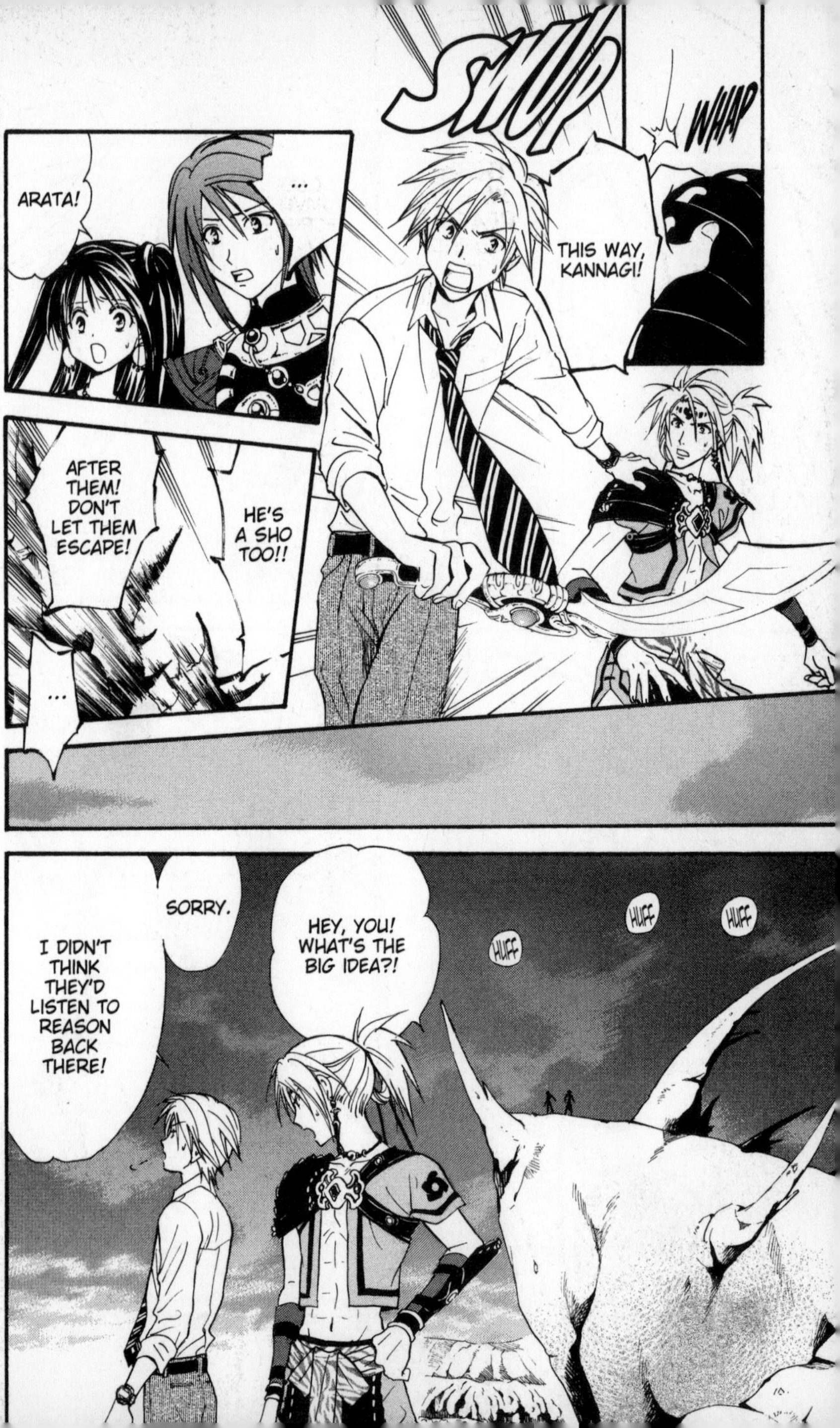
WHAP
SWOP
THIS WAY, KANNAGI!
...
ARATA!
HE'S A SHO TOO!!
AFTER THEM! DON'T LET THEM ESCAPE!
...
HUFF
HUFF
HUFF
HEY, YOU! WHAT'S THE BIG IDEA?!
SORRY.
I DIDN'T THINK THEY'D LISTEN TO REASON BACK THERE!

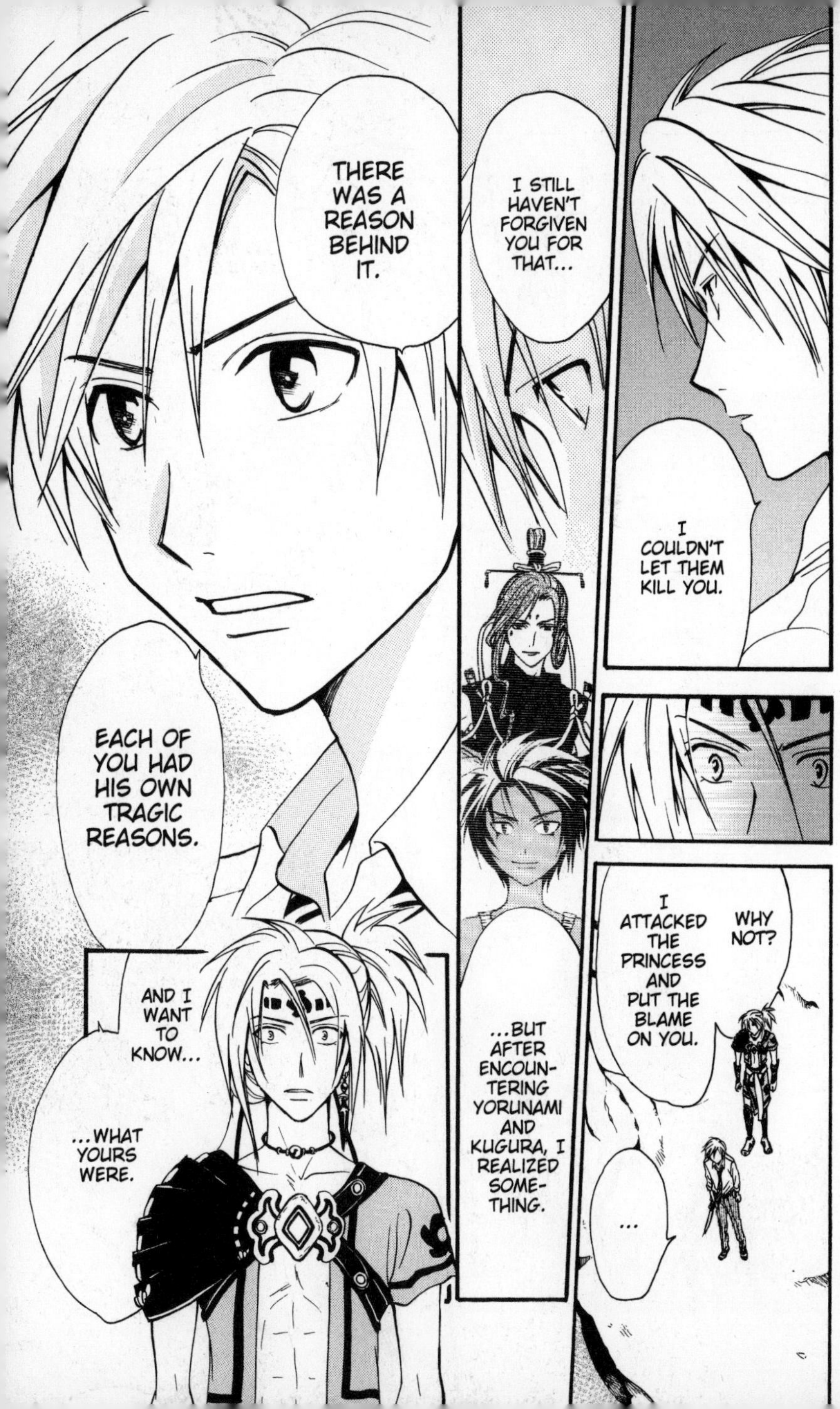
I COULDN'T LET THEM KILL YOU.
WHY NOT?
I ATTACKED THE PRINCESS AND PUT THE BLAME ON YOU.
...
I STILL HAVEN'T FORGIVEN YOU FOR THAT...
...BUT AFTER ENCOUN-TERING YORUNAMI AND KUGURA, I REALIZED SOME-THING.
THERE WAS A REASON BEHIND IT.
EACH OF YOU HAD HIS OWN TRAGIC REASONS.
AND I WANT TO KNOW...
...WHAT YOURS WERE.

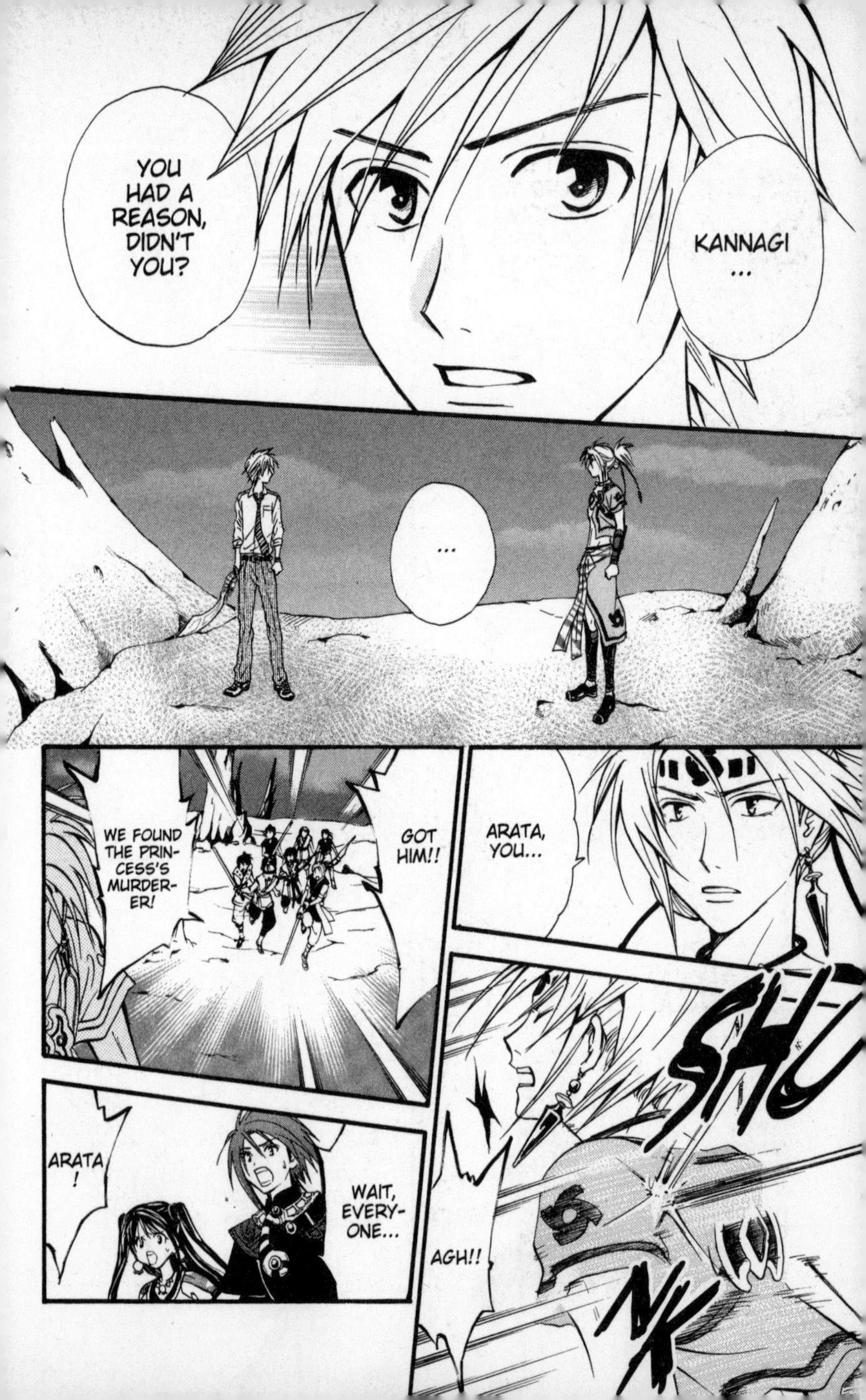

KANNAGI ...
YOU HAD A REASON, DIDN'T YOU?
...
ARATA, YOU...
GOT HIM!!
WE FOUND THE PRIN-CESS'S MURDER-ER!
SHUNK
AGH!!
WAIT, EVERY-ONE...
ARATA!

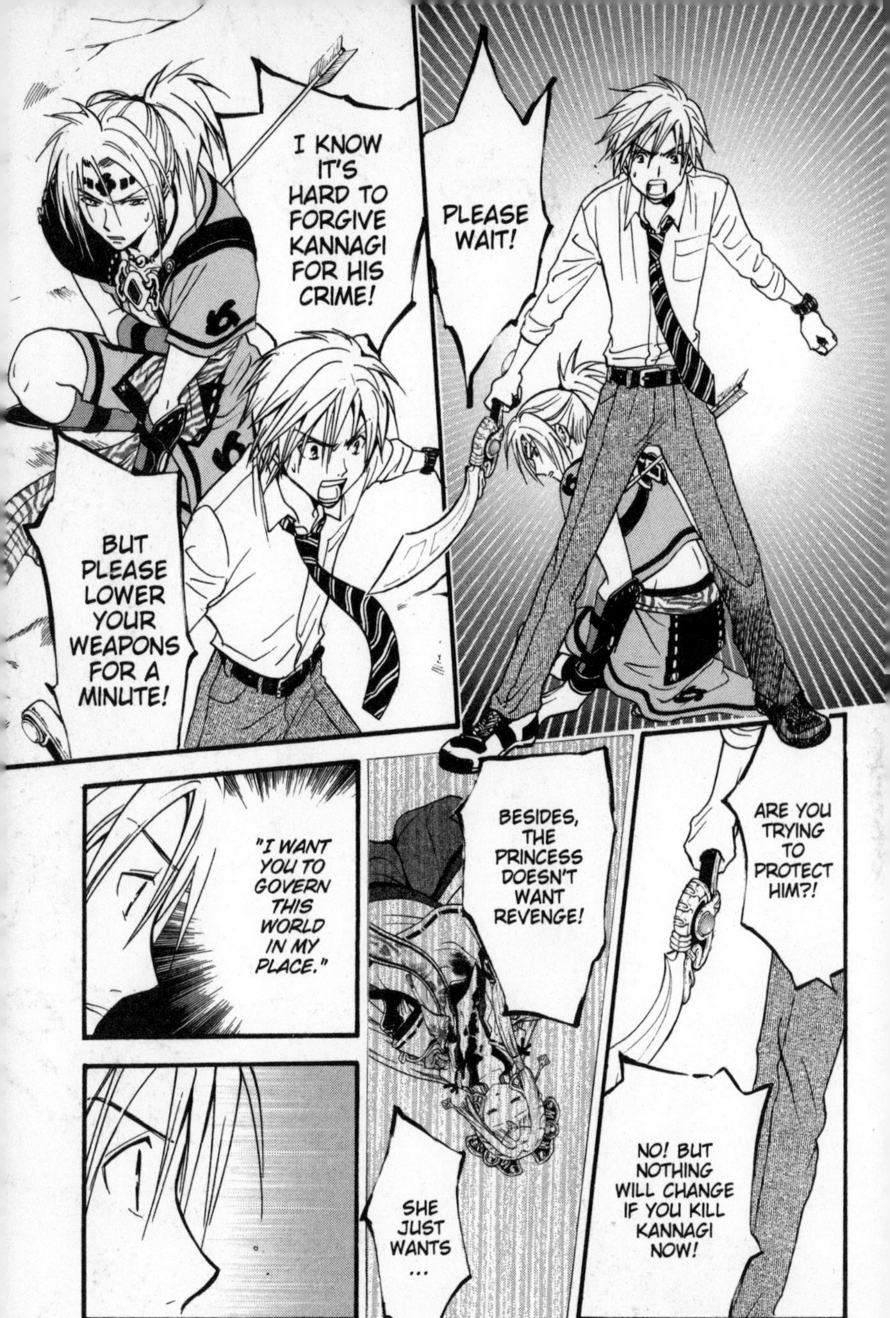
PLEASE WAIT!
I KNOW IT'S HARD TO FORGIVE KANNAGI FOR HIS CRIME!
BUT PLEASE LOWER YOUR WEAPONS FOR A MINUTE!
ARE YOU TRYING TO PROTECT HIM?!
NO! BUT NOTHING WILL CHANGE IF YOU KILL KANNAGI NOW!
BESIDES, THE PRINCESS DOESN'T WANT REVENGE!
SHE JUST WANTS ...
"I WANT YOU TO GOVERN THIS WORLD IN MY PLACE."

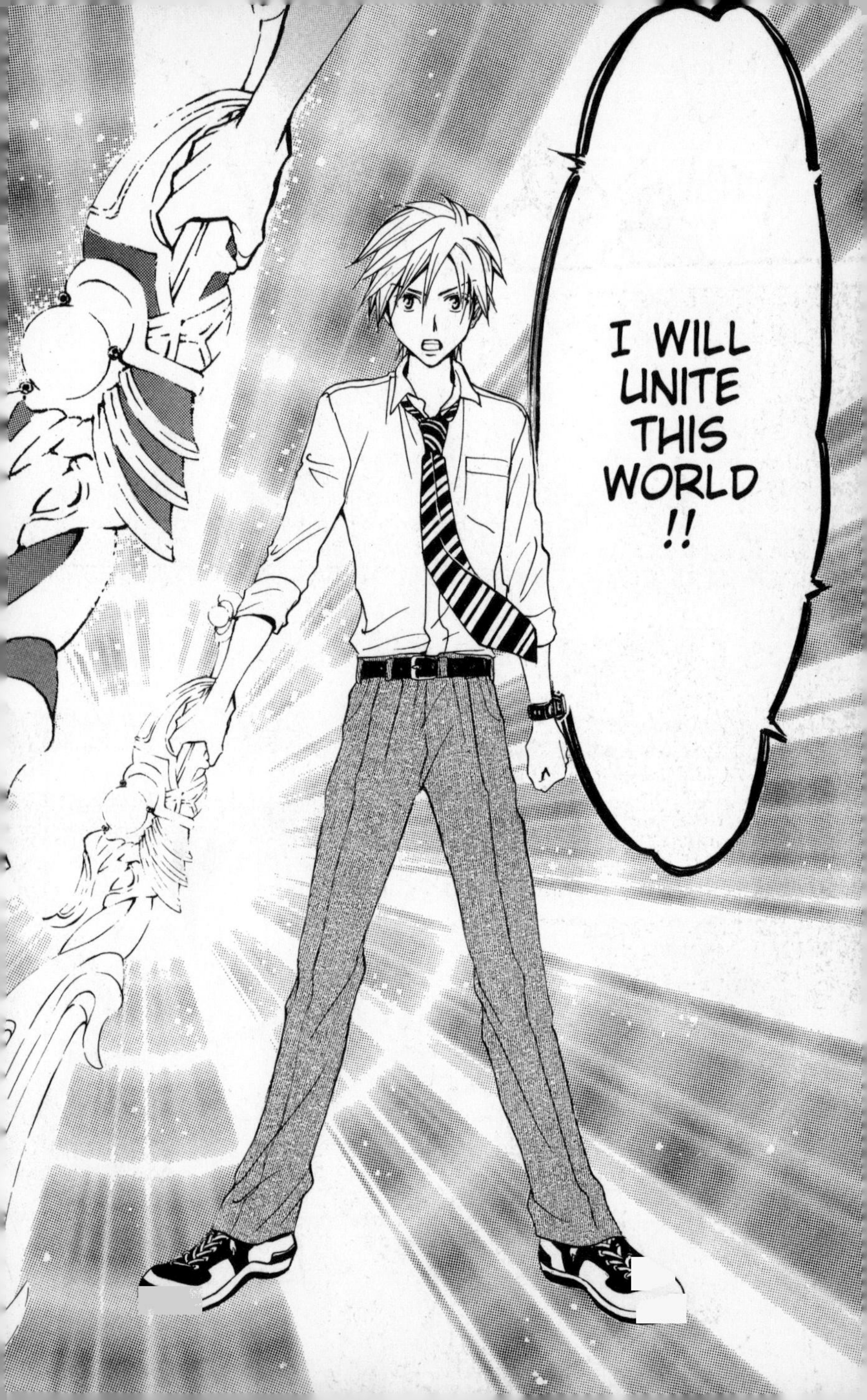
I WILL UNITE THIS WORLD !!

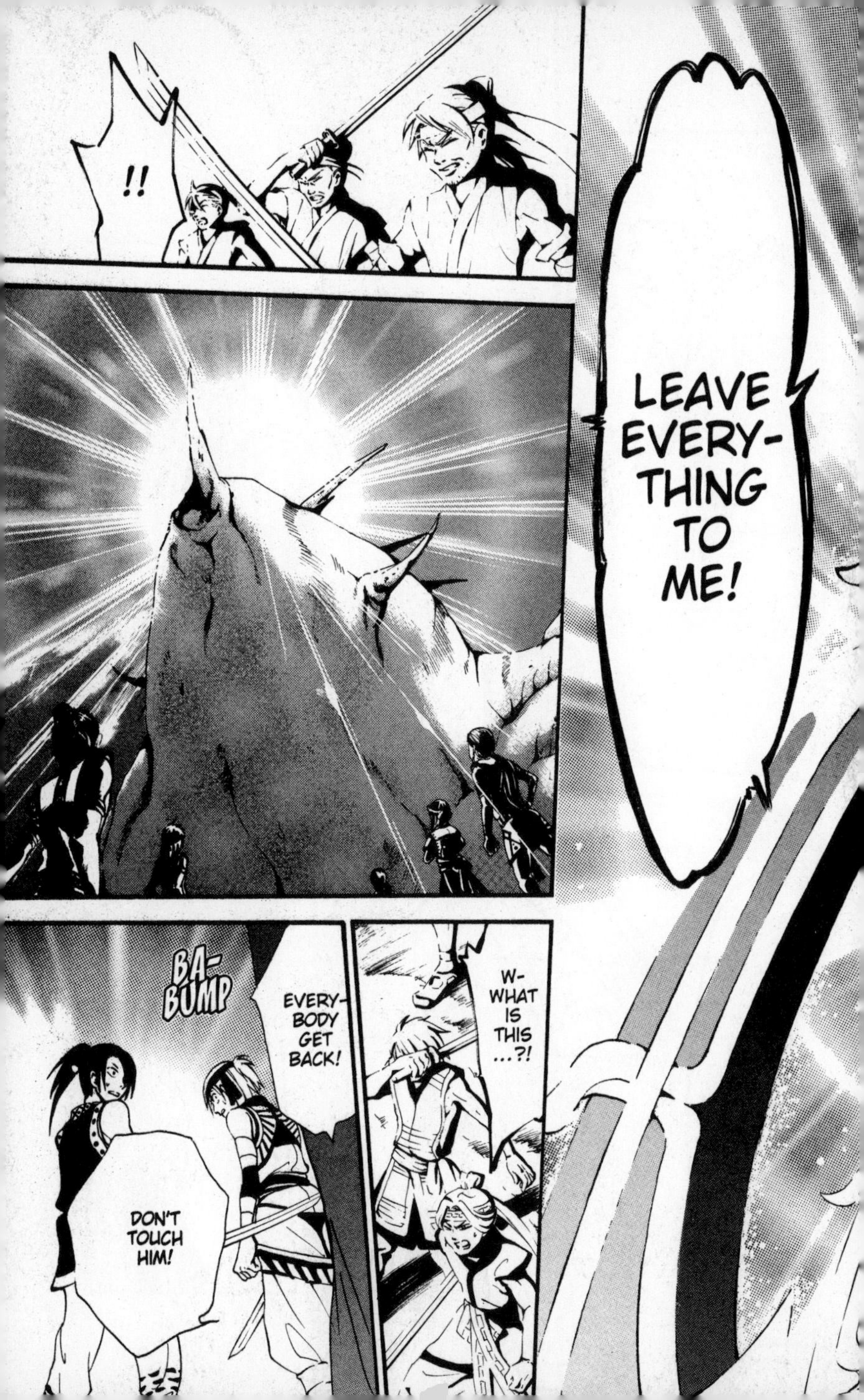
LEAVE EVERY-THING TO ME!
!!
W-WHAT IS THIS ...?!
BA-BUMP
EVERY-BODY GET BACK!
DON'T TOUCH HIM!

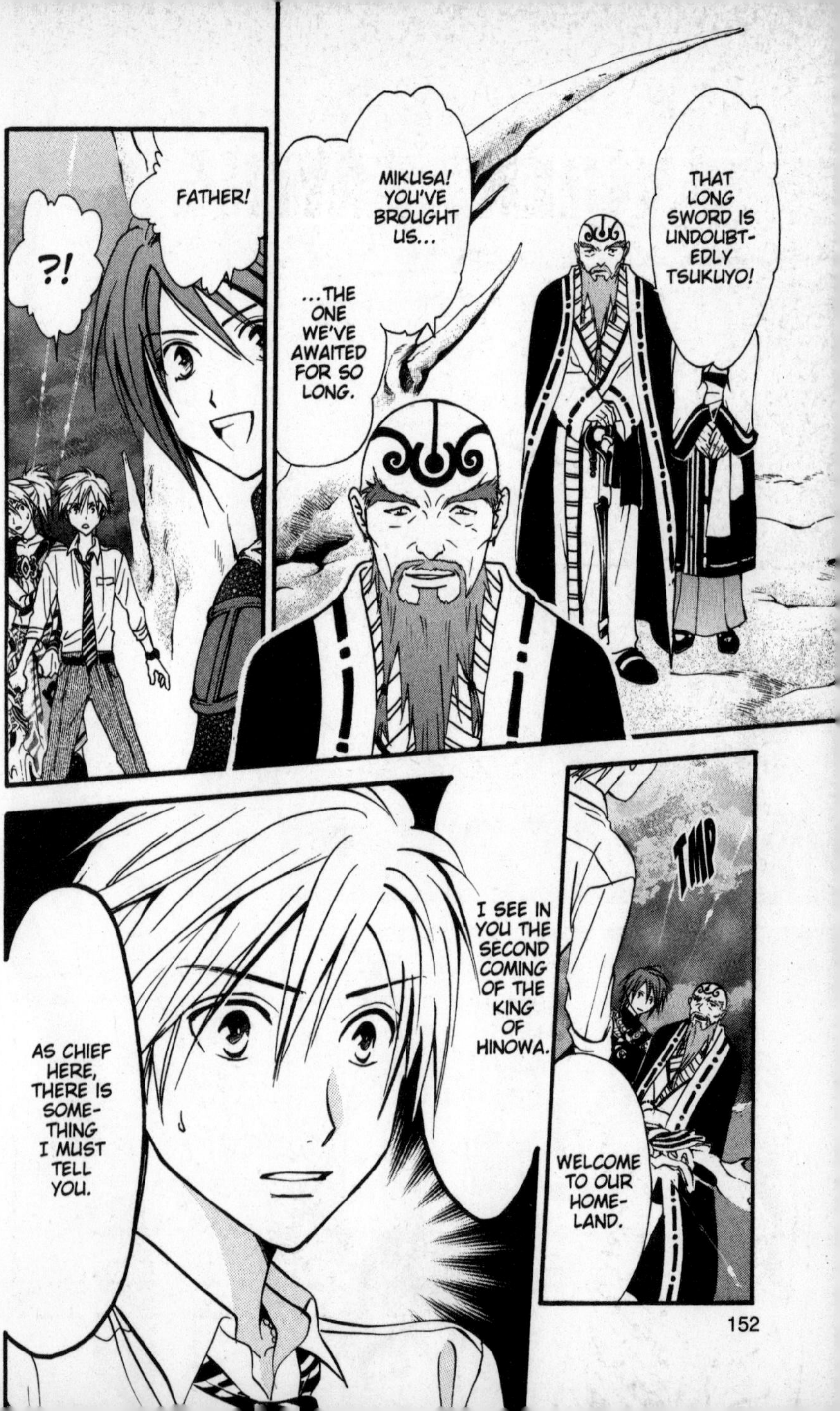
THAT LONG SWORD IS UNDOUBTEDLY TSUKUYO!
MIKUSA! YOU'VE BROUGHT US...
...THE ONE WE'VE AWAITED FOR SO LONG.
FATHER!
?!
TMP
WELCOME TO OUR HOMELAND.
I SEE IN YOU THE SECOND COMING OF THE KING OF HINOWA.
AS CHIEF HERE, THERE IS SOMETHING I MUST TELL YOU.

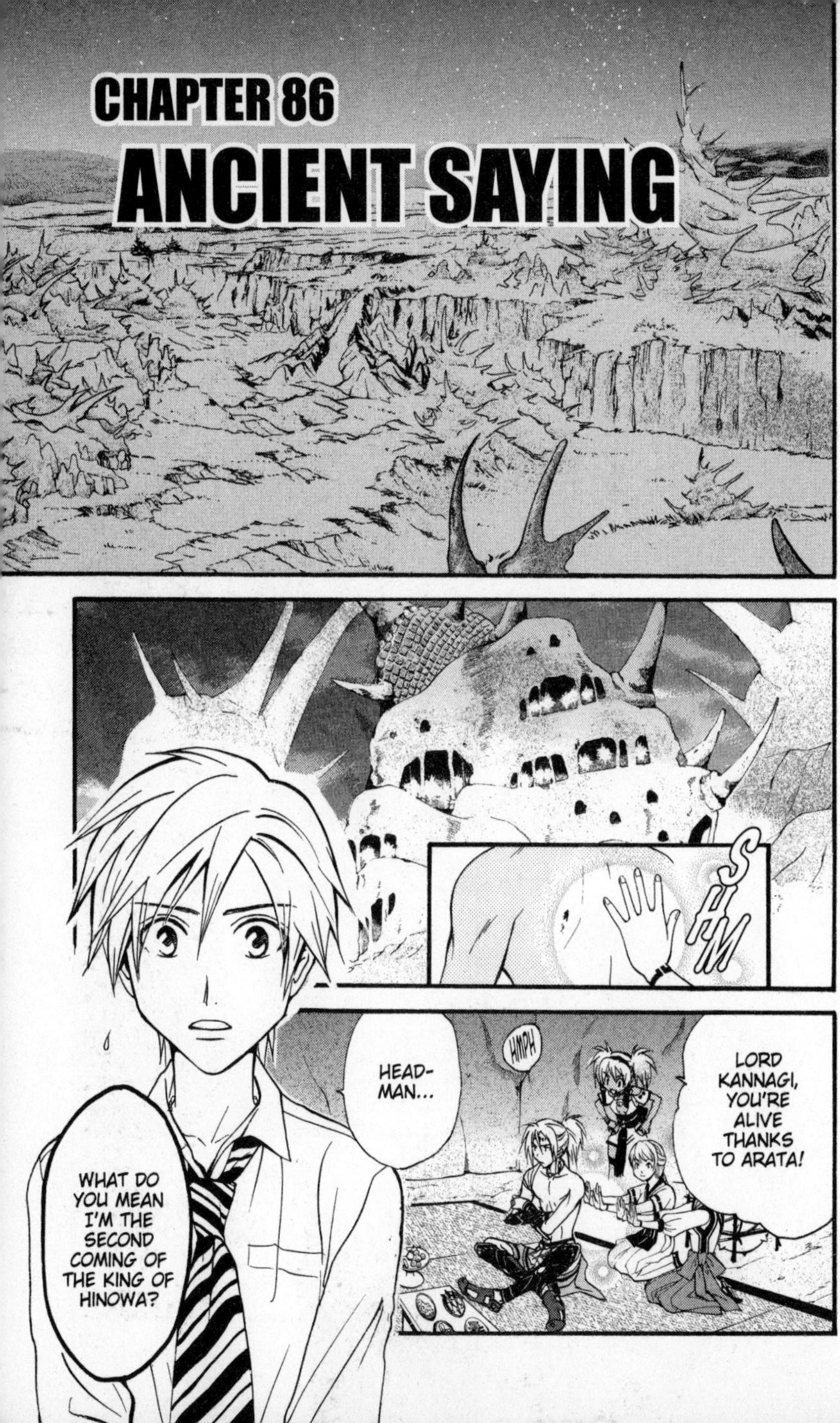
CHAPTER 86
ANCIENT SAYING
SHM
LORD KANNAGI, YOU'RE ALIVE THANKS TO ARATA!
HMPH
HEAD-MAN...
WHAT DO YOU MEAN I'M THE SECOND COMING OF THE KING OF HINOWA?

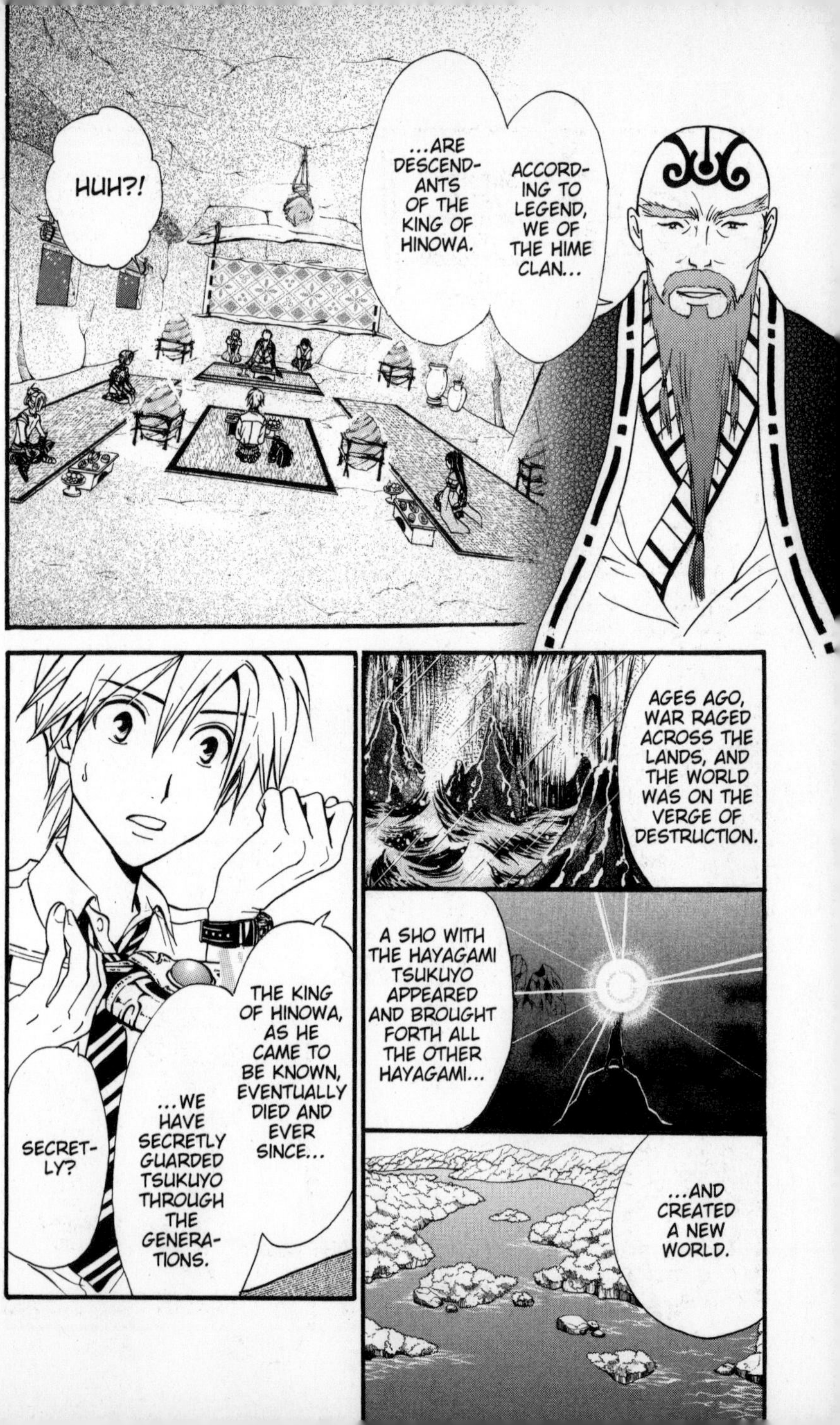
ACCORD-ING TO LEGEND, WE OF THE HIME CLAN...
...ARE DESCEND-ANTS OF THE KING OF HINOWA.
HUH?!
AGES AGO, WAR RAGED ACROSS THE LANDS, AND THE WORLD WAS ON THE VERGE OF DESTRUCTION.
A SHO WITH THE HAYAGAMI TSUKUYO APPEARED AND BROUGHT FORTH ALL THE OTHER HAYAGAMI...
...AND CREATED A NEW WORLD.
THE KING OF HINOWA, AS HE CAME TO BE KNOWN, EVENTUALLY DIED AND EVER SINCE...
...WE HAVE SECRETLY GUARDED TSUKUYO THROUGH THE GENERA-TIONS.
SECRET-LY?

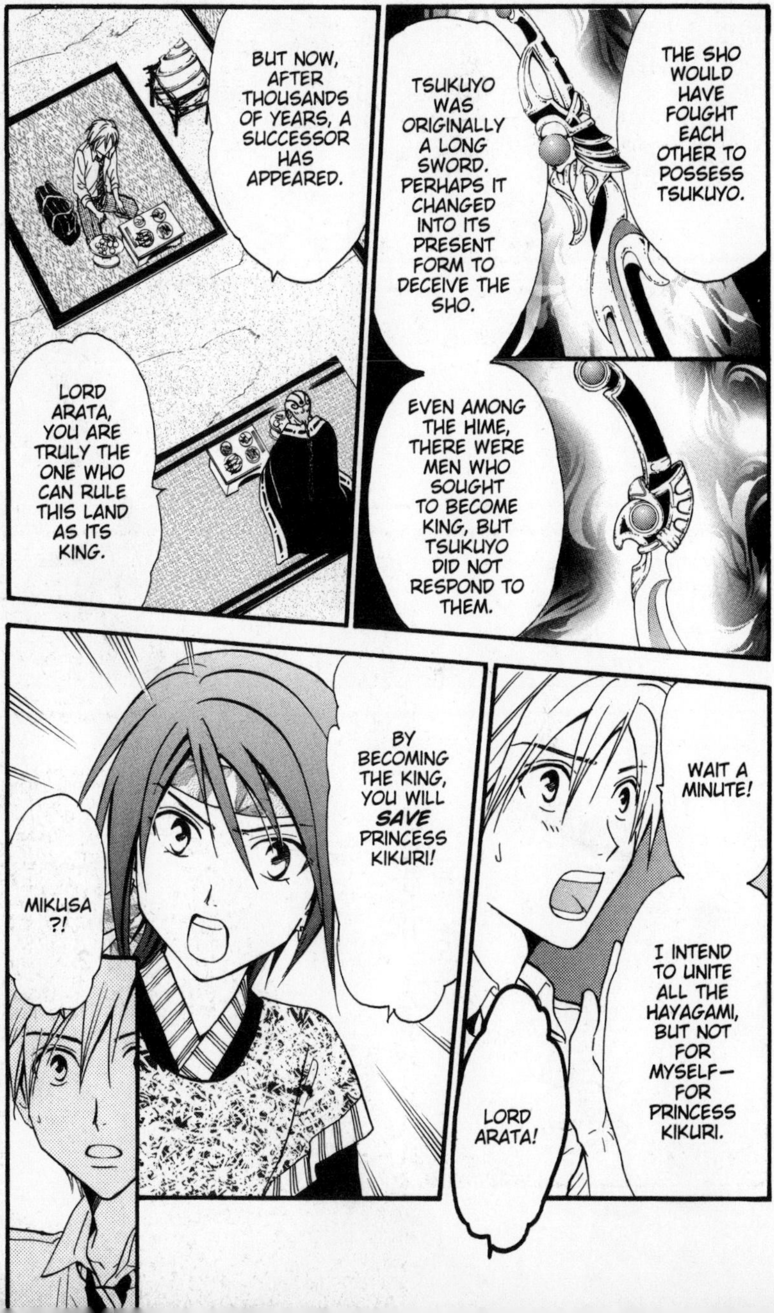
THE SHO WOULD HAVE FOUGHT EACH OTHER TO POSSESS TSUKUYO.
TSUKUYO WAS ORIGINALLY A LONG SWORD. PERHAPS IT CHANGED INTO ITS PRESENT FORM TO DECEIVE THE SHO.
EVEN AMONG THE HIME, THERE WERE MEN WHO SOUGHT TO BECOME KING, BUT TSUKUYO DID NOT RESPOND TO THEM.
BUT NOW, AFTER THOUSANDS OF YEARS, A SUCCESSOR HAS APPEARED.
LORD ARATA, YOU ARE TRULY THE ONE WHO CAN RULE THIS LAND AS ITS KING.
WAIT A MINUTE!
I INTEND TO UNITE ALL THE HAYAGAMI, BUT NOT FOR MYSELF—FOR PRINCESS KIKURI.
LORD ARATA!
BY BECOMING THE KING, YOU WILL *SAVE* PRINCESS KIKURI!
MIKUSA ?!

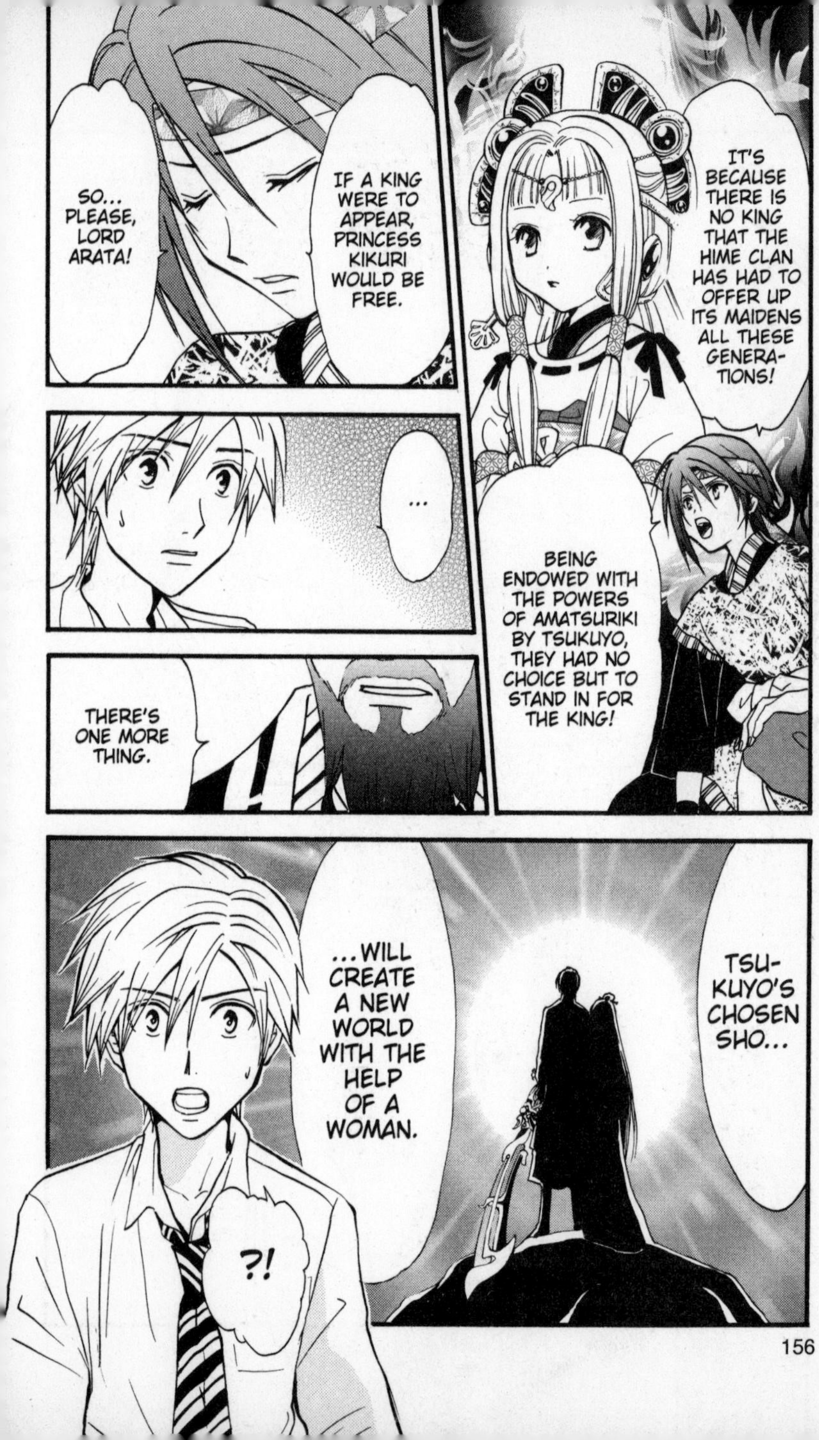
IT'S BECAUSE THERE IS NO KING THAT THE HIME CLAN HAS HAD TO OFFER UP ITS MAIDENS ALL THESE GENERATIONS!
BEING ENDOWED WITH THE POWERS OF AMATSURIKI BY TSUKUYO, THEY HAD NO CHOICE BUT TO STAND IN FOR THE KING!
IF A KING WERE TO APPEAR, PRINCESS KIKURI WOULD BE FREE.
SO... PLEASE, LORD ARATA!
...
THERE'S ONE MORE THING.
TSU-KUYO'S CHOSEN SHO...
...WILL CREATE A NEW WORLD WITH THE HELP OF A WOMAN.
?!

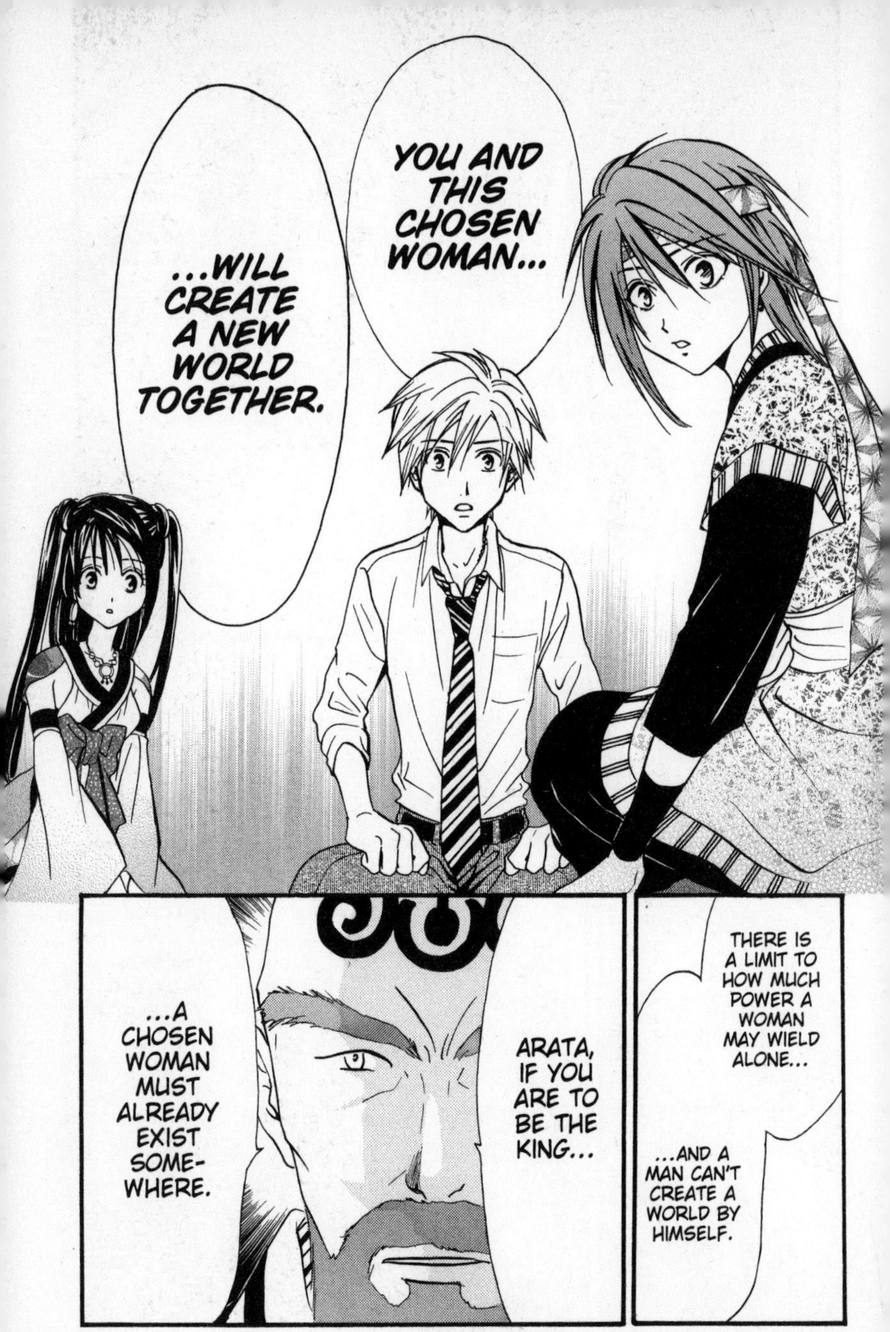
YOU AND THIS CHOSEN WOMAN...
...WILL CREATE A NEW WORLD TOGETHER.
THERE IS A LIMIT TO HOW MUCH POWER A WOMAN MAY WIELD ALONE...
...AND A MAN CAN'T CREATE A WORLD BY HIMSELF.
ARATA, IF YOU ARE TO BE THE KING...
...A CHOSEN WOMAN MUST ALREADY EXIST SOME-WHERE.

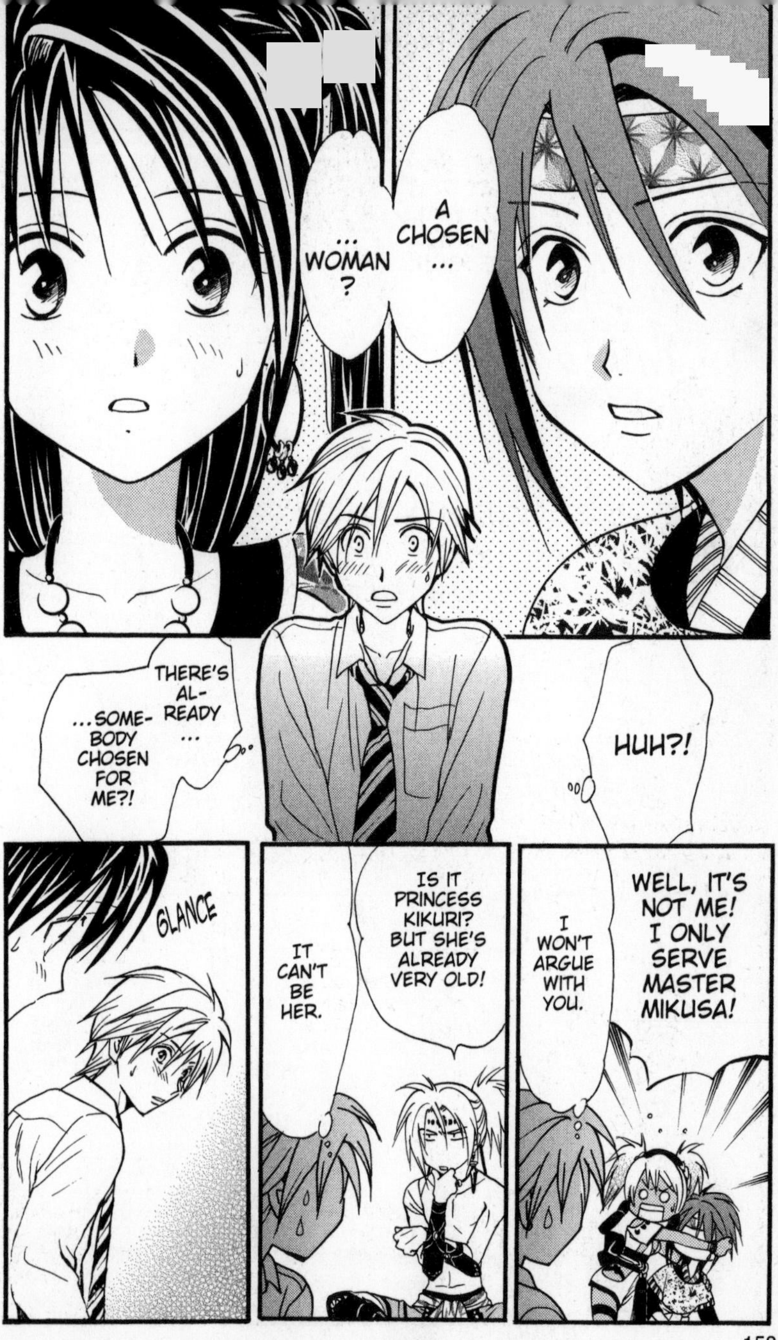
A CHOSEN ...
... WOMAN ?
HUH?!
THERE'S AL- READY ... ...SOME- BODY CHOSEN FOR ME?!
WELL, IT'S NOT ME! I ONLY SERVE MASTER MIKUSA!
I WON'T ARGUE WITH YOU.
IS IT PRINCESS KIKURI? BUT SHE'S ALREADY VERY OLD!
IT CAN'T BE HER.
GLANCE

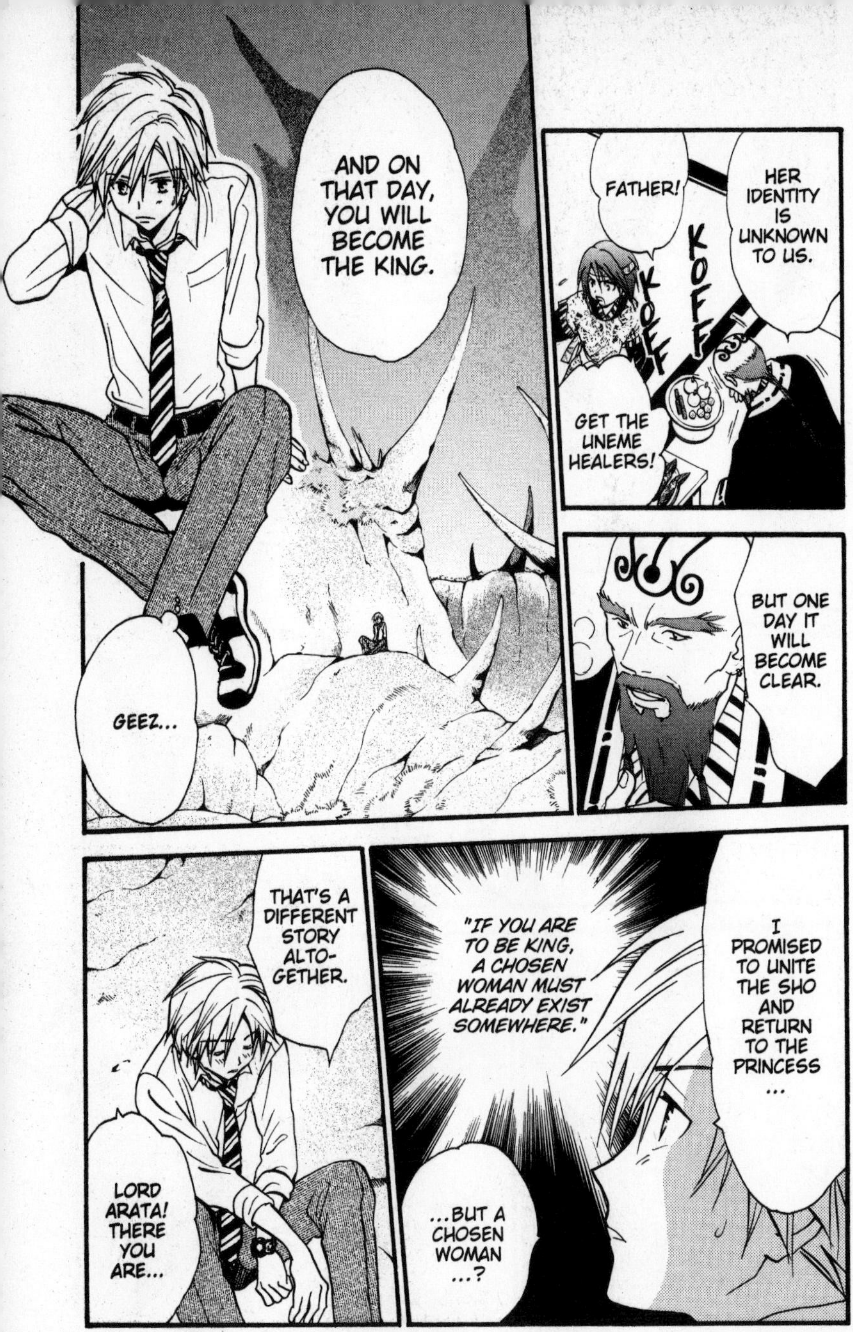
HER IDENTITY IS UNKNOWN TO US.
FATHER!
KOFF KOFF
GET THE UNEME HEALERS!
BUT ONE DAY IT WILL BECOME CLEAR.
AND ON THAT DAY, YOU WILL BECOME THE KING.
GEEZ...
I PROMISED TO UNITE THE SHO AND RETURN TO THE PRINCESS...
"IF YOU ARE TO BE KING, A CHOSEN WOMAN MUST ALREADY EXIST SOMEWHERE."
...BUT A CHOSEN WOMAN...?
THAT'S A DIFFERENT STORY ALTO-GETHER.
LORD ARATA! THERE YOU ARE...

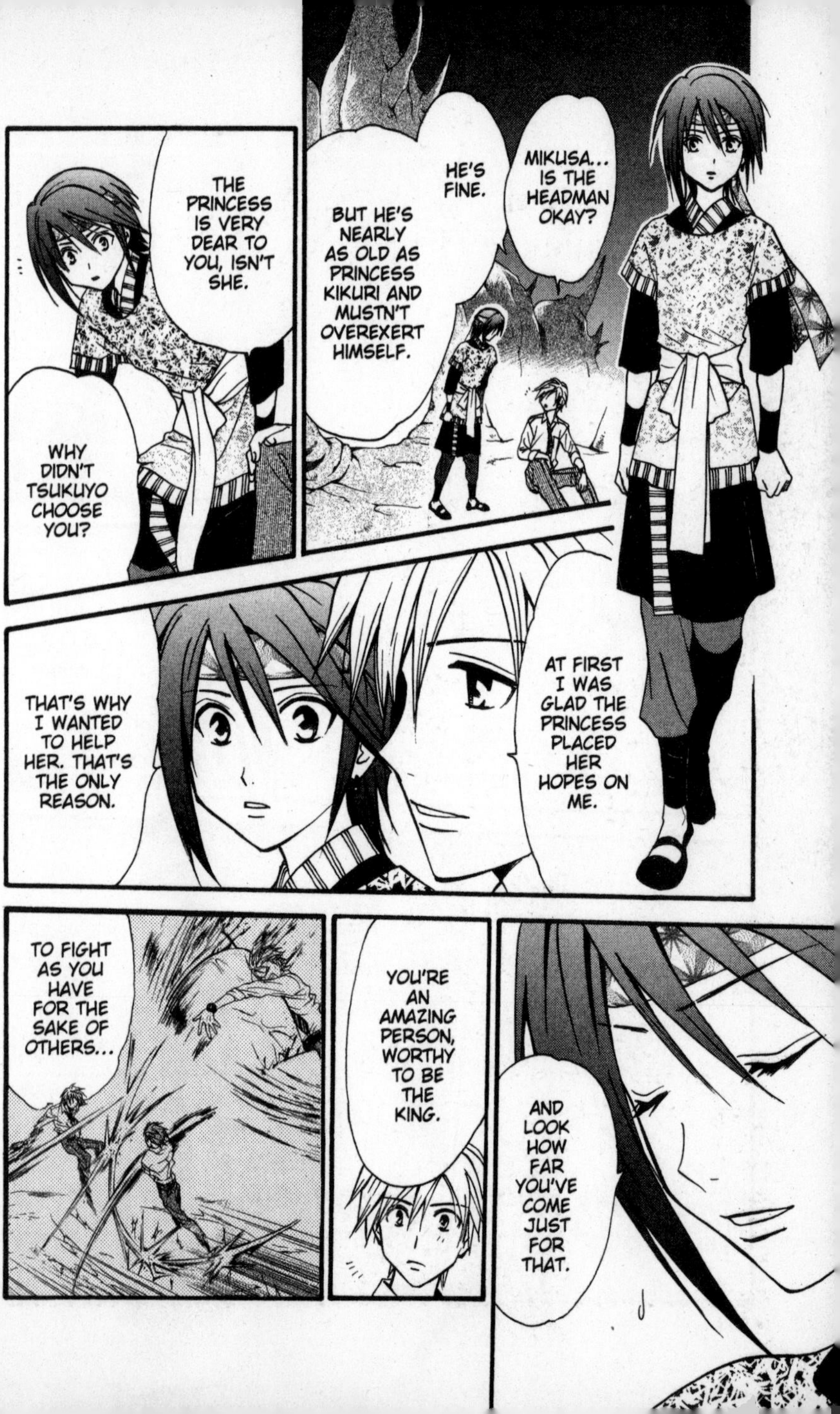
MIKUSA... IS THE HEADMAN OKAY?
HE'S FINE.
BUT HE'S NEARLY AS OLD AS PRINCESS KIKURI AND MUSTN'T OVEREXERT HIMSELF.
THE PRINCESS IS VERY DEAR TO YOU, ISN'T SHE.
WHY DIDN'T TSUKUYO CHOOSE YOU?
AT FIRST I WAS GLAD THE PRINCESS PLACED HER HOPES ON ME.
THAT'S WHY I WANTED TO HELP HER. THAT'S THE ONLY REASON.
AND LOOK HOW FAR YOU'VE COME JUST FOR THAT.
YOU'RE AN AMAZING PERSON, WORTHY TO BE THE KING.
TO FIGHT AS YOU HAVE FOR THE SAKE OF OTHERS...

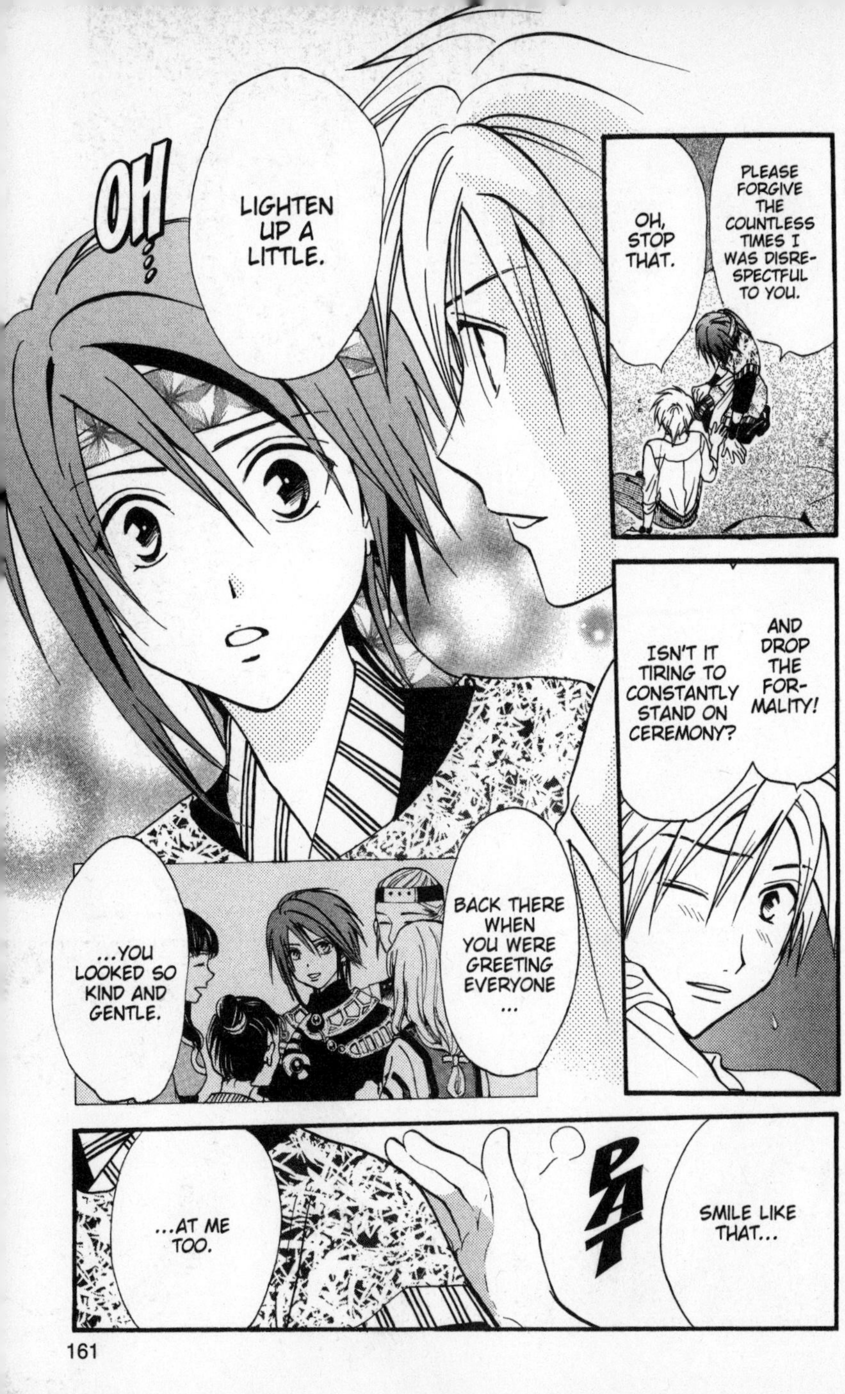
PLEASE FORGIVE THE COUNTLESS TIMES I WAS DISRE-SPECTFUL TO YOU.
OH, STOP THAT.
AND DROP THE FOR-MALITY!
ISN'T IT TIRING TO CONSTANTLY STAND ON CEREMONY?
OH
LIGHTEN UP A LITTLE.
BACK THERE WHEN YOU WERE GREETING EVERYONE ...
...YOU LOOKED SO KIND AND GENTLE.
SMILE LIKE THAT...
PAT
...AT ME TOO.

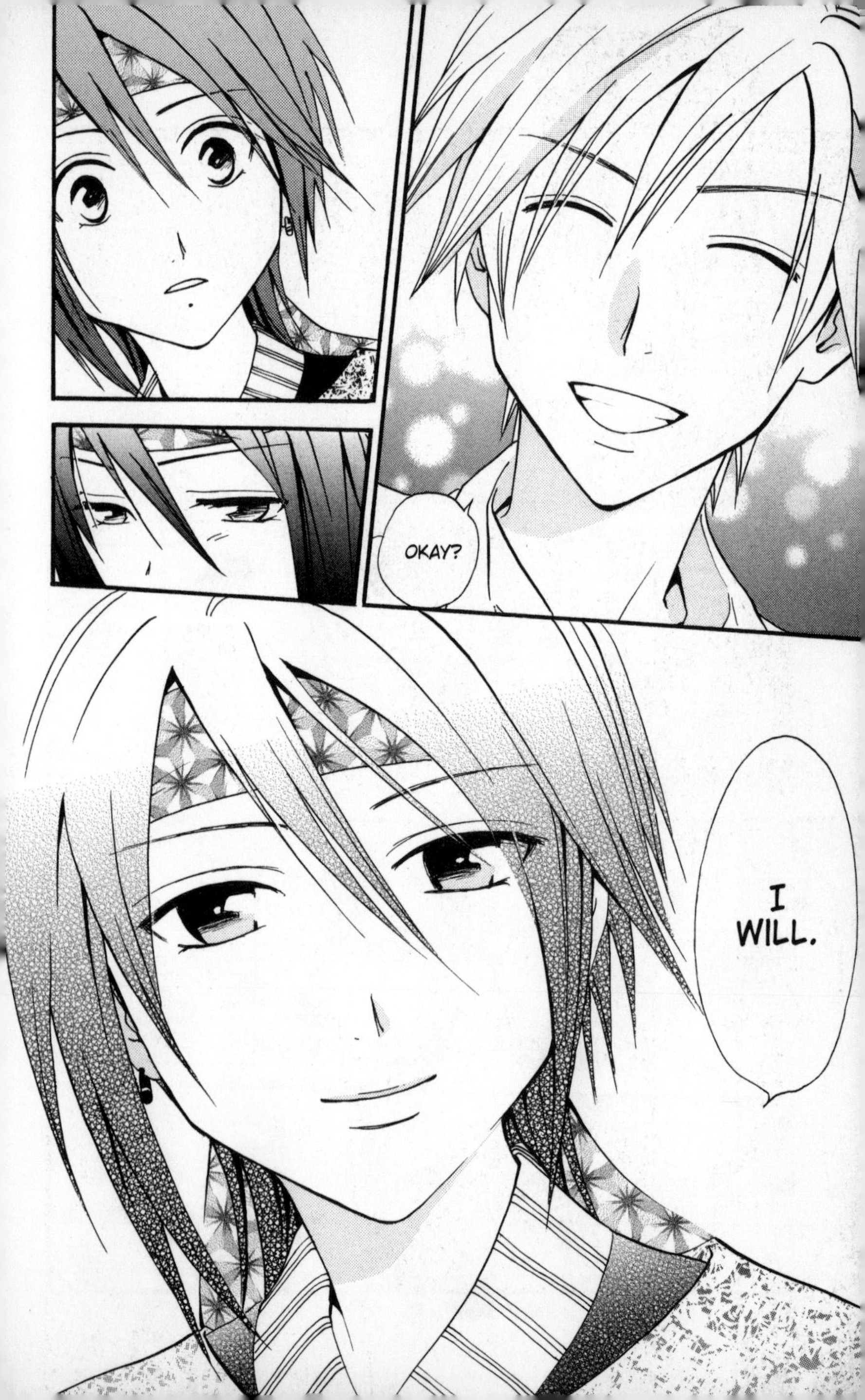
OKAY?
I WILL.

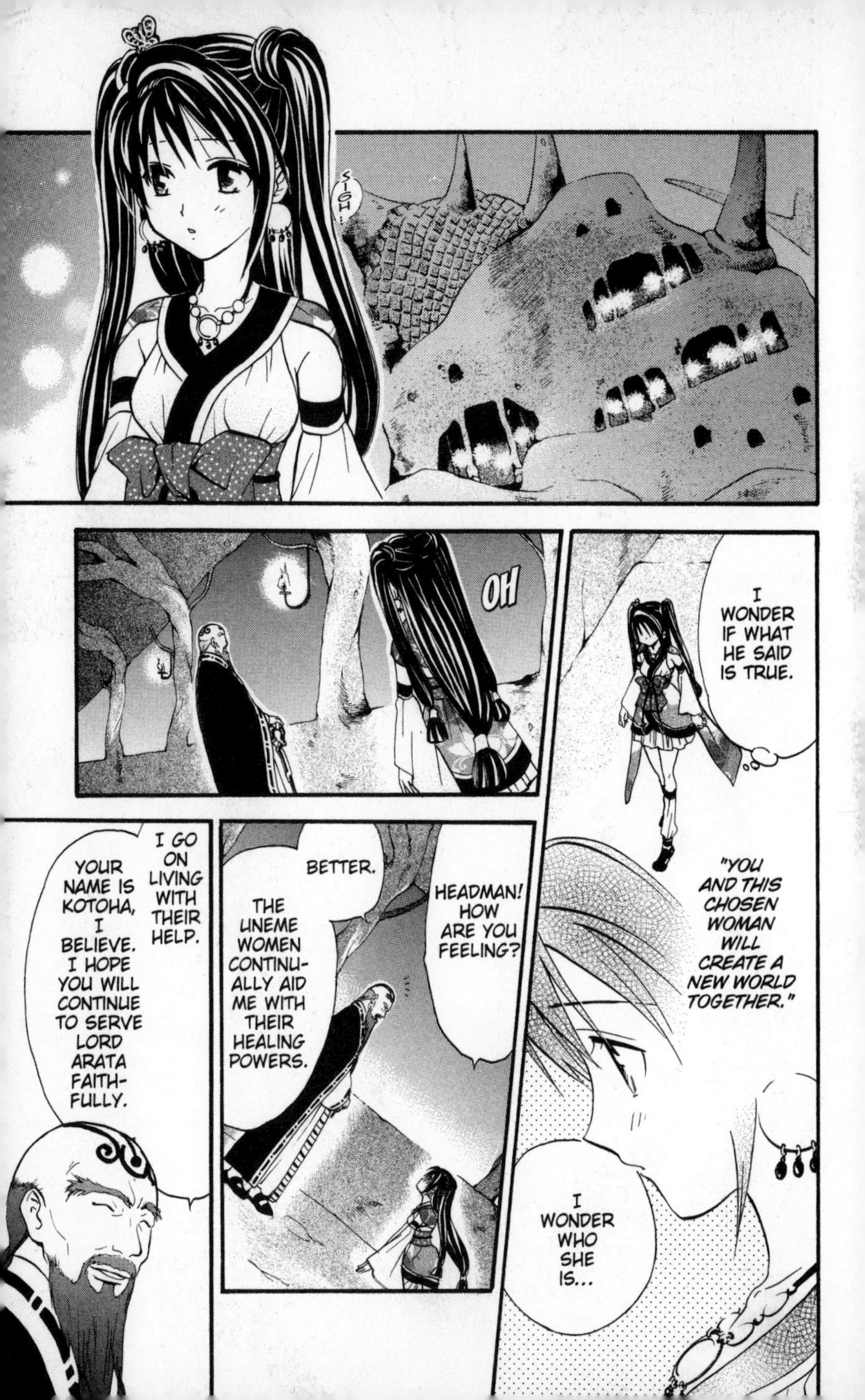
SIGH...
I WONDER IF WHAT HE SAID IS TRUE.
"YOU AND THIS CHOSEN WOMAN WILL CREATE A NEW WORLD TOGETHER."
I WONDER WHO SHE IS...
OH
HEADMAN! HOW ARE YOU FEELING?
BETTER.
THE UNEME WOMEN CONTINU-ALLY AID ME WITH THEIR HEALING POWERS.
I GO ON LIVING WITH THEIR HELP.
YOUR NAME IS KOTOHA, I BELIEVE. I HOPE YOU WILL CONTINUE TO SERVE LORD ARATA FAITH-FULLY.

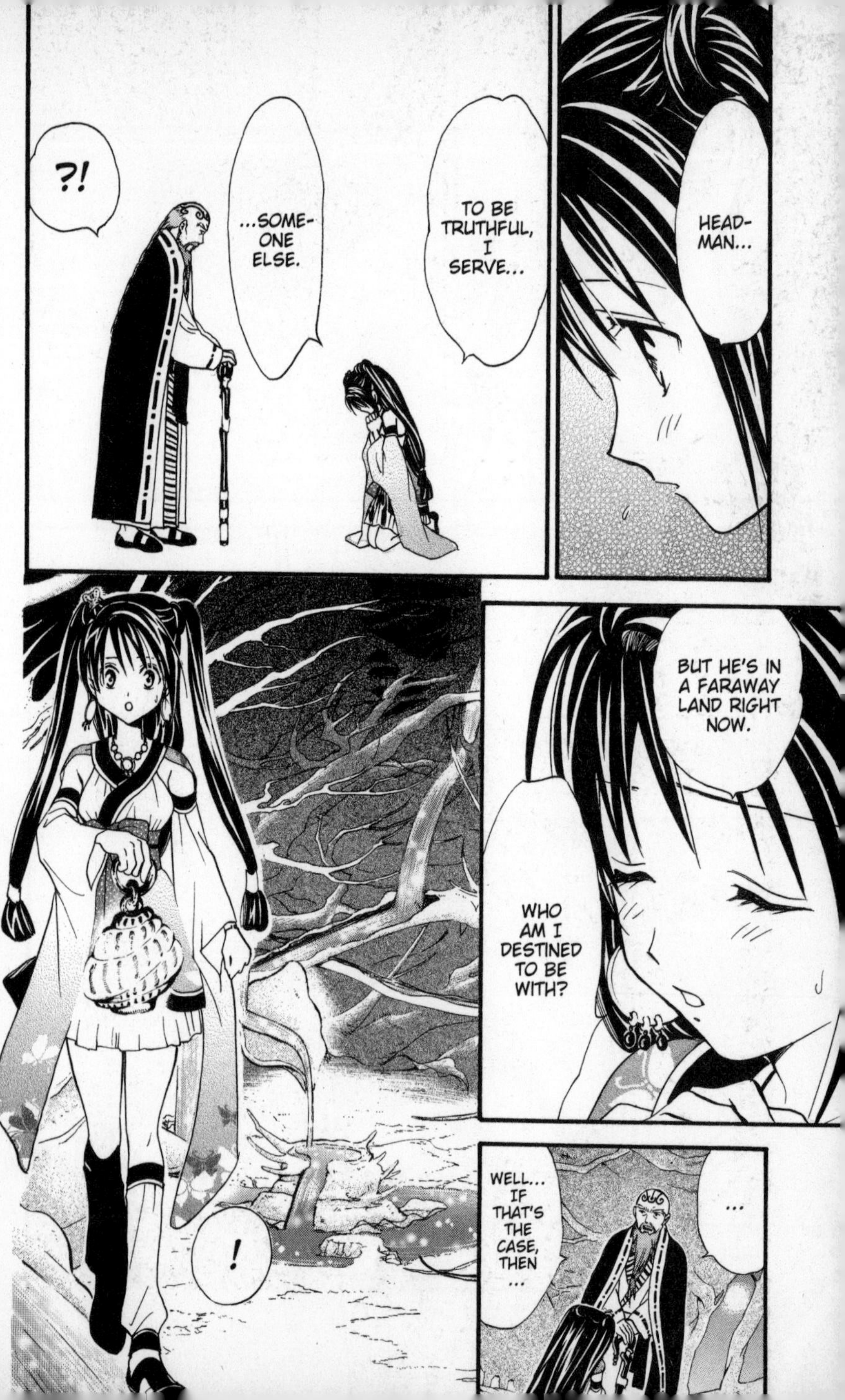
HEAD-MAN...
TO BE TRUTHFUL, I SERVE...
...SOME-ONE ELSE.
?!
BUT HE'S IN A FARAWAY LAND RIGHT NOW.
WHO AM I DESTINED TO BE WITH?
...
WELL... IF THAT'S THE CASE, THEN ...
!

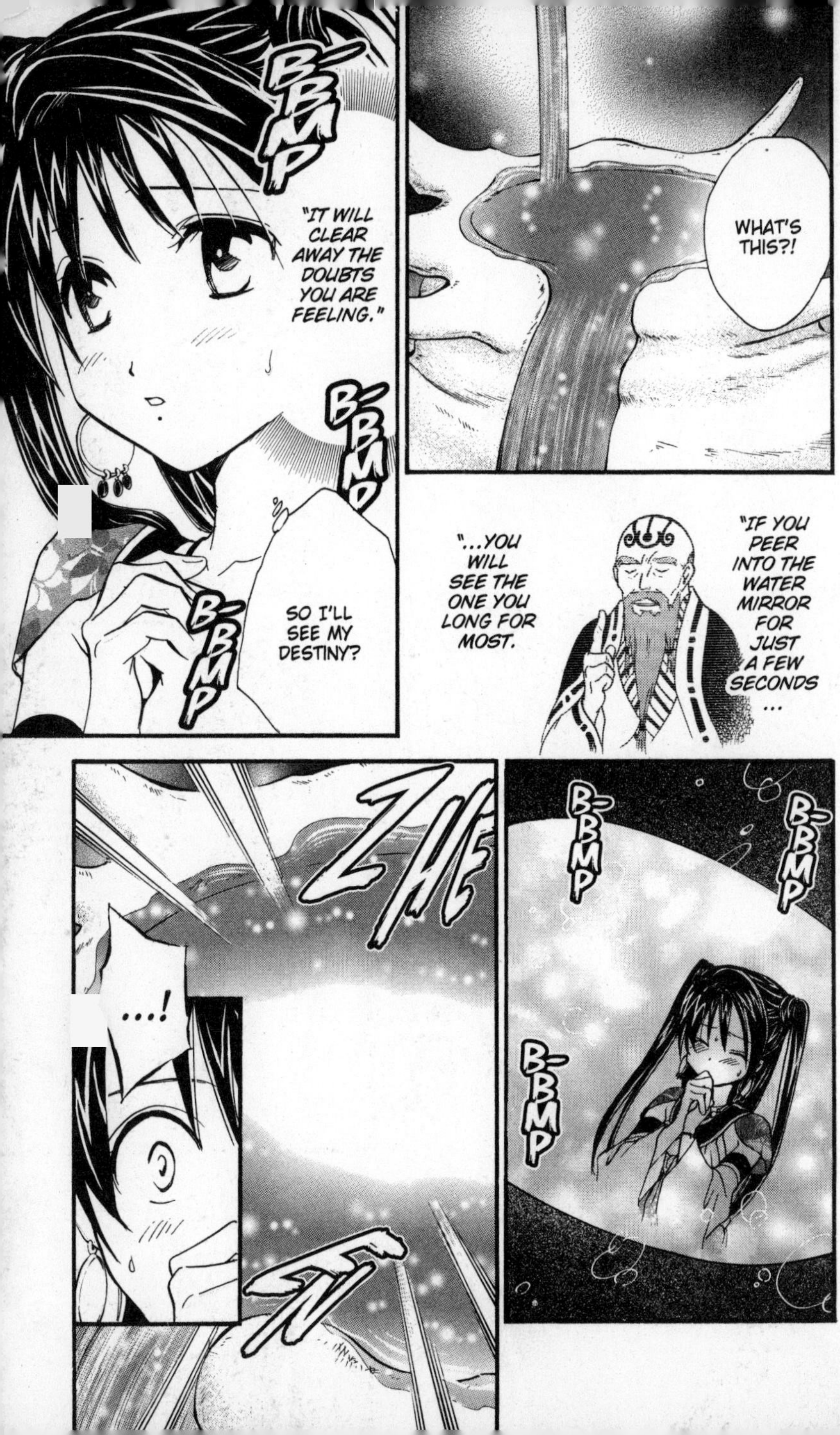
WHAT'S THIS?!
"IF YOU PEER INTO THE WATER MIRROR FOR JUST A FEW SECONDS...
"...YOU WILL SEE THE ONE YOU LONG FOR MOST.
B-BMP
"IT WILL CLEAR AWAY THE DOUBTS YOU ARE FEELING."
B-BMP
SO I'LL SEE MY DESTINY?
B-BMP
B-BMP
B-BMP
B-BMP
ZHE
...!

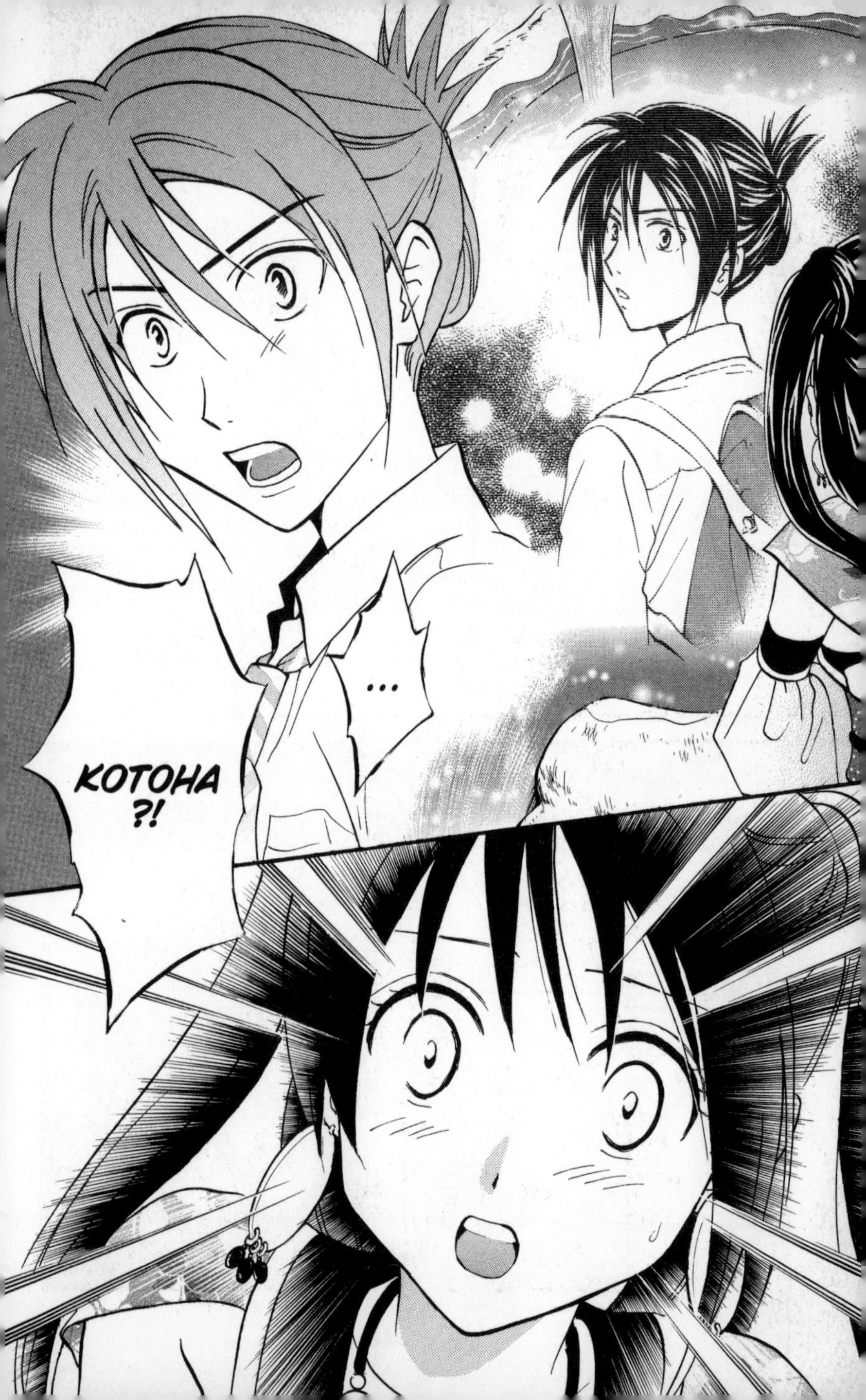
...
KOTOHA ?!

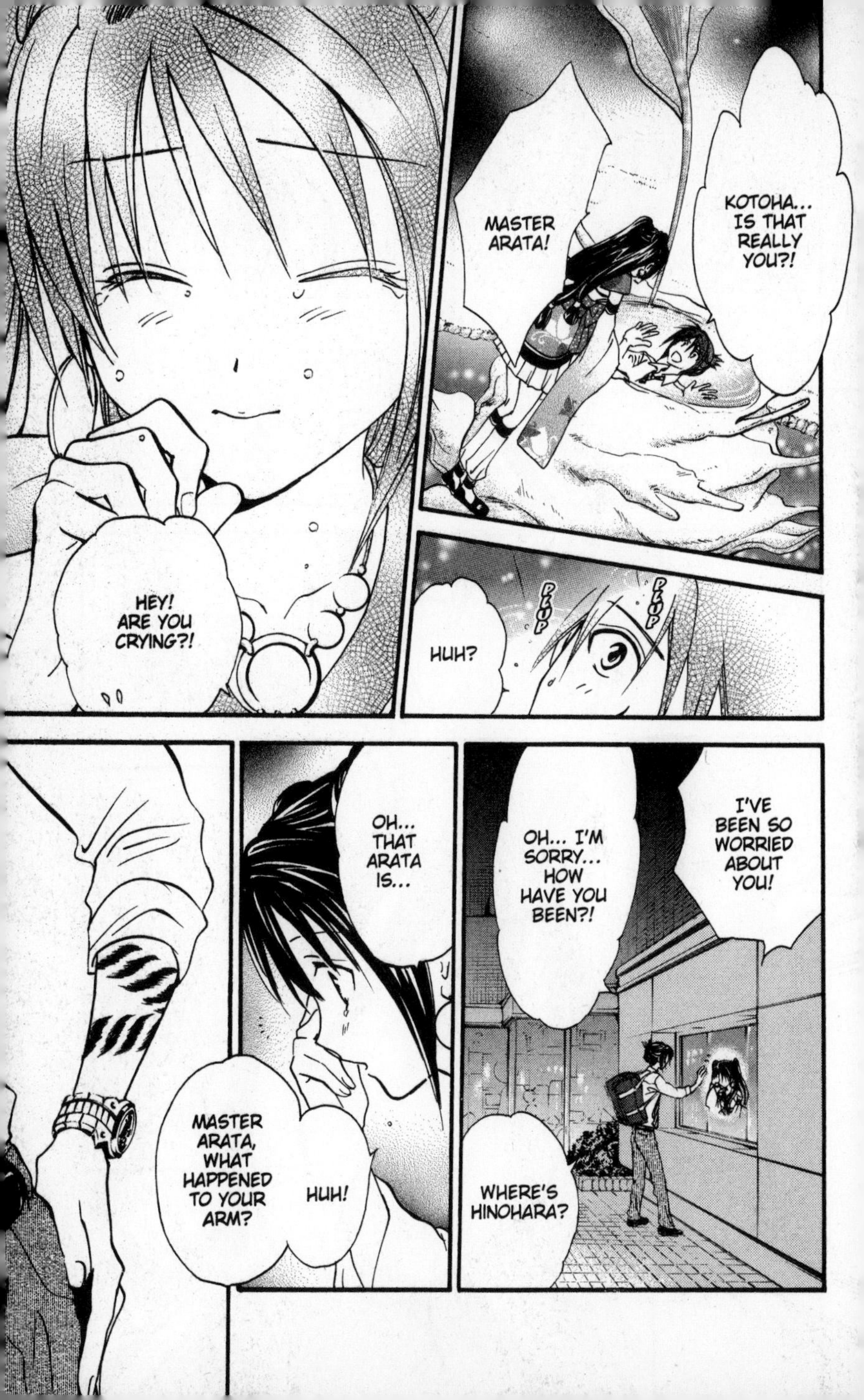
KOTOHA... IS THAT REALLY YOU?!
MASTER ARATA!
PLUP
PLUP
HUH?
HEY! ARE YOU CRYING?!
I'VE BEEN SO WORRIED ABOUT YOU!
OH... I'M SORRY... HOW HAVE YOU BEEN?!
WHERE'S HINOHARA?
OH... THAT ARATA IS...
HUH!
MASTER ARATA, WHAT HAPPENED TO YOUR ARM?

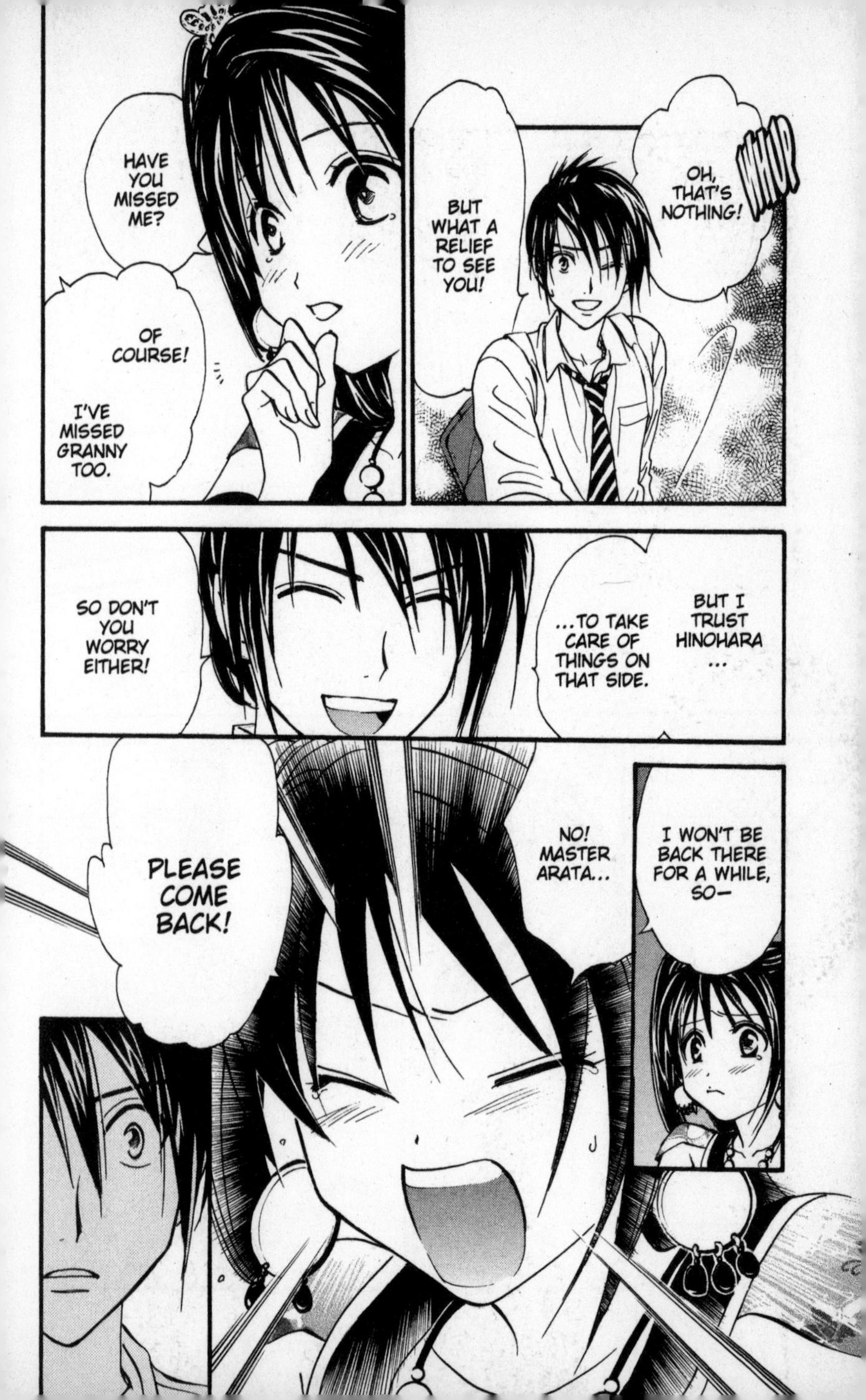
WHUP
OH, THAT'S NOTHING!
BUT WHAT A RELIEF TO SEE YOU!
HAVE YOU MISSED ME?
OF COURSE!
I'VE MISSED GRANNY TOO.
BUT I TRUST HINOHARA ...
...TO TAKE CARE OF THINGS ON THAT SIDE.
SO DON'T YOU WORRY EITHER!
I WON'T BE BACK THERE FOR A WHILE, SO—
NO! MASTER ARATA...
PLEASE COME BACK!

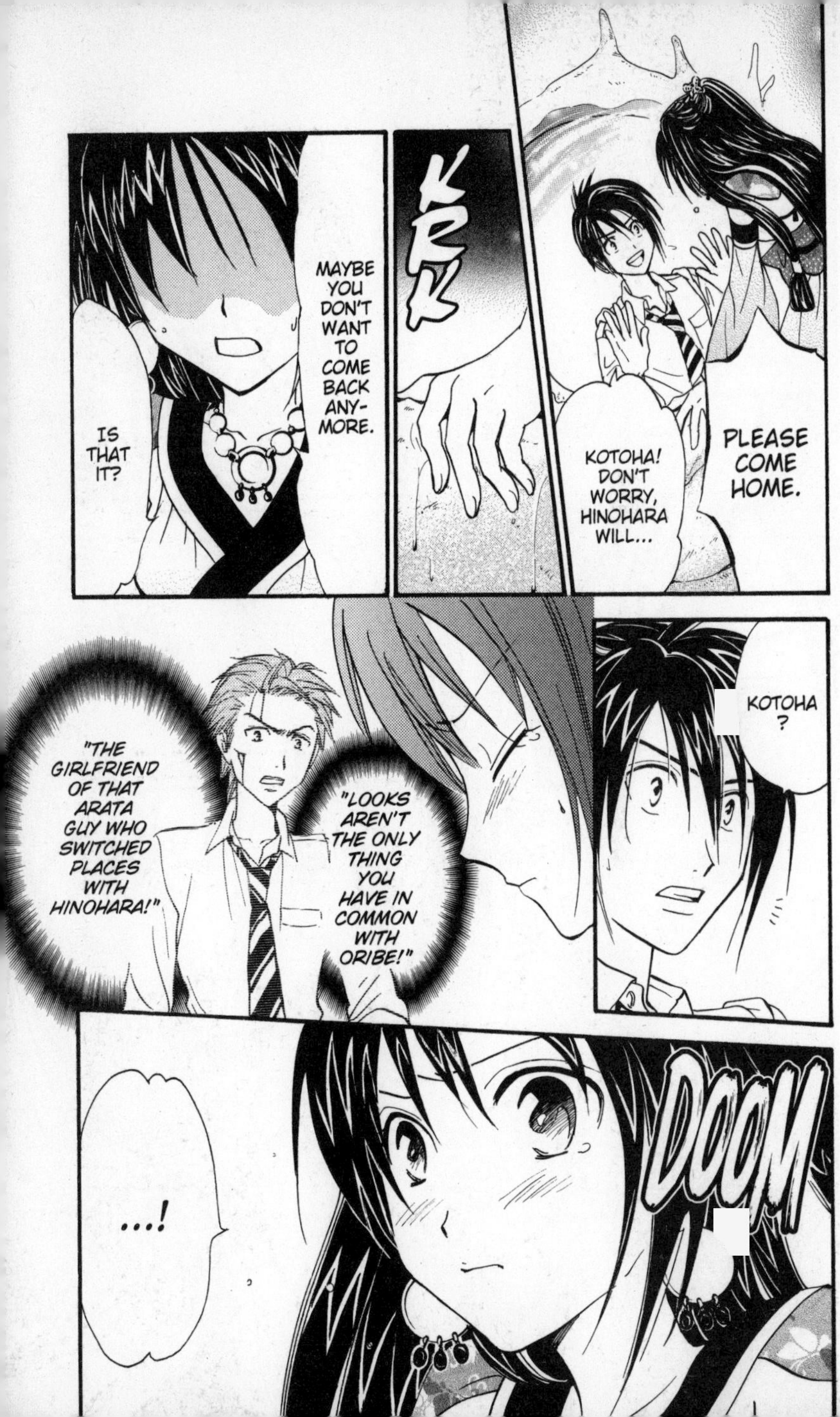
PLEASE COME HOME.
KOTOHA! DON'T WORRY, HINOHARA WILL...
KRK
MAYBE YOU DON'T WANT TO COME BACK ANYMORE.
IS THAT IT?
KOTOHA?
"LOOKS AREN'T THE ONLY THING YOU HAVE IN COMMON WITH ORIBE!"
"THE GIRLFRIEND OF THAT ARATA GUY WHO SWITCHED PLACES WITH HINOHARA!"
DOOM
...!

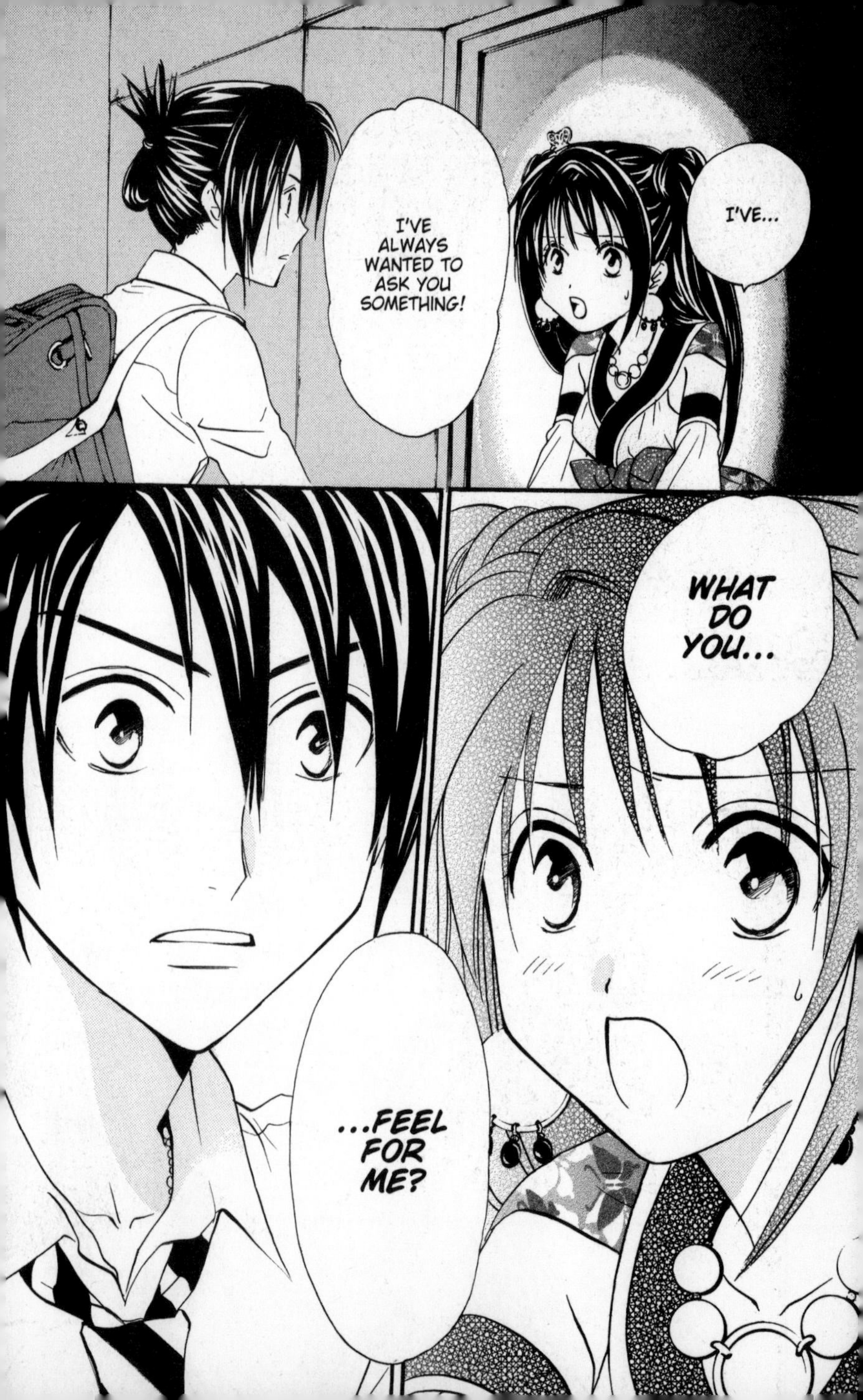
I'VE...
I'VE ALWAYS WANTED TO ASK YOU SOMETHING!
WHAT DO YOU...
...FEEL FOR ME?

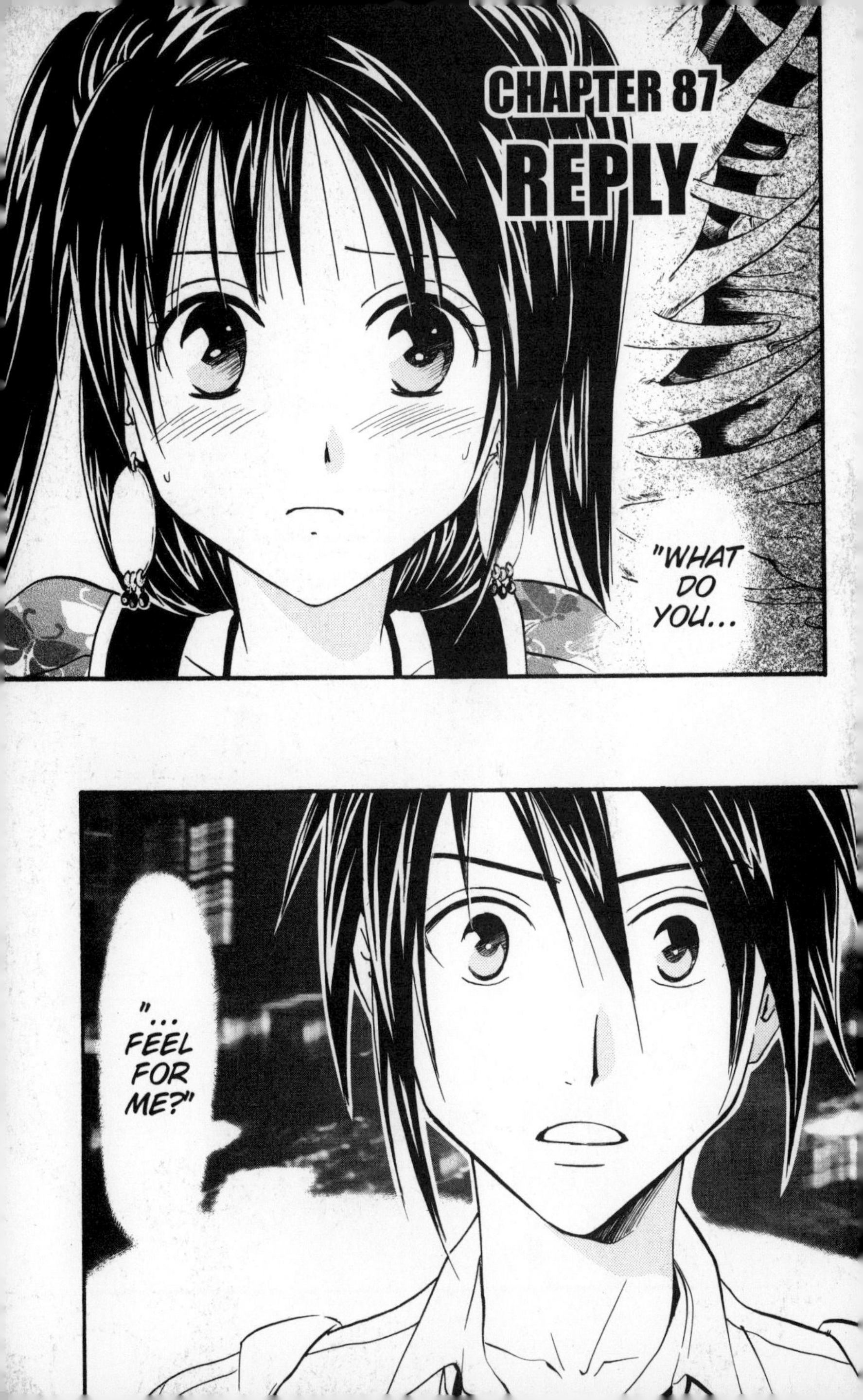
CHAPTER 87
REPLY
"WHAT DO YOU...
"... FEEL FOR ME?"

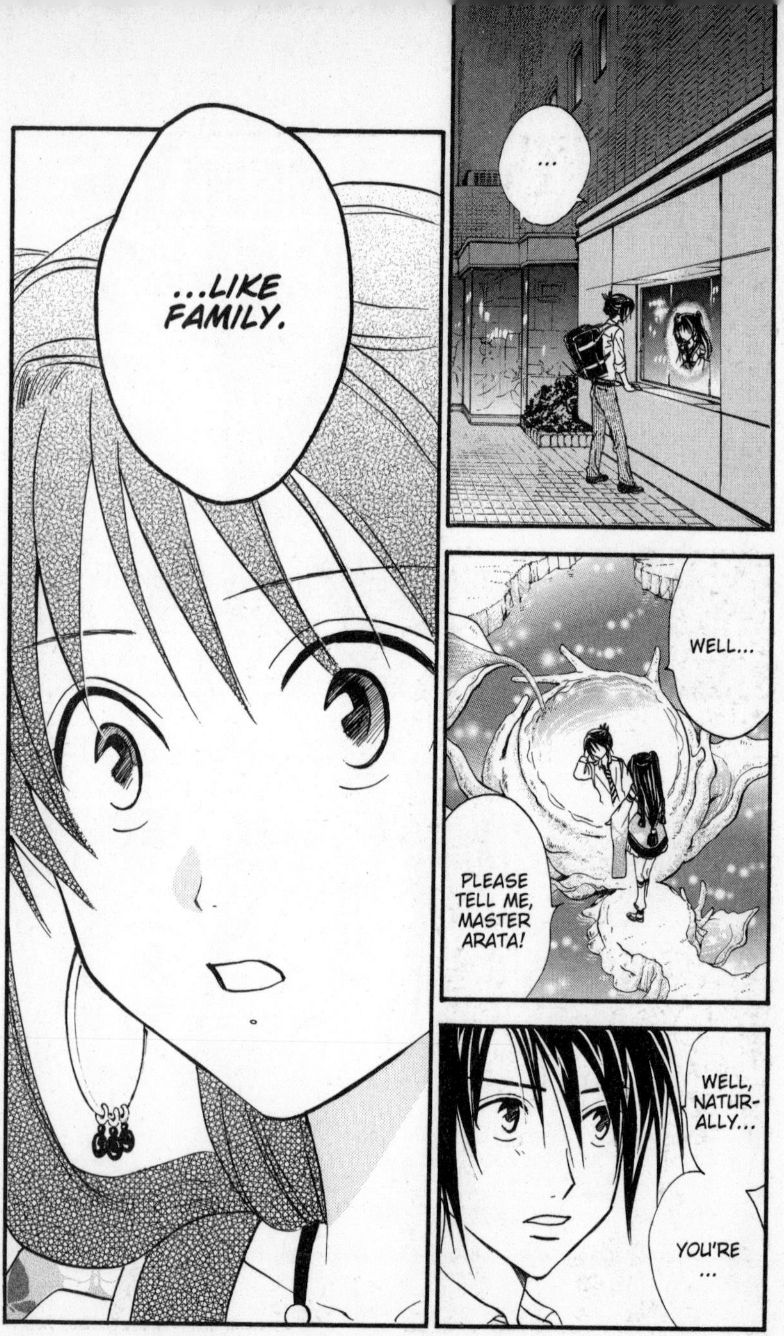
...
WELL...
PLEASE TELL ME, MASTER ARATA!
WELL, NATUR-ALLY...
YOU'RE ...
...LIKE FAMILY.

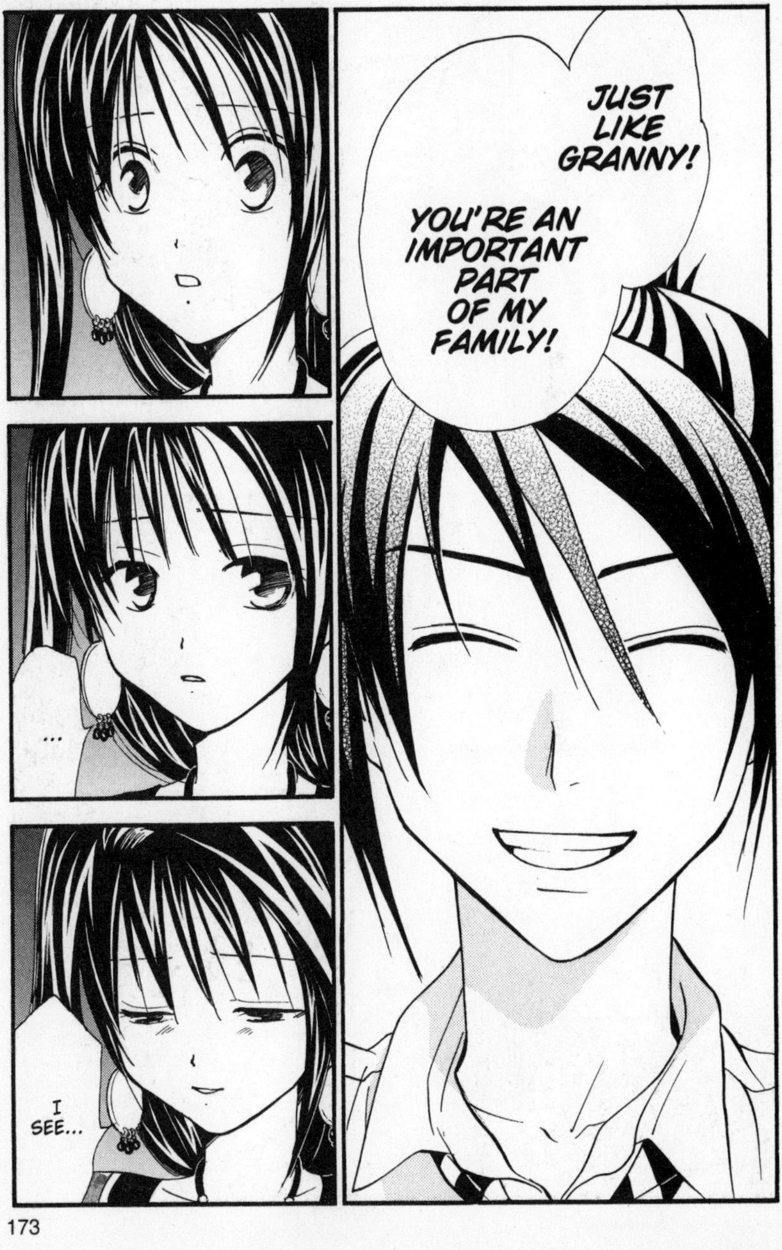
JUST LIKE GRANNY!
YOU'RE AN IMPORTANT PART OF MY FAMILY!
...
I SEE...

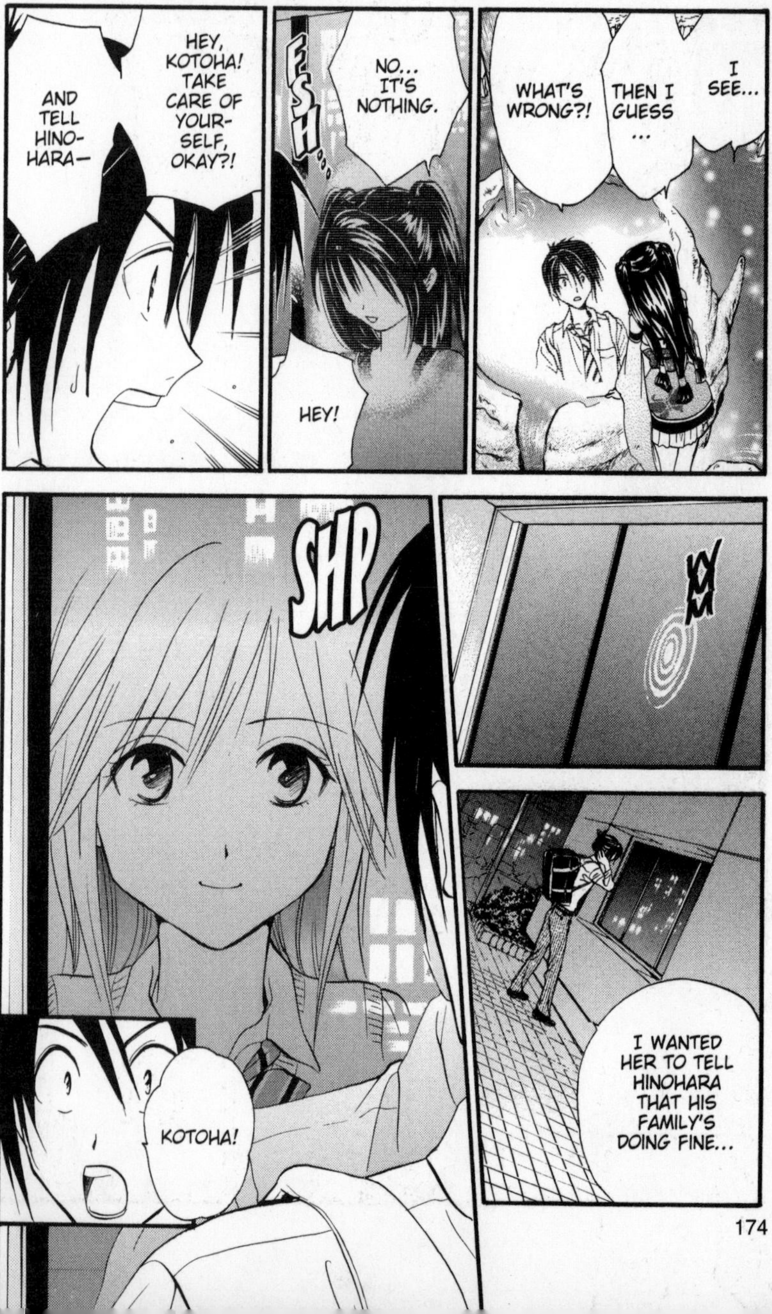
I SEE...
THEN I GUESS ...
WHAT'S WRONG?!
NO... IT'S NOTHING.
FSH...
HEY!
HEY, KOTOHA! TAKE CARE OF YOUR-SELF, OKAY?!
AND TELL HINO-HARA—
I WANTED HER TO TELL HINOHARA THAT HIS FAMILY'S DOING FINE...
SHP
KOTOHA!

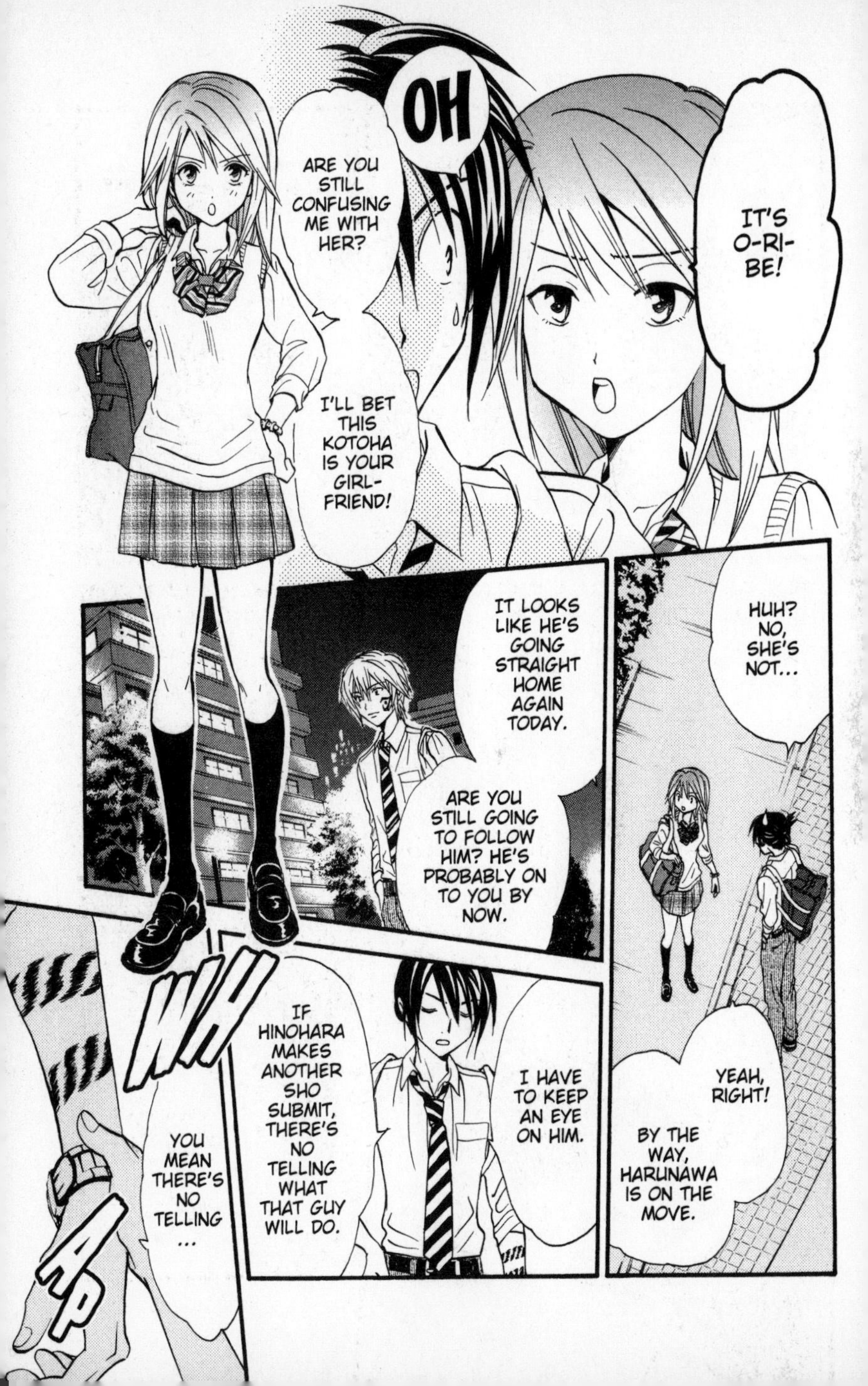
IT'S O-RI-BE!
OH
ARE YOU STILL CONFUSING ME WITH HER?
I'LL BET THIS KOTOHA IS YOUR GIRL-FRIEND!
HUH? NO, SHE'S NOT...
YEAH, RIGHT!
BY THE WAY, HARUNAWA IS ON THE MOVE.
IT LOOKS LIKE HE'S GOING STRAIGHT HOME AGAIN TODAY.
ARE YOU STILL GOING TO FOLLOW HIM? HE'S PROBABLY ON TO YOU BY NOW.
I HAVE TO KEEP AN EYE ON HIM.
IF HINOHARA MAKES ANOTHER SHO SUBMIT, THERE'S NO TELLING WHAT THAT GUY WILL DO.
YOU MEAN THERE'S NO TELLING ...
WH
AP

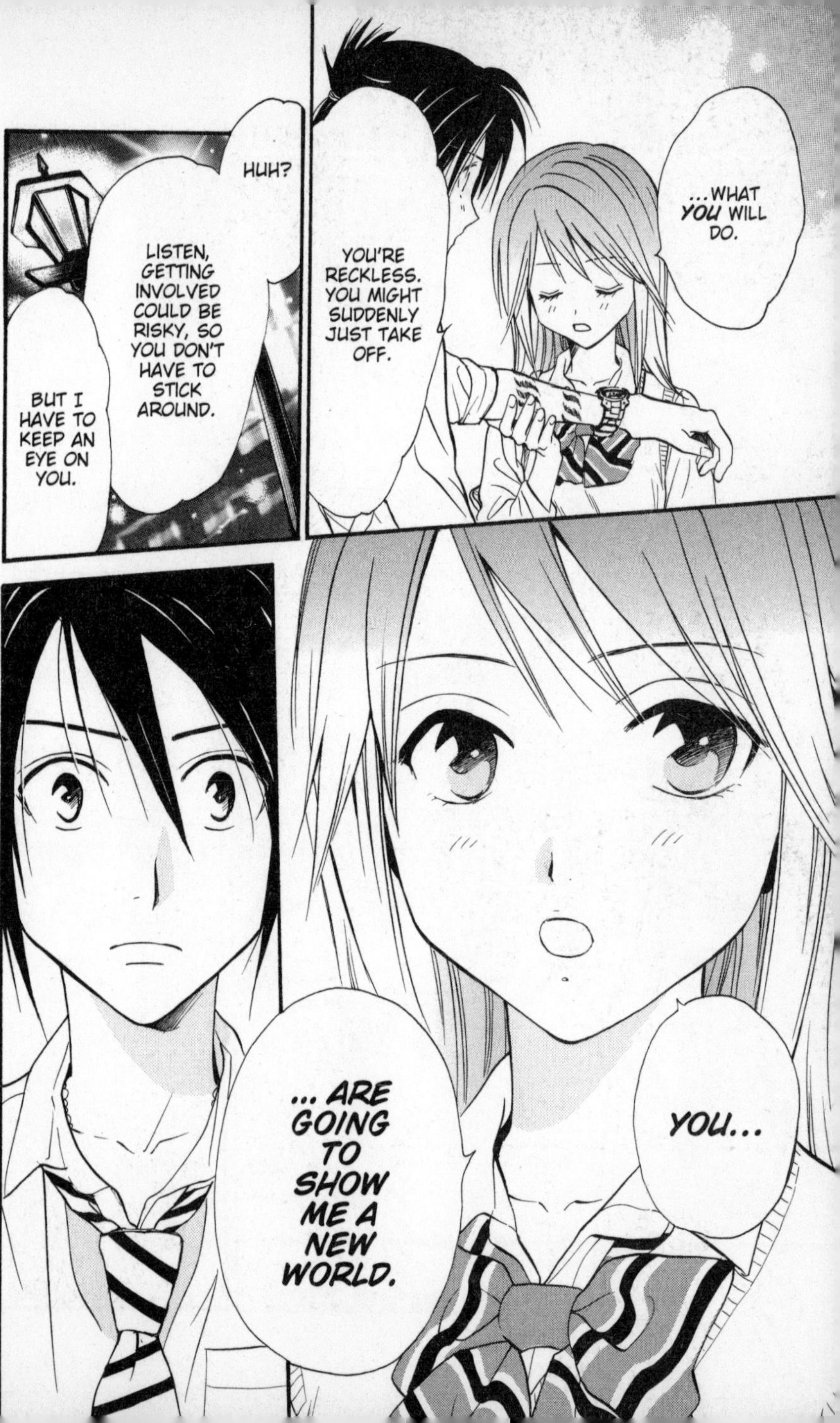
...WHAT *YOU* WILL DO.
YOU'RE RECKLESS. YOU MIGHT SUDDENLY JUST TAKE OFF.
HUH?
LISTEN, GETTING INVOLVED COULD BE RISKY, SO YOU DON'T HAVE TO STICK AROUND.
BUT I HAVE TO KEEP AN EYE ON YOU.
YOU...
...ARE GOING TO SHOW ME A NEW WORLD.

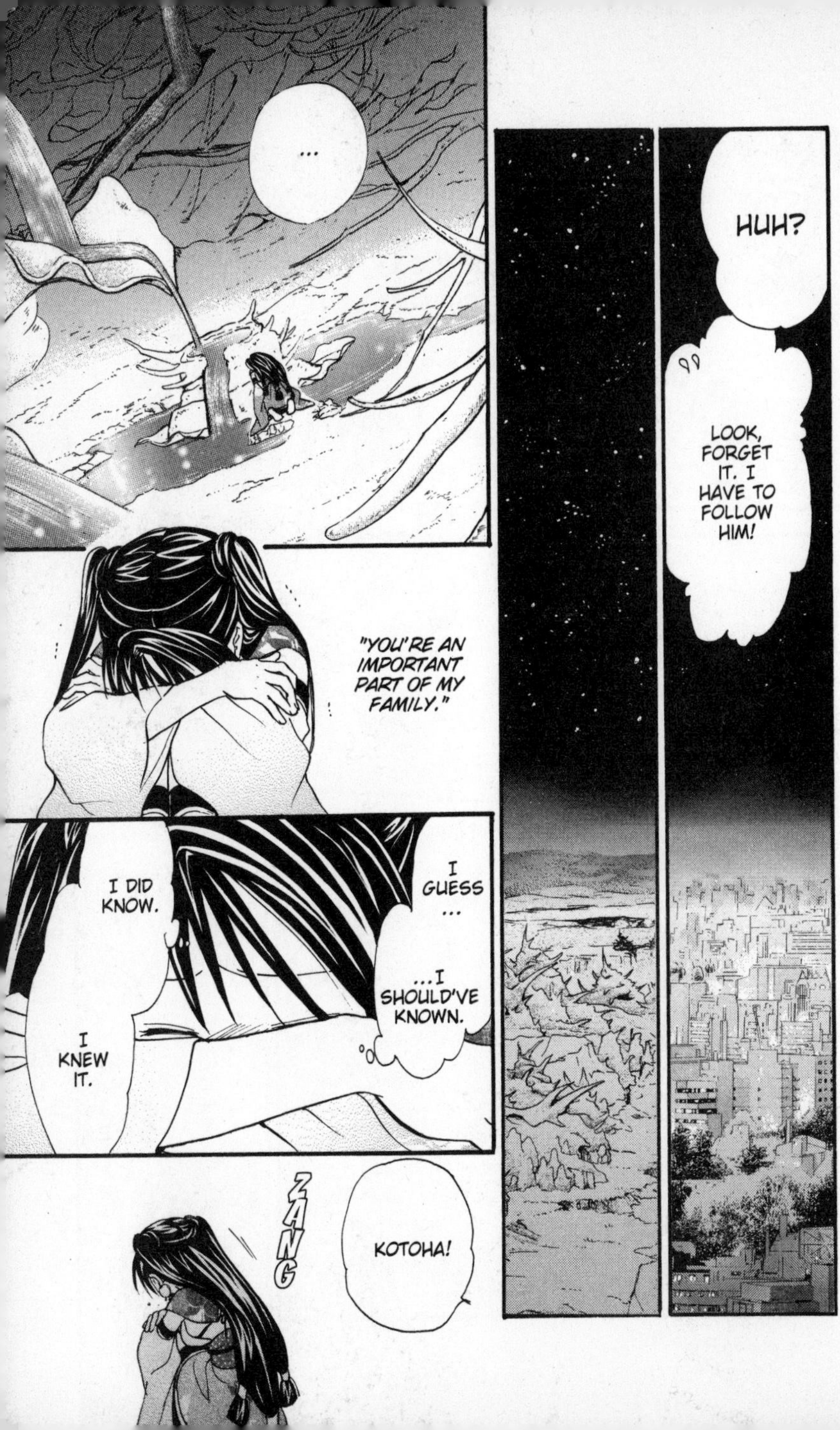
...
"YOU'RE AN IMPORTANT PART OF MY FAMILY."
I GUESS ...
...I SHOULD'VE KNOWN.
I DID KNOW.
I KNEW IT.
ZANG
KOTOHA!
HUH?
LOOK, FORGET IT. I HAVE TO FOLLOW HIM!

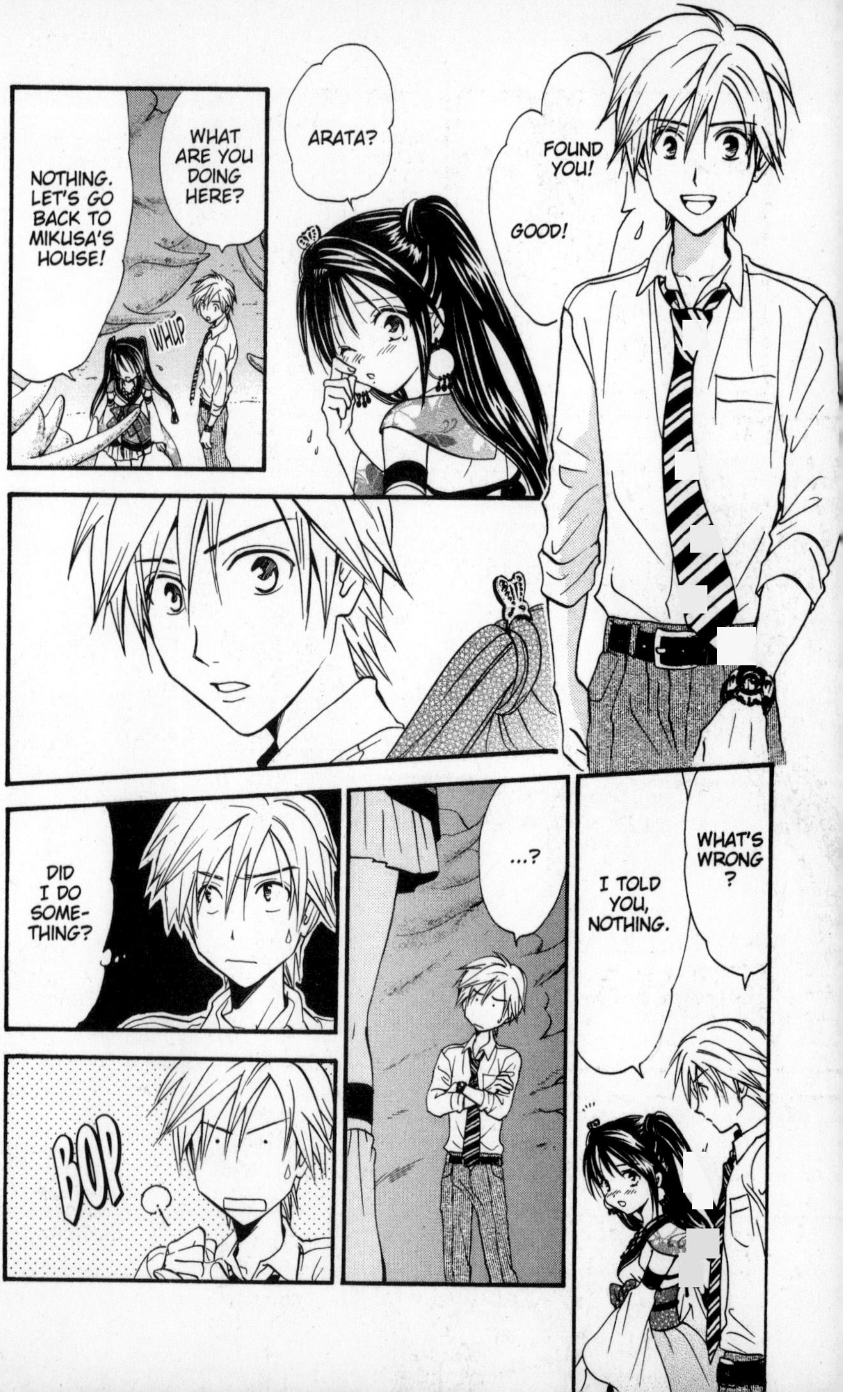
FOUND YOU!
GOOD!
ARATA?
WHAT ARE YOU DOING HERE?
NOTHING. LET'S GO BACK TO MIKUSA'S HOUSE!
WHUP
WHAT'S WRONG?
I TOLD YOU, NOTHING.
...?
DID I DO SOME-THING?
BOP

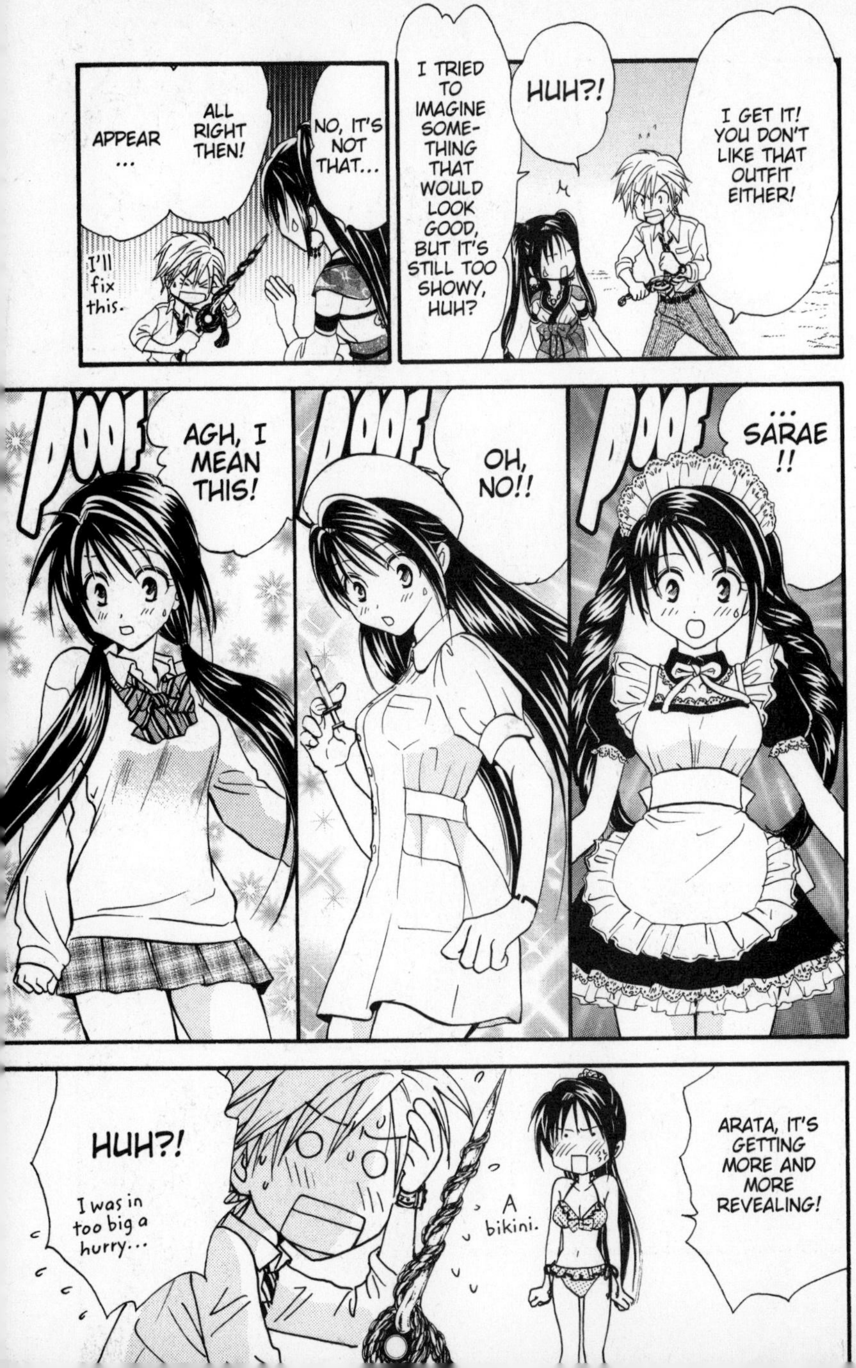
I GET IT! YOU DON'T LIKE THAT OUTFIT EITHER!
HUH?!
I TRIED TO IMAGINE SOMETHING THAT WOULD LOOK GOOD, BUT IT'S STILL TOO SHOWY, HUH?
NO, IT'S NOT THAT...
ALL RIGHT THEN!
APPEAR ...
I'll fix this.
POOF
... SARAE !!
POOF
OH, NO!!
POOF
AGH, I MEAN THIS!
ARATA, IT'S GETTING MORE AND MORE REVEALING!
A bikini.
HUH?!
I was in too big a hurry...

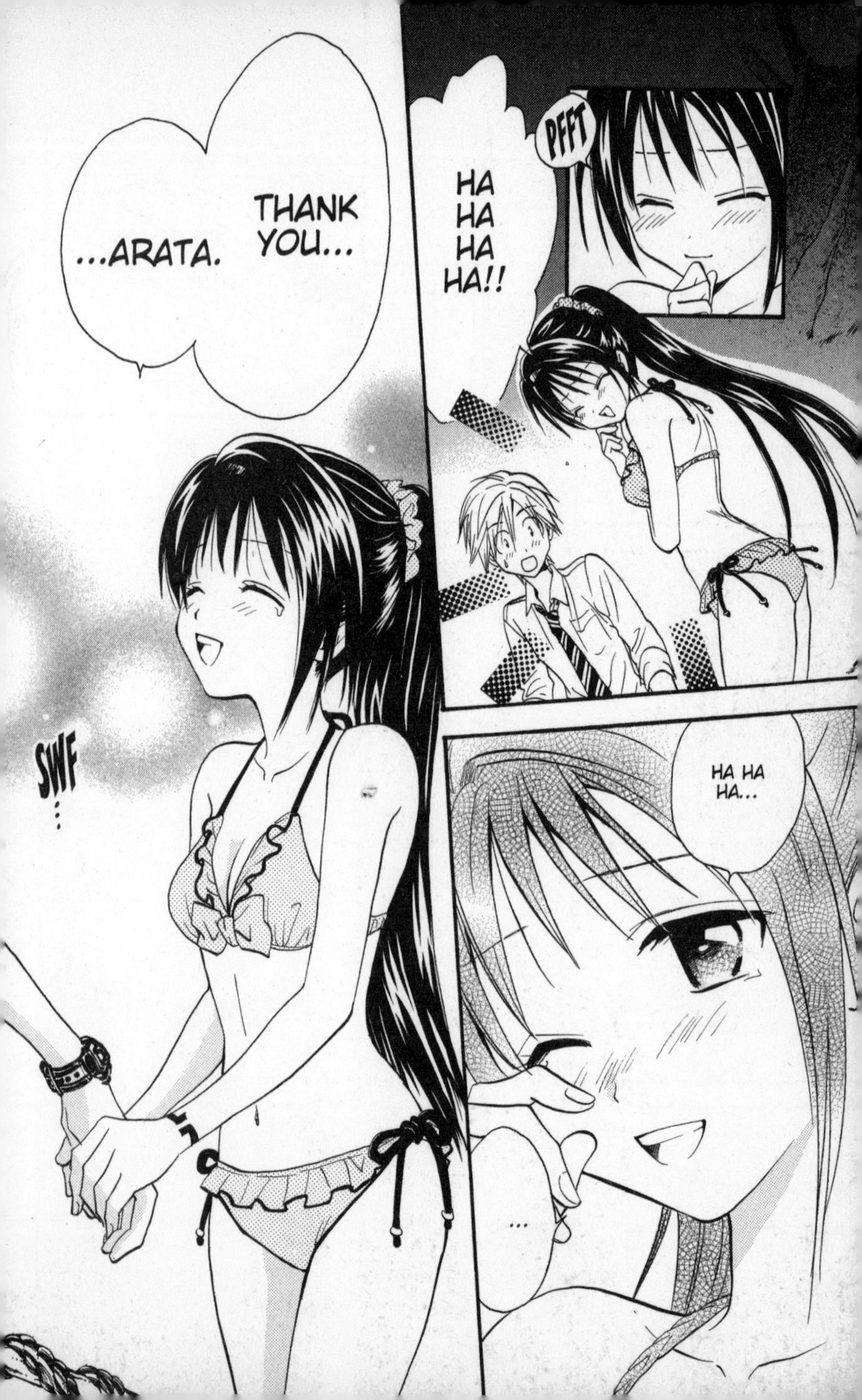
PFFT
HA HA HA HA!!
HA HA HA...
...
THANK YOU...
...ARATA.
SWF

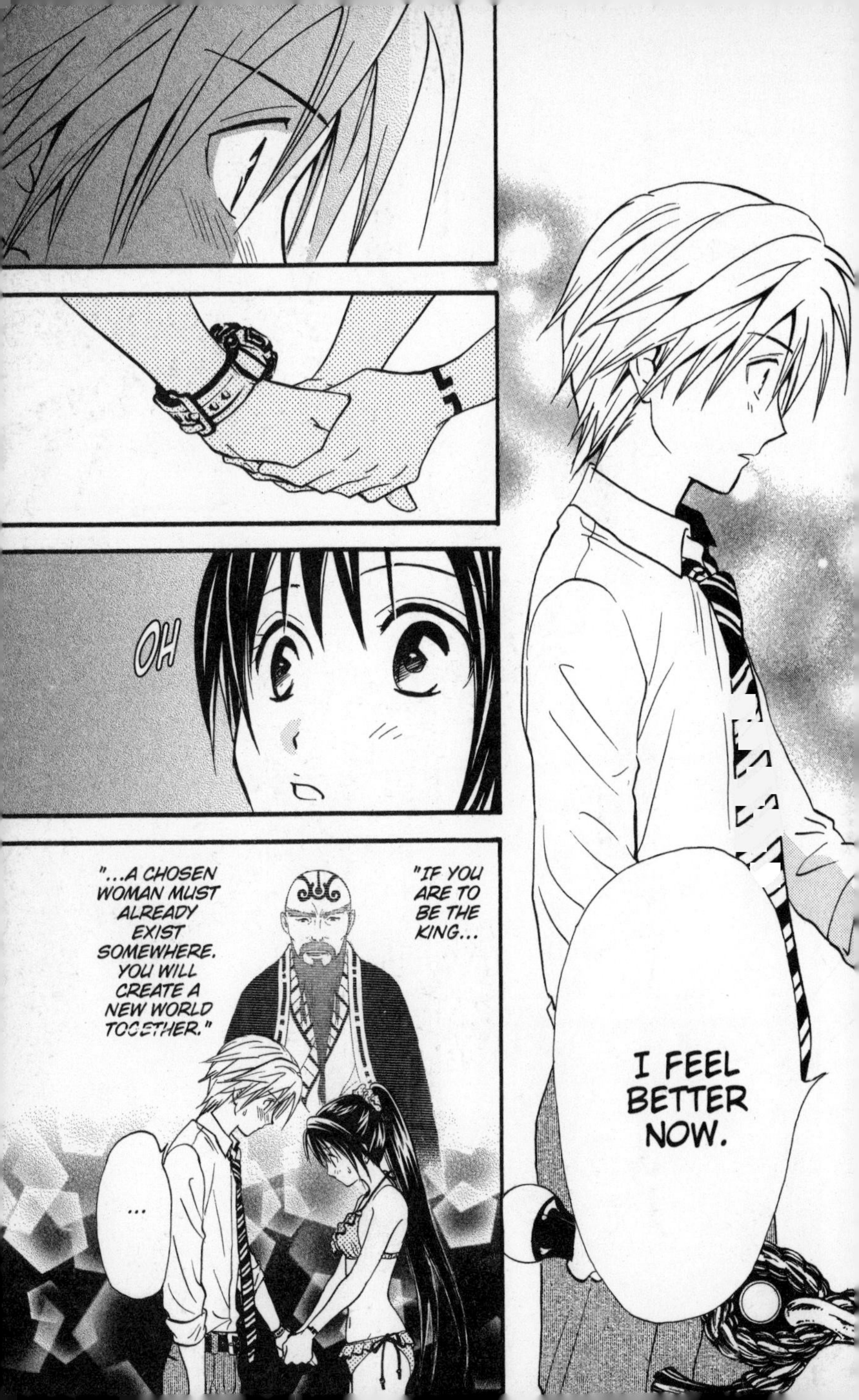
I FEEL BETTER NOW.
OH
"IF YOU ARE TO BE THE KING...
"...A CHOSEN WOMAN MUST ALREADY EXIST SOMEWHERE. YOU WILL CREATE A NEW WORLD TOGETHER."
...

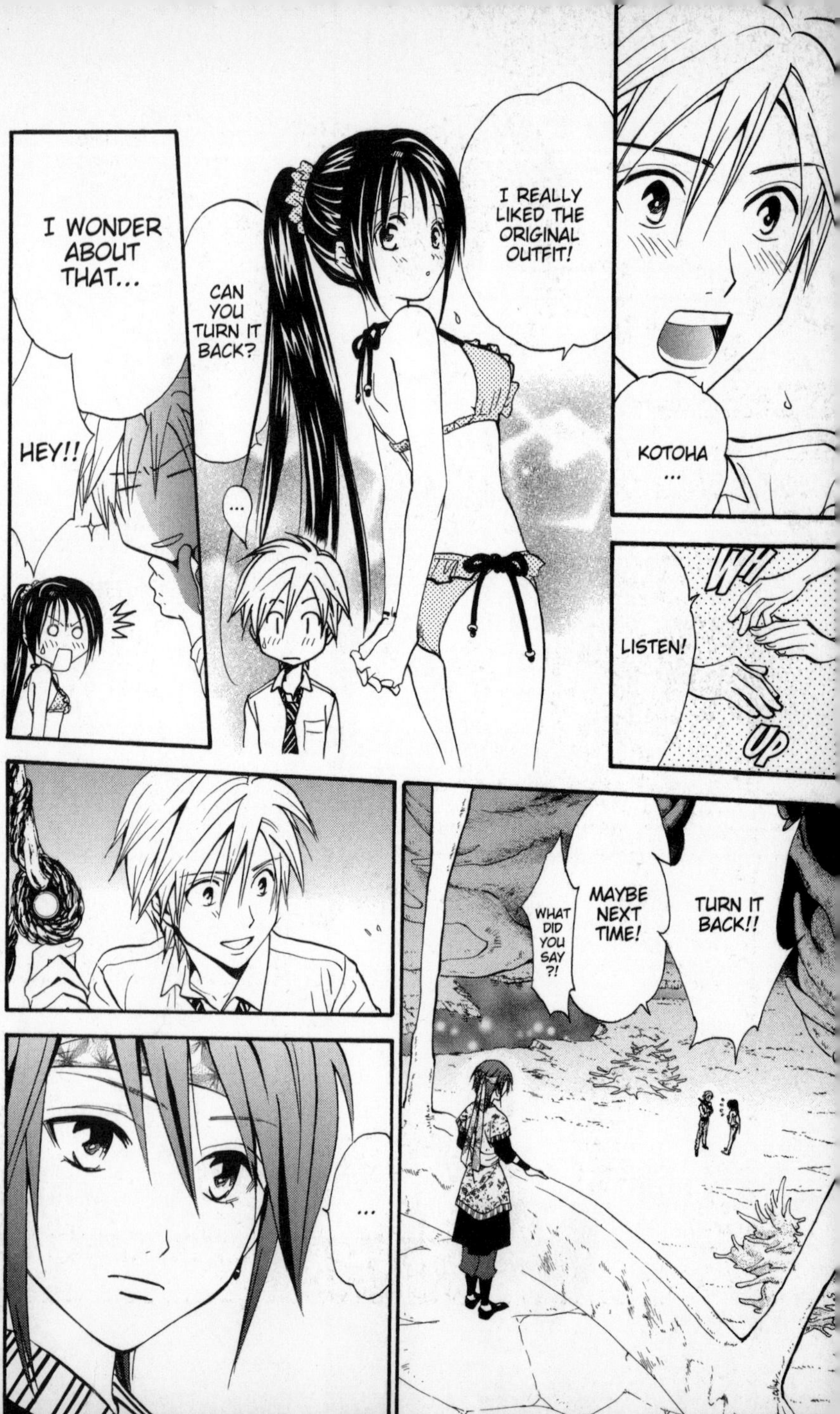
KOTOHA ...
WH
LISTEN!
UP
I REALLY LIKED THE ORIGINAL OUTFIT!
CAN YOU TURN IT BACK?
...
I WONDER ABOUT THAT...
HEY!!
MM
TURN IT BACK!!
MAYBE NEXT TIME!
WHAT DID YOU SAY ?!
...

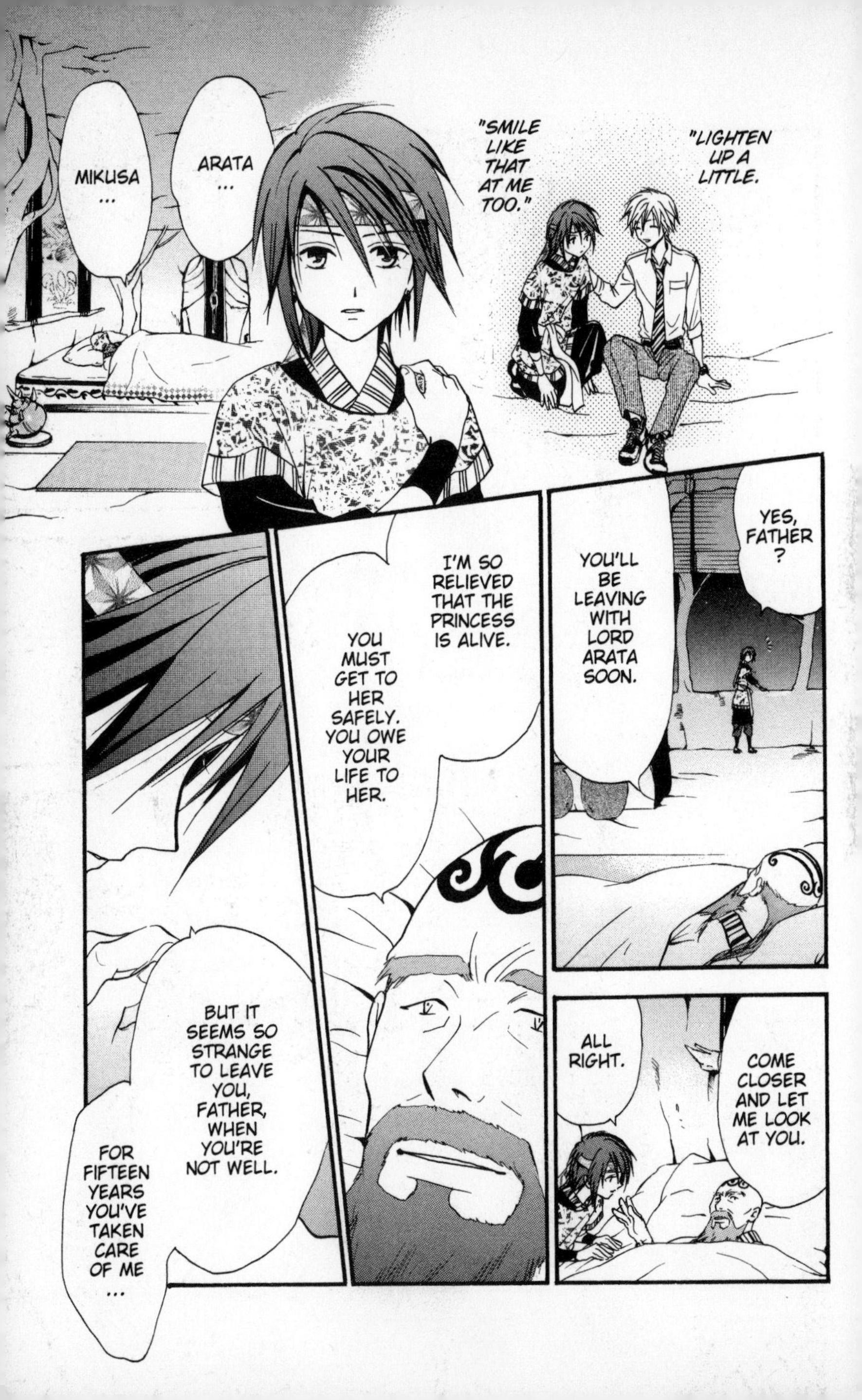
"LIGHTEN UP A LITTLE.
"SMILE LIKE THAT AT ME TOO."
ARATA ...
MIKUSA ...
YES, FATHER?
YOU'LL BE LEAVING WITH LORD ARATA SOON.
COME CLOSER AND LET ME LOOK AT YOU.
ALL RIGHT.
I'M SO RELIEVED THAT THE PRINCESS IS ALIVE.
YOU MUST GET TO HER SAFELY. YOU OWE YOUR LIFE TO HER.
BUT IT SEEMS SO STRANGE TO LEAVE YOU, FATHER, WHEN YOU'RE NOT WELL.
FOR FIFTEEN YEARS YOU'VE TAKEN CARE OF ME ...

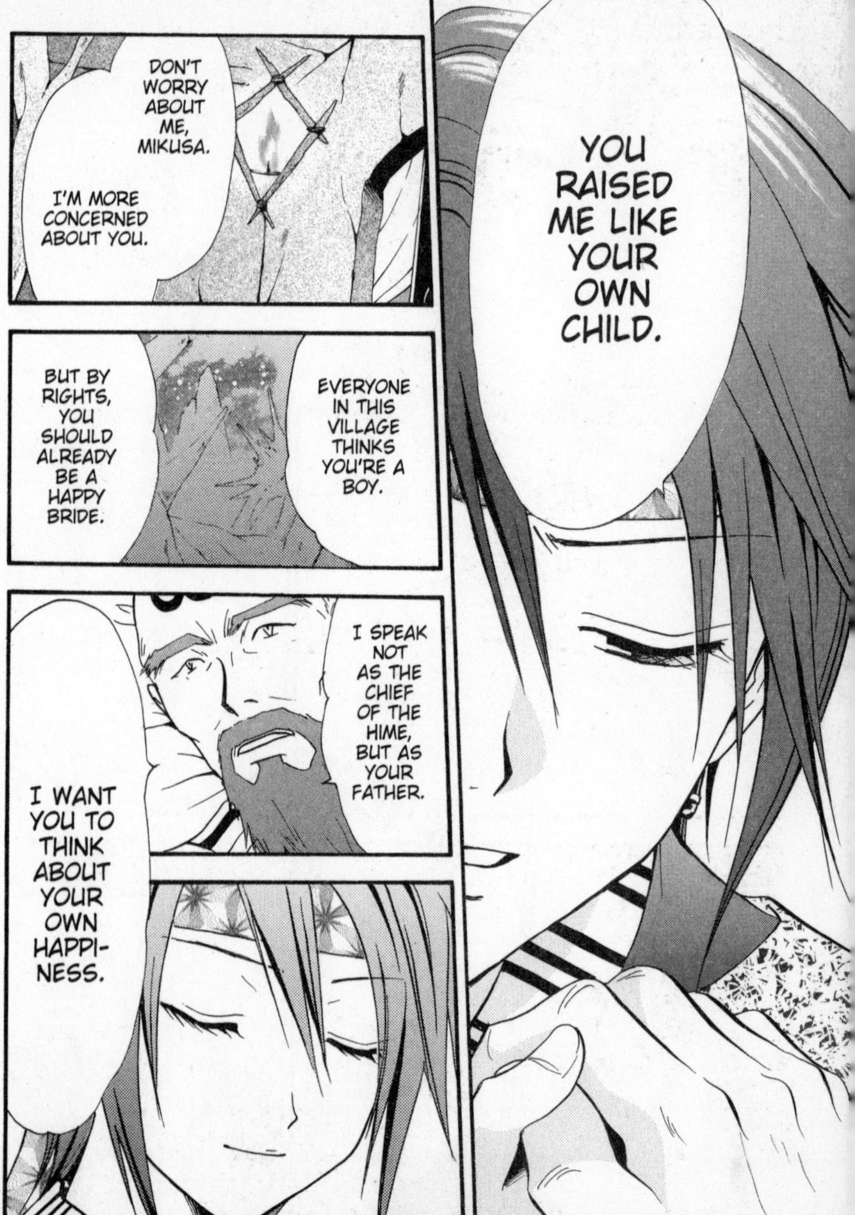
YOU RAISED ME LIKE YOUR OWN CHILD.
DON'T WORRY ABOUT ME, MIKUSA.
I'M MORE CONCERNED ABOUT YOU.
EVERYONE IN THIS VILLAGE THINKS YOU'RE A BOY.
BUT BY RIGHTS, YOU SHOULD ALREADY BE A HAPPY BRIDE.
I SPEAK NOT AS THE CHIEF OF THE HIME, BUT AS YOUR FATHER.
I WANT YOU TO THINK ABOUT YOUR OWN HAPPI-NESS.

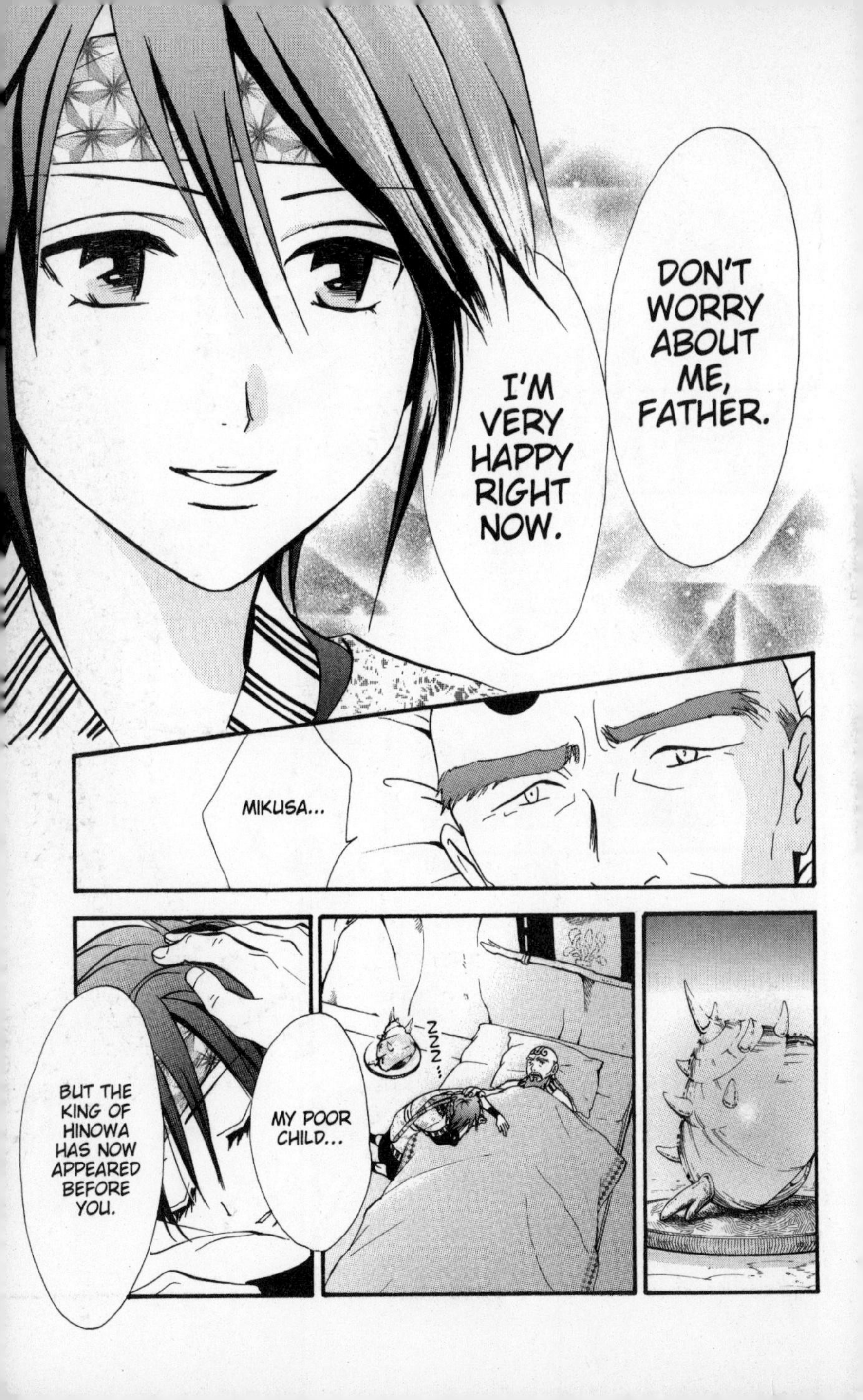
DON'T WORRY ABOUT ME, FATHER.
I'M VERY HAPPY RIGHT NOW.
MIKUSA...
ZZZ...
MY POOR CHILD...
BUT THE KING OF HINOWA HAS NOW APPEARED BEFORE YOU.

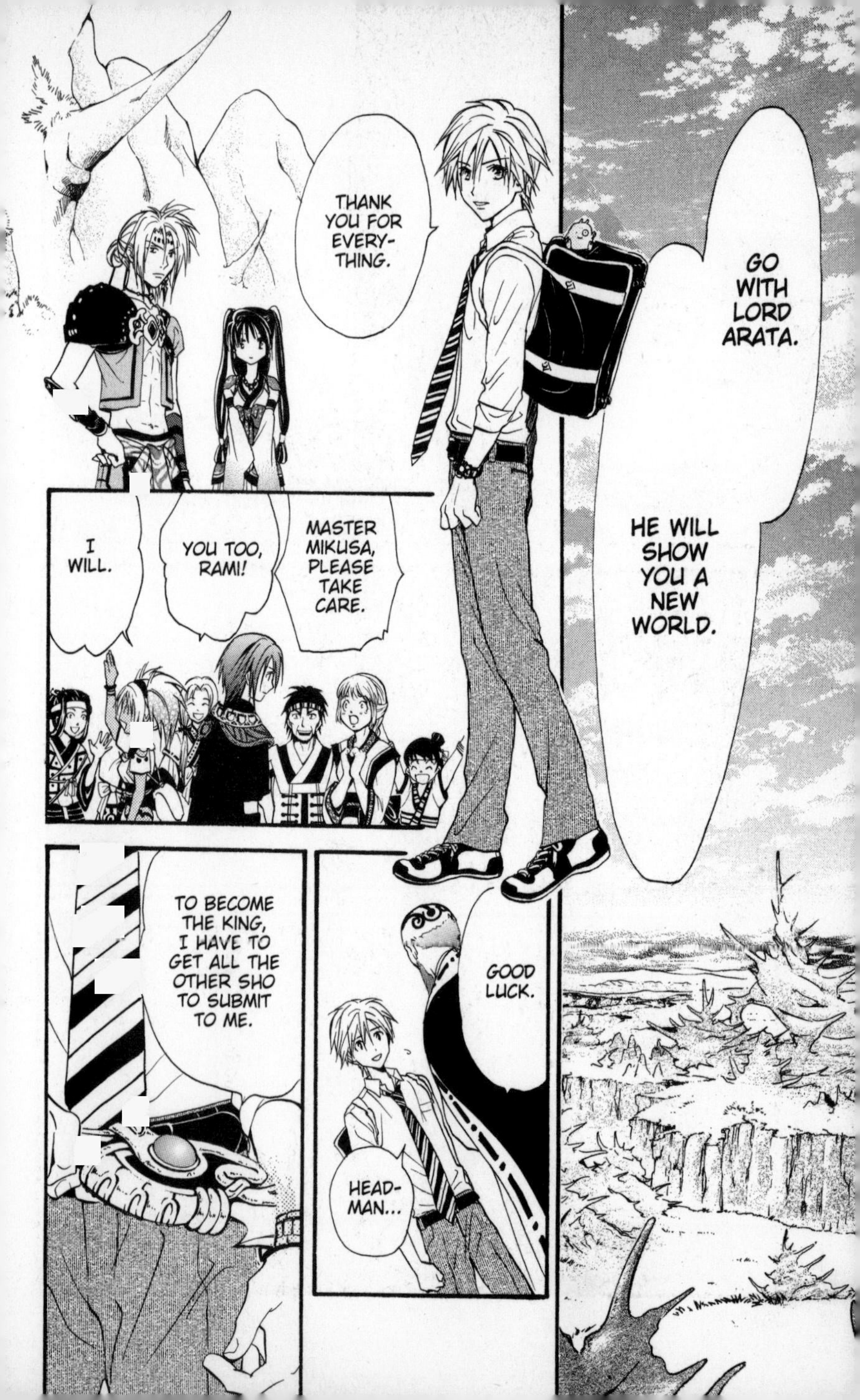
GO WITH LORD ARATA.
HE WILL SHOW YOU A NEW WORLD.
THANK YOU FOR EVERY-THING.
MASTER MIKUSA, PLEASE TAKE CARE.
YOU TOO, RAMI!
I WILL.
GOOD LUCK.
HEAD-MAN...
TO BECOME THE KING, I HAVE TO GET ALL THE OTHER SHO TO SUBMIT TO ME.

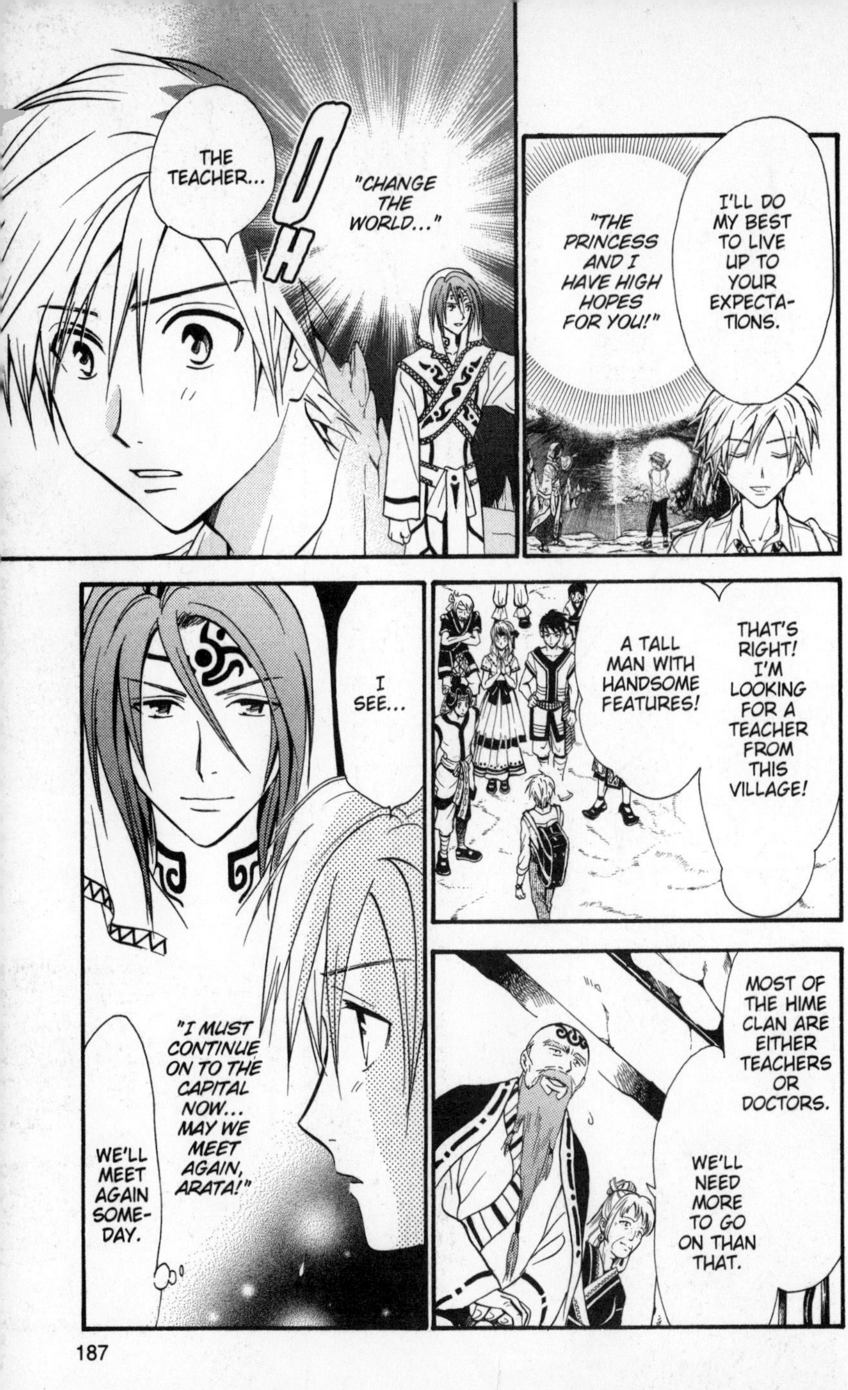
I'LL DO MY BEST TO LIVE UP TO YOUR EXPECTATIONS.
"THE PRINCESS AND I HAVE HIGH HOPES FOR YOU!"
"CHANGE THE WORLD..."
OH
THE TEACHER...
THAT'S RIGHT! I'M LOOKING FOR A TEACHER FROM THIS VILLAGE!
A TALL MAN WITH HANDSOME FEATURES!
MOST OF THE HIME CLAN ARE EITHER TEACHERS OR DOCTORS.
WE'LL NEED MORE TO GO ON THAN THAT.
I SEE...
"I MUST CONTINUE ON TO THE CAPITAL NOW... MAY WE MEET AGAIN, ARATA!"
WE'LL MEET AGAIN SOMEDAY.

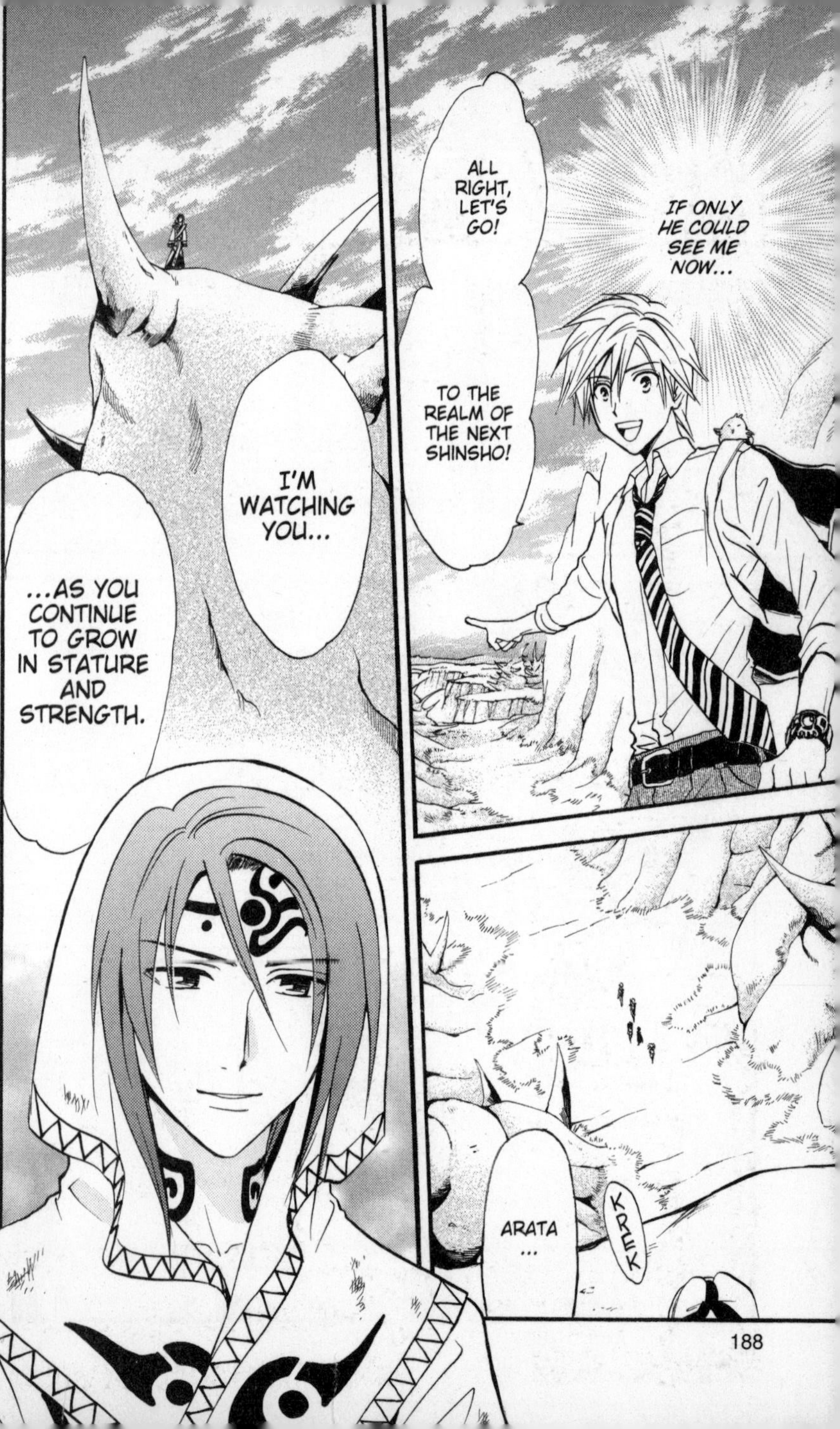
IF ONLY HE COULD SEE ME NOW...
ALL RIGHT, LET'S GO!
TO THE REALM OF THE NEXT SHINSHO!
KREK
ARATA ...
I'M WATCHING YOU...
...AS YOU CONTINUE TO GROW IN STATURE AND STRENGTH.

ARATA: THE LEGEND 9 (THE END)

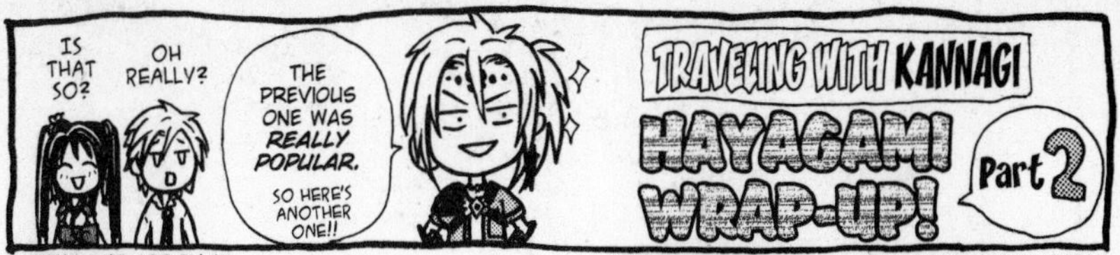
TRAVELING WITH KANNAGI
HAYAGAMI WRAP-UP!
Part 2
THE PREVIOUS ONE WAS REALLY POPULAR.
SO HERE'S ANOTHER ONE!!
OH REALLY?
IS THAT SO?

TEXT AND ART BY M.

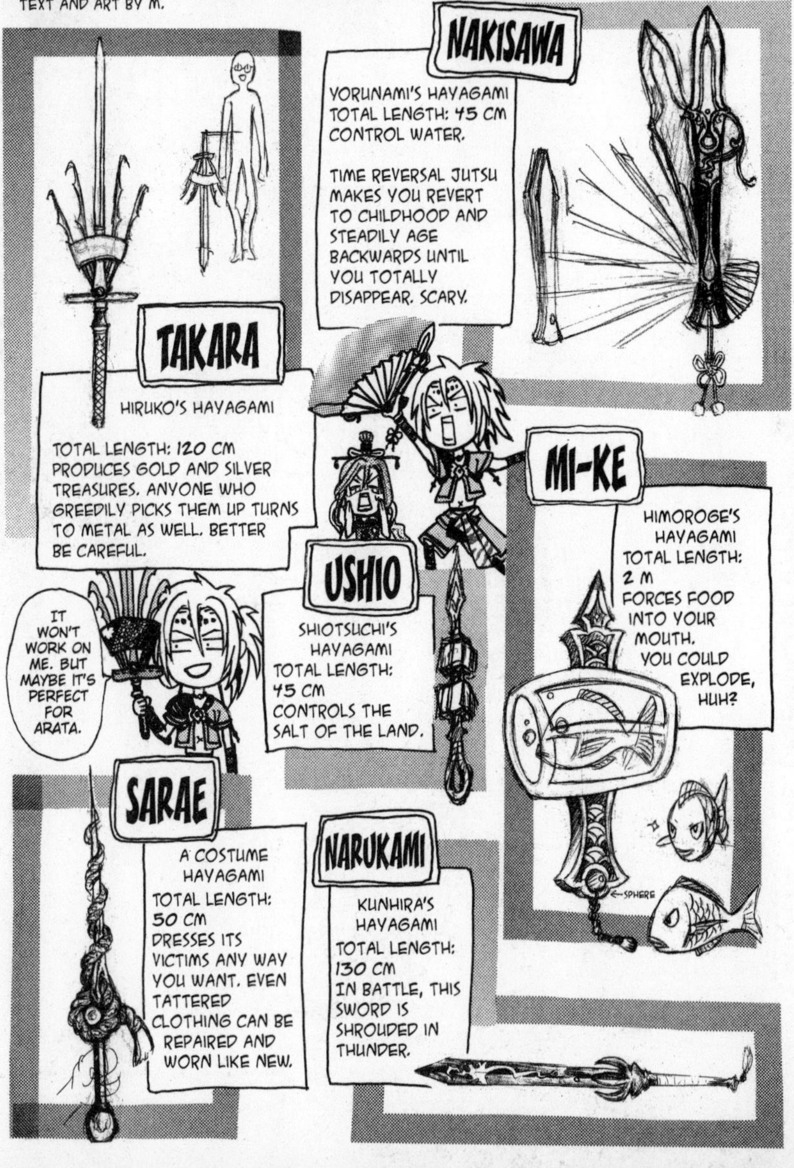
NAKISAWA
YORUNAMI'S HAYAGAMI
TOTAL LENGTH: 45 CM
CONTROL WATER.
TIME REVERSAL JUTSU MAKES YOU REVERT TO CHILDHOOD AND STEADILY AGE BACKWARDS UNTIL YOU TOTALLY DISAPPEAR. SCARY.
TAKARA
HIRUKO'S HAYAGAMI
TOTAL LENGTH: 120 CM
PRODUCES GOLD AND SILVER TREASURES. ANYONE WHO GREEDILY PICKS THEM UP TURNS TO METAL AS WELL. BETTER BE CAREFUL.
MI-KE
HIMOROGE'S HAYAGAMI
TOTAL LENGTH: 2 M
FORCES FOOD INTO YOUR MOUTH. YOU COULD EXPLODE, HUH?
←SPHERE
USHIO
SHIOTSUCHI'S HAYAGAMI
TOTAL LENGTH: 45 CM
CONTROLS THE SALT OF THE LAND.
IT WON'T WORK ON ME. BUT MAYBE IT'S PERFECT FOR ARATA.
NARUKAMI
KUNHIRA'S HAYAGAMI
TOTAL LENGTH: 130 CM
IN BATTLE, THIS SWORD IS SHROUDED IN THUNDER.
SARAE
A COSTUME HAYAGAMI
TOTAL LENGTH: 50 CM
DRESSES ITS VICTIMS ANY WAY YOU WANT. EVEN TATTERED CLOTHING CAN BE REPAIRED AND WORN LIKE NEW.

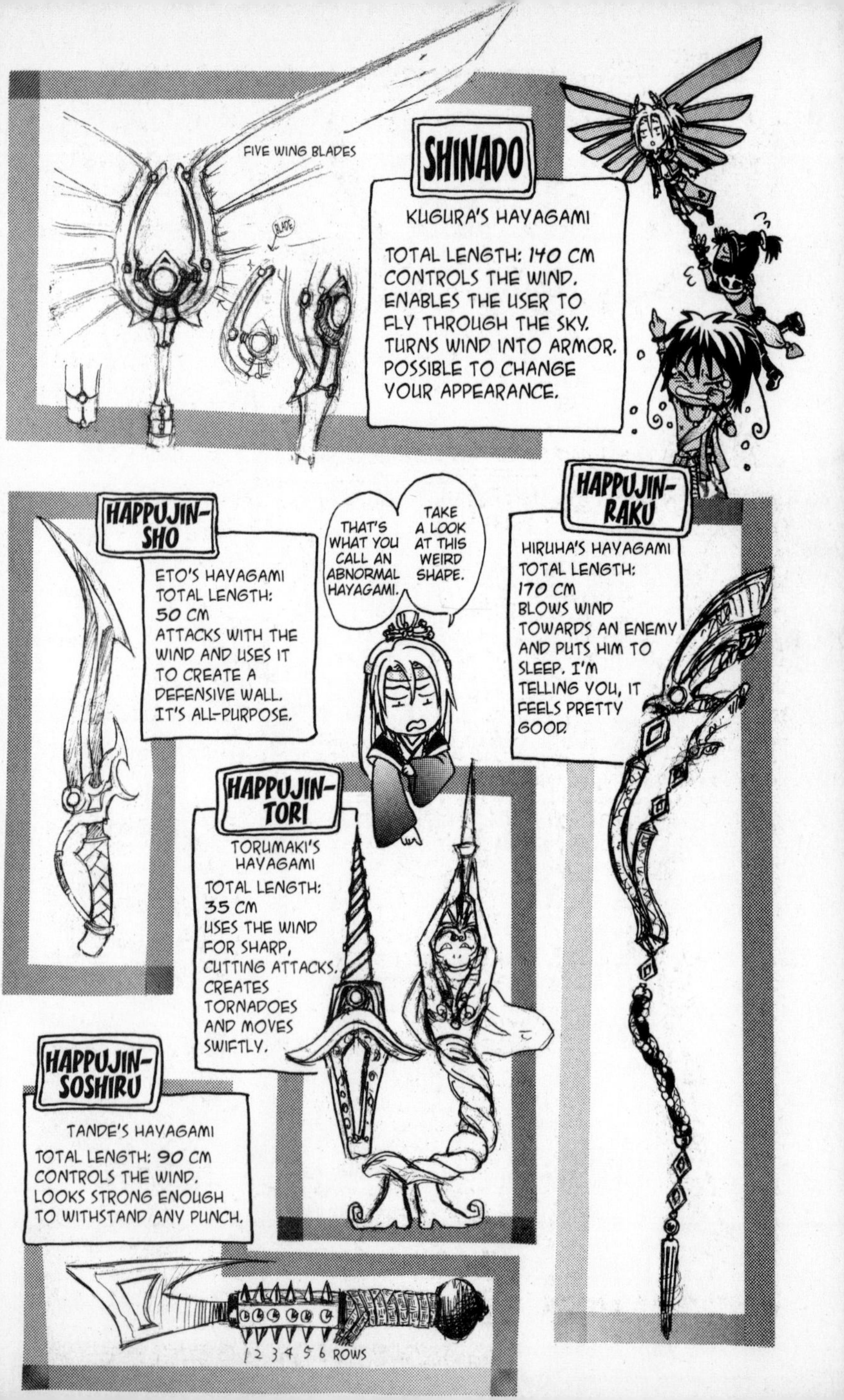
SHINADO
KUGURA'S HAYAGAMI
TOTAL LENGTH: 140 CM
CONTROLS THE WIND. ENABLES THE USER TO FLY THROUGH THE SKY. TURNS WIND INTO ARMOR. POSSIBLE TO CHANGE YOUR APPEARANCE.
FIVE WING BLADES
BLADE
HAPPUJIN-RAKU
HIRUHA'S HAYAGAMI
TOTAL LENGTH: 170 CM
BLOWS WIND TOWARDS AN ENEMY AND PUTS HIM TO SLEEP. I'M TELLING YOU, IT FEELS PRETTY GOOD.
TAKE A LOOK AT THIS WEIRD SHAPE.
THAT'S WHAT YOU CALL AN ABNORMAL HAYAGAMI.
HAPPUJIN-SHO
ETO'S HAYAGAMI
TOTAL LENGTH: 50 CM
ATTACKS WITH THE WIND AND USES IT TO CREATE A DEFENSIVE WALL. IT'S ALL-PURPOSE.
HAPPUJIN-TORI
TORUMAKI'S HAYAGAMI
TOTAL LENGTH: 35 CM
USES THE WIND FOR SHARP, CUTTING ATTACKS. CREATES TORNADOES AND MOVES SWIFTLY.
HAPPUJIN-SOSHIRU
TANDE'S HAYAGAMI
TOTAL LENGTH: 90 CM
CONTROLS THE WIND. LOOKS STRONG ENOUGH TO WITHSTAND ANY PUNCH.
1 2 3 4 5 6 ROWS

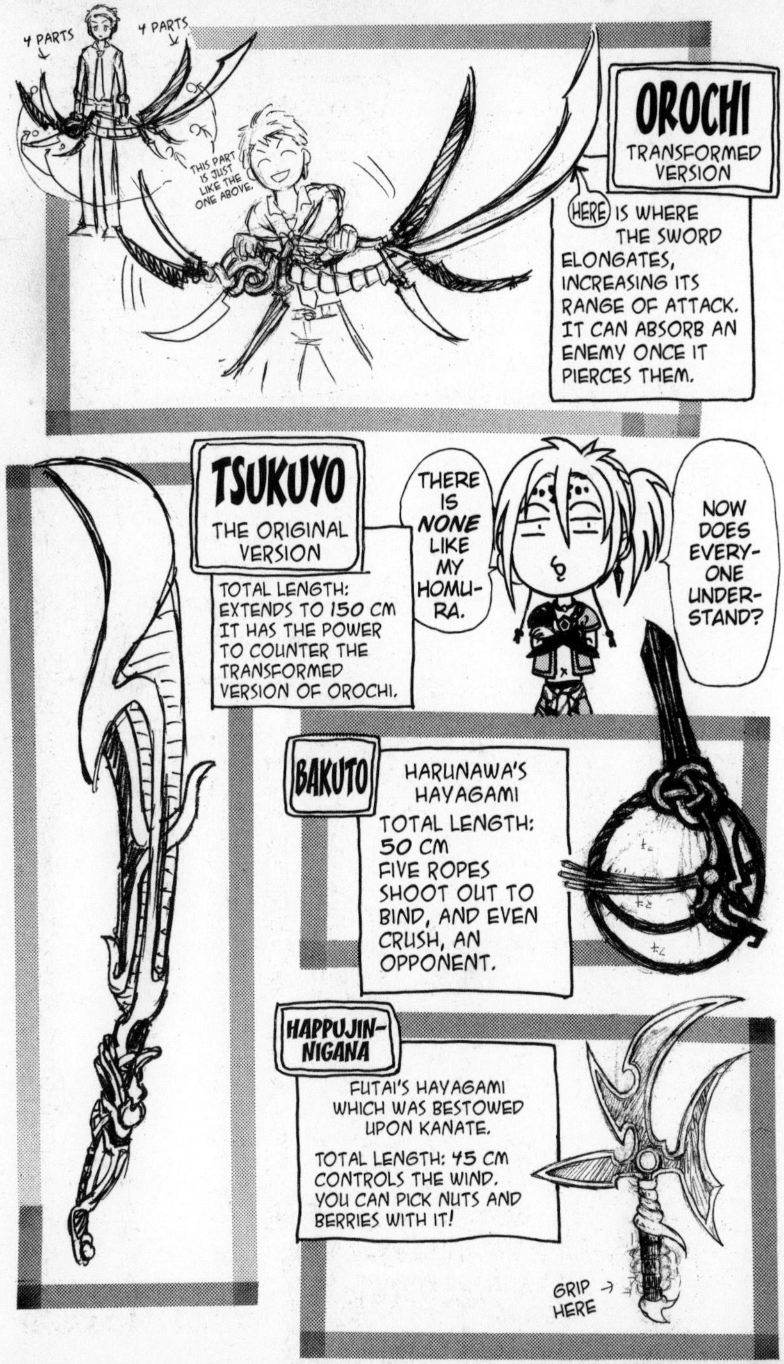

OROCHI
TRANSFORMED VERSION
HERE IS WHERE THE SWORD ELONGATES, INCREASING ITS RANGE OF ATTACK. IT CAN ABSORB AN ENEMY ONCE IT PIERCES THEM.
4 PARTS
4 PARTS
THIS PART IS JUST LIKE THE ONE ABOVE.
NOW DOES EVERYONE UNDERSTAND?
THERE IS NONE LIKE MY HOMURA.
TSUKUYO
THE ORIGINAL VERSION
TOTAL LENGTH: EXTENDS TO 150 CM IT HAS THE POWER TO COUNTER THE TRANSFORMED VERSION OF OROCHI.
BAKUTO
HARUNAWA'S HAYAGAMI
TOTAL LENGTH: 50 CM FIVE ROPES SHOOT OUT TO BIND, AND EVEN CRUSH, AN OPPONENT.
HAPPUJIN-NIGANA
FUTAI'S HAYAGAMI WHICH WAS BESTOWED UPON KANATE.
TOTAL LENGTH: 45 CM CONTROLS THE WIND. YOU CAN PICK NUTS AND BERRIES WITH IT!
GRIP HERE

I recently started a blog on Ameba. I even have a really cute pig avatar. I actually enjoy playing with the characters I create more than the one that represents me. Anyway, I'm kind of thrilled that there are so many possible emoticons. I wasn't able to use my cell phone to post my last blog for various reasons (none of which are worth mentioning). Maybe I should try it more often? Anyway, I'm basically an analog person, but I'm slowly learning.

–Yuu Watase

AUTHOR BIO

Born March 5 in Osaka, Yuu Watase debuted in the *Shôjo Comic* manga anthology in 1989. She won the 43rd Shogakukan Manga Award with *Ceres: Celestial Legend*. One of her most famous works is *Fushigi Yûgi*, a series that has inspired the prequel *Fushigi Yûgi: Genbu Kaiden*. In 2008, *Arata: The Legend* started serialization in *Shonen Sunday*.

ARATA: THE LEGEND

Volume 9
Shonen Sunday Edition

Story and Art by YUU WATASE

© 2009 Yuu WATASE/Shogakukan
All rights reserved.
Original Japanese edition "ARATAKANGATARI"
published by SHOGAKUKAN Inc.

English Adaptation: Lance Caselman
Translation: JN Productions
Touch-up Art & Lettering: Rina Mapa
Design: Ronnie Casson
Editor: Amy Yu

Printed in the U.S.A.

Published by VIZ Media, LLC
P.O. Box 77010
San Francisco, CA 94107

10 9 8 7 6 5 4 3 2 1
First printing, March 2012

www.viz.com

WWW.SHONENSUNDAY.COM

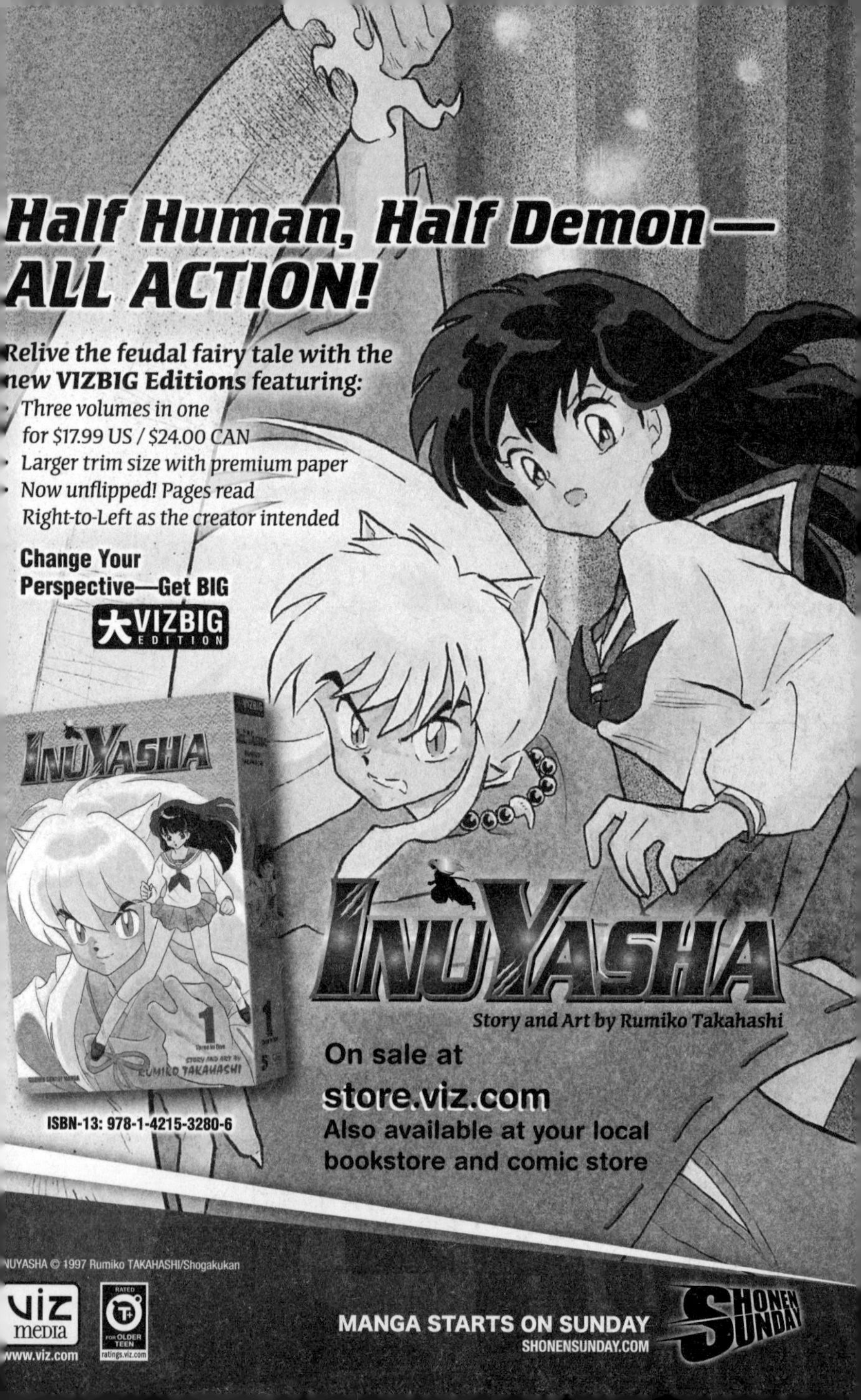
Half Human, Half Demon—
ALL ACTION!
Relive the feudal fairy tale with the new VIZBIG Editions featuring:
• Three volumes in one for $17.99 US / $24.00 CAN
• Larger trim size with premium paper
• Now unflipped! Pages read Right-to-Left as the creator intended
Change Your Perspective—Get BIG
大 VIZBIG EDITION
INUYASHA
1
RUMIKO TAKAHASHI
ISBN-13: 978-1-4215-3280-6
INUYASHA
Story and Art by Rumiko Takahashi
On sale at
store.viz.com
Also available at your local bookstore and comic store
INUYASHA © 1997 Rumiko TAKAHASHI/Shogakukan
viz media
www.viz.com
RATED T+ FOR OLDER TEEN
ratings.viz.com
MANGA STARTS ON SUNDAY
SHONENSUNDAY.COM
SHONEN SUNDAY

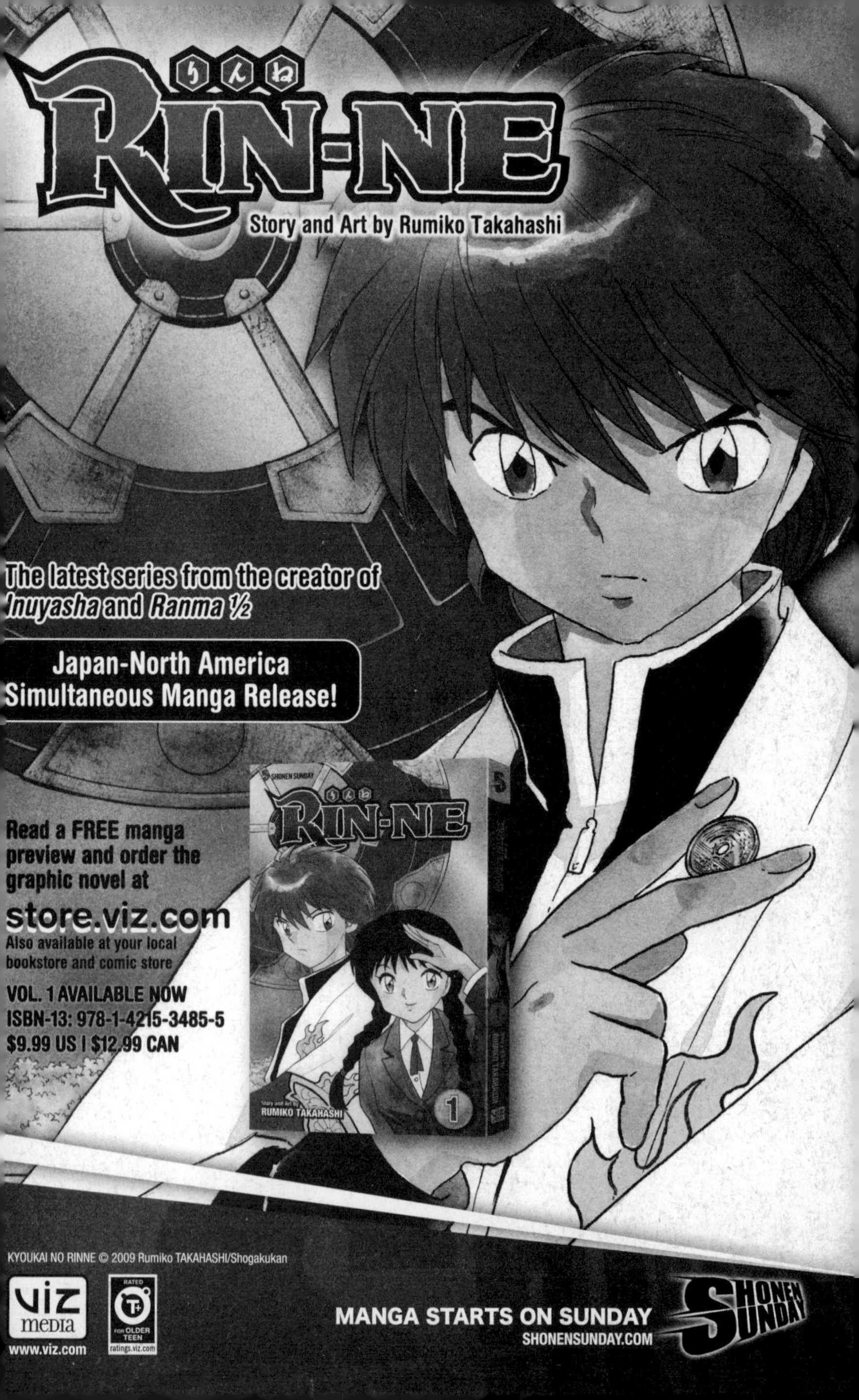

RIN-NE
Story and Art by Rumiko Takahashi
The latest series from the creator of *Inuyasha* and *Ranma ½*
Japan-North America Simultaneous Manga Release!
SHONEN SUNDAY
RIN-NE
Story and Art by RUMIKO TAKAHASHI
1
Read a FREE manga preview and order the graphic novel at
store.viz.com
Also available at your local bookstore and comic store
VOL. 1 AVAILABLE NOW
ISBN-13: 978-1-4215-3485-5
$9.99 US | $12.99 CAN
KYOUKAI NO RINNE © 2009 Rumiko TAKAHASHI/Shogakukan
viz media
www.viz.com
RATED T+ FOR OLDER TEEN
ratings.viz.com
MANGA STARTS ON SUNDAY
SHONENSUNDAY.COM
SHONEN SUNDAY

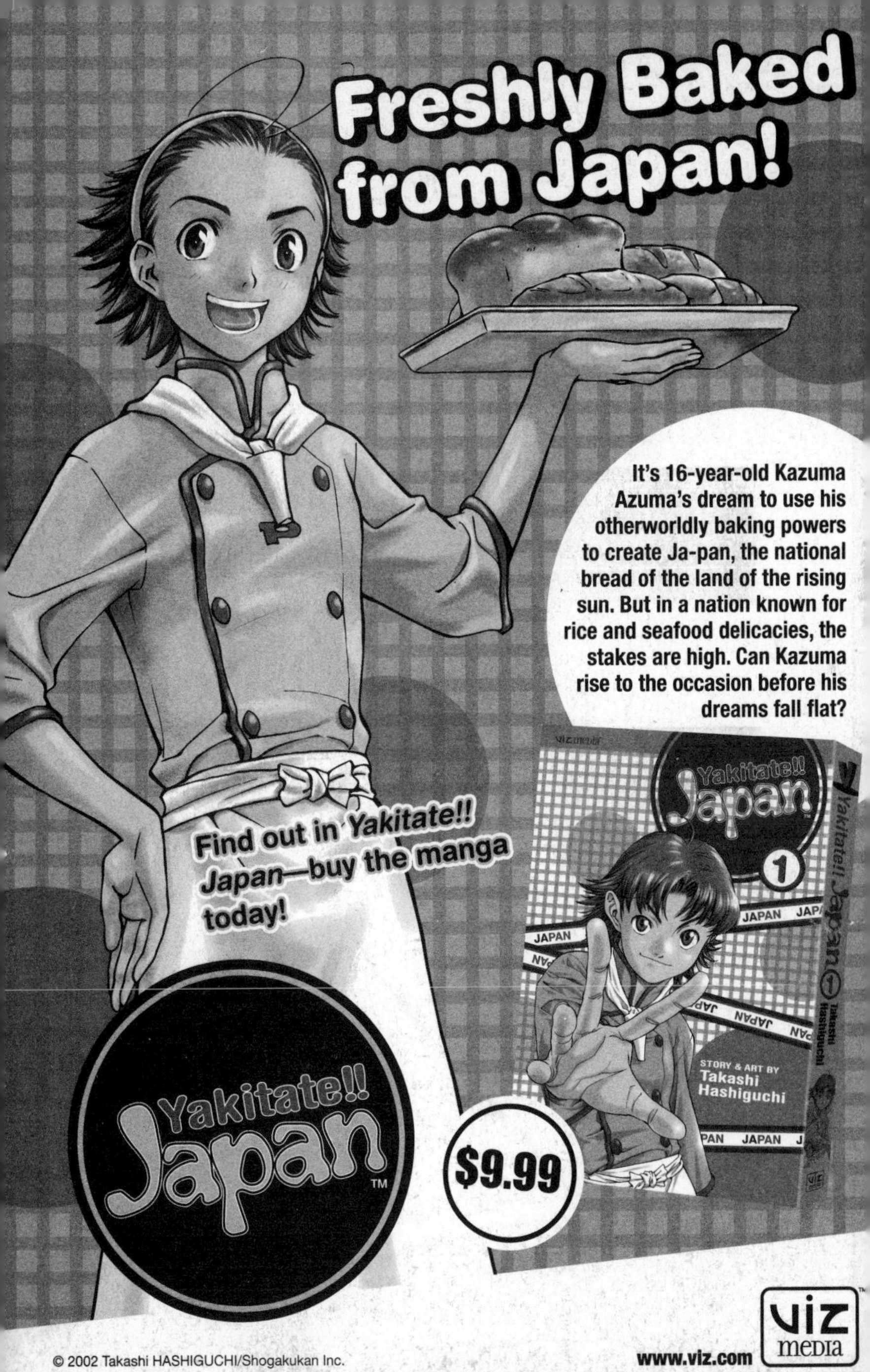
Freshly Baked from Japan!
It's 16-year-old Kazuma Azuma's dream to use his otherworldly baking powers to create Ja-pan, the national bread of the land of the rising sun. But in a nation known for rice and seafood delicacies, the stakes are high. Can Kazuma rise to the occasion before his dreams fall flat?
Find out in Yakitate!! Japan—buy the manga today!
Yakitate!! Japan™
Yakitate!! Japan™ 1
STORY & ART BY Takashi Hashiguchi
$9.99
viz media
www.viz.com